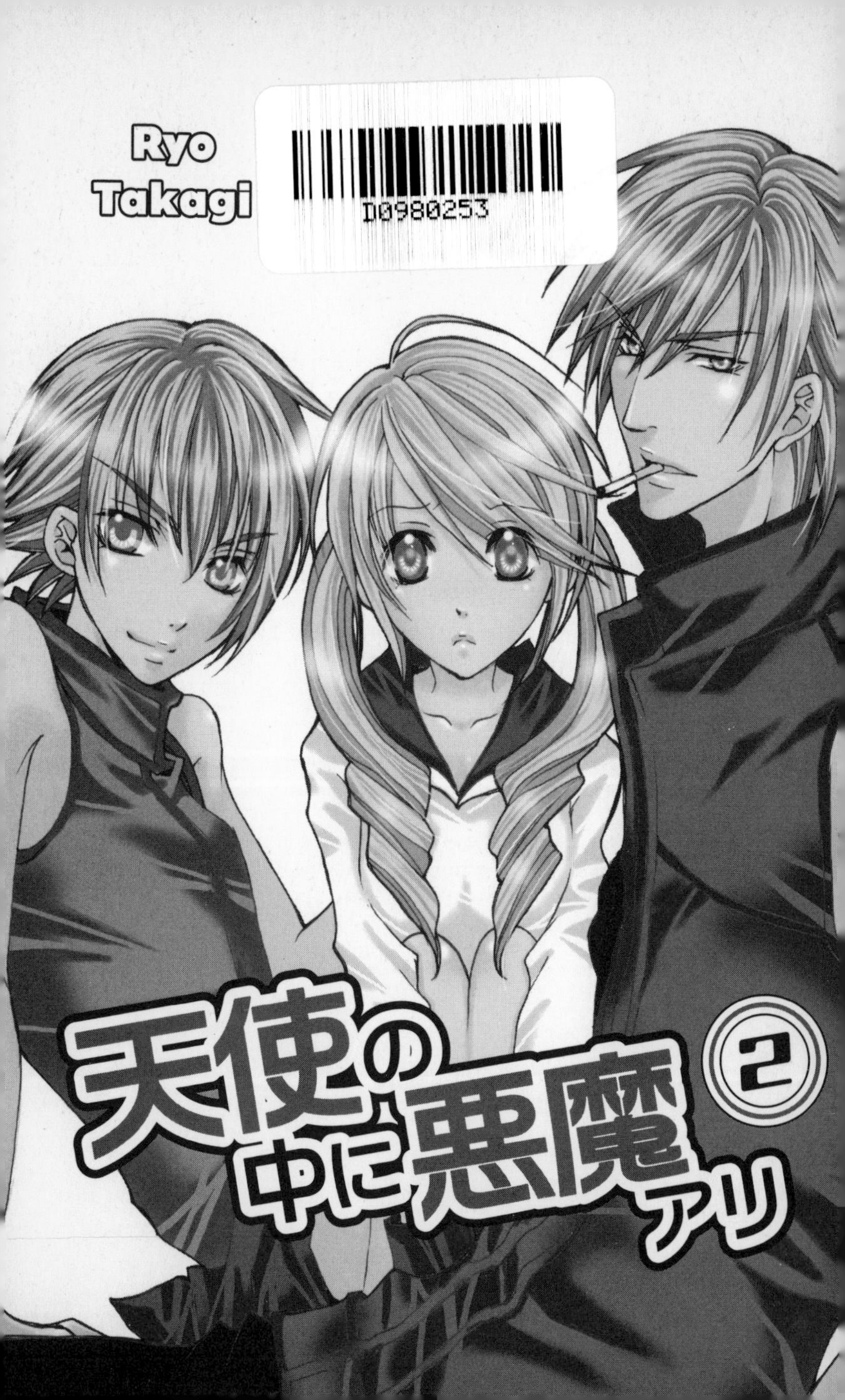
Ryo Takagi
天使の中に悪魔アリ
2

Translation – Christine Schilling
Adaptation – Brynne Chandler
Editorial Assistant – Mallory Reaves
Lettering & Retouch – Jennifer Skarupa
Production Manager – James Dashiell
Editor – Brynne Chandler


A Go! Comi manga

Published by Go! Media Entertainment, LLC

Tenshi no Naka ni Akuma Ari Volume 2
© 2005 RYO TAKAGI
All rights reserved.
First published in Japan in 2005 by SHINSHOKAN Co., Ltd. Tokyo
English Version published by Go! Media Entertainment, LLC under license
from SHINSHOKAN Co., Ltd.

Visit us online at www.gocomi.com
e-mail: info@gocomi.com


ISBN 978-1-933617-45-9

First printed in November 2007

1  2  3  4  5  6  7  8  9

Manufactured in the United States of America.

# STORY AND ART BY

# Ryo Takagi

## VOLUME 2

# go!comi

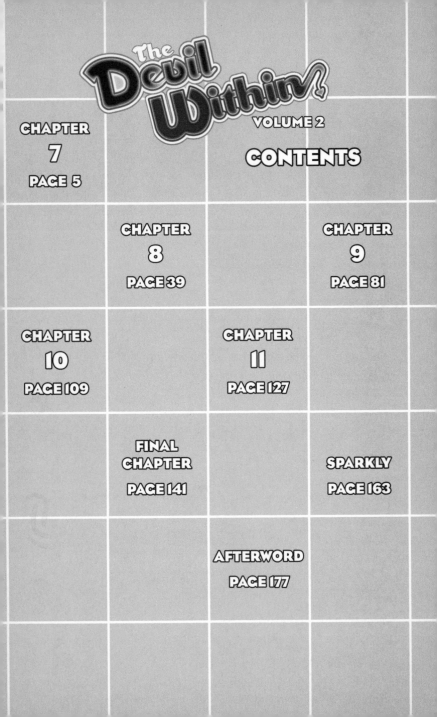

# The Devil Within

**VOLUME 2**

# CONTENTS

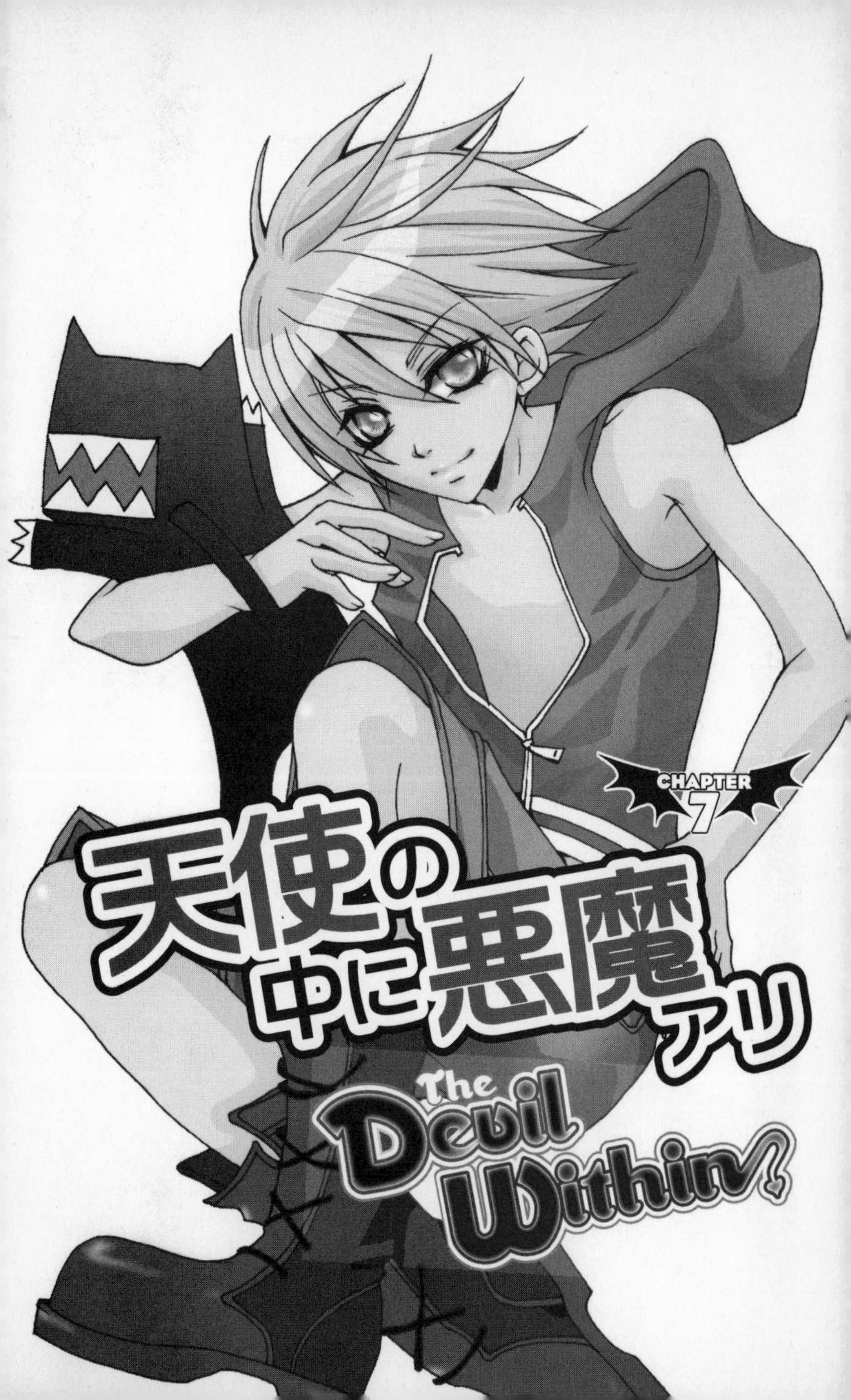
CHAPTER 7
天使の中に悪魔アリ
The Devil Within!

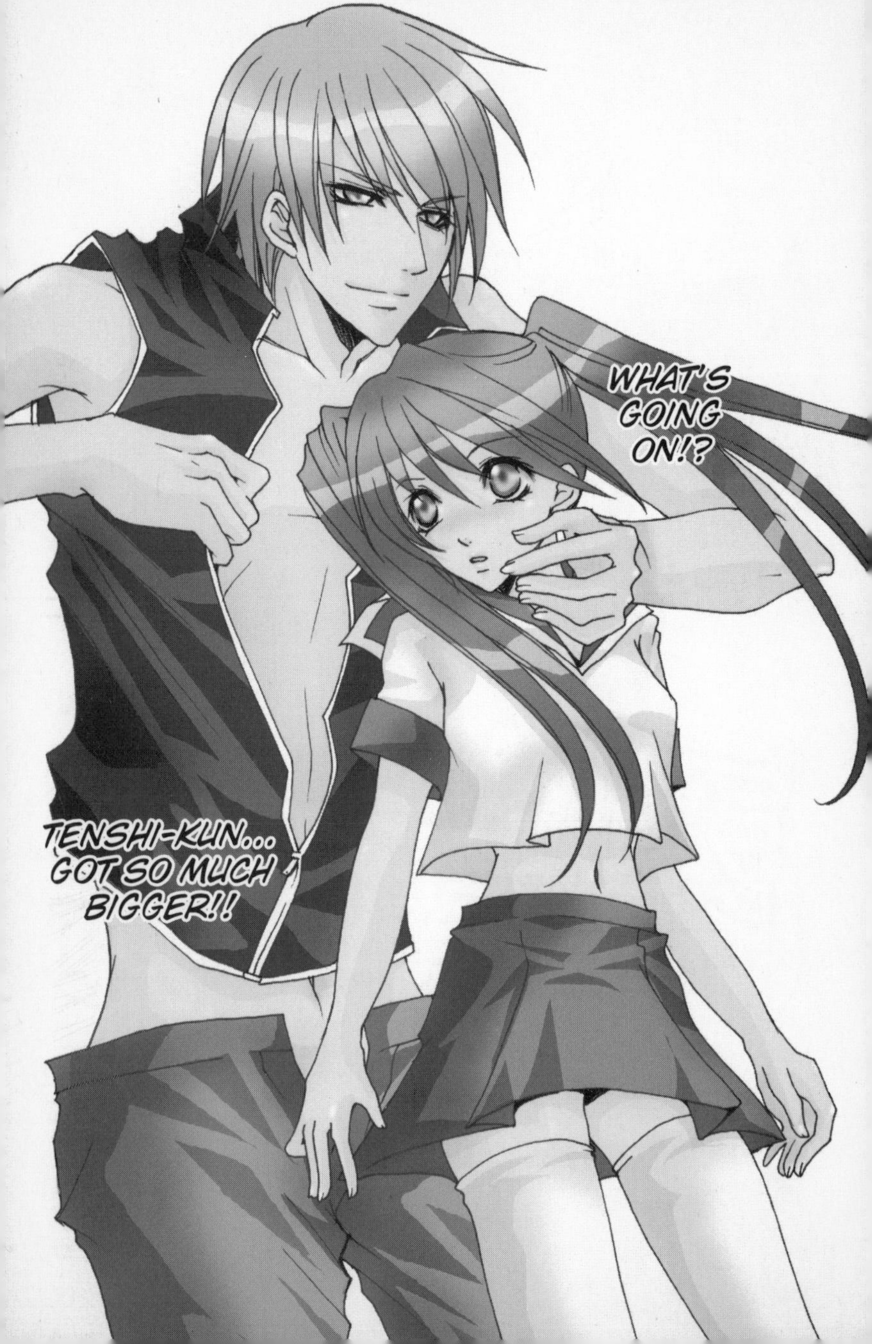
WHAT'S GOING ON!?
TENSHI-KUN... GOT SO MUCH BIGGER!!

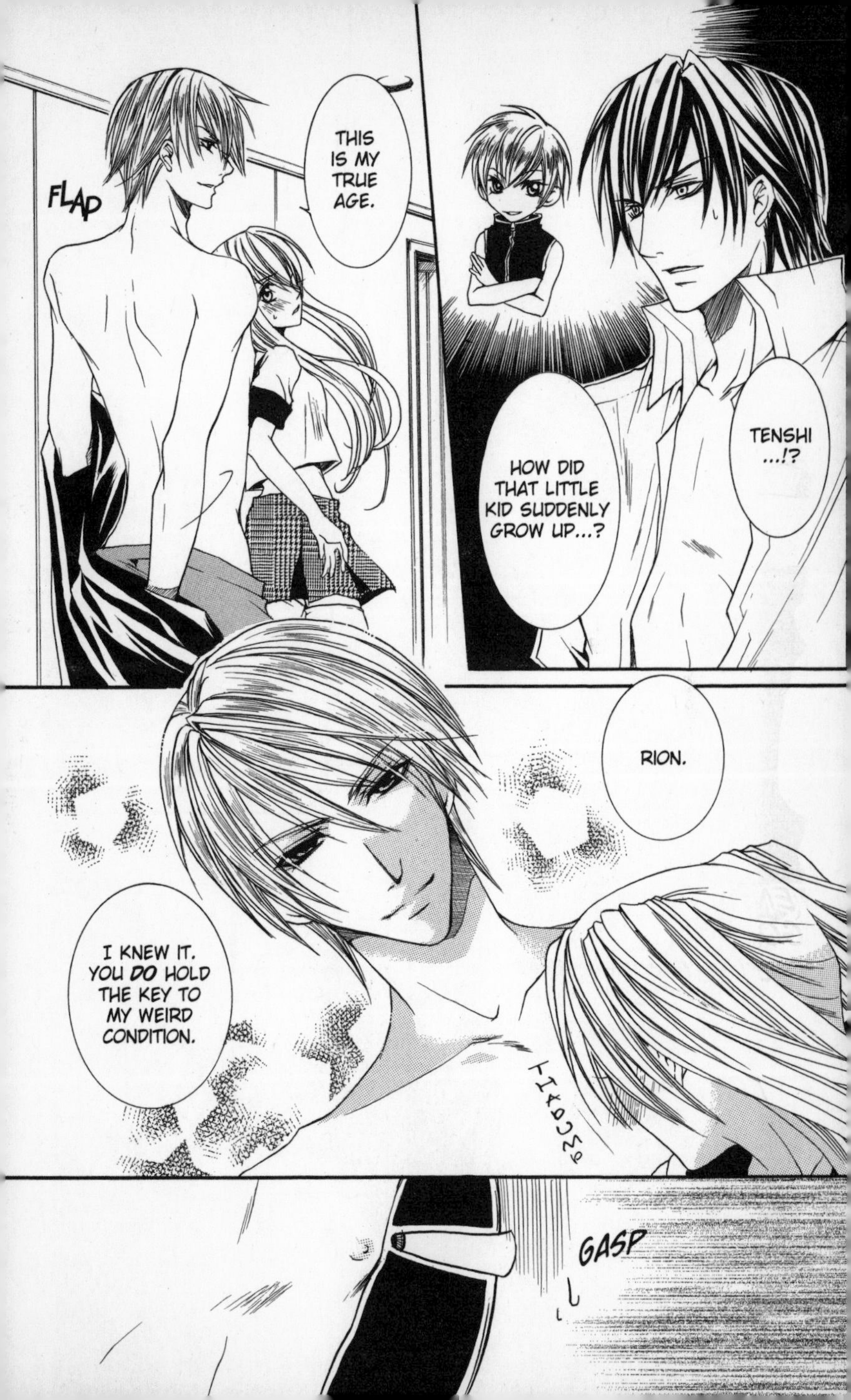
TENSHI ...!?
HOW DID THAT LITTLE KID SUDDENLY GROW UP...?
THIS IS MY TRUE AGE.
FLAP
RION.
I KNEW IT. YOU DO HOLD THE KEY TO MY WEIRD CONDITION.
GASP

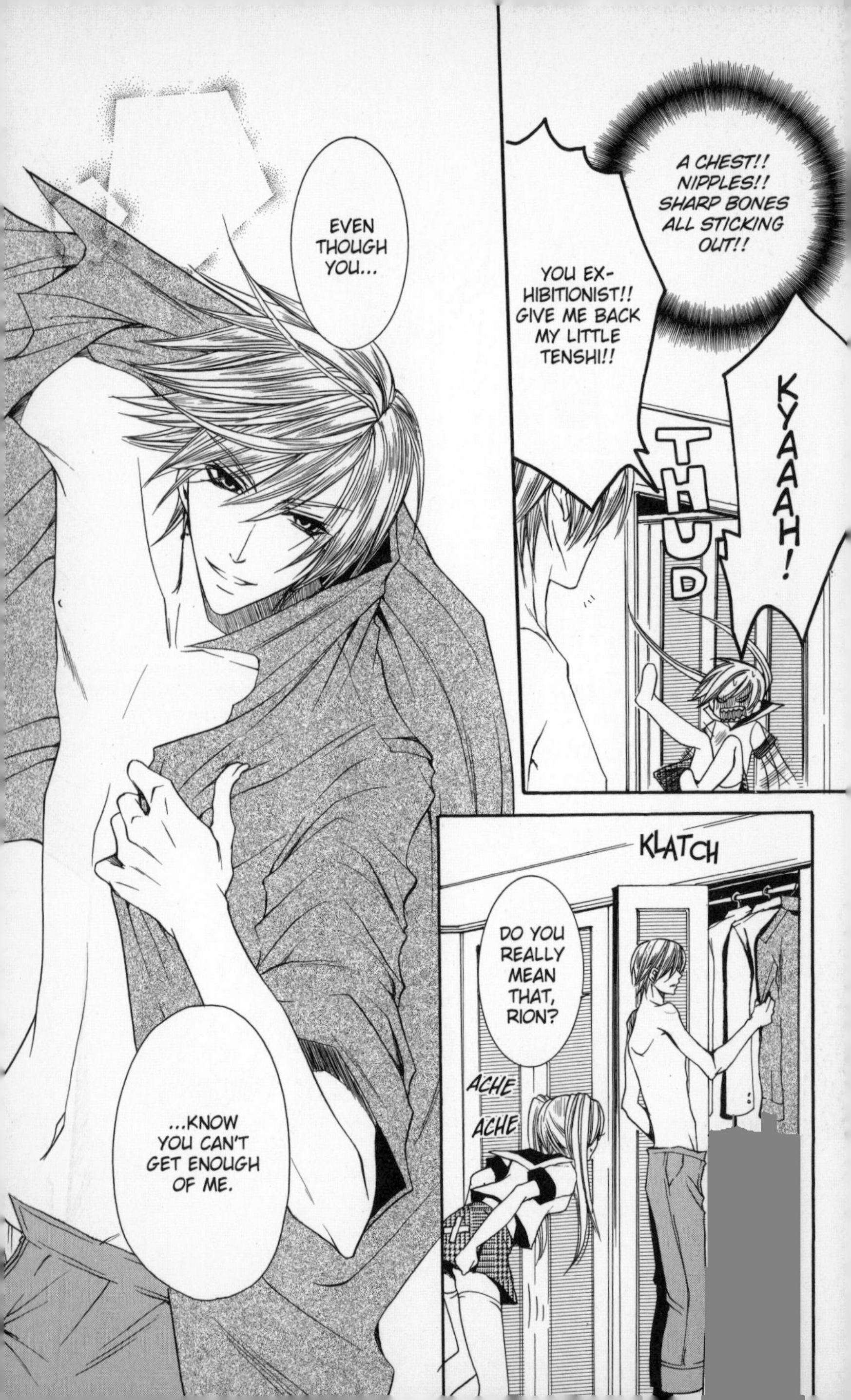
A CHEST!! NIPPLES!! SHARP BONES ALL STICKING OUT!!
YOU EX-HIBITIONIST!! GIVE ME BACK MY LITTLE TENSHI!!
KYAAAH!
THUD
KLATCH
DO YOU REALLY MEAN THAT, RION?
ACHE
ACHE
EVEN THOUGH YOU...
...KNOW YOU CAN'T GET ENOUGH OF ME.

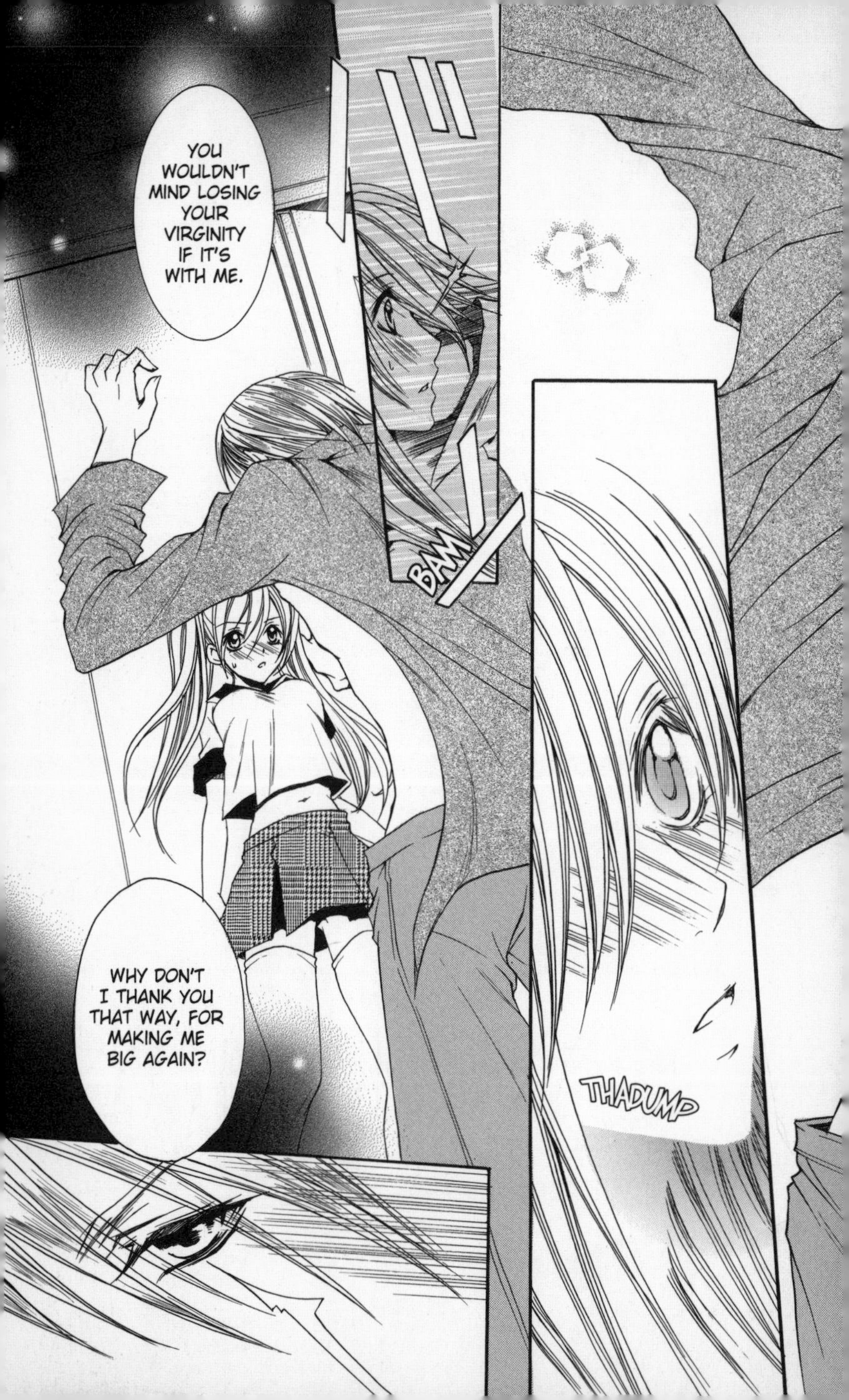
BAM
YOU WOULDN'T MIND LOSING YOUR VIRGINITY IF IT'S WITH ME.
WHY DON'T I THANK YOU THAT WAY, FOR MAKING ME BIG AGAIN?
THADUMP

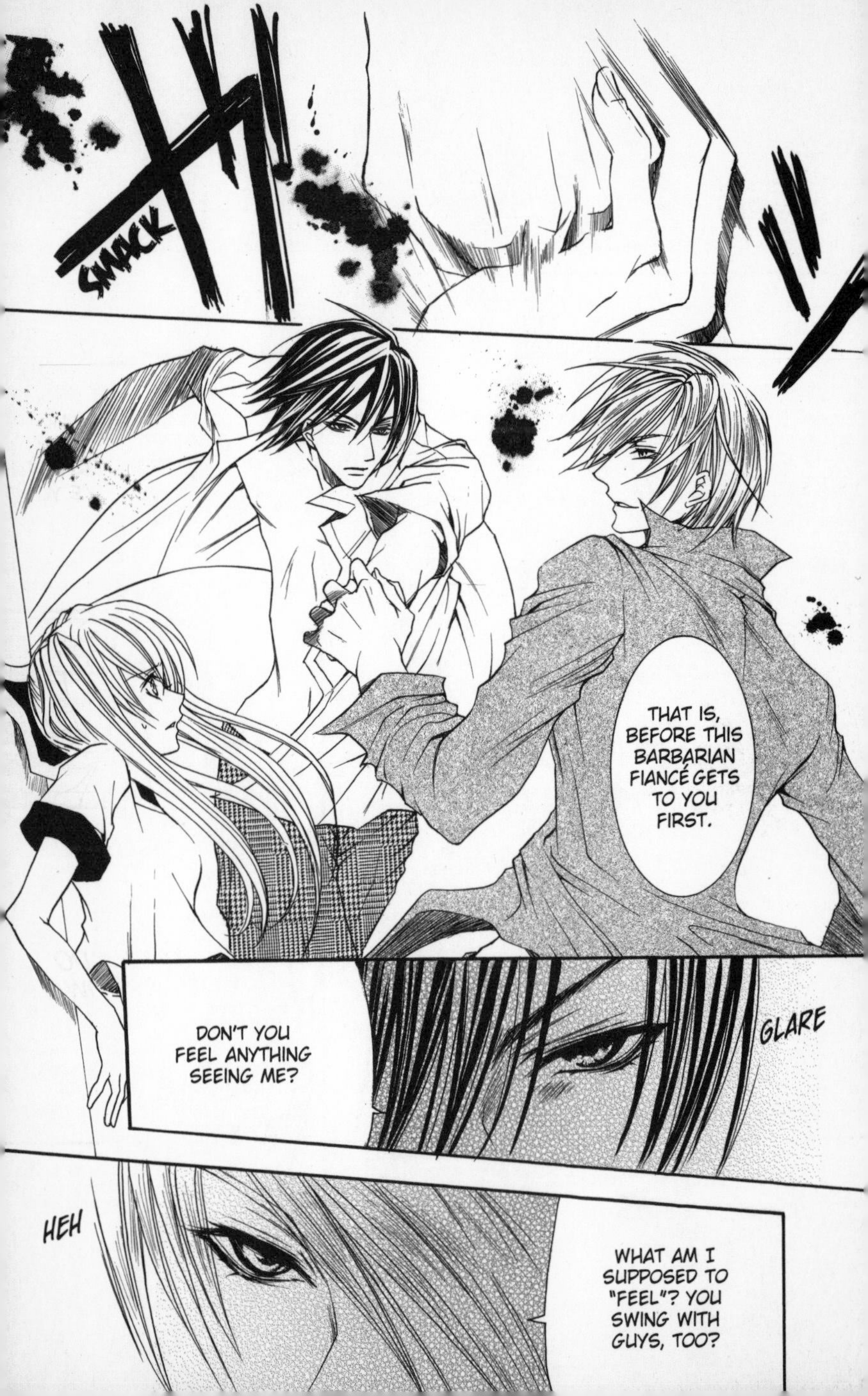
SMACK
THAT IS, BEFORE THIS BARBARIAN FIANCÉ GETS TO YOU FIRST.
GLARE
DON'T YOU FEEL ANYTHING SEEING ME?
WHAT AM I SUPPOSED TO "FEEL"? YOU SWING WITH GUYS, TOO?
HEH

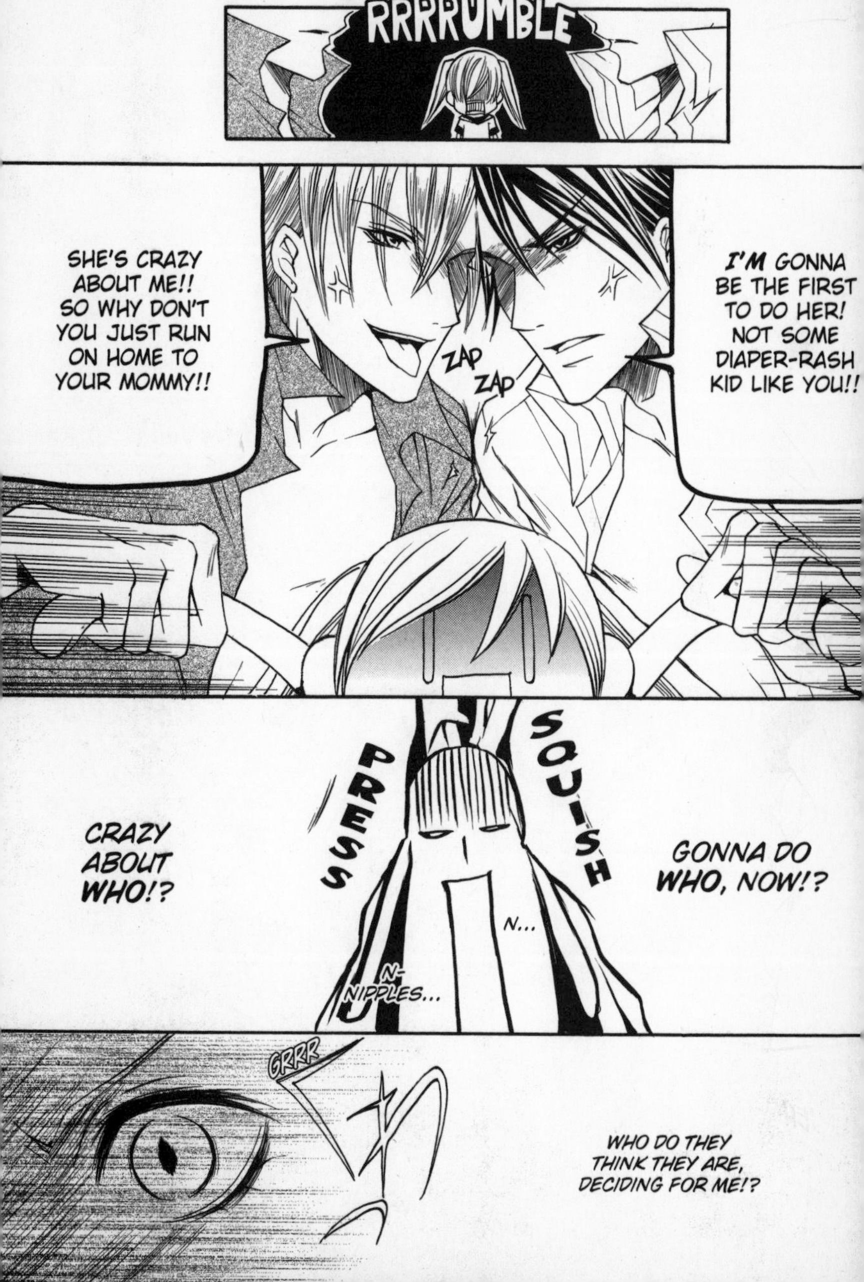
RRRRUMBLE
I'M GONNA BE THE FIRST TO DO HER! NOT SOME DIAPER-RASH KID LIKE YOU!!
ZAP
ZAP
SHE'S CRAZY ABOUT ME!! SO WHY DON'T YOU JUST RUN ON HOME TO YOUR MOMMY!!
GONNA DO WHO, NOW!?
SQUISH
PRESS
CRAZY ABOUT WHO!?
N...
N-NIPPLES...
GRRR
WHO DO THEY THINK THEY ARE, DECIDING FOR ME!?

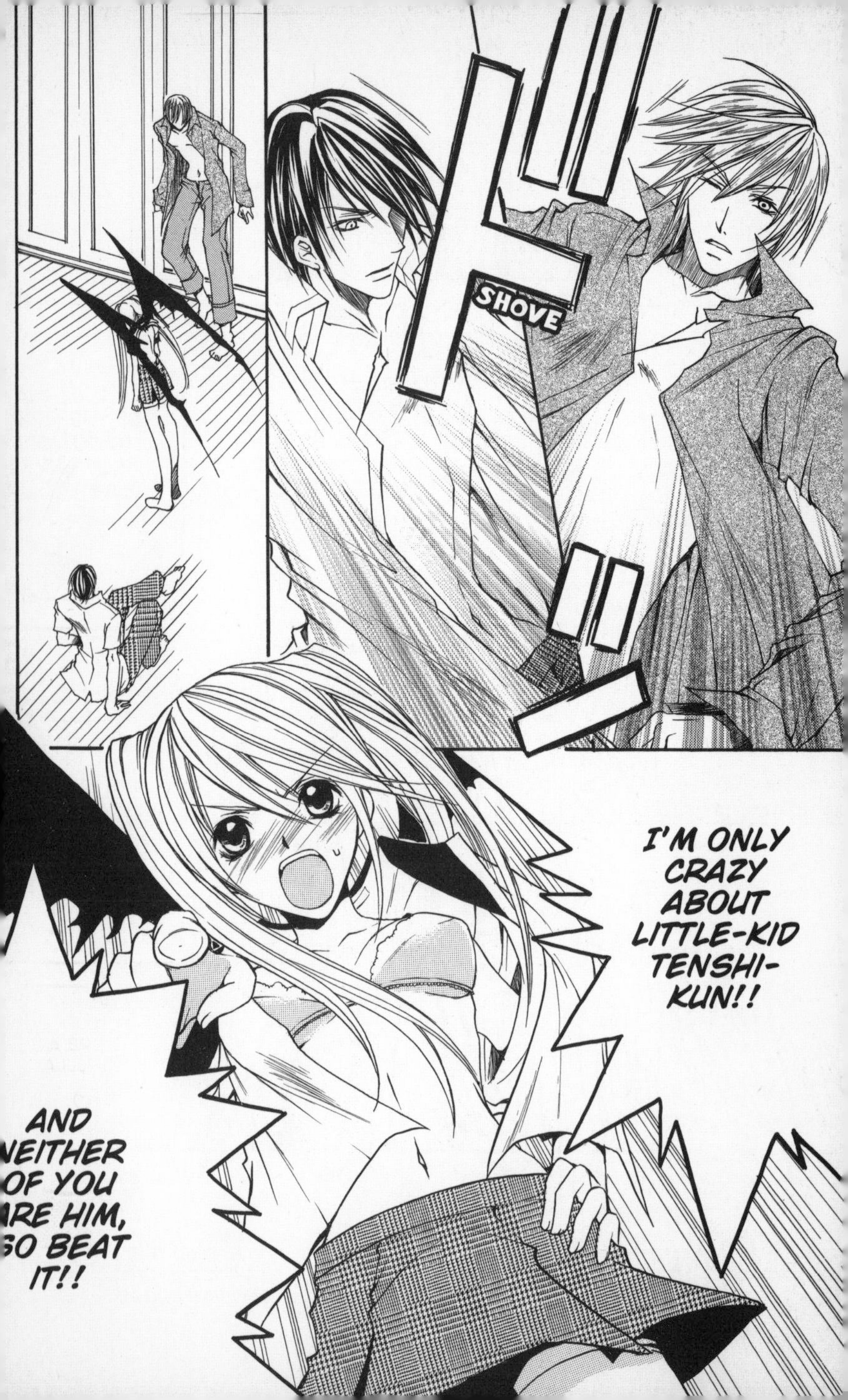
SHOVE
I'M ONLY CRAZY ABOUT LITTLE-KID TENSHI-KUN!!
AND NEITHER OF YOU ARE HIM, SO BEAT IT!!

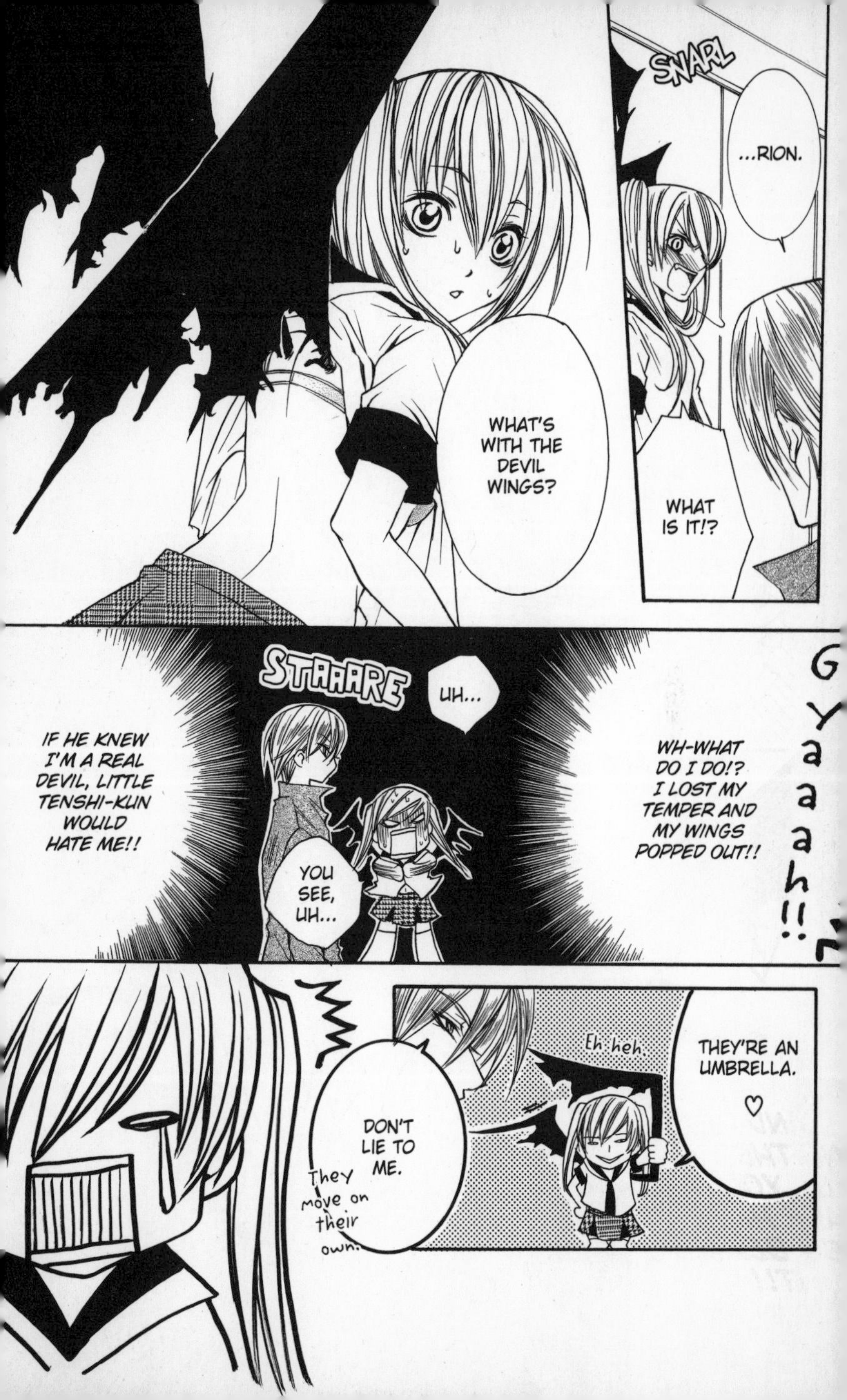
SNARL
...RION.
WHAT IS IT!?
WHAT'S WITH THE DEVIL WINGS?
Gyaaah!!
WH-WHAT DO I DO!? I LOST MY TEMPER AND MY WINGS POPPED OUT!!
STAAARE
UH...
YOU SEE, UH...
IF HE KNEW I'M A REAL DEVIL, LITTLE TENSHI-KUN WOULD HATE ME!!
THEY'RE AN UMBRELLA. ♡
Eh heh.
DON'T LIE TO ME.
They move on their own.

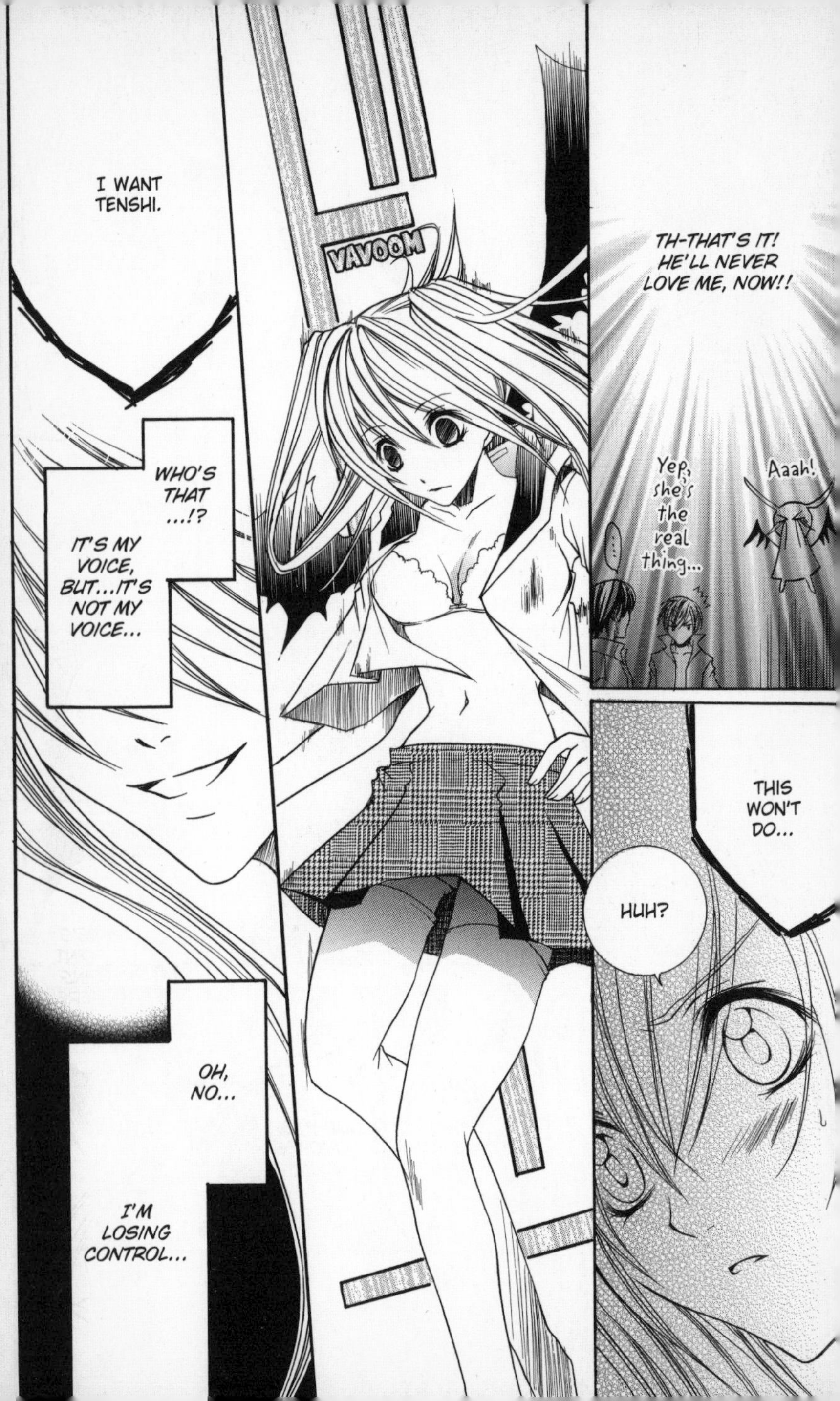
TH-THAT'S IT! HE'LL NEVER LOVE ME, NOW!!
Aaah!
Yep, she's the real thing...
THIS WON'T DO...
HUH?
VAVOOM
I WANT TENSHI.
WHO'S THAT ...!?
IT'S MY VOICE, BUT...IT'S NOT MY VOICE...
OH, NO...
I'M LOSING CONTROL...

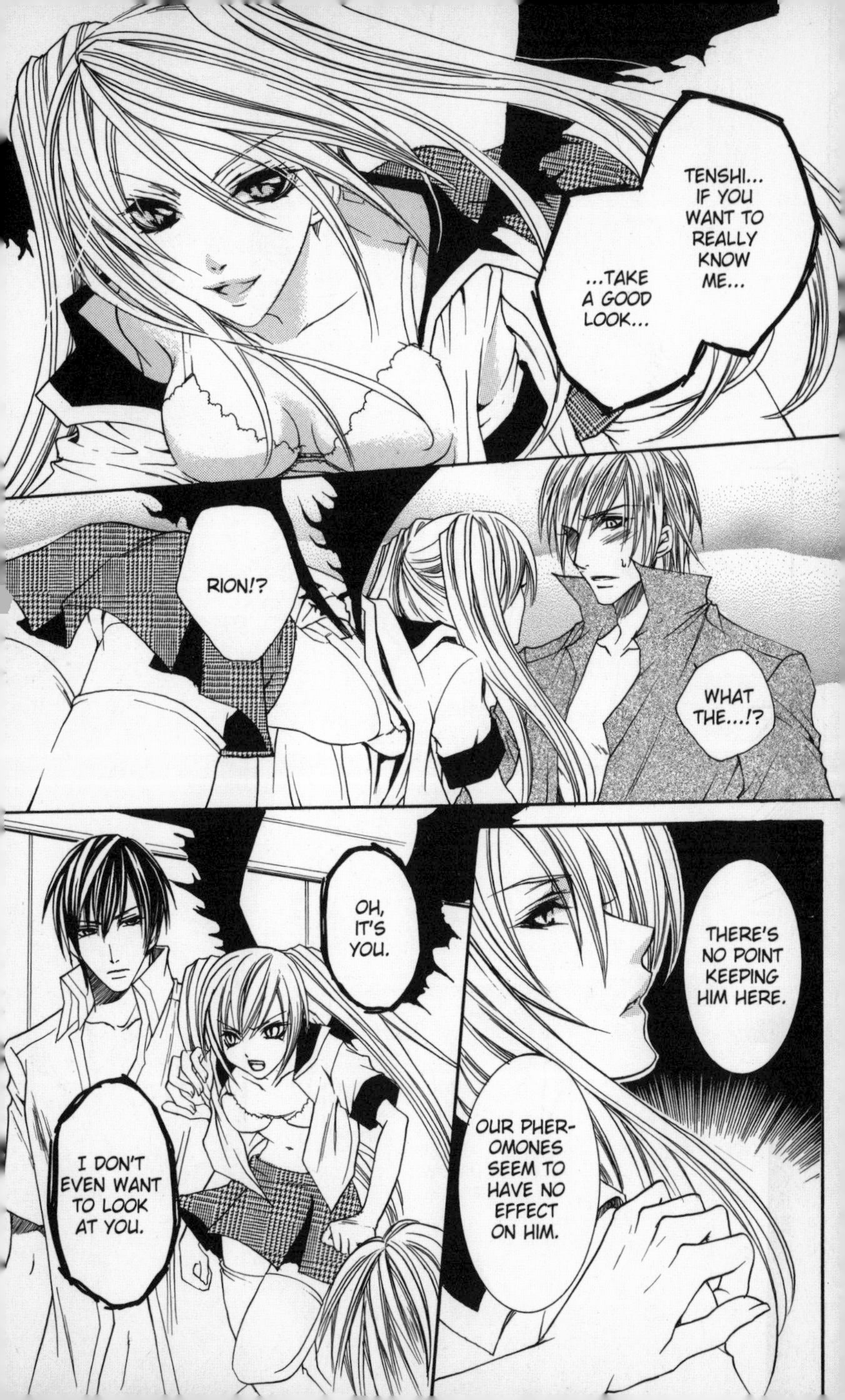
TENSHI... IF YOU WANT TO REALLY KNOW ME...
...TAKE A GOOD LOOK...
RION!?
WHAT THE...!?
THERE'S NO POINT KEEPING HIM HERE.
OUR PHER-OMONES SEEM TO HAVE NO EFFECT ON HIM.
OH, IT'S YOU.
I DON'T EVEN WANT TO LOOK AT YOU.

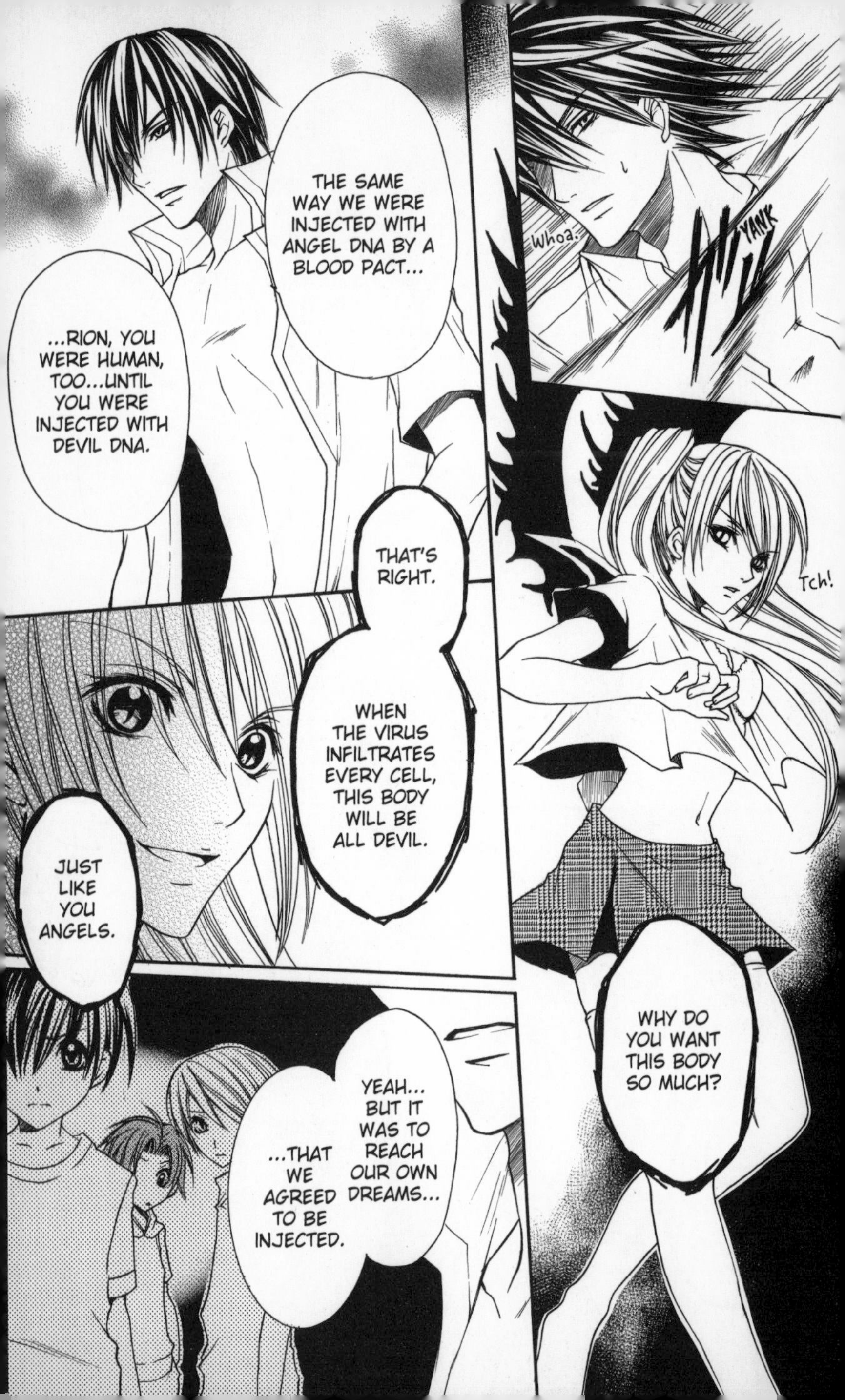

Whoa.
YANK
Tch!
WHY DO YOU WANT THIS BODY SO MUCH?
THE SAME WAY WE WERE INJECTED WITH ANGEL DNA BY A BLOOD PACT...
...RION, YOU WERE HUMAN, TOO...UNTIL YOU WERE INJECTED WITH DEVIL DNA.
THAT'S RIGHT.
WHEN THE VIRUS INFILTRATES EVERY CELL, THIS BODY WILL BE ALL DEVIL.
JUST LIKE YOU ANGELS.
YEAH... BUT IT WAS TO REACH OUR OWN DREAMS...
...THAT WE AGREED TO BE INJECTED.

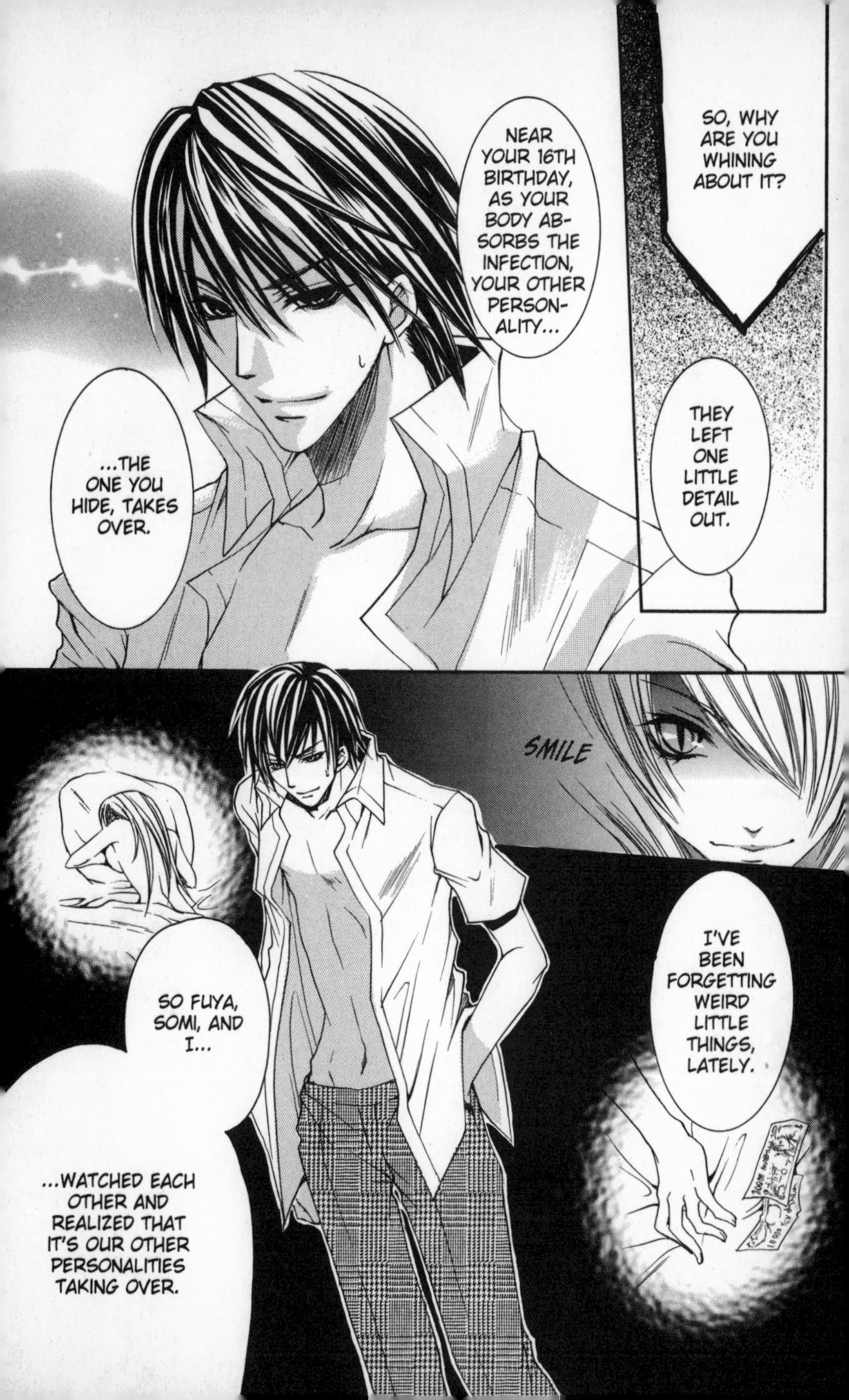
SO, WHY ARE YOU WHINING ABOUT IT?
THEY LEFT ONE LITTLE DETAIL OUT.
NEAR YOUR 16TH BIRTHDAY, AS YOUR BODY AB-SORBS THE INFECTION, YOUR OTHER PERSON-ALITY...
...THE ONE YOU HIDE, TAKES OVER.
SMILE
I'VE BEEN FORGETTING WEIRD LITTLE THINGS, LATELY.
SO FUYA, SOMI, AND I...
...WATCHED EACH OTHER AND REALIZED THAT IT'S OUR OTHER PERSONALITIES TAKING OVER.

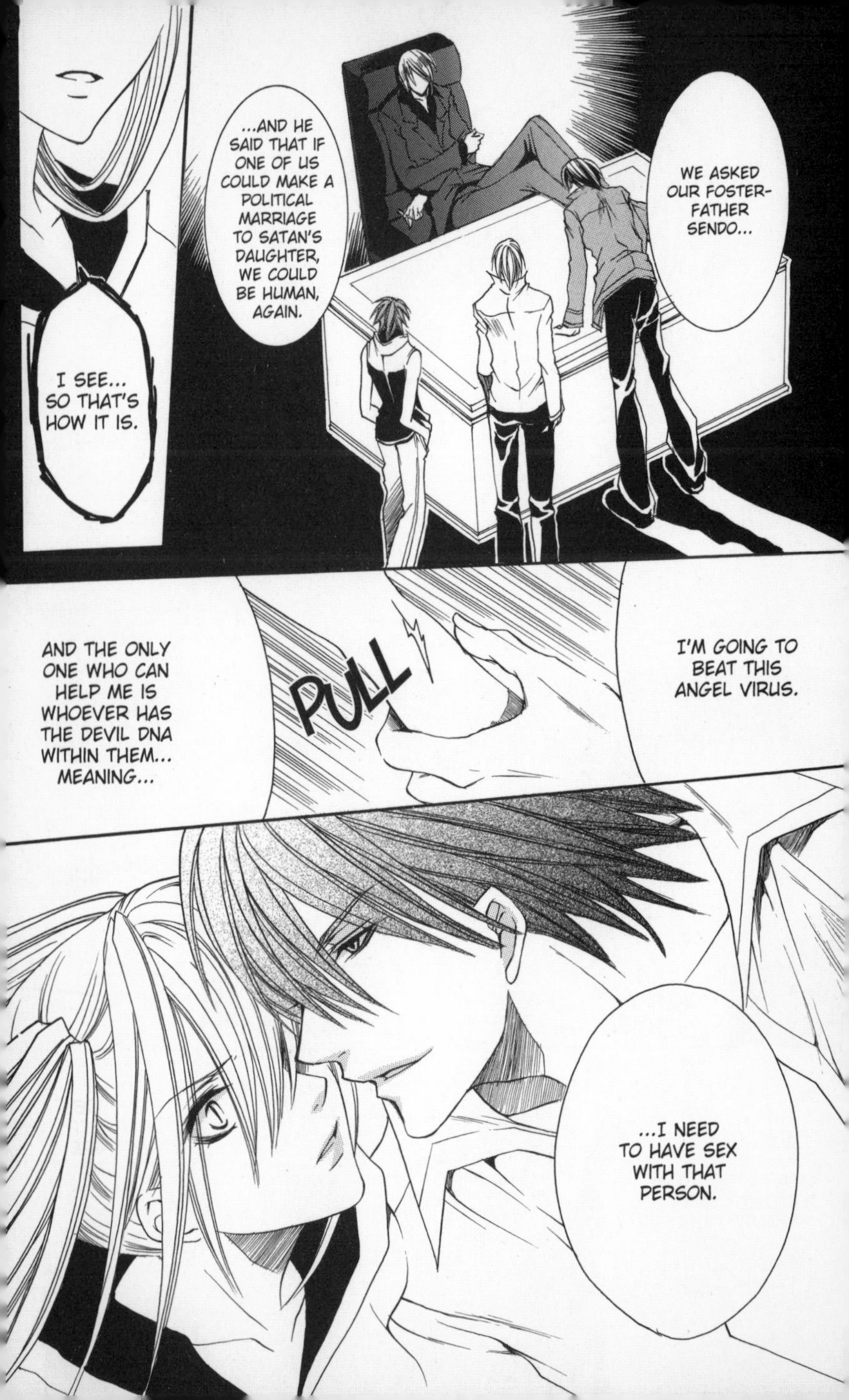
WE ASKED OUR FOSTER-FATHER SENDO...
...AND HE SAID THAT IF ONE OF US COULD MAKE A POLITICAL MARRIAGE TO SATAN'S DAUGHTER, WE COULD BE HUMAN, AGAIN.
I SEE... SO THAT'S HOW IT IS.
I'M GOING TO BEAT THIS ANGEL VIRUS.
PULL
AND THE ONLY ONE WHO CAN HELP ME IS WHOEVER HAS THE DEVIL DNA WITHIN THEM... MEANING...
...I NEED TO HAVE SEX WITH THAT PERSON.

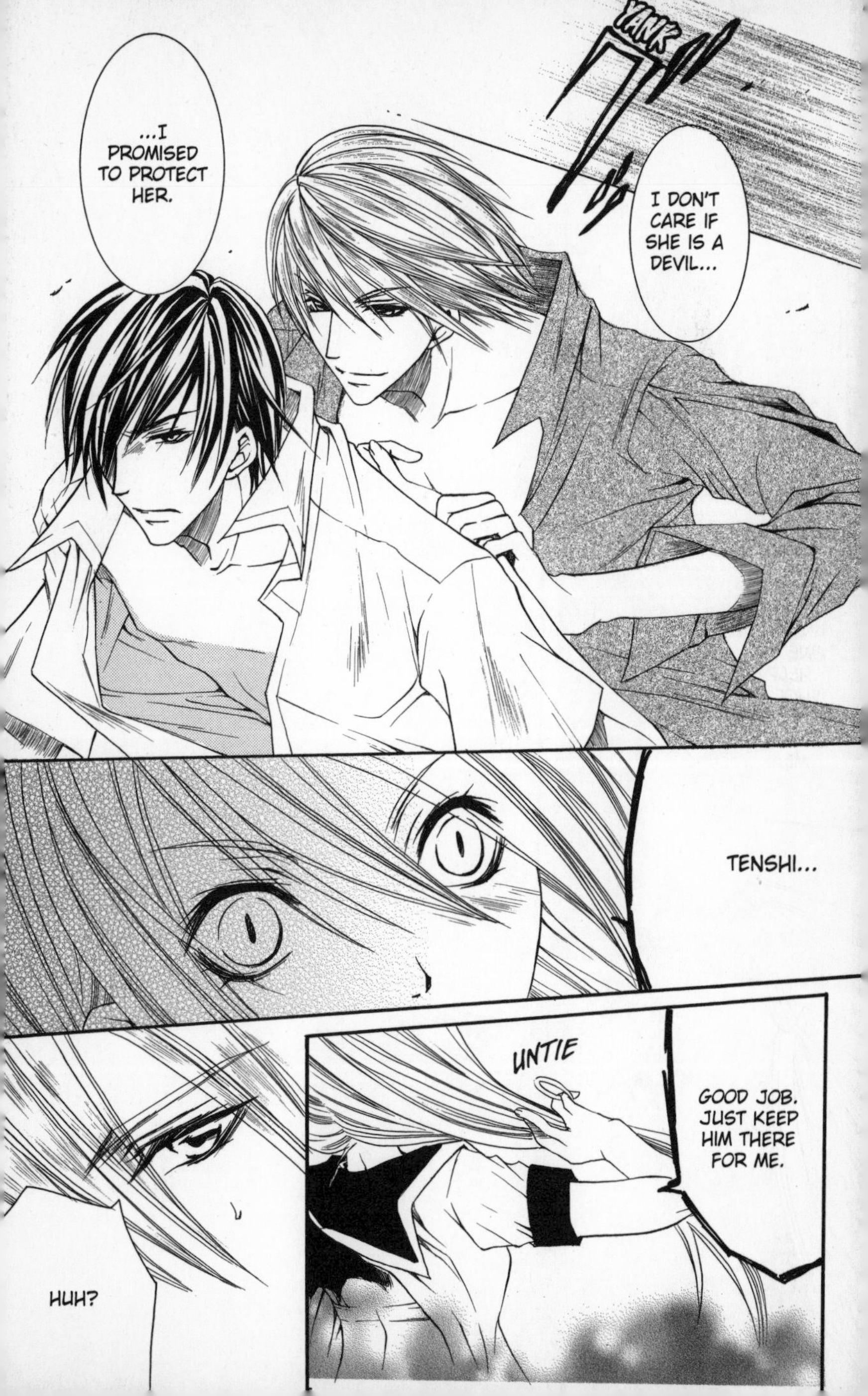
YANK
I DON'T CARE IF SHE IS A DEVIL...
...I PROMISED TO PROTECT HER.
TENSHI...
UNTIE
GOOD JOB. JUST KEEP HIM THERE FOR ME.
HUH?

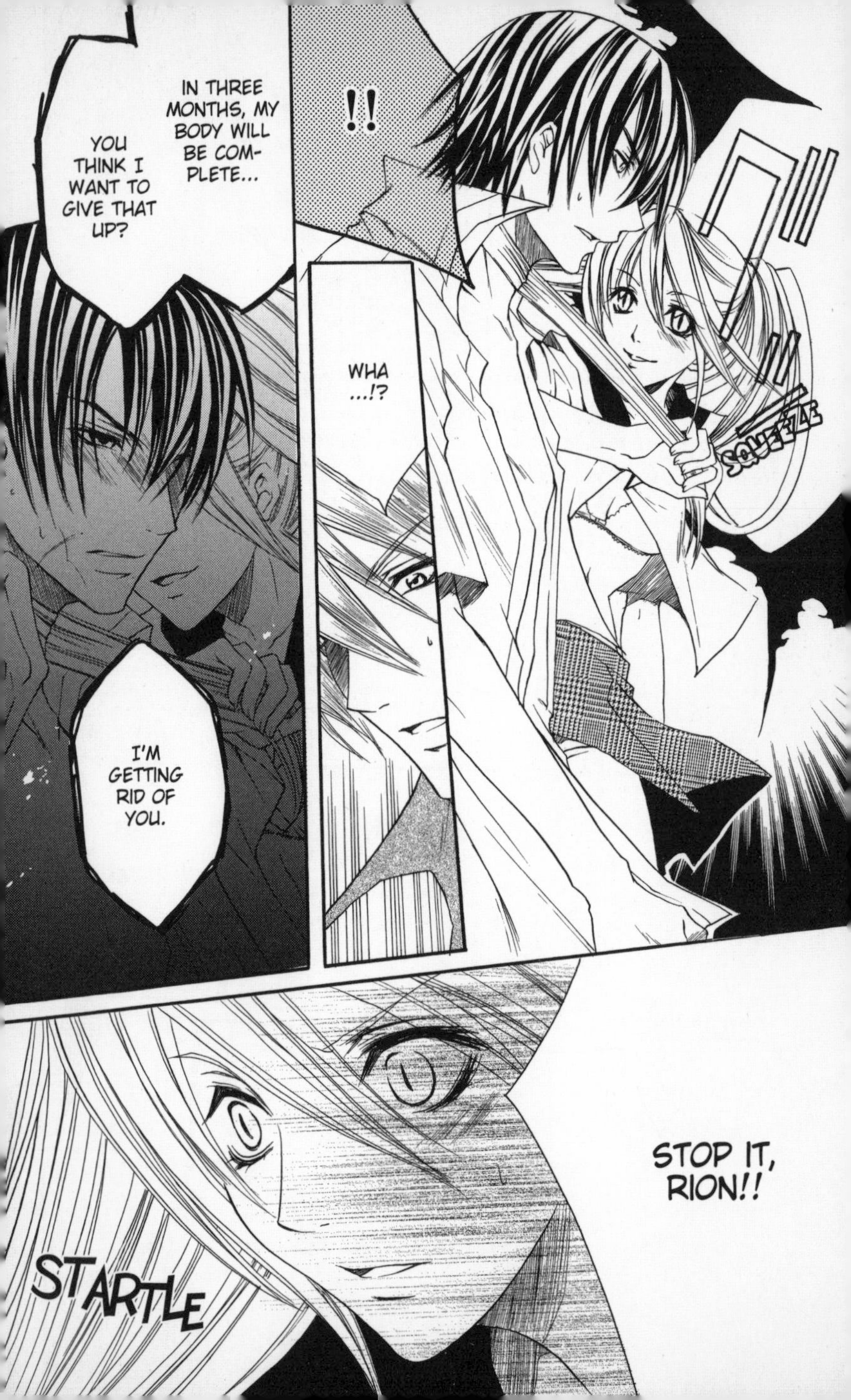
!!
SQUEEZE
WHA...!?
IN THREE MONTHS, MY BODY WILL BE COMPLETE...
YOU THINK I WANT TO GIVE THAT UP?
I'M GETTING RID OF YOU.
STOP IT, RION!!
STARTLE

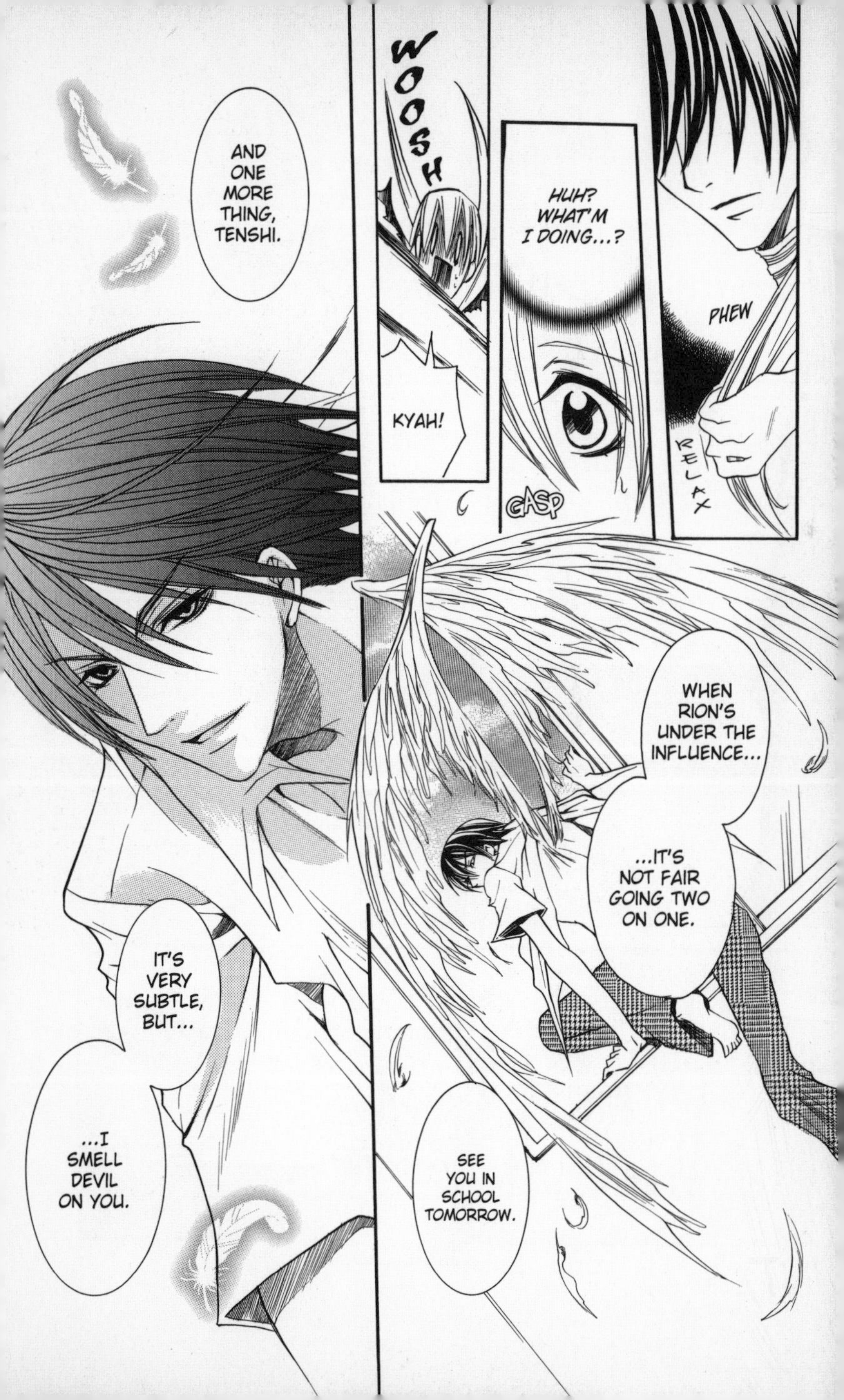
PHEW
RELAX
HUH? WHAT'M I DOING...?
GASP
WOOSH
KYAH!
WHEN RION'S UNDER THE INFLUENCE...
...IT'S NOT FAIR GOING TWO ON ONE.
SEE YOU IN SCHOOL TOMORROW.
AND ONE MORE THING, TENSHI.
IT'S VERY SUBTLE, BUT...
...I SMELL DEVIL ON YOU.

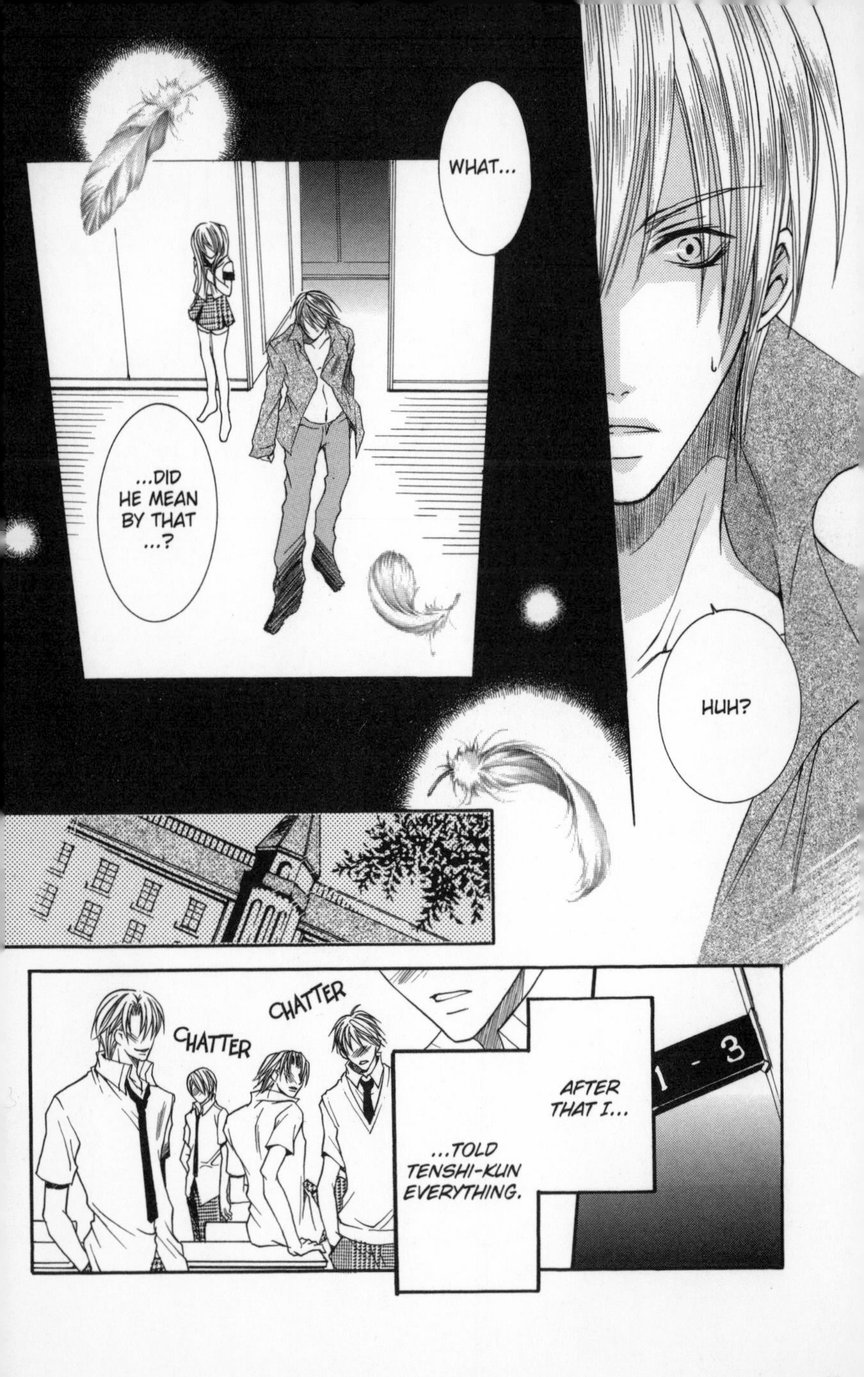
WHAT...
...DID HE MEAN BY THAT ...?
HUH?
1 - 3
AFTER THAT I...
...TOLD TENSHI-KUN EVERYTHING.
CHATTER
CHATTER

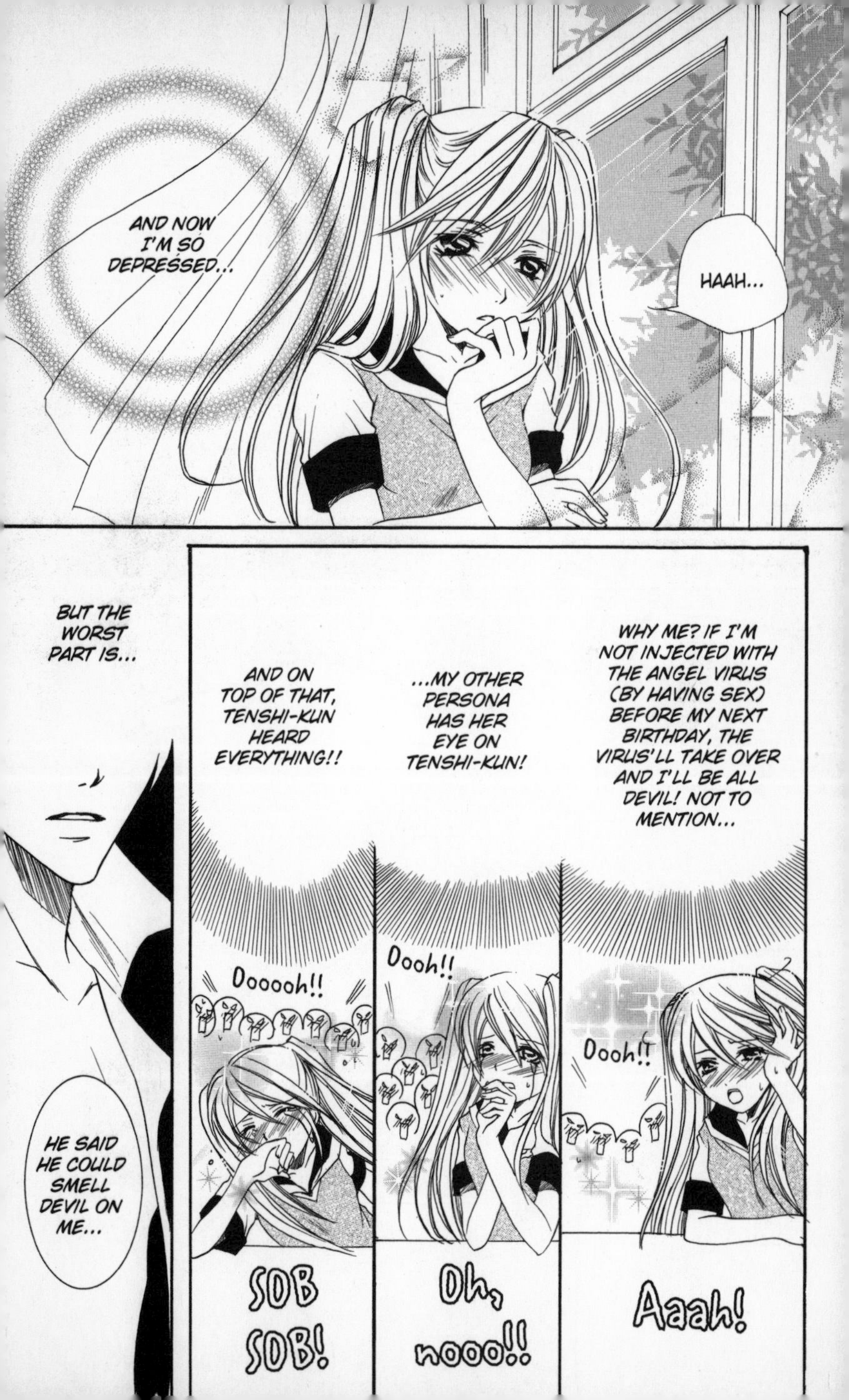
HAAH...
AND NOW I'M SO DEPRESSED...
WHY ME? IF I'M NOT INJECTED WITH THE ANGEL VIRUS (BY HAVING SEX) BEFORE MY NEXT BIRTHDAY, THE VIRUS'LL TAKE OVER AND I'LL BE ALL DEVIL! NOT TO MENTION...
Oooh!!
Aaah!
...MY OTHER PERSONA HAS HER EYE ON TENSHI-KUN!
Oooh!!
Oh, nooo!!
AND ON TOP OF THAT, TENSHI-KUN HEARD EVERYTHING!!
Oooooh!!
SOB SOB!
BUT THE WORST PART IS...
HE SAID HE COULD SMELL DEVIL ON ME...

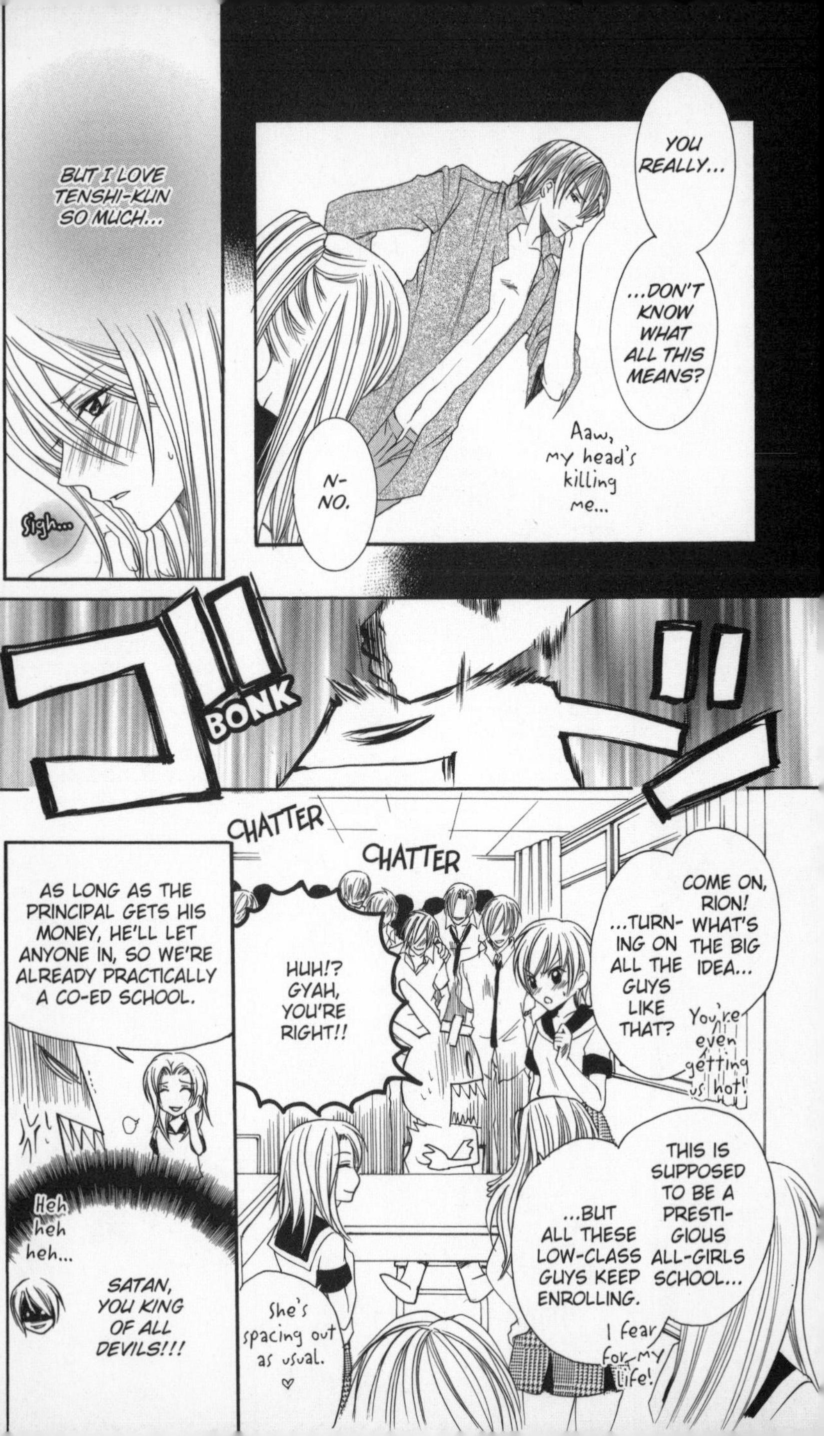
YOU REALLY...
...DON'T KNOW WHAT ALL THIS MEANS?
Aaw, my head's killing me...
N-NO.
BUT I LOVE TENSHI-KUN SO MUCH...
Sigh...
BONK
CHATTER
CHATTER
COME ON, RION! WHAT'S THE BIG IDEA...
...TURNING ON ALL THE GUYS LIKE THAT?
You're even getting us hot!
HUH!? GYAH, YOU'RE RIGHT!!
THIS IS SUPPOSED TO BE A PRESTIGIOUS ALL-GIRLS SCHOOL...
...BUT ALL THESE LOW-CLASS GUYS KEEP ENROLLING.
I fear for my life!
She's spacing out as usual. ♡
AS LONG AS THE PRINCIPAL GETS HIS MONEY, HE'LL LET ANYONE IN, SO WE'RE ALREADY PRACTICALLY A CO-ED SCHOOL.
Heh heh heh...
SATAN, YOU KING OF ALL DEVILS!!!

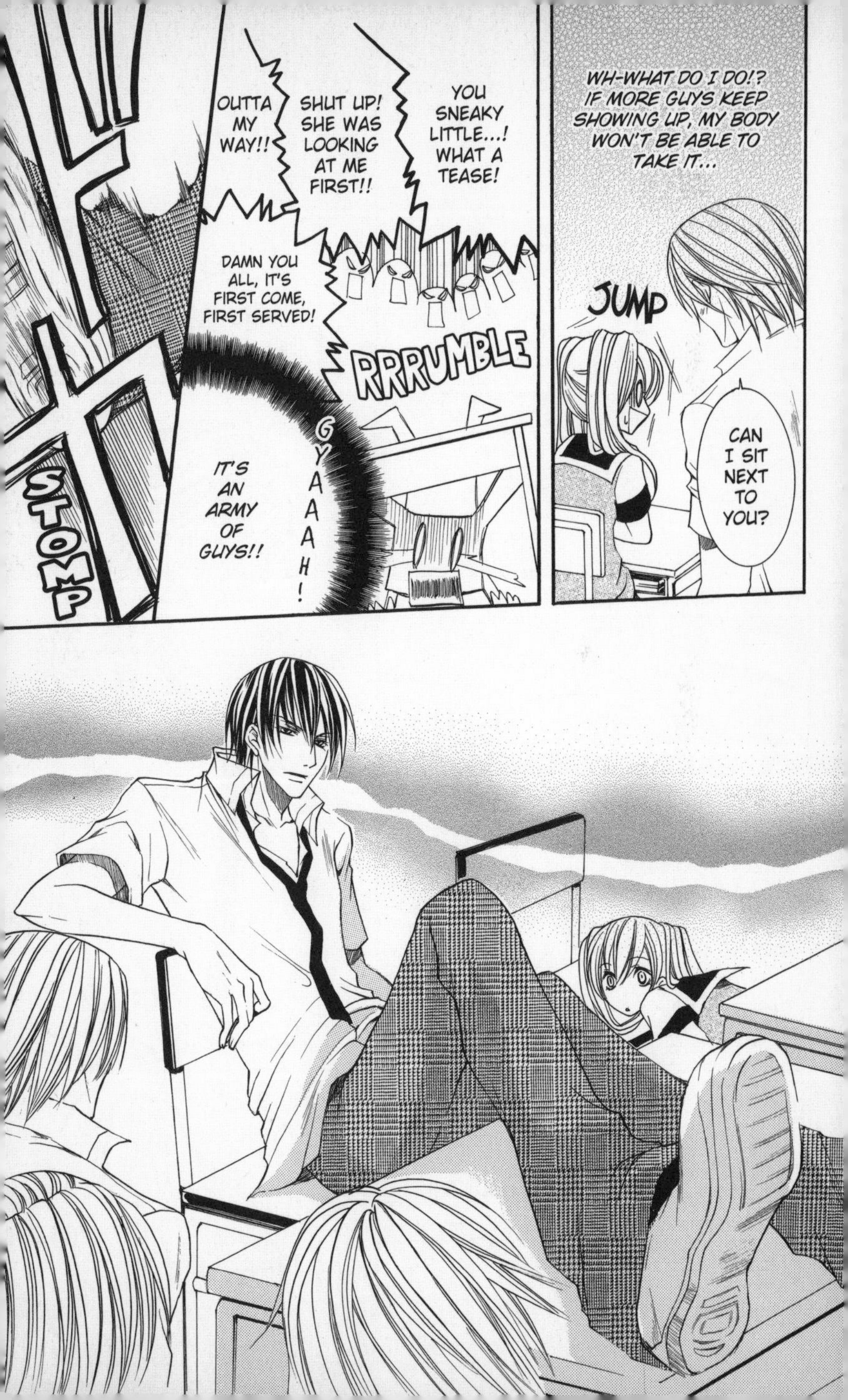
WH-WHAT DO I DO!? IF MORE GUYS KEEP SHOWING UP, MY BODY WON'T BE ABLE TO TAKE IT...
JUMP
CAN I SIT NEXT TO YOU?
YOU SNEAKY LITTLE...! WHAT A TEASE!
SHUT UP! SHE WAS LOOKING AT ME FIRST!!
OUTTA MY WAY!!
DAMN YOU ALL, IT'S FIRST COME, FIRST SERVED!
RRRUMBLE
GYAAAAH!
IT'S AN ARMY OF GUYS!!
STOMP

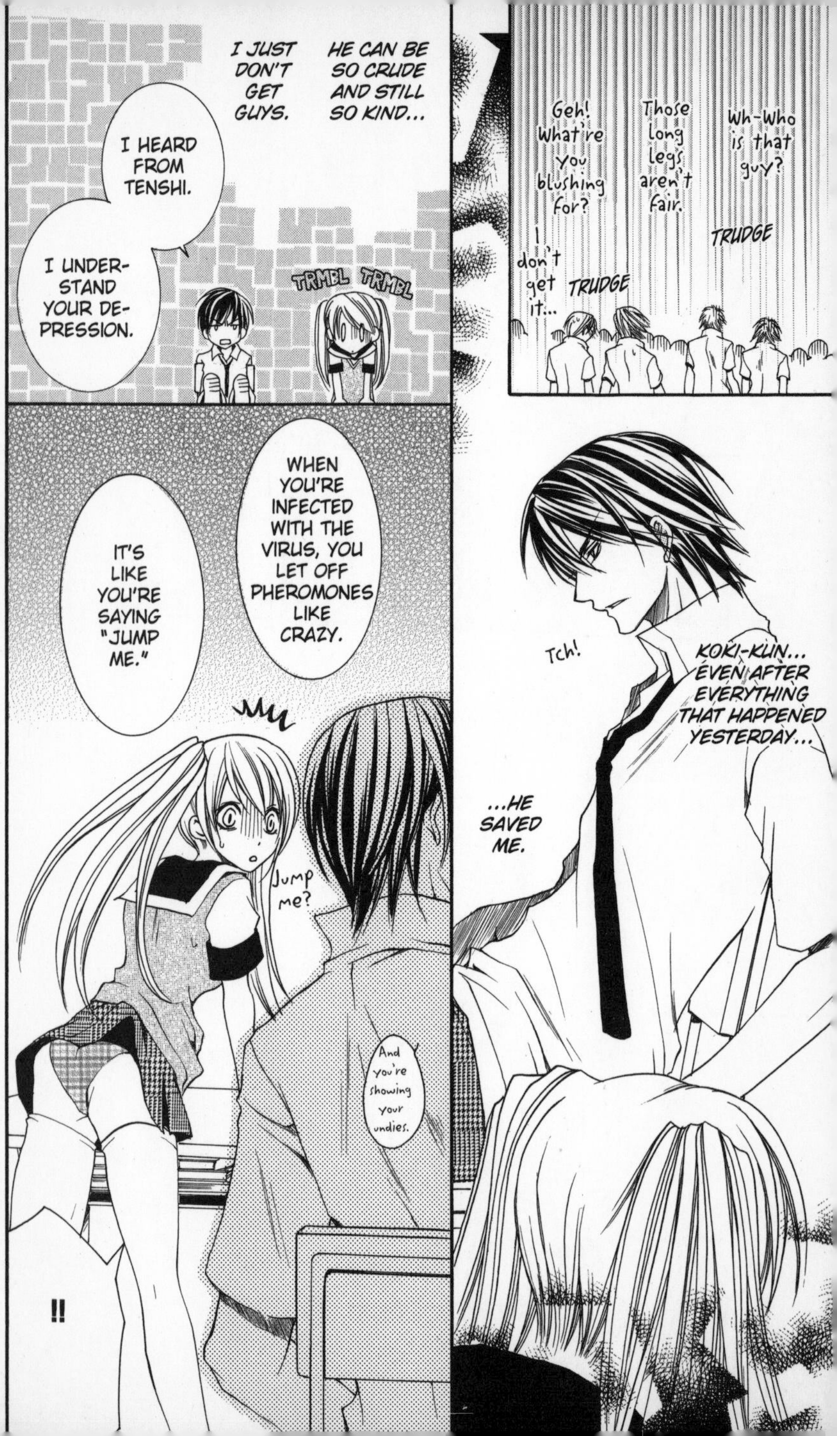
Wh-Who is that guy?
TRUDGE
Those long legs aren't fair.
Geh! What're you blushing for?
I don't get it...
TRUDGE
KOKI-KUN... EVEN AFTER EVERYTHING THAT HAPPENED YESTERDAY...
Tch!
...HE SAVED ME.
HE CAN BE SO CRUDE AND STILL SO KIND...
I JUST DON'T GET GUYS.
I HEARD FROM TENSHI.
I UNDER-STAND YOUR DE-PRESSION.
TRMBL TRMBL
WHEN YOU'RE INFECTED WITH THE VIRUS, YOU LET OFF PHEROMONES LIKE CRAZY.
IT'S LIKE YOU'RE SAYING "JUMP ME."
Jump me?
And you're showing your undies.
!!

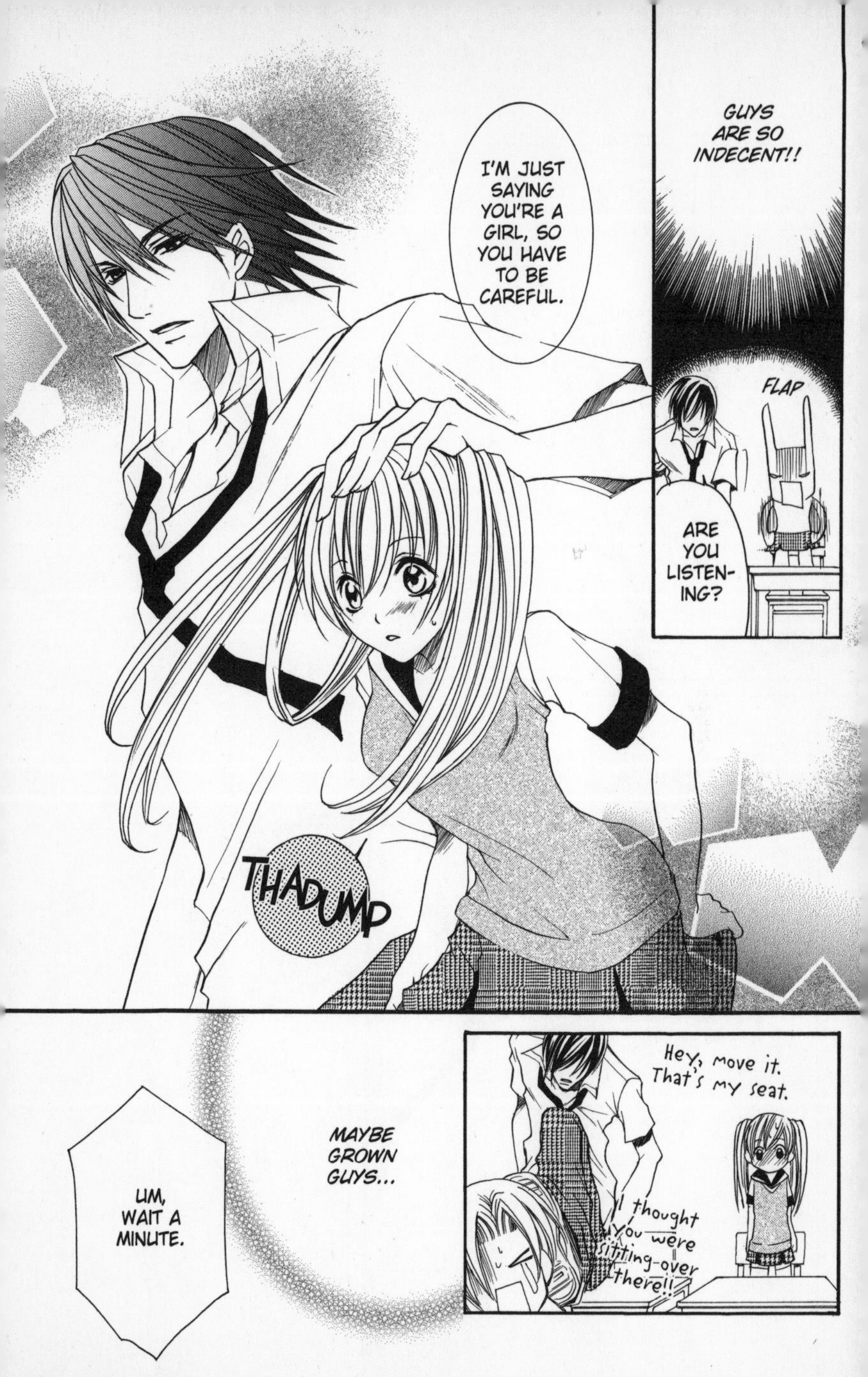
GUYS ARE SO INDECENT!!
FLAP
ARE YOU LISTEN-ING?
I'M JUST SAYING YOU'RE A GIRL, SO YOU HAVE TO BE CAREFUL.
THADUMP
Hey, move it. That's my seat.
I thought you were sitting over there!!
MAYBE GROWN GUYS...
UM, WAIT A MINUTE.

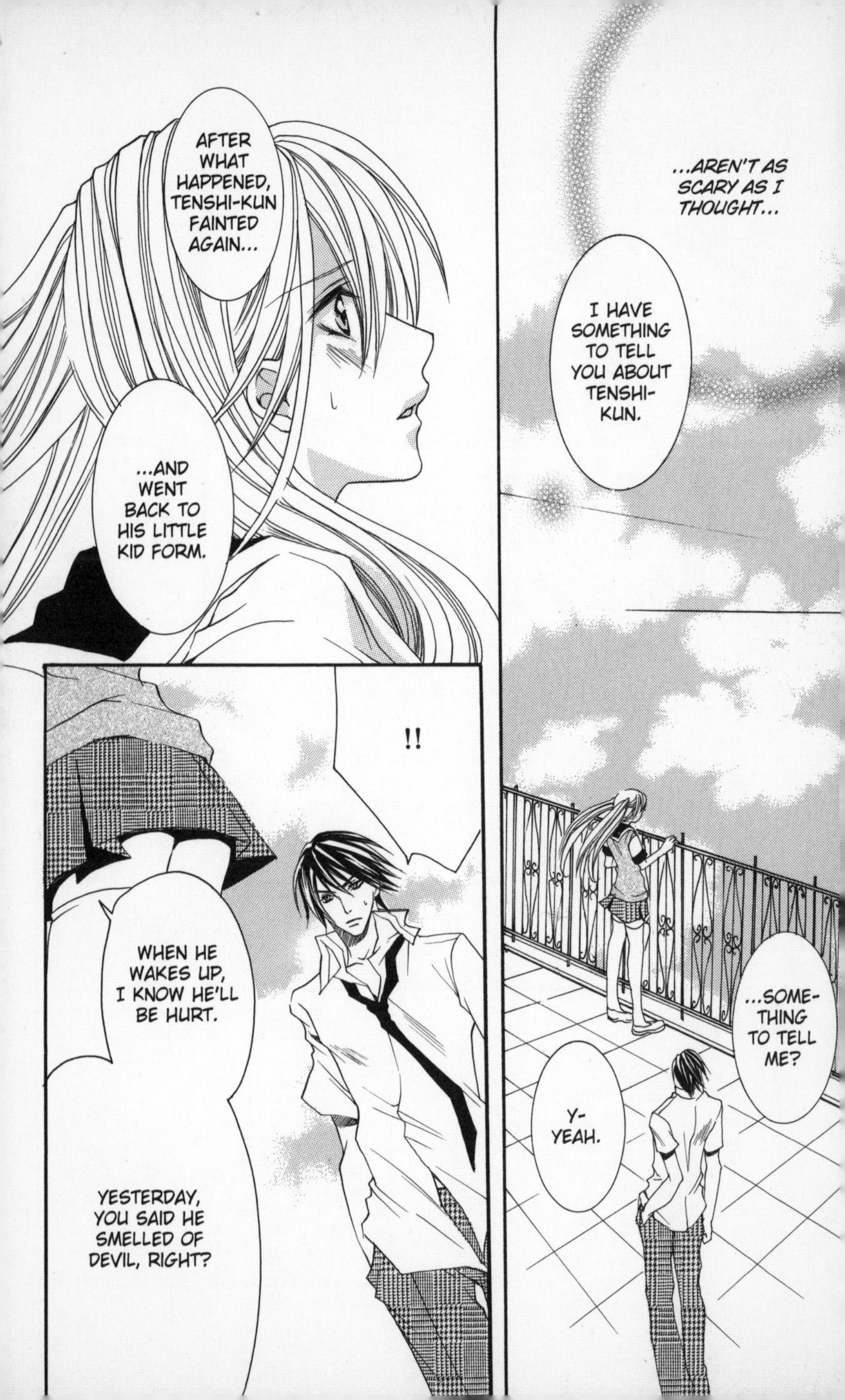
...AREN'T AS SCARY AS I THOUGHT...
I HAVE SOMETHING TO TELL YOU ABOUT TENSHI-KUN.
...SOME-THING TO TELL ME?
Y-YEAH.
AFTER WHAT HAPPENED, TENSHI-KUN FAINTED AGAIN...
...AND WENT BACK TO HIS LITTLE KID FORM.
!!
WHEN HE WAKES UP, I KNOW HE'LL BE HURT.
YESTERDAY, YOU SAID HE SMELLED OF DEVIL, RIGHT?

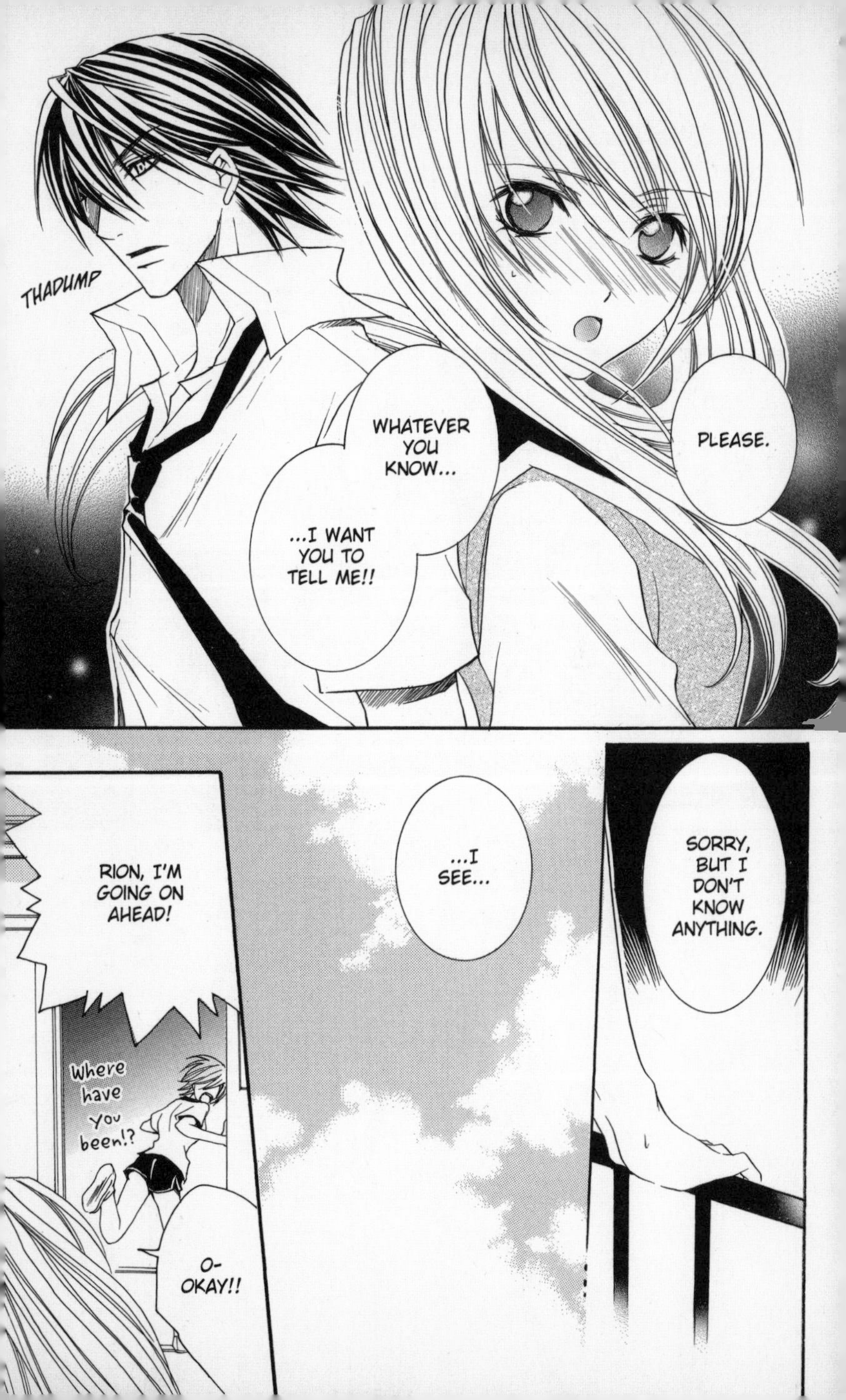
PLEASE.
WHATEVER YOU KNOW...
...I WANT YOU TO TELL ME!!
THADUMP
SORRY, BUT I DON'T KNOW ANYTHING.
...I SEE...
RION, I'M GOING ON AHEAD!
Where have you been!?
O- OKAY!!

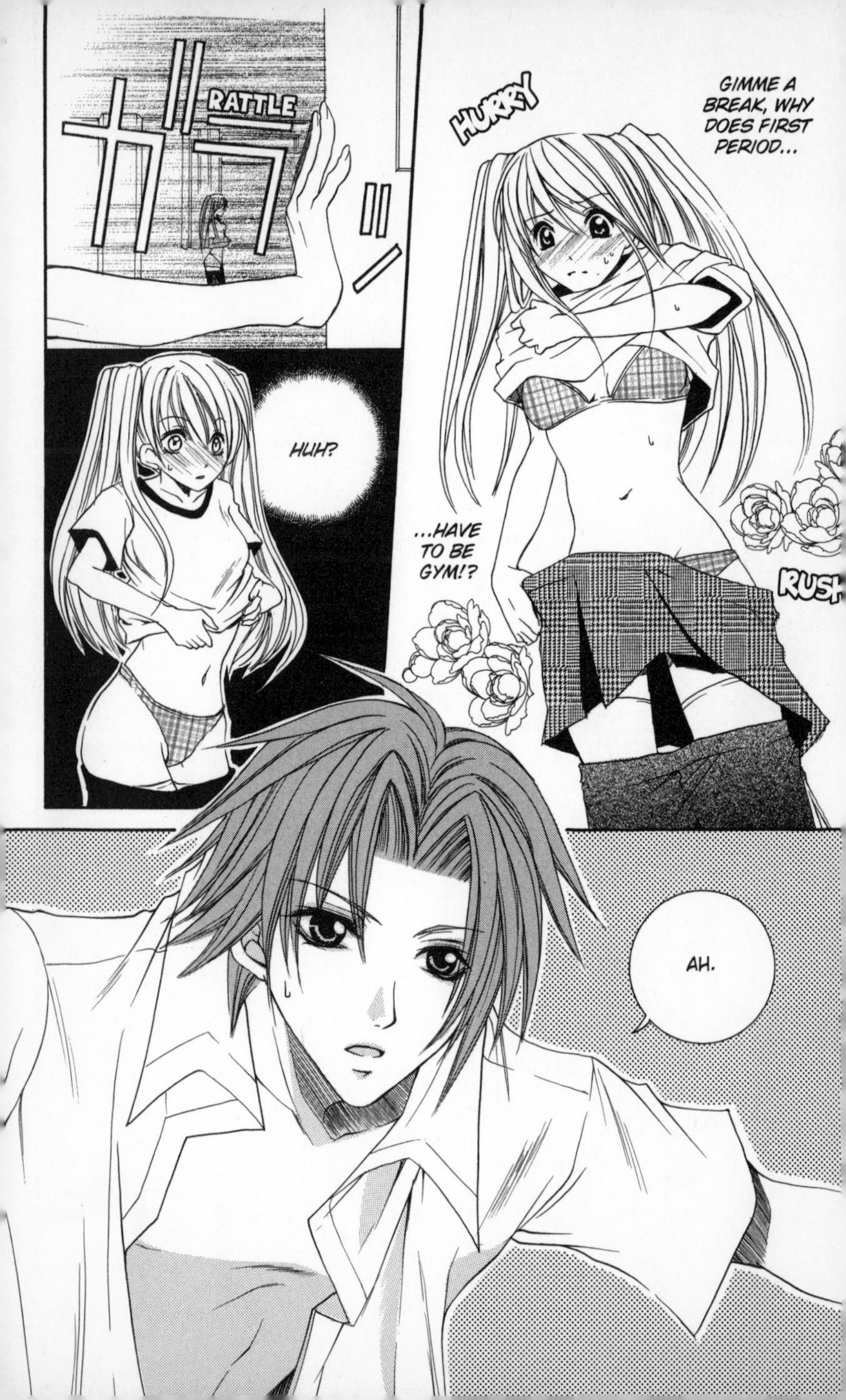

GIMME A BREAK, WHY DOES FIRST PERIOD...
HURRY
...HAVE TO BE GYM!?
RUSH
RATTLE
HUH?
AH.

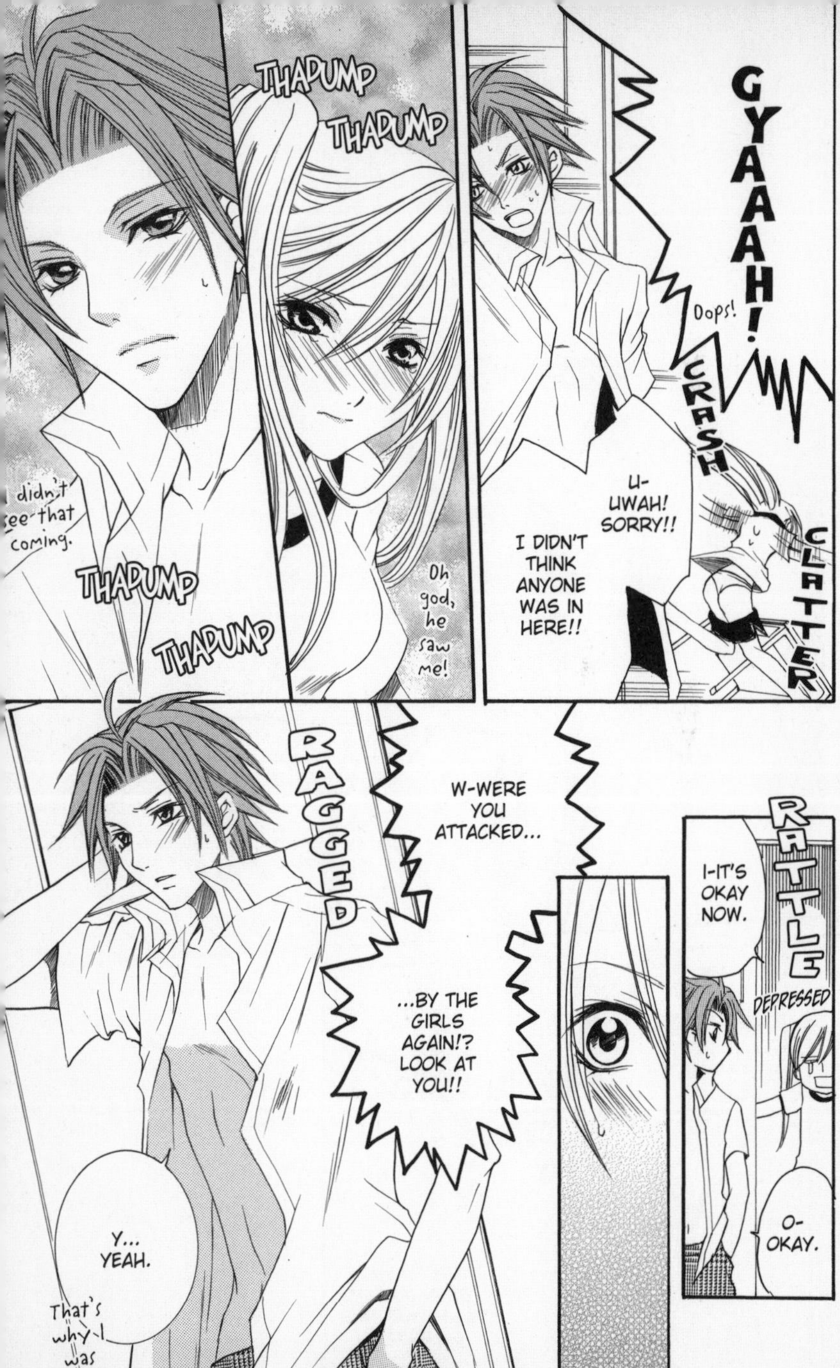
GYAAAH!
Oops!
CRASH
U-UWAH! SORRY!!
I DIDN'T THINK ANYONE WAS IN HERE!!
CLATTER
THADUMP
THADUMP
Oh god, he saw me!
didn't see that coming.
THADUMP
THADUMP
RATTLE
I-IT'S OKAY NOW.
DEPRESSED
O-OKAY.
W-WERE YOU ATTACKED...
...BY THE GIRLS AGAIN!? LOOK AT YOU!!
RAGGED
Y... YEAH.
That's why I was late.

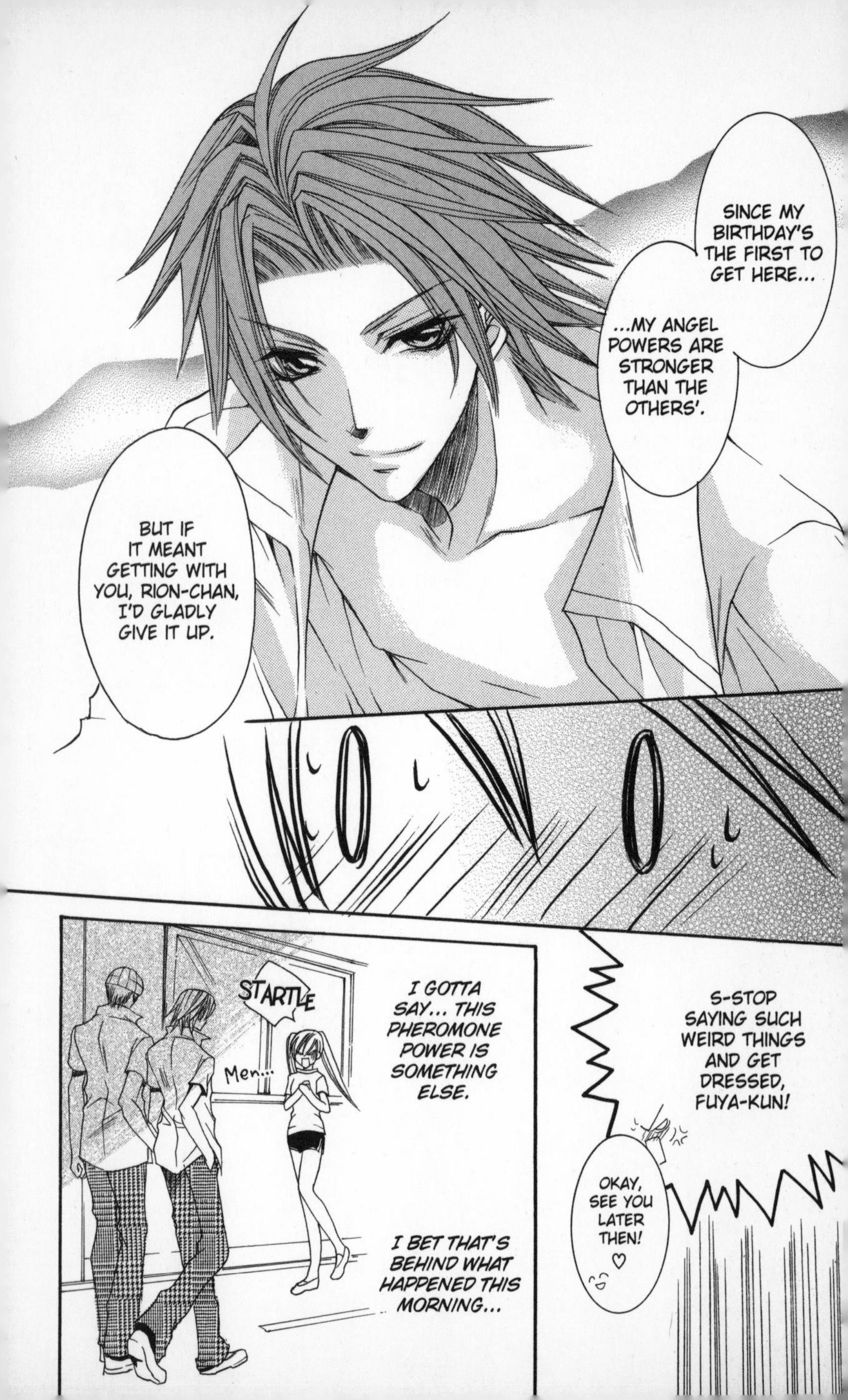
SINCE MY BIRTHDAY'S THE FIRST TO GET HERE...
...MY ANGEL POWERS ARE STRONGER THAN THE OTHERS'.
BUT IF IT MEANT GETTING WITH YOU, RION-CHAN, I'D GLADLY GIVE IT UP.
S-STOP SAYING SUCH WEIRD THINGS AND GET DRESSED, FUYA-KUN!
OKAY, SEE YOU LATER THEN! ♡
I GOTTA SAY... THIS PHEROMONE POWER IS SOMETHING ELSE.
STARTLE
Men...
I BET THAT'S BEHIND WHAT HAPPENED THIS MORNING...

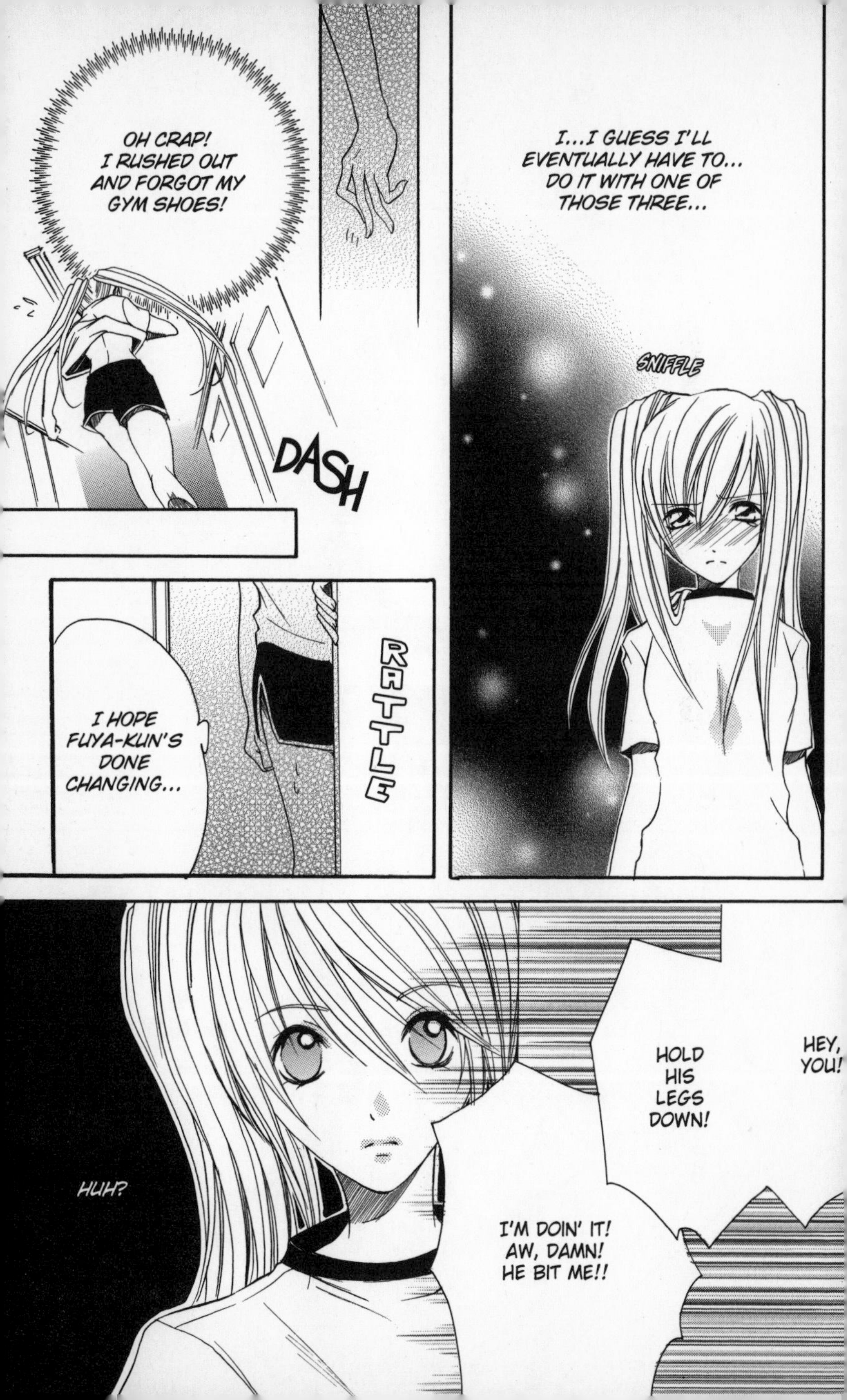
I...I GUESS I'LL EVENTUALLY HAVE TO... DO IT WITH ONE OF THOSE THREE...
SNIFFLE
OH CRAP! I RUSHED OUT AND FORGOT MY GYM SHOES!
DASH
RATTLE
I HOPE FUYA-KUN'S DONE CHANGING...
HEY, YOU!
HOLD HIS LEGS DOWN!
I'M DOIN' IT! AW, DAMN! HE BIT ME!!
HUH?

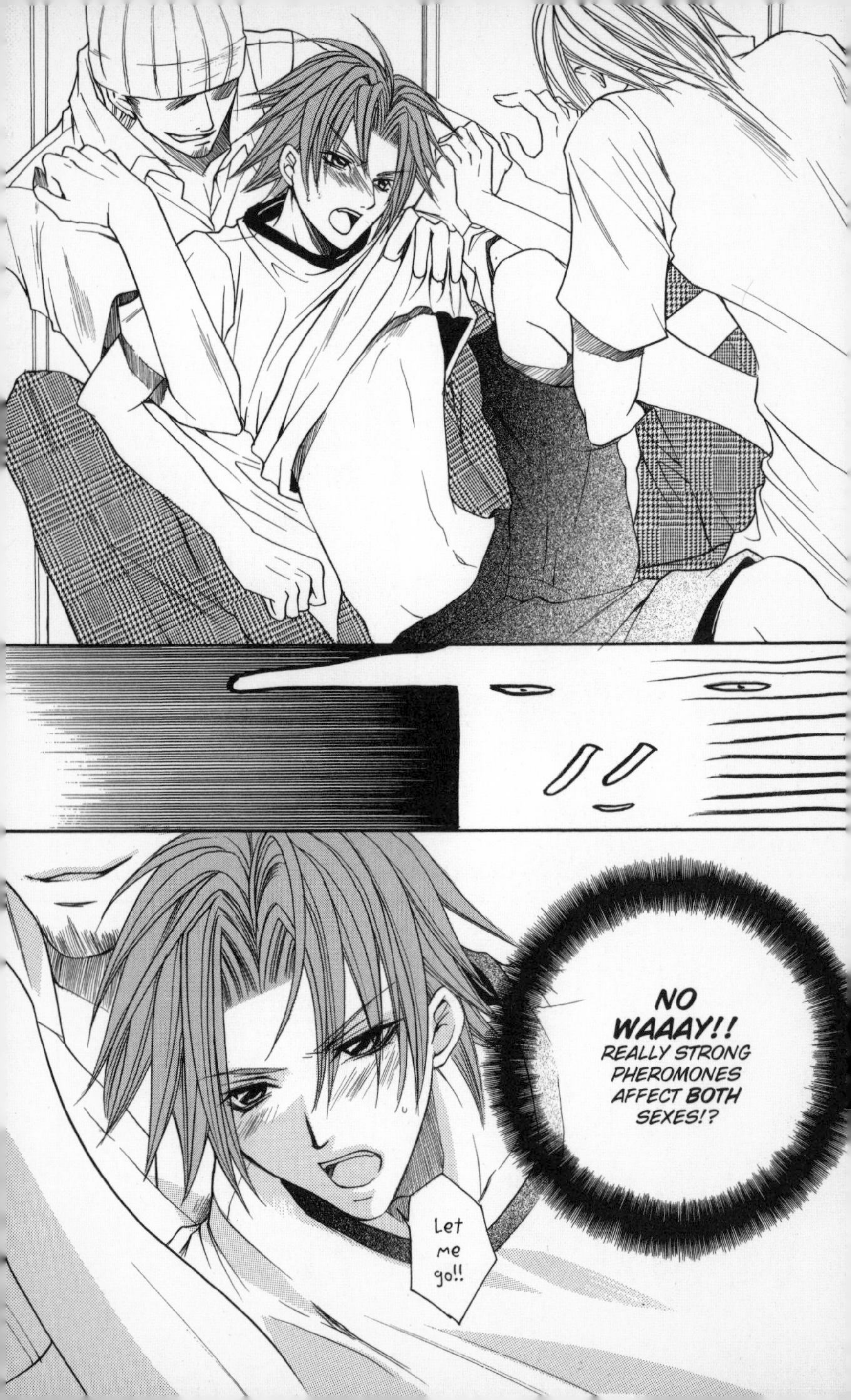
NO WAAAY!! REALLY STRONG PHEROMONES AFFECT BOTH SEXES!?
Let me go!!

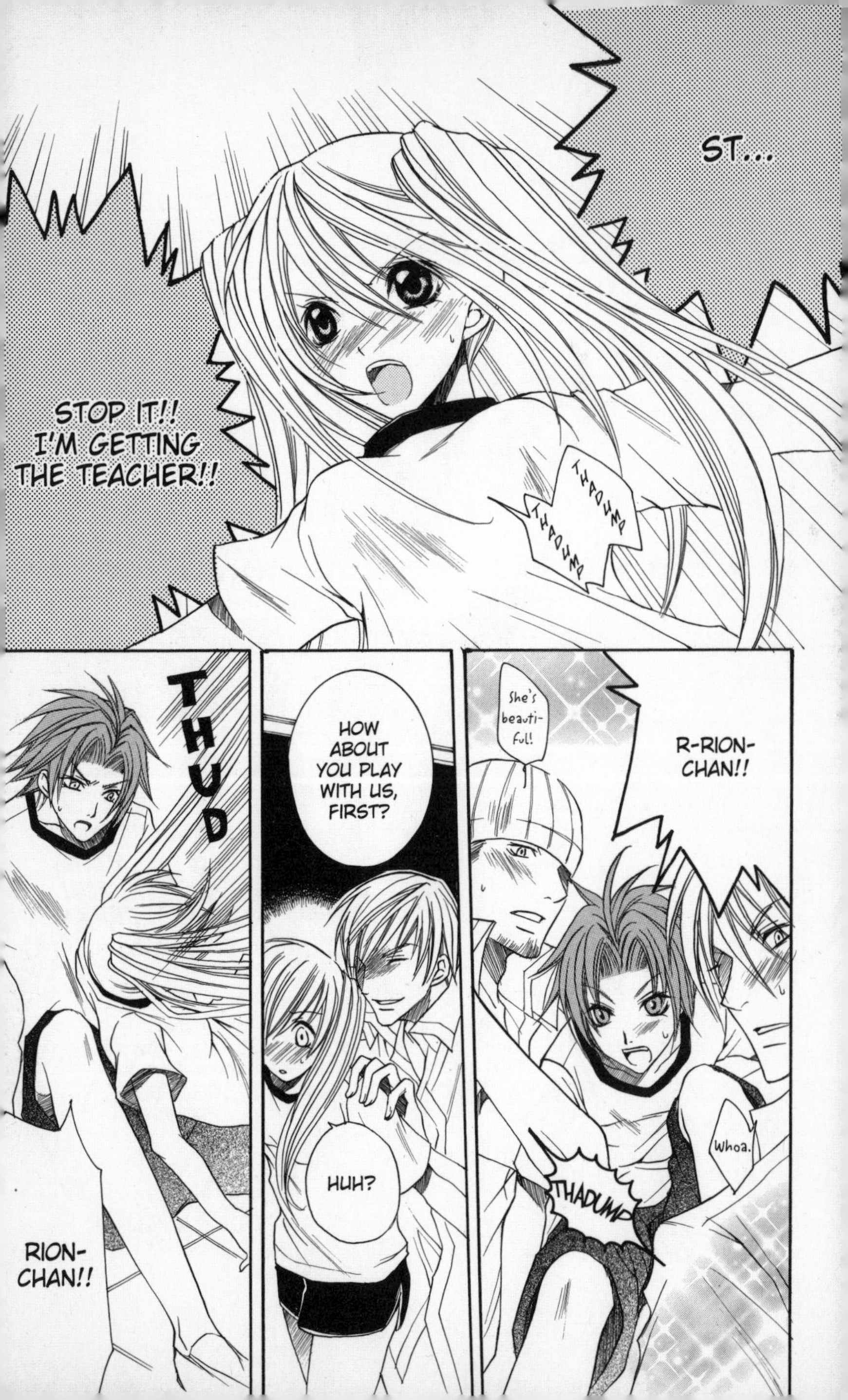
ST...
THADUMP THADUMP
STOP IT!! I'M GETTING THE TEACHER!!
R-RION-CHAN!!
She's beauti-ful!
Whoa.
THADUMP
HOW ABOUT YOU PLAY WITH US, FIRST?
HUH?
THUD
RION-CHAN!!

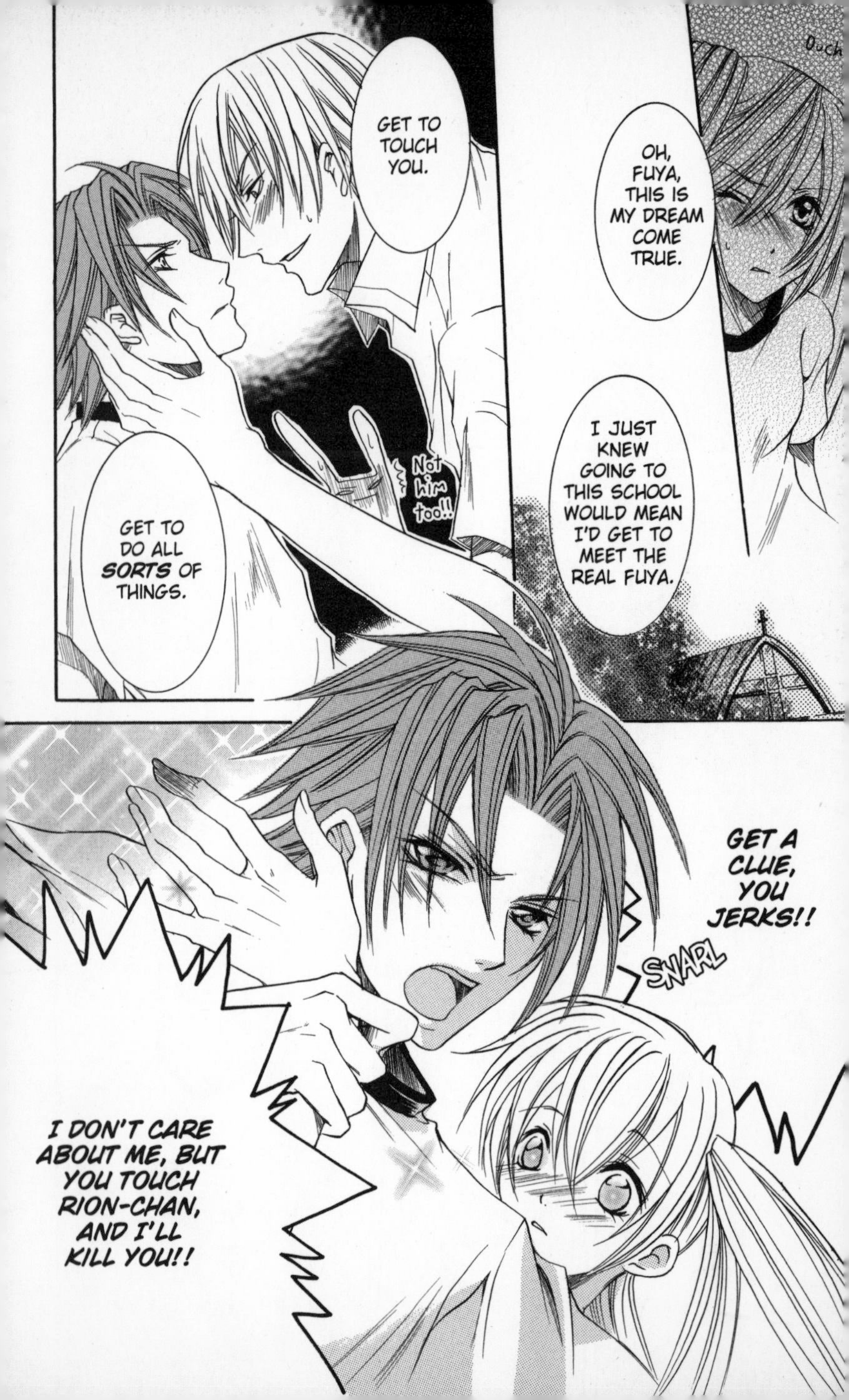
Ouch
OH, FUYA, THIS IS MY DREAM COME TRUE.
I JUST KNEW GOING TO THIS SCHOOL WOULD MEAN I'D GET TO MEET THE REAL FUYA.
GET TO TOUCH YOU.
GET TO DO ALL SORTS OF THINGS.
Not him too!!
GET A CLUE, YOU JERKS!!
SNARL
I DON'T CARE ABOUT ME, BUT YOU TOUCH RION-CHAN, AND I'LL KILL YOU!!

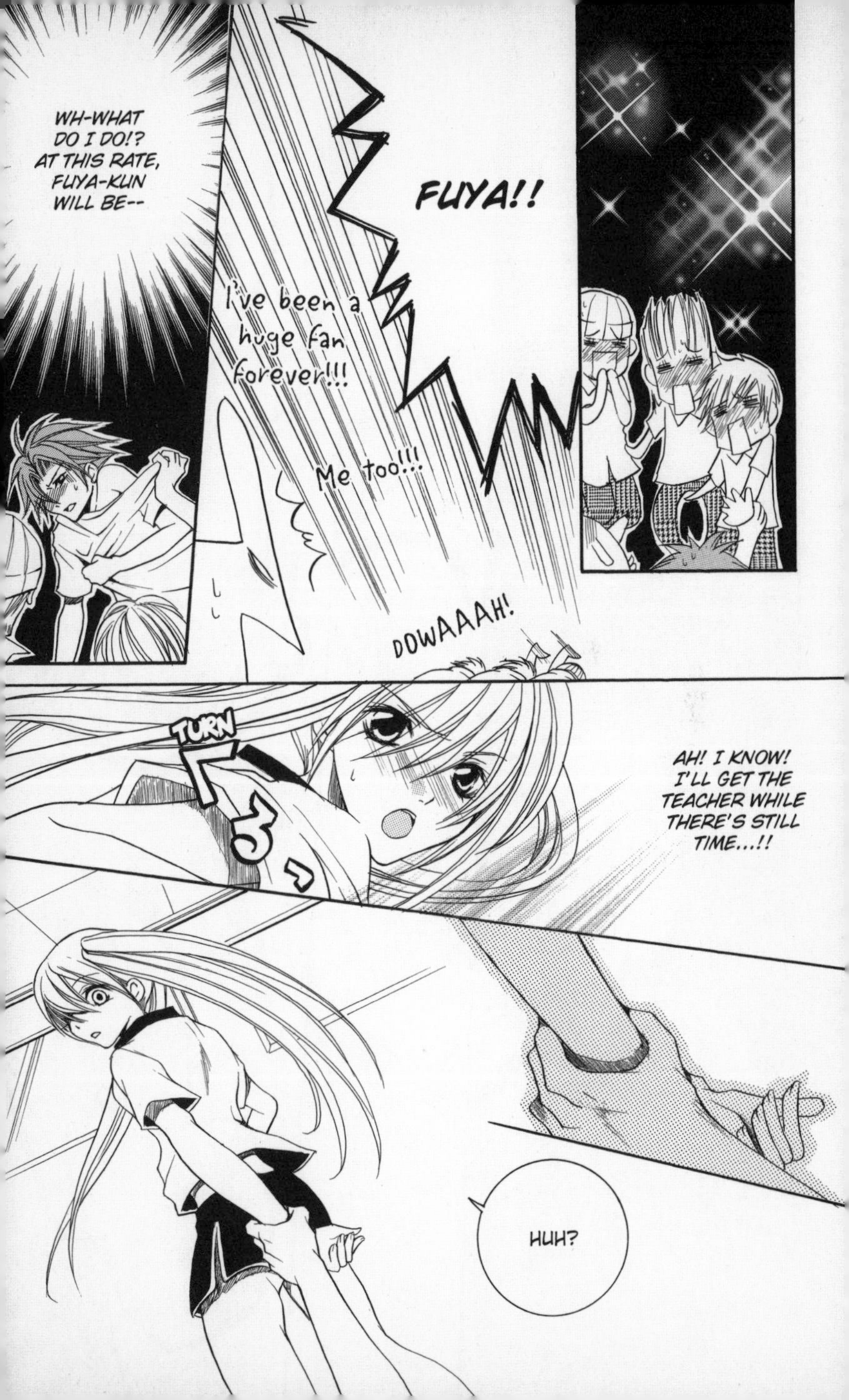
FUYA!!
I've been a huge fan forever!!!
Me too!!!
DOWAAAH!
WH-WHAT DO I DO!? AT THIS RATE, FUYA-KUN WILL BE--
AH! I KNOW! I'LL GET THE TEACHER WHILE THERE'S STILL TIME...!!
TURN
HUH?

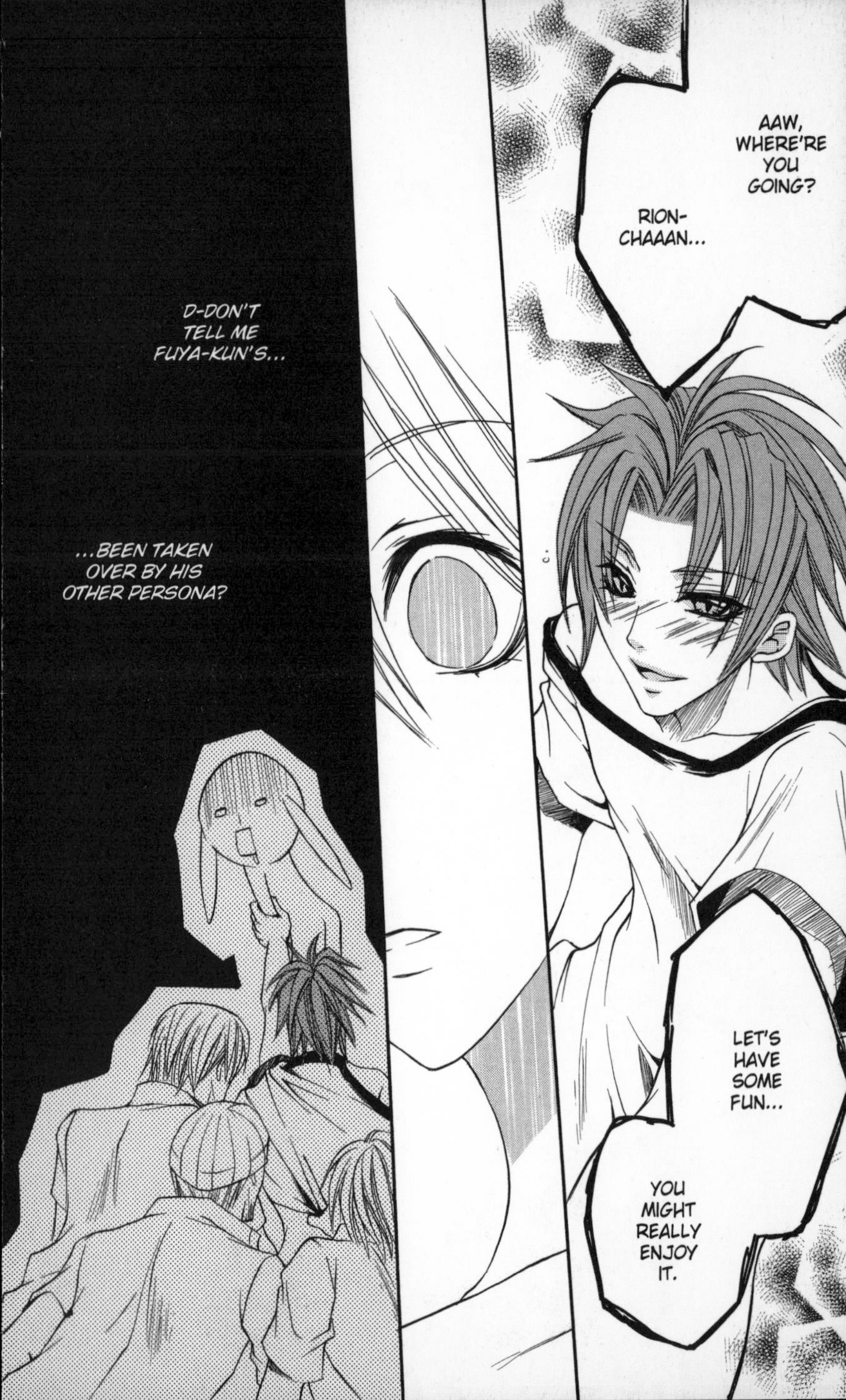
AAW, WHERE'RE YOU GOING?
RION-CHAAAN...
LET'S HAVE SOME FUN...
YOU MIGHT REALLY ENJOY IT.
D-DON'T TELL ME FUYA-KUN'S...
...BEEN TAKEN OVER BY HIS OTHER PERSONA?

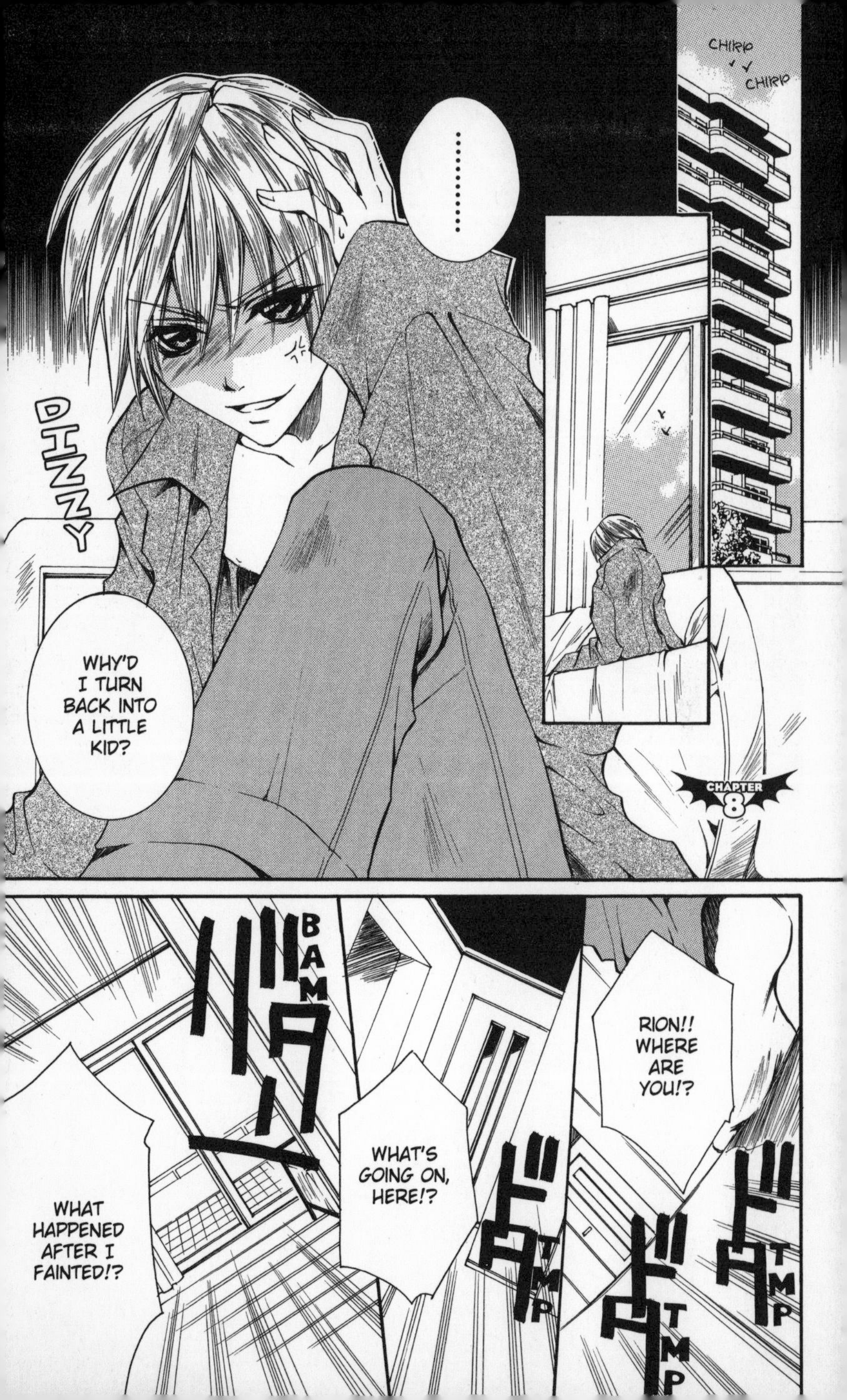
CHIRP
CHIRP
CHAPTER 8
......
DIZZY
WHY'D I TURN BACK INTO A LITTLE KID?
RION!! WHERE ARE YOU!?
TMP
TMP
TMP
WHAT'S GOING ON, HERE!?
BAM
WHAT HAPPENED AFTER I FAINTED!?

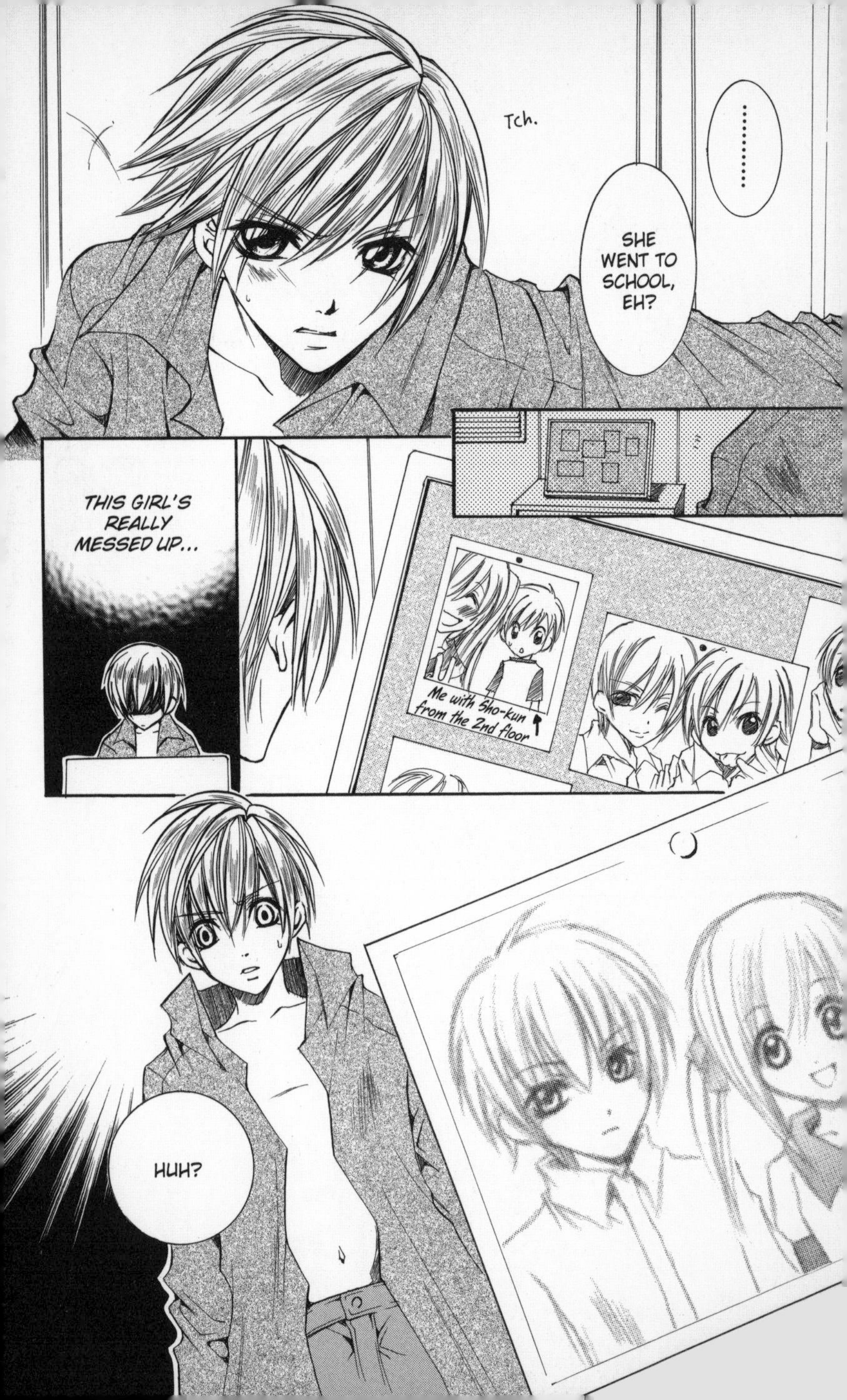
……
SHE WENT TO SCHOOL, EH?
Tch.
Me with Sho-kun from the 2nd floor
THIS GIRL'S REALLY MESSED UP...
HUH?

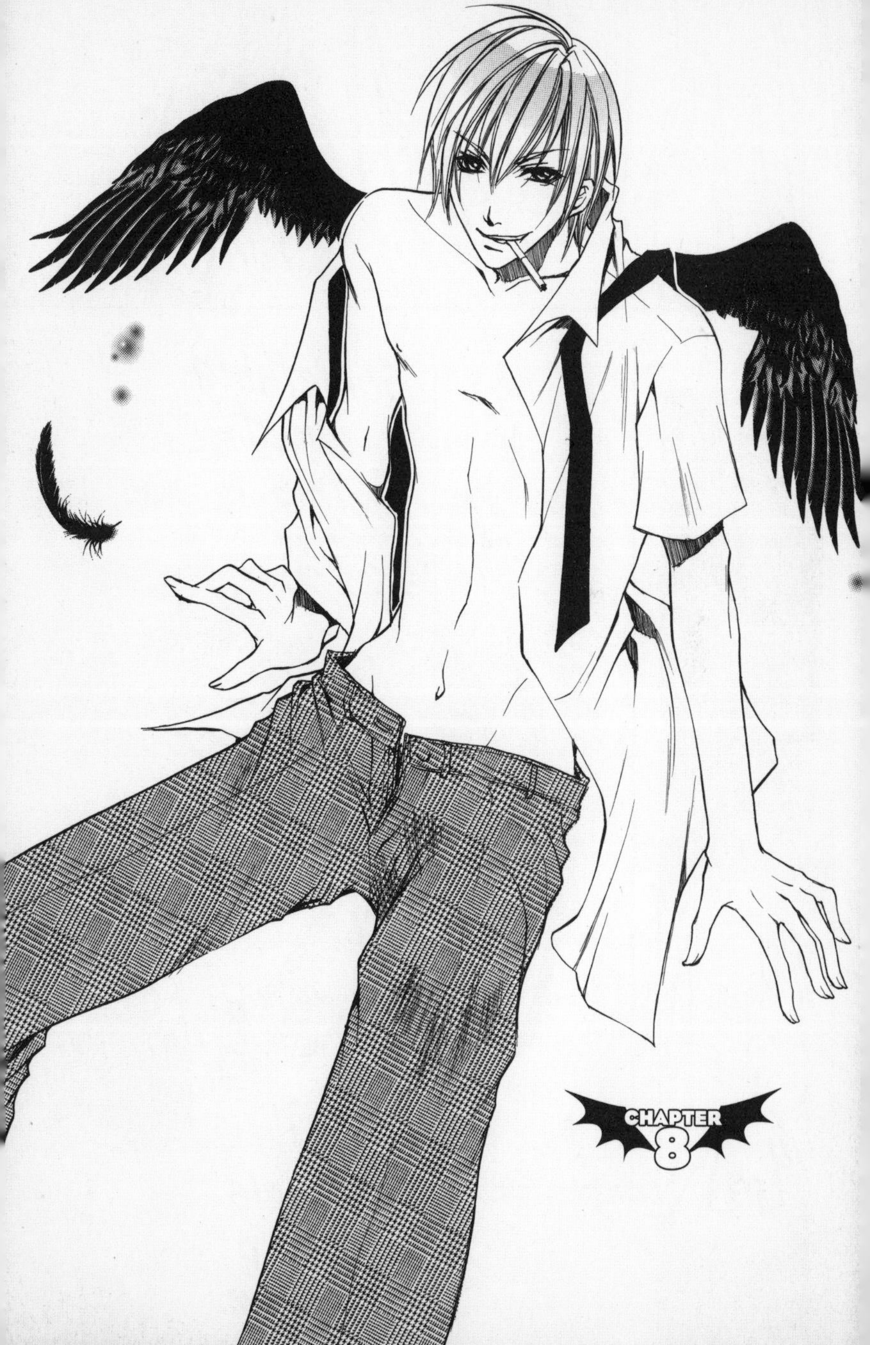
CHAPTER
8

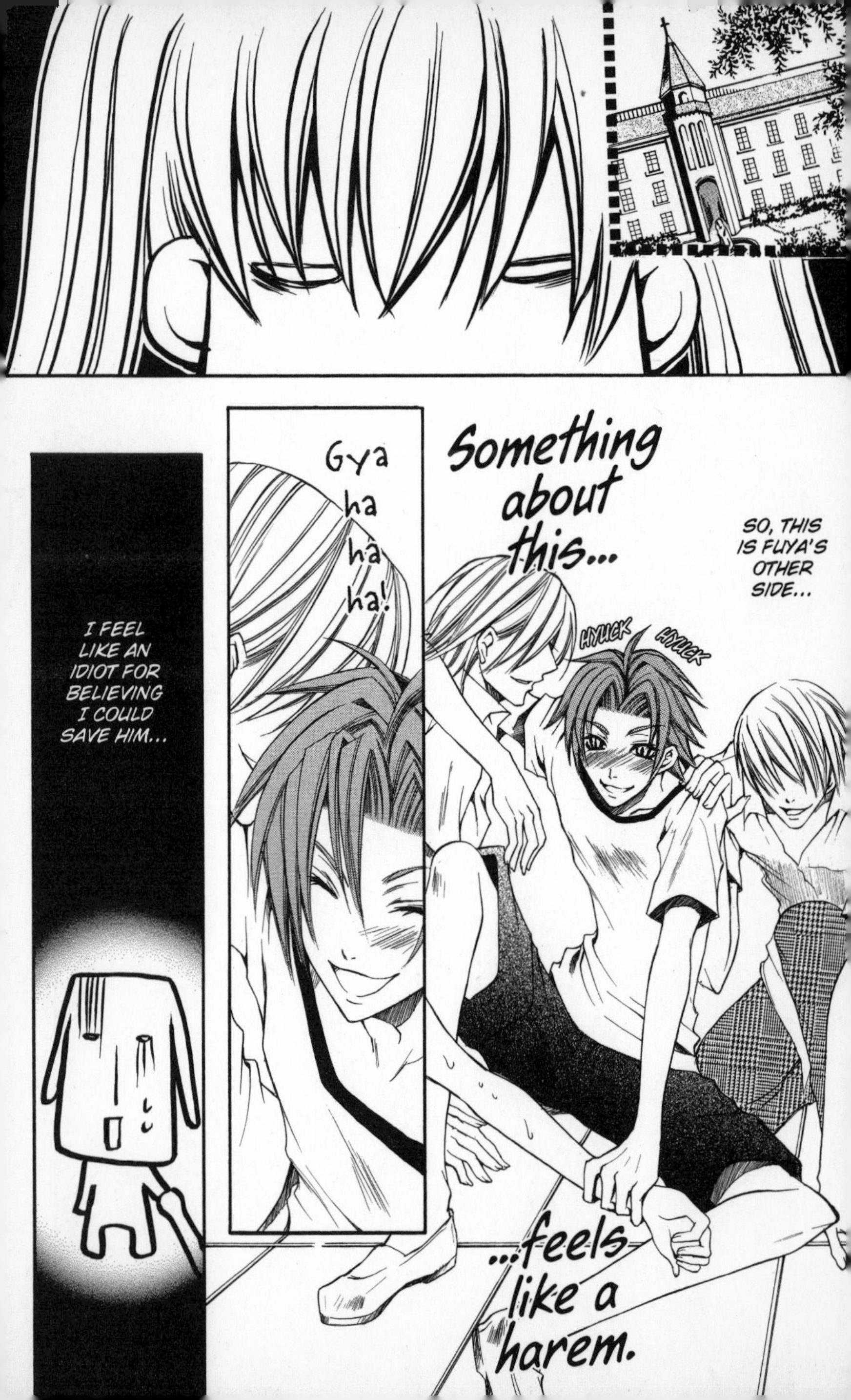
SO, THIS IS FUYA'S OTHER SIDE...
Something about this...
HYUCK HYUCK
Gya ha ha ha!
...feels like a harem.
I FEEL LIKE AN IDIOT FOR BELIEVING I COULD SAVE HIM...

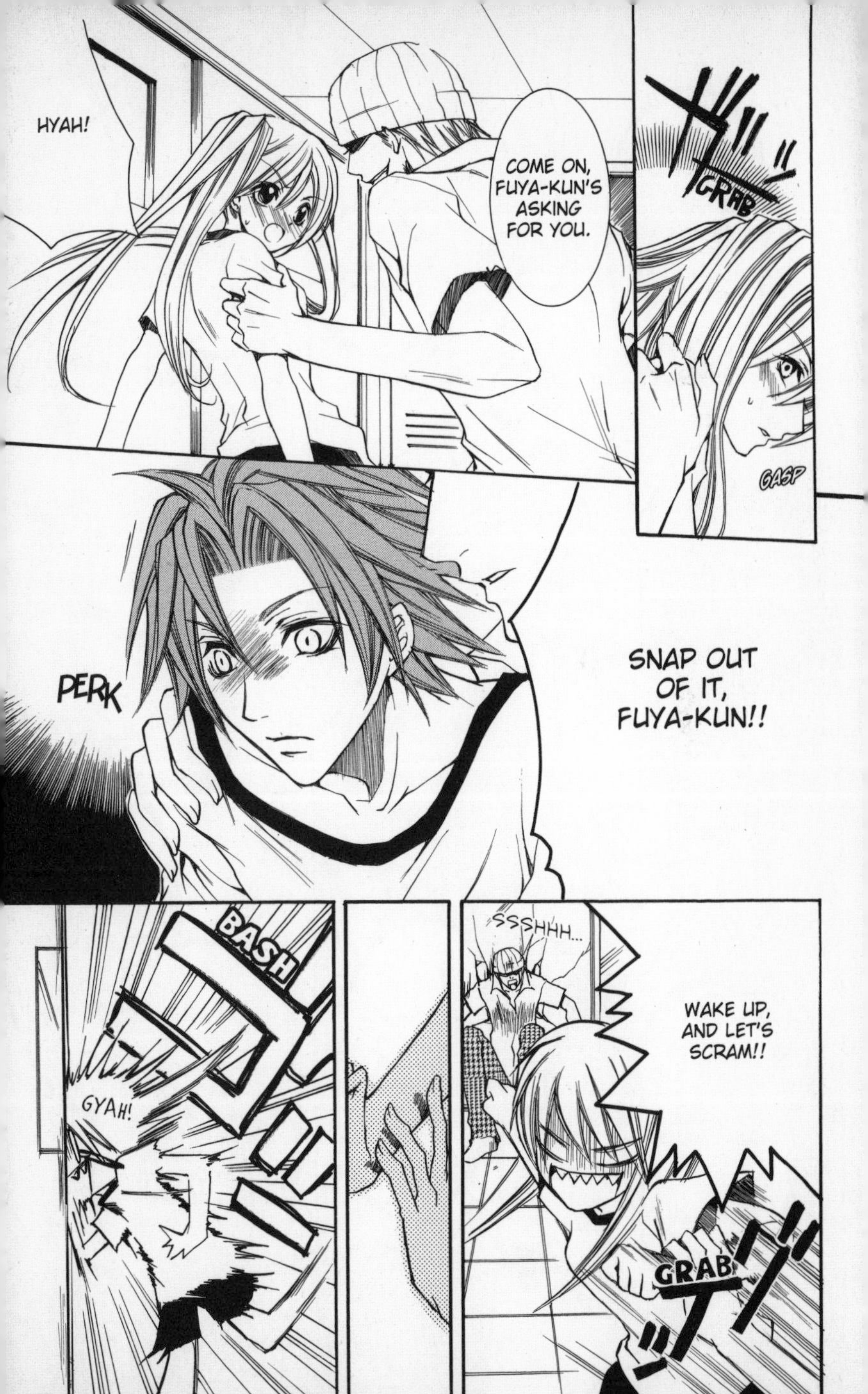
GRAB
GASP
COME ON, FUYA-KUN'S ASKING FOR YOU.
HYAH!
SNAP OUT OF IT, FUYA-KUN!!
PERK
SSSHHH...
WAKE UP, AND LET'S SCRAM!!
GRAB
BASH
GYAH!

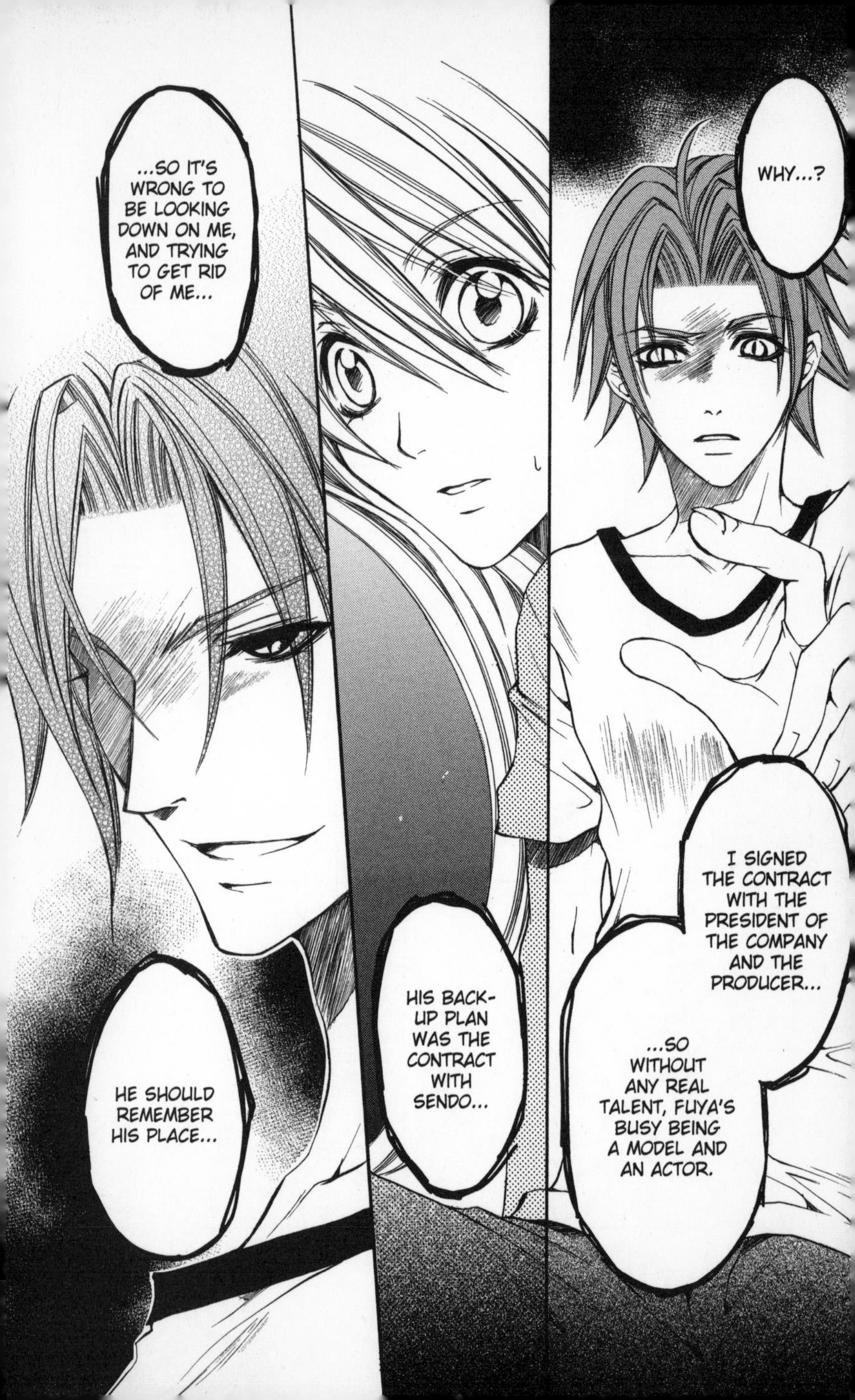
WHY...?
I SIGNED THE CONTRACT WITH THE PRESIDENT OF THE COMPANY AND THE PRODUCER...
...SO WITHOUT ANY REAL TALENT, FUYA'S BUSY BEING A MODEL AND AN ACTOR.
HIS BACK-UP PLAN WAS THE CONTRACT WITH SENDO...
...SO IT'S WRONG TO BE LOOKING DOWN ON ME, AND TRYING TO GET RID OF ME...
HE SHOULD REMEMBER HIS PLACE...

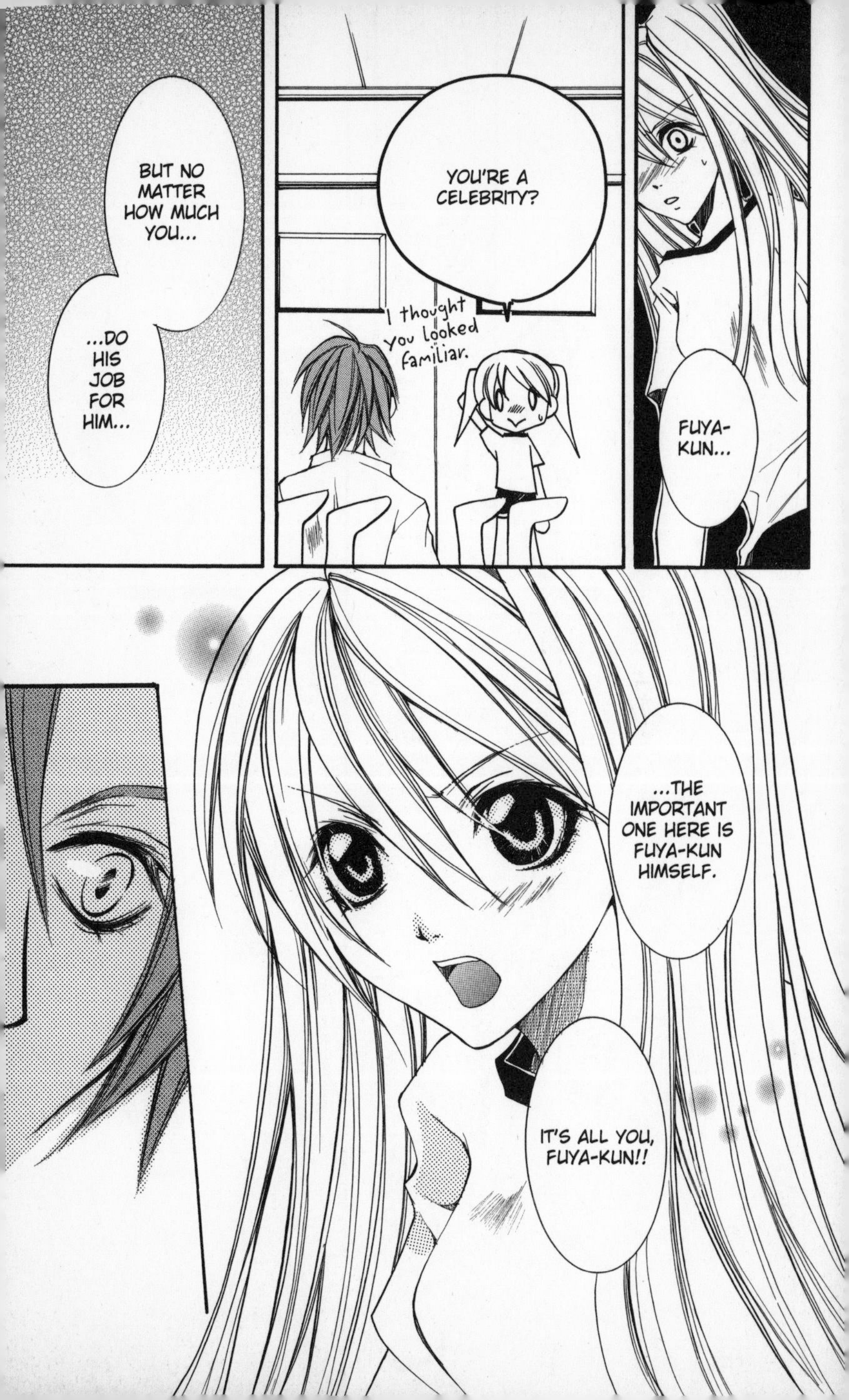
FUYA-KUN...
YOU'RE A CELEBRITY?
I thought you looked familiar.
BUT NO MATTER HOW MUCH YOU...
...DO HIS JOB FOR HIM...
...THE IMPORTANT ONE HERE IS FUYA-KUN HIMSELF.
IT'S ALL YOU, FUYA-KUN!!

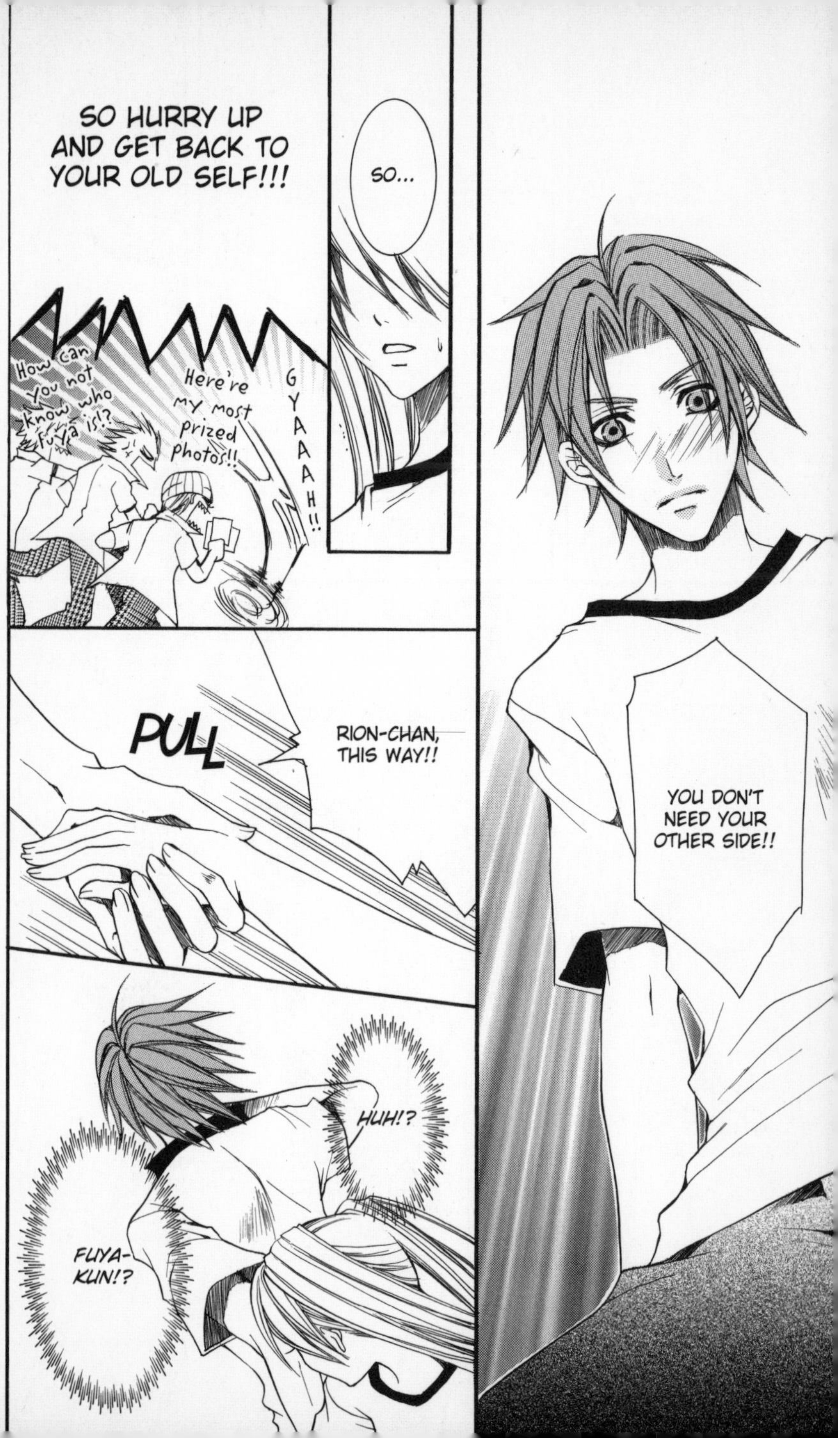
YOU DON'T NEED YOUR OTHER SIDE!!
SO...
SO HURRY UP AND GET BACK TO YOUR OLD SELF!!!
GYAAAAH!!
Here're my most prized photos!!
How can you not know who Fuya is!?
PULL
RION-CHAN, THIS WAY!!
HUH!?
FUYA-KUN!?

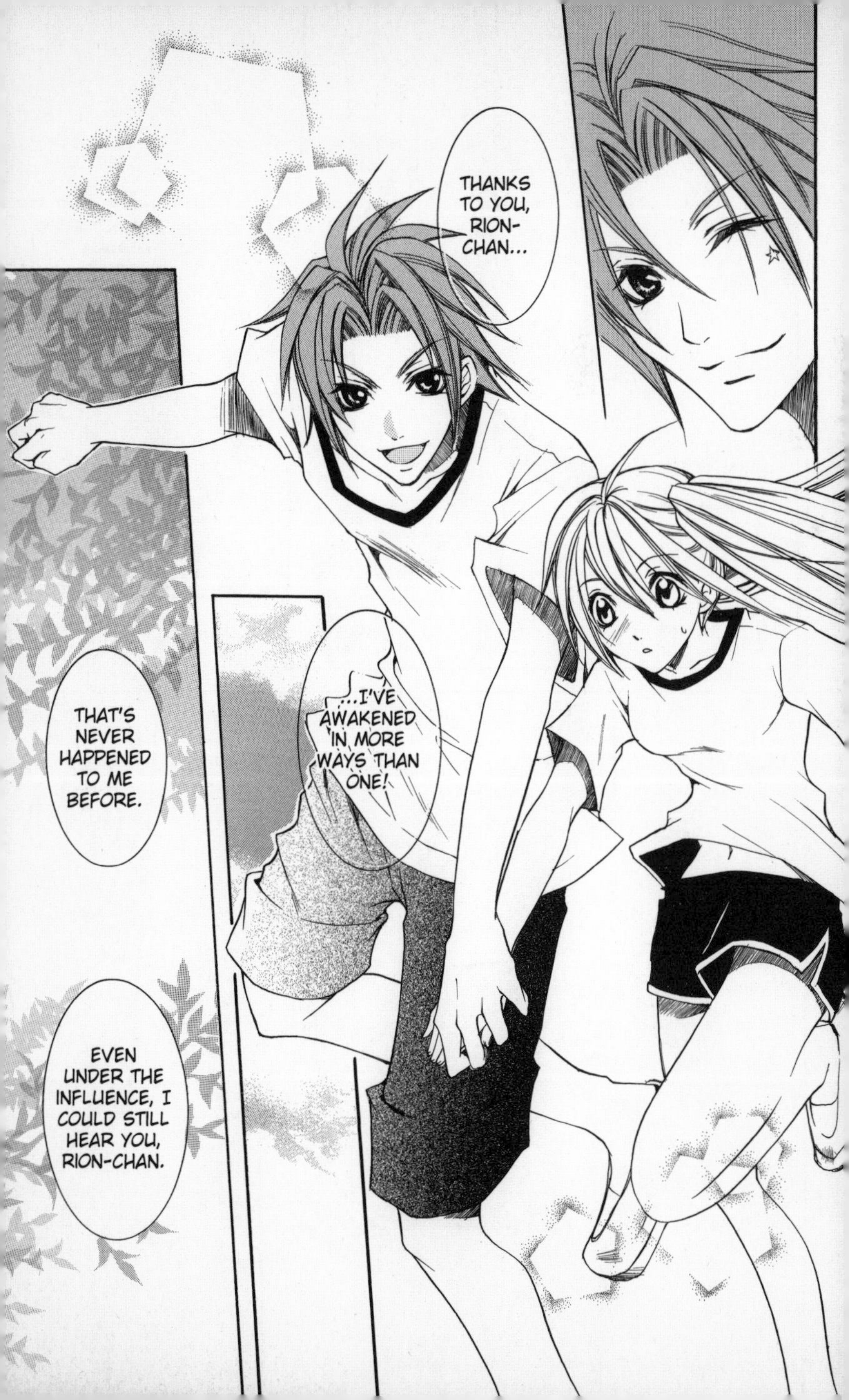
THANKS TO YOU, RION-CHAN...
...I'VE AWAKENED IN MORE WAYS THAN ONE!
THAT'S NEVER HAPPENED TO ME BEFORE.
EVEN UNDER THE INFLUENCE, I COULD STILL HEAR YOU, RION-CHAN.

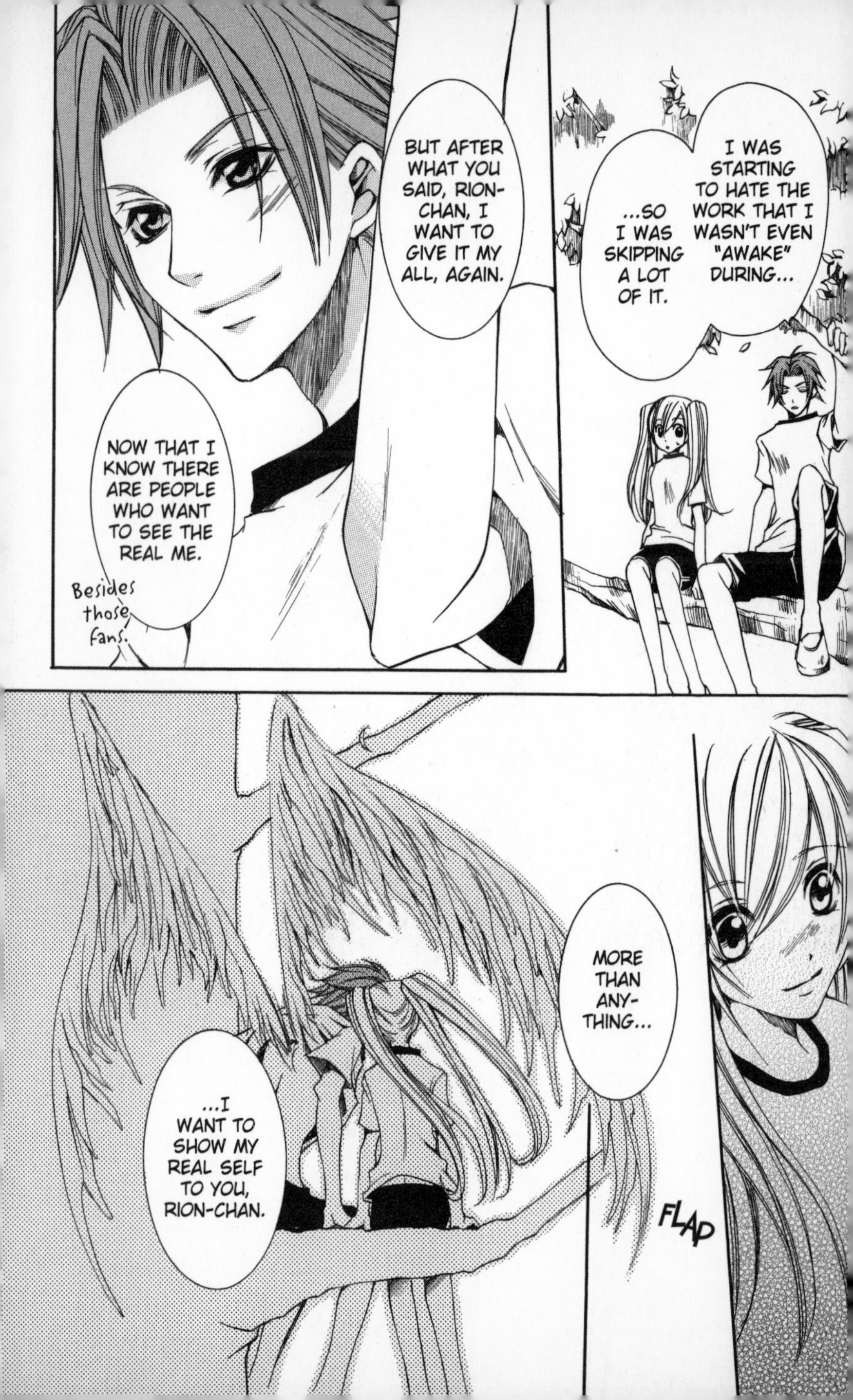
I WAS STARTING TO HATE THE WORK THAT I WASN'T EVEN "AWAKE" DURING...
...SO I WAS SKIPPING A LOT OF IT.
BUT AFTER WHAT YOU SAID, RION-CHAN, I WANT TO GIVE IT MY ALL, AGAIN.
NOW THAT I KNOW THERE ARE PEOPLE WHO WANT TO SEE THE REAL ME.
Besides those fans.
MORE THAN ANY-THING...
FLAP
...I WANT TO SHOW MY REAL SELF TO YOU, RION-CHAN.

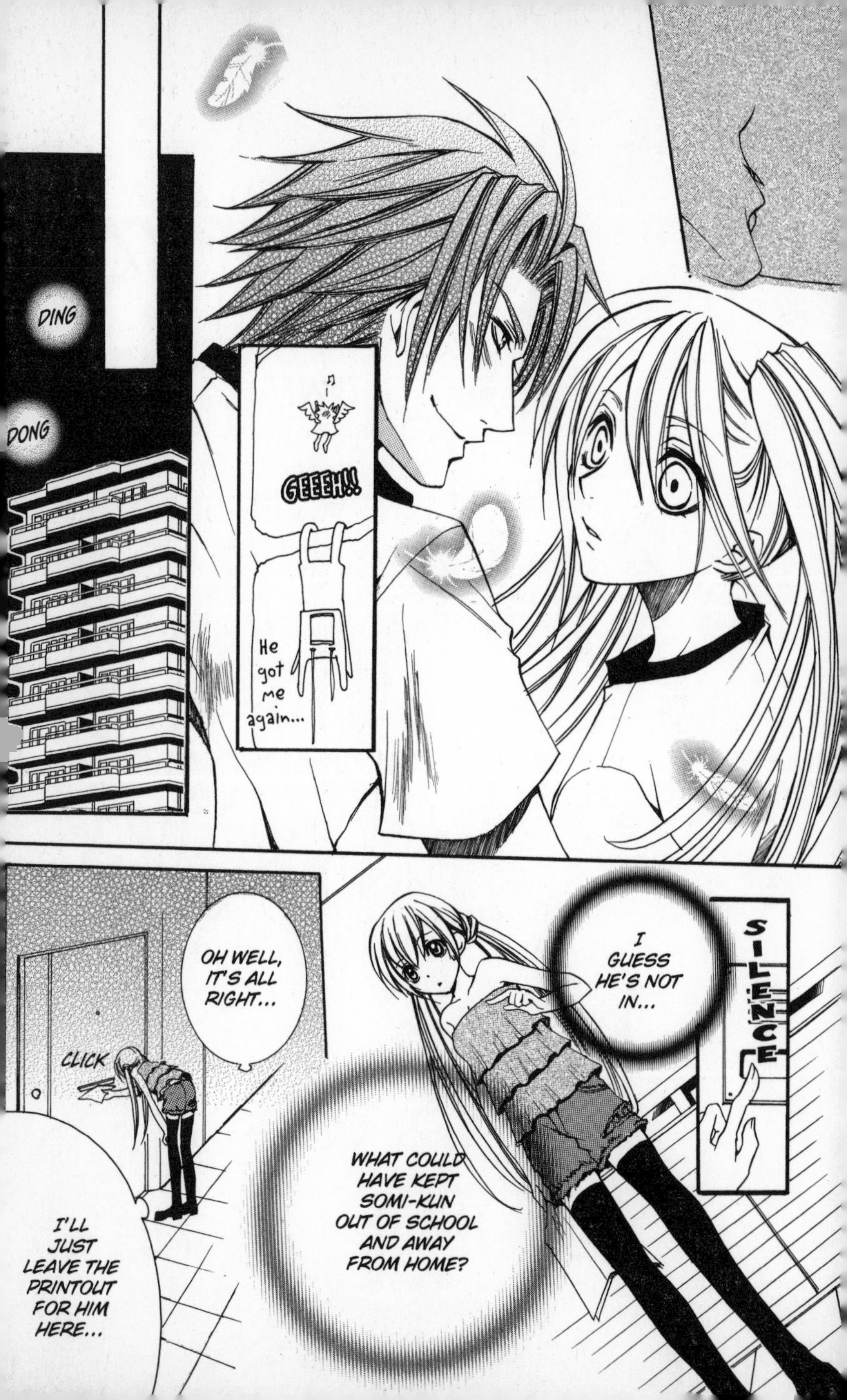
GEEEH!!
He got me again...
DING
DONG
SILENCE
I GUESS HE'S NOT IN...
WHAT COULD HAVE KEPT SOMI-KUN OUT OF SCHOOL AND AWAY FROM HOME?
OH WELL, IT'S ALL RIGHT...
CLICK
I'LL JUST LEAVE THE PRINTOUT FOR HIM HERE...

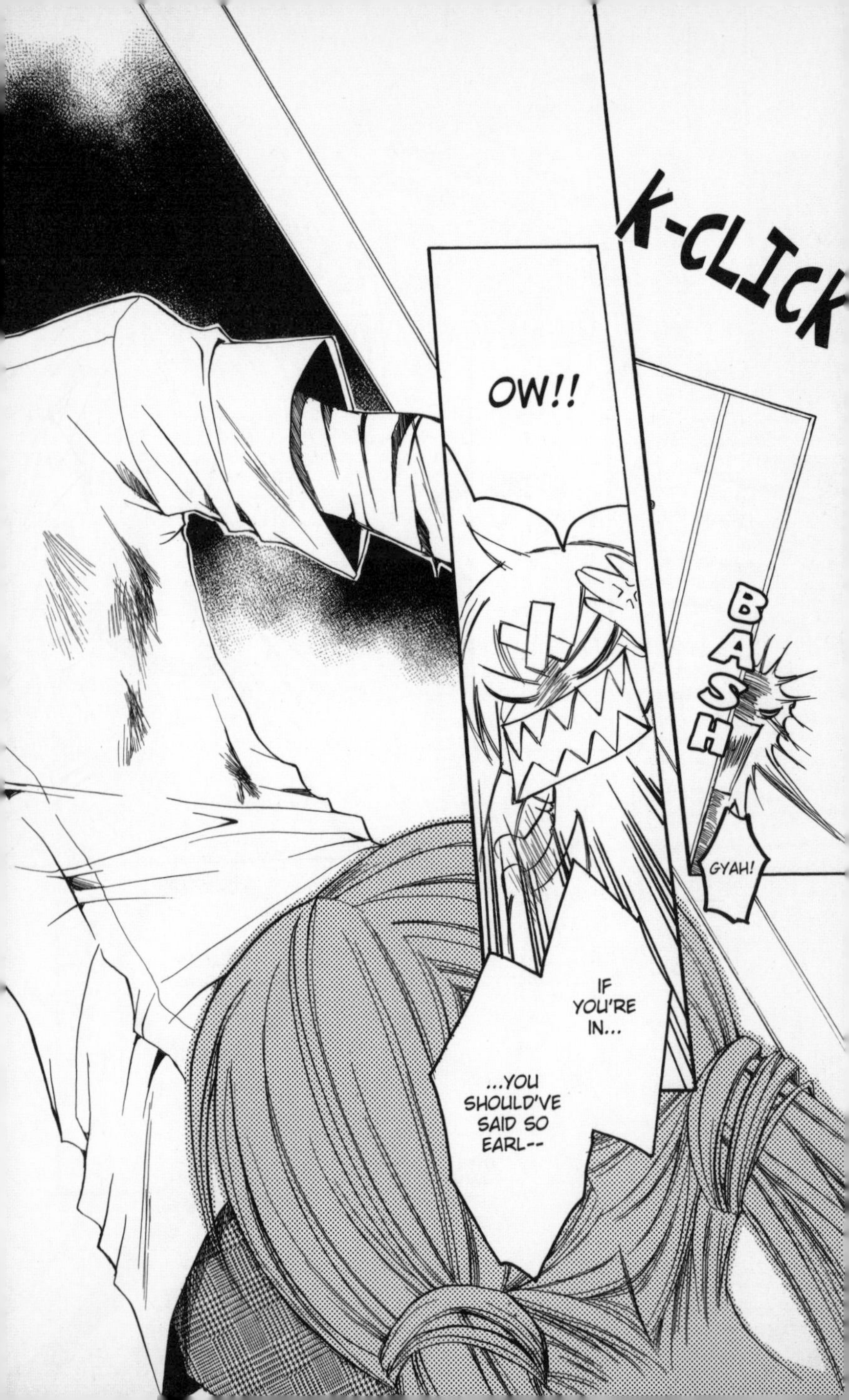
K-CLICK
OW!!
BASH
GYAH!
IF YOU'RE IN...
...YOU SHOULD'VE SAID SO EARL--

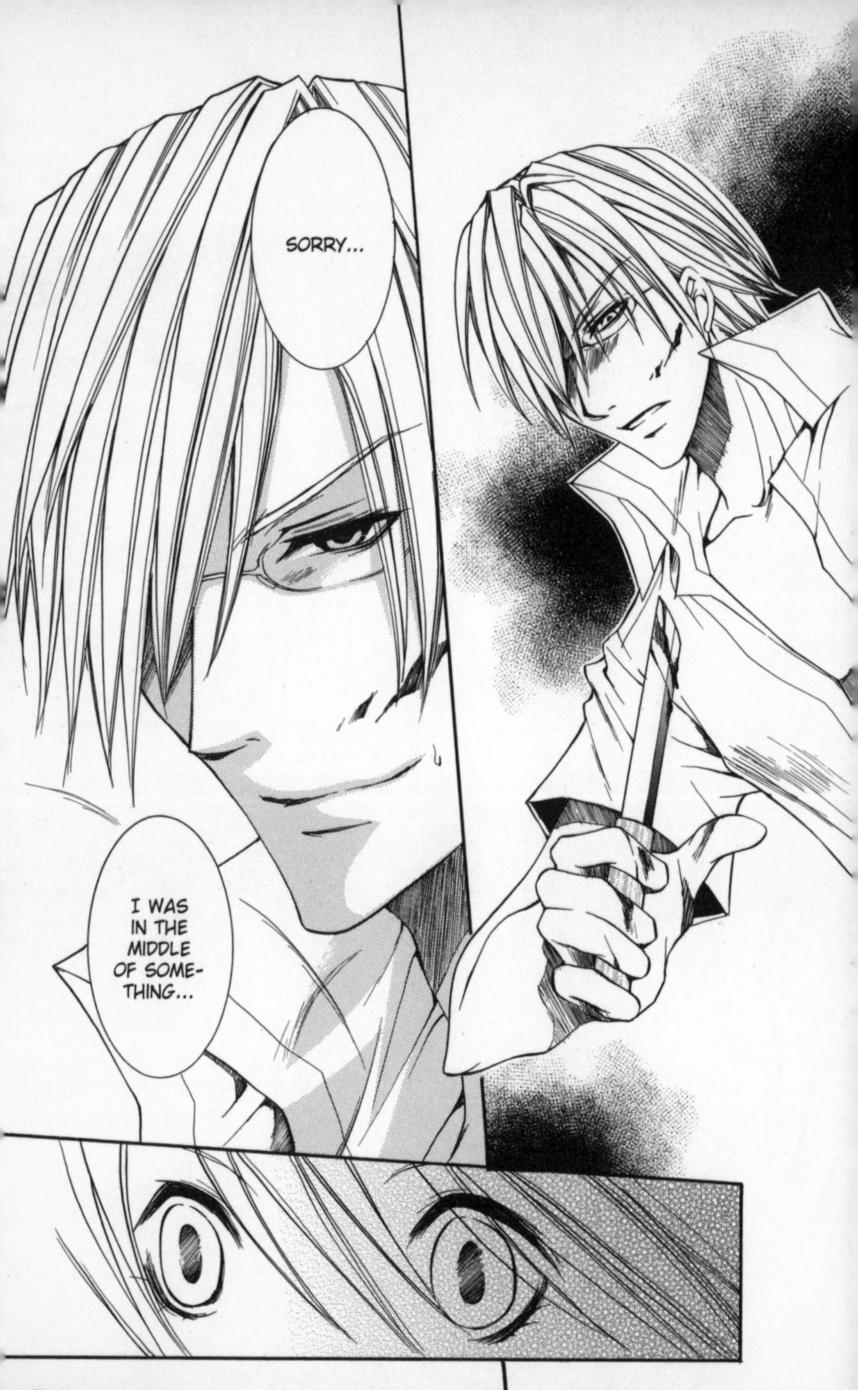
SORRY...
I WAS IN THE MIDDLE OF SOME-THING...

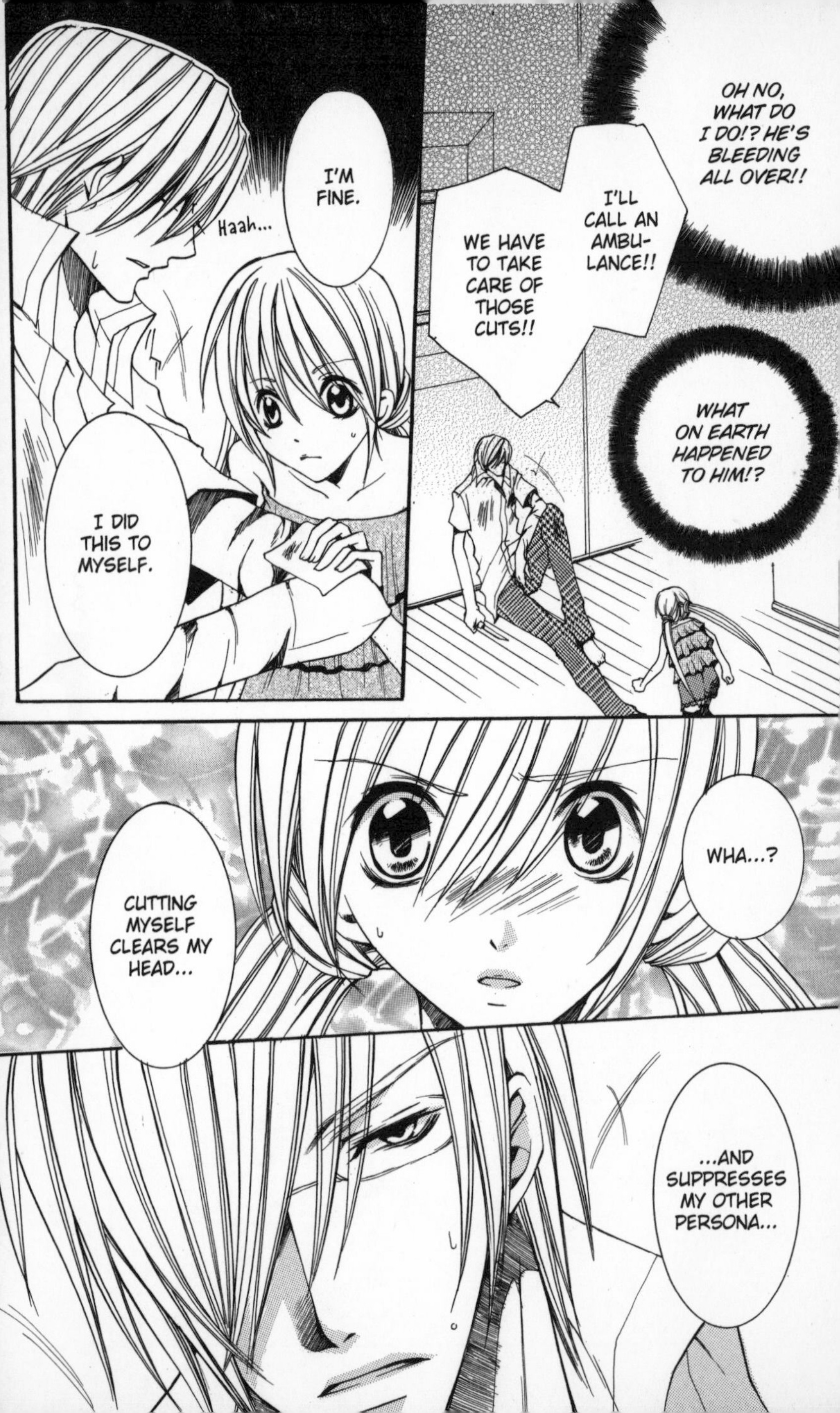
OH NO, WHAT DO I DO!? HE'S BLEEDING ALL OVER!!
I'LL CALL AN AMBULANCE!!
WE HAVE TO TAKE CARE OF THOSE CUTS!!
WHAT ON EARTH HAPPENED TO HIM!?
I'M FINE.
Haaah...
I DID THIS TO MYSELF.
WHA...?
CUTTING MYSELF CLEARS MY HEAD...
...AND SUPPRESSES MY OTHER PERSONA...

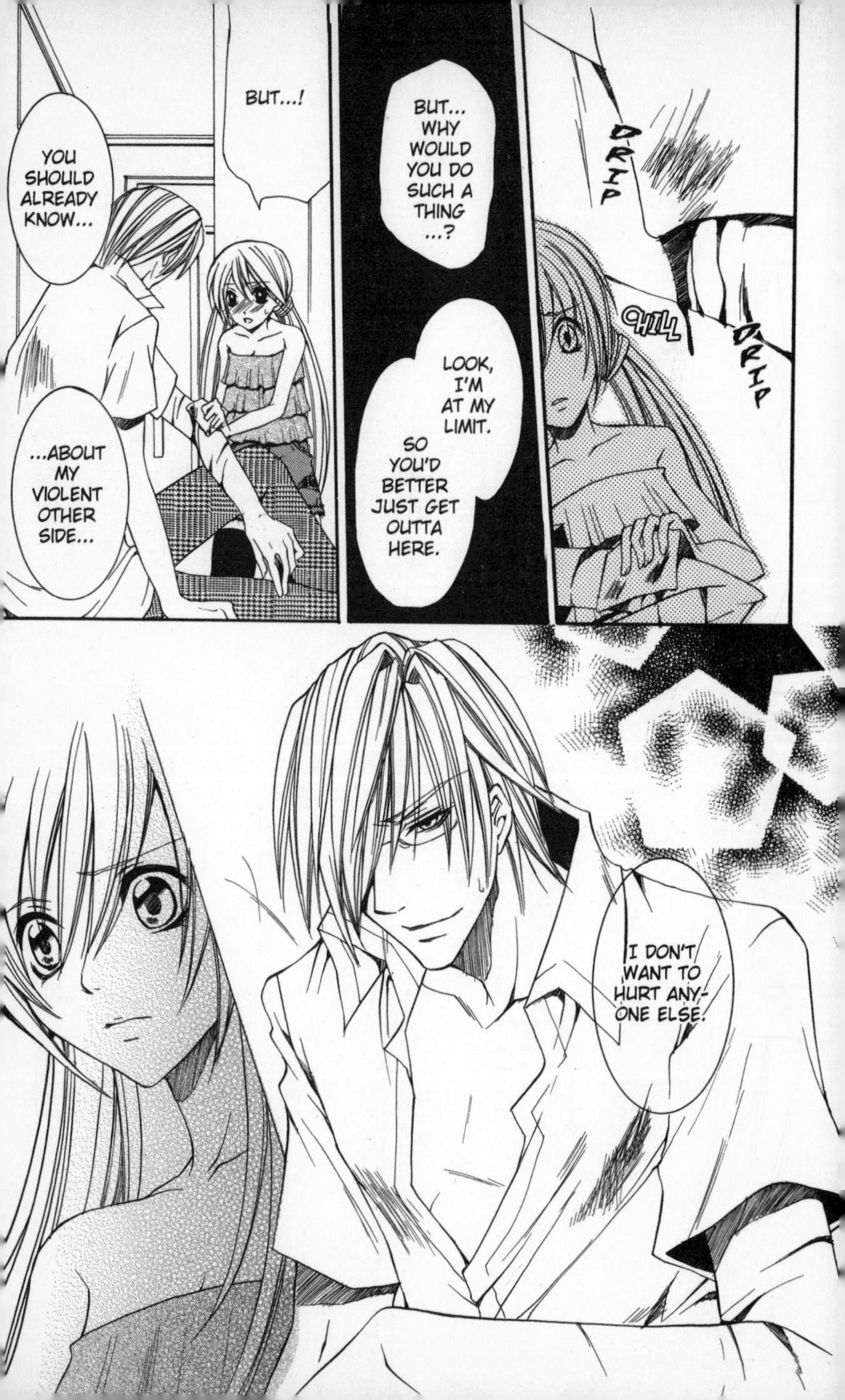
DRIP
CHILL
DRIP
BUT... WHY WOULD YOU DO SUCH A THING ...?
LOOK, I'M AT MY LIMIT.
SO YOU'D BETTER JUST GET OUTTA HERE.
BUT...!
YOU SHOULD ALREADY KNOW...
...ABOUT MY VIOLENT OTHER SIDE...
I DON'T WANT TO HURT ANY-ONE ELSE.

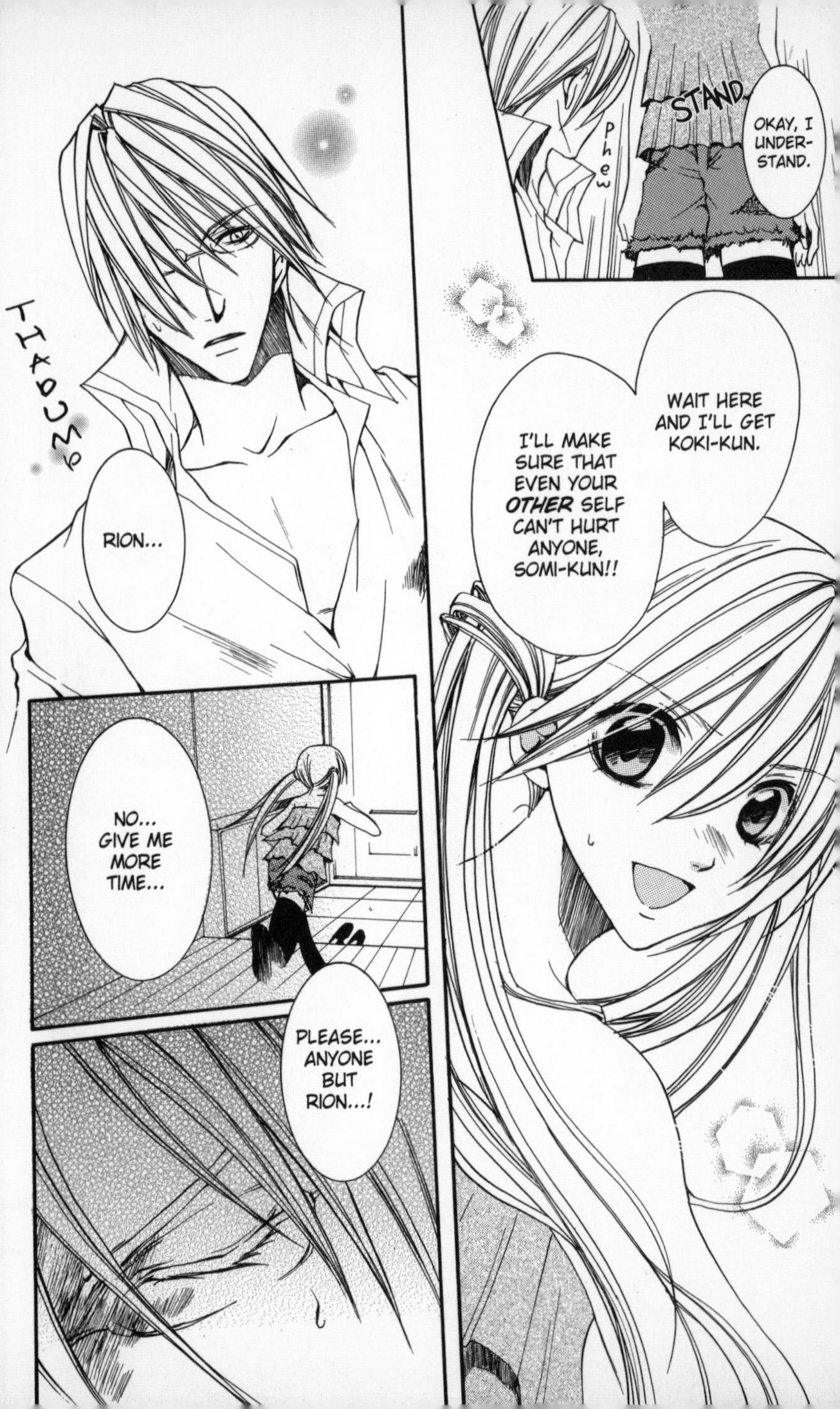
OKAY, I UNDER-STAND.
STAND
Phew
WAIT HERE AND I'LL GET KOKI-KUN.
I'LL MAKE SURE THAT EVEN YOUR OTHER SELF CAN'T HURT ANYONE, SOMI-KUN!!
THADUMP
RION...
NO... GIVE ME MORE TIME...
PLEASE... ANYONE BUT RION...!

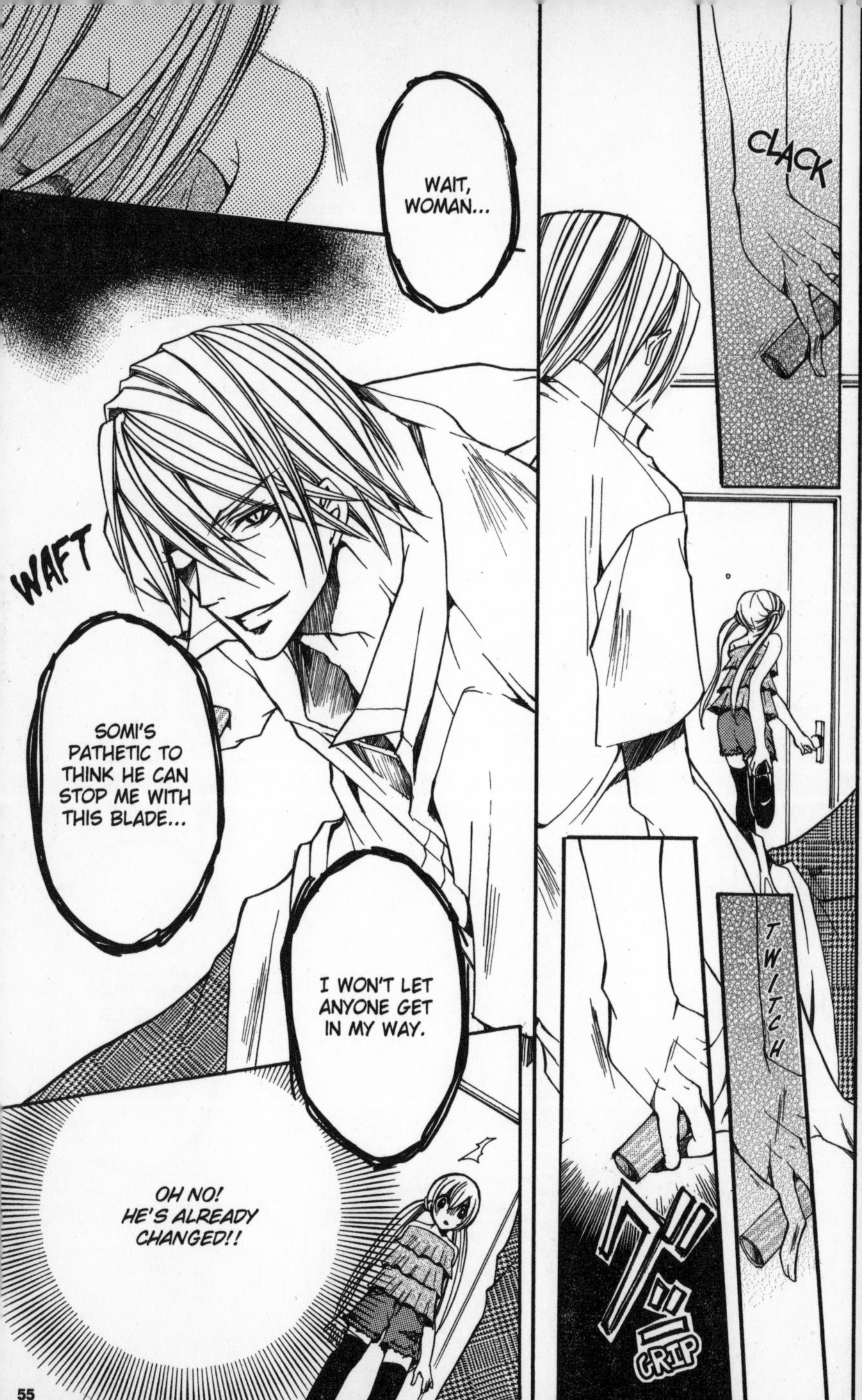
CLACK
TWITCH
GRIP
WAIT, WOMAN...
WAFT
SOMI'S PATHETIC TO THINK HE CAN STOP ME WITH THIS BLADE...
I WON'T LET ANYONE GET IN MY WAY.
OH NO! HE'S ALREADY CHANGED!!

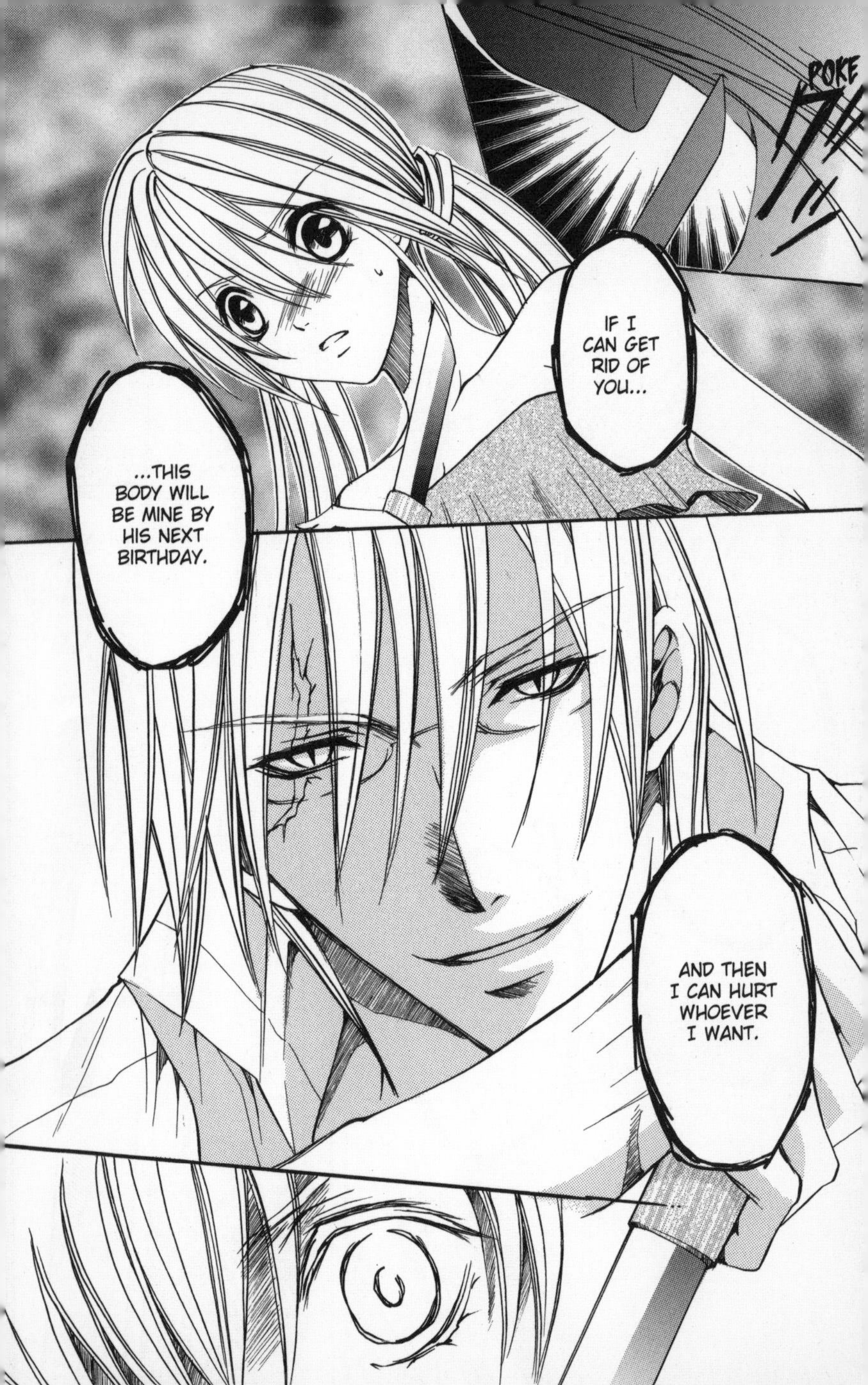
POKE
IF I CAN GET RID OF YOU...
...THIS BODY WILL BE MINE BY HIS NEXT BIRTHDAY.
AND THEN I CAN HURT WHOEVER I WANT.

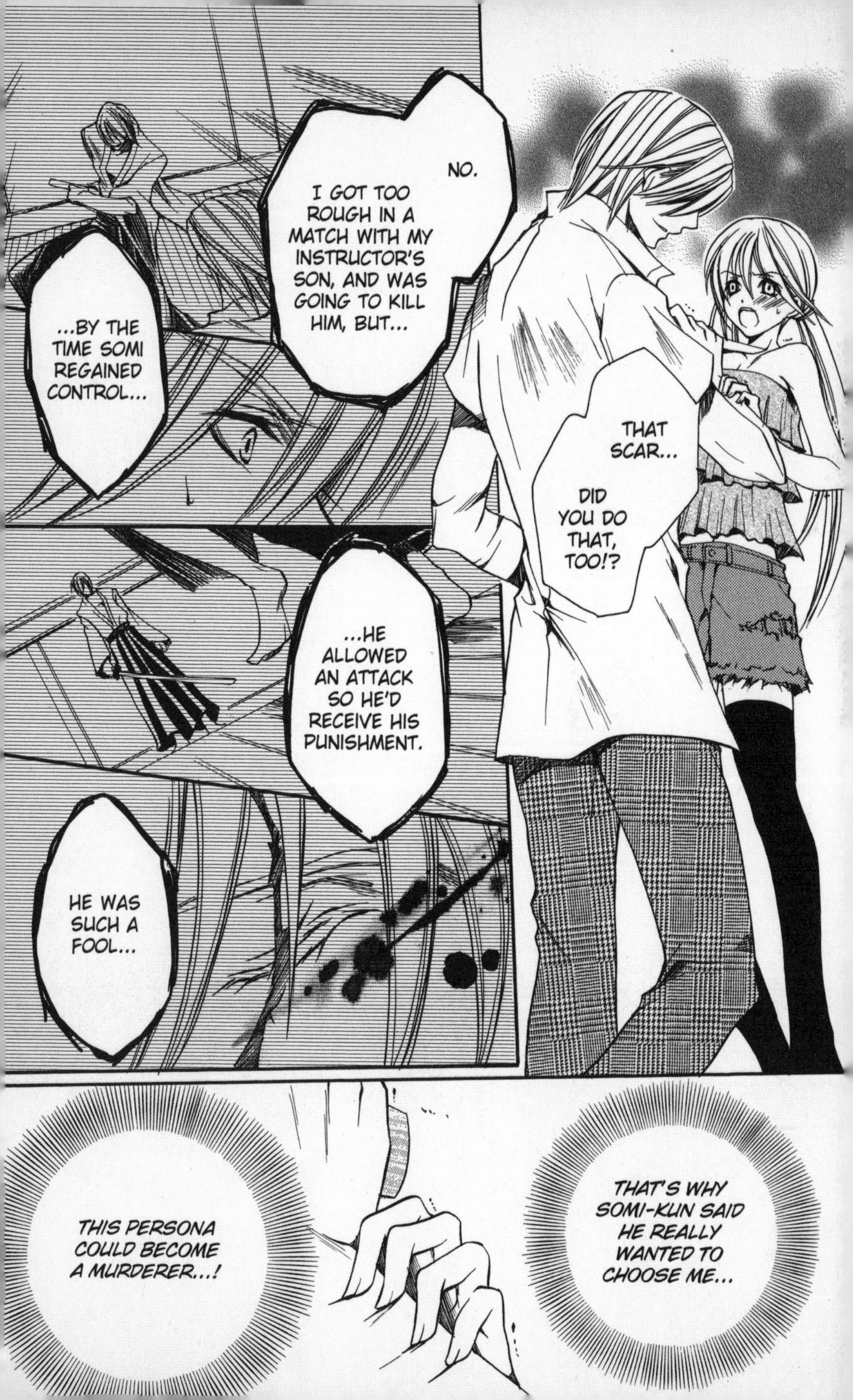
THAT SCAR...
DID YOU DO THAT, TOO!?
NO.
I GOT TOO ROUGH IN A MATCH WITH MY INSTRUCTOR'S SON, AND WAS GOING TO KILL HIM, BUT...
...BY THE TIME SOMI REGAINED CONTROL...
...HE ALLOWED AN ATTACK SO HE'D RECEIVE HIS PUNISHMENT.
HE WAS SUCH A FOOL...
THAT'S WHY SOMI-KUN SAID HE REALLY WANTED TO CHOOSE ME...
THIS PERSONA COULD BECOME A MURDERER...!

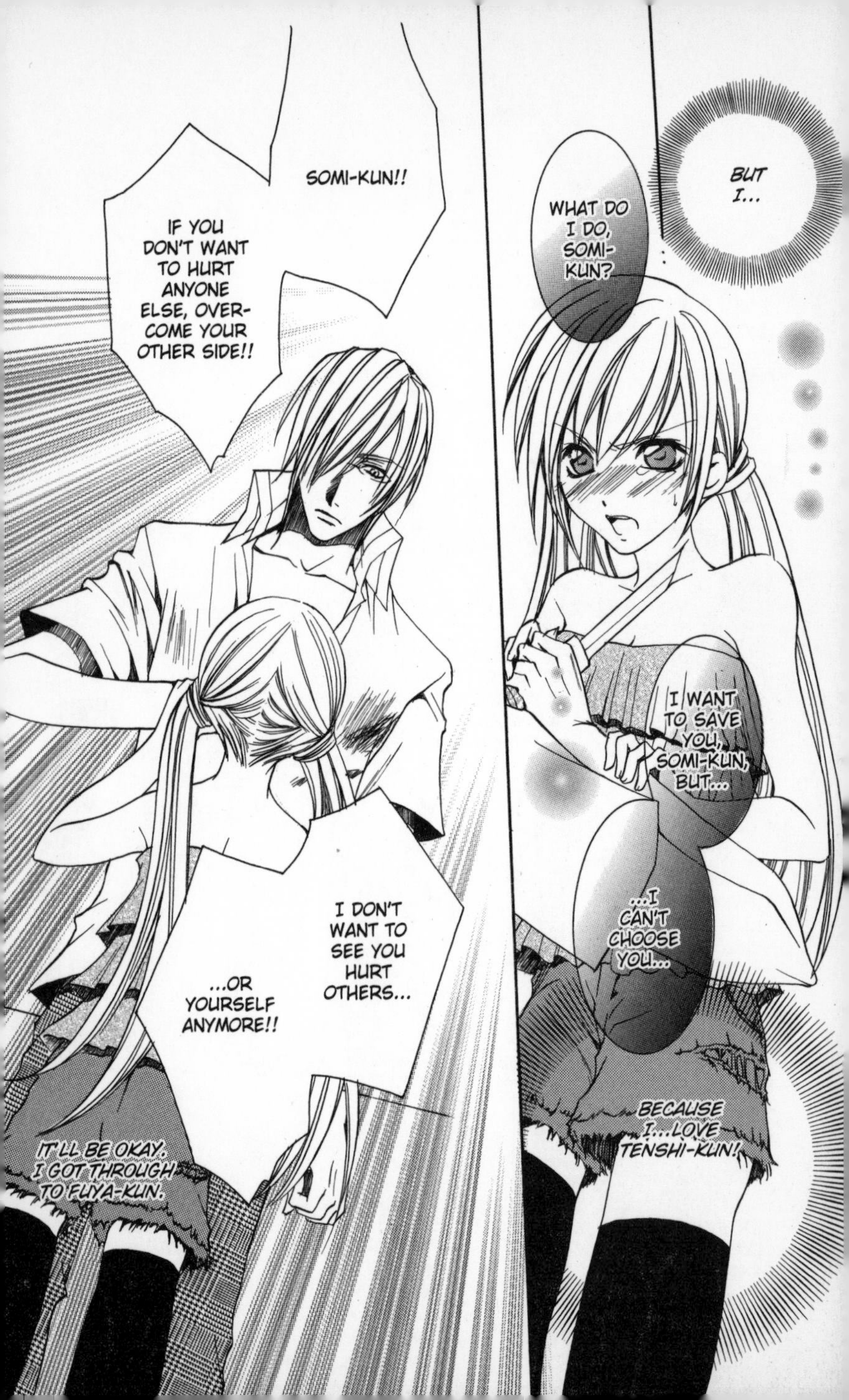

BUT I...
WHAT DO I DO, SOMI-KUN?
I WANT TO SAVE YOU, SOMI-KUN, BUT...
...I CAN'T CHOOSE YOU...
BECAUSE I...LOVE TENSHI-KUN!
SOMI-KUN!!
IF YOU DON'T WANT TO HURT ANYONE ELSE, OVER-COME YOUR OTHER SIDE!!
I DON'T WANT TO SEE YOU HURT OTHERS...
...OR YOURSELF ANYMORE!!
IT'LL BE OKAY. I GOT THROUGH TO FUYA-KUN.

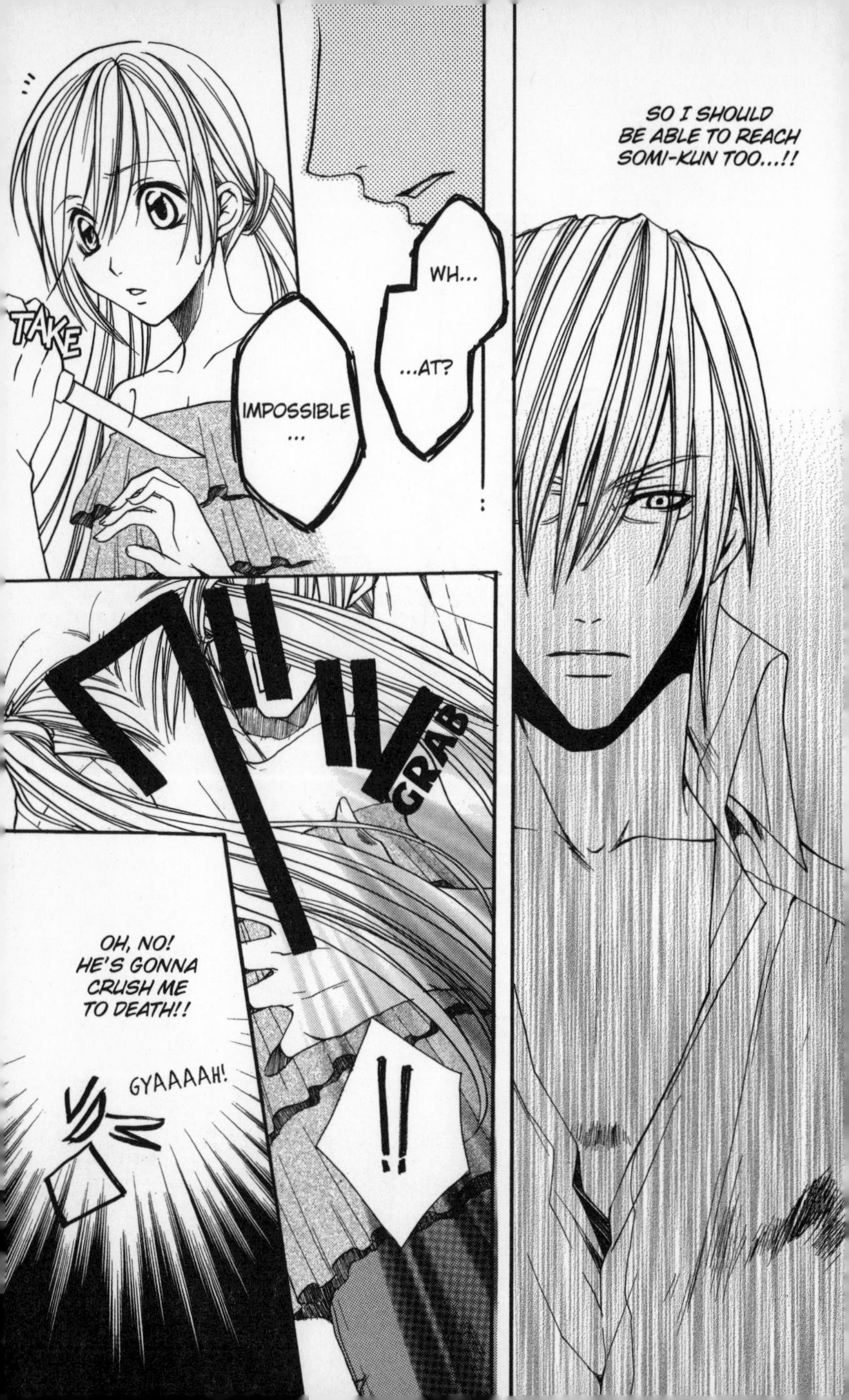
SO I SHOULD BE ABLE TO REACH SOMI-KUN TOO...!!
WH...
...AT?
IMPOSSIBLE ...
TAKE
GRAB
!!
OH, NO! HE'S GONNA CRUSH ME TO DEATH!!
GYAAAAH!

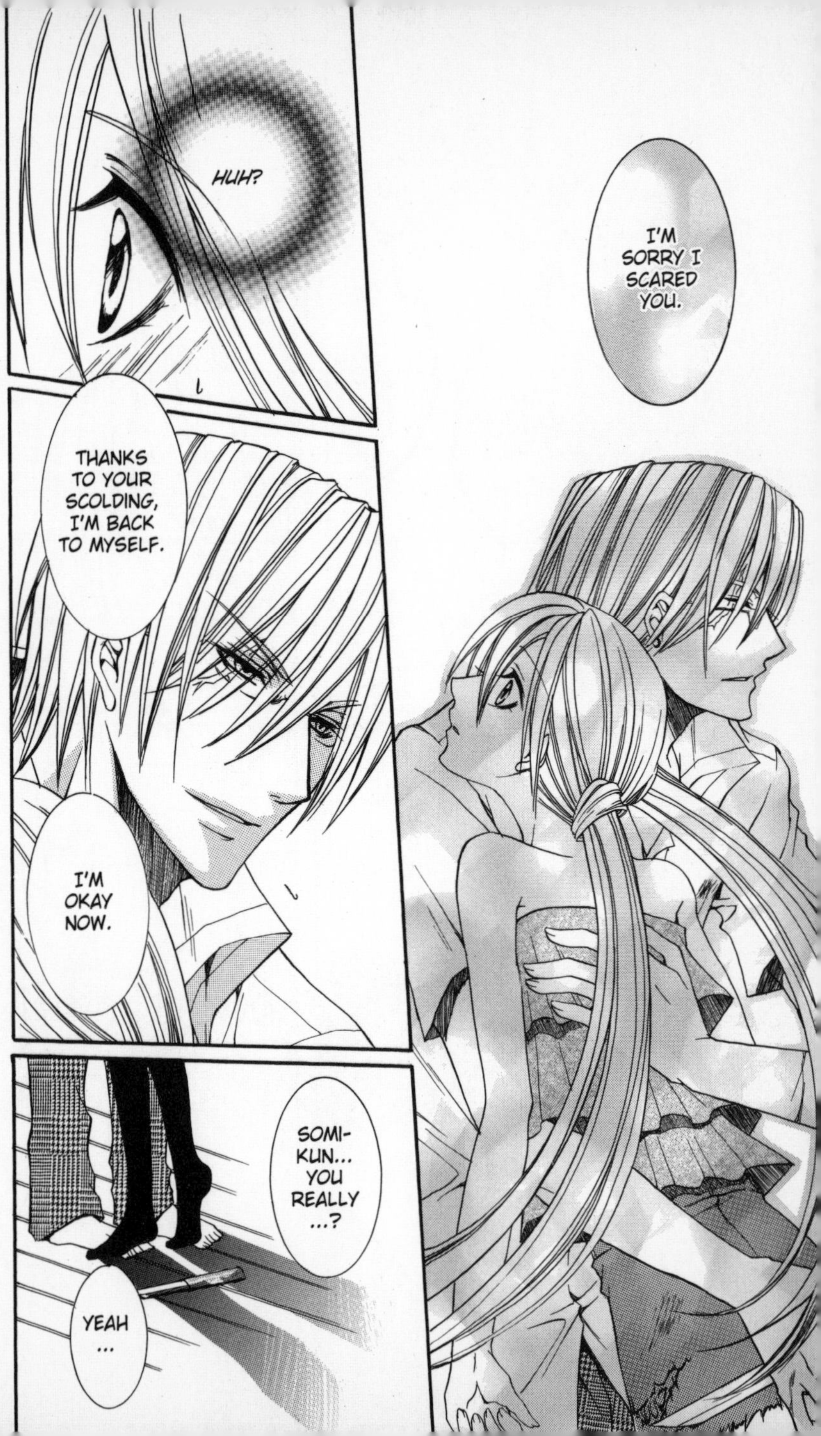
I'M SORRY I SCARED YOU.
HUH?
THANKS TO YOUR SCOLDING, I'M BACK TO MYSELF.
I'M OKAY NOW.
SOMI-KUN... YOU REALLY ...?
YEAH ...

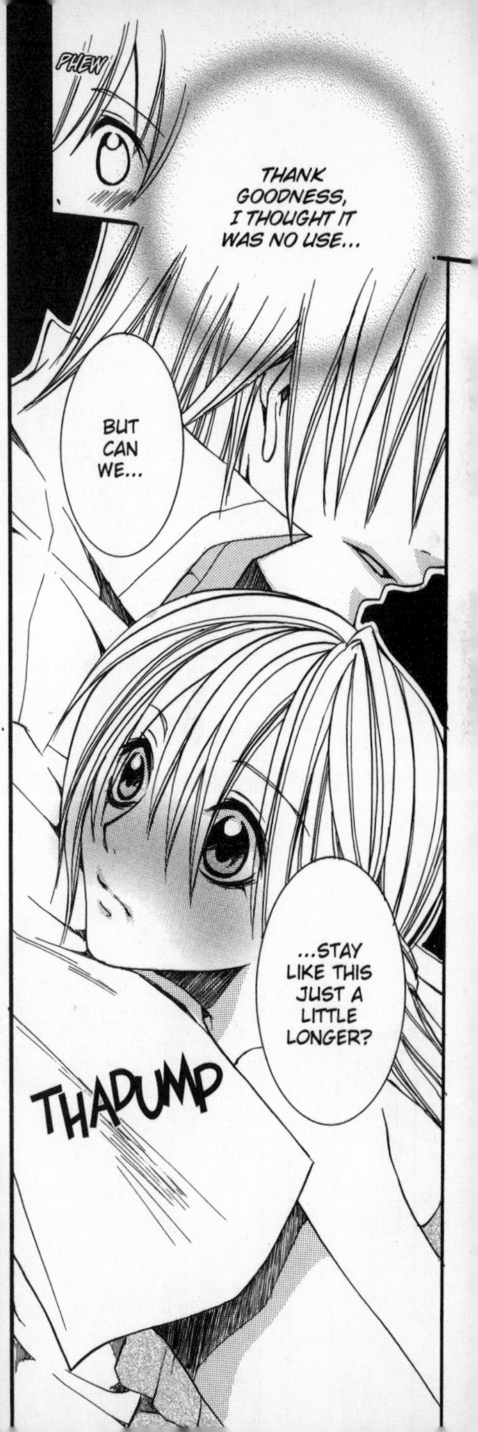
PHEW
THANK GOODNESS, I THOUGHT IT WAS NO USE...
BUT CAN WE...
...STAY LIKE THIS JUST A LITTLE LONGER?
THADUMP

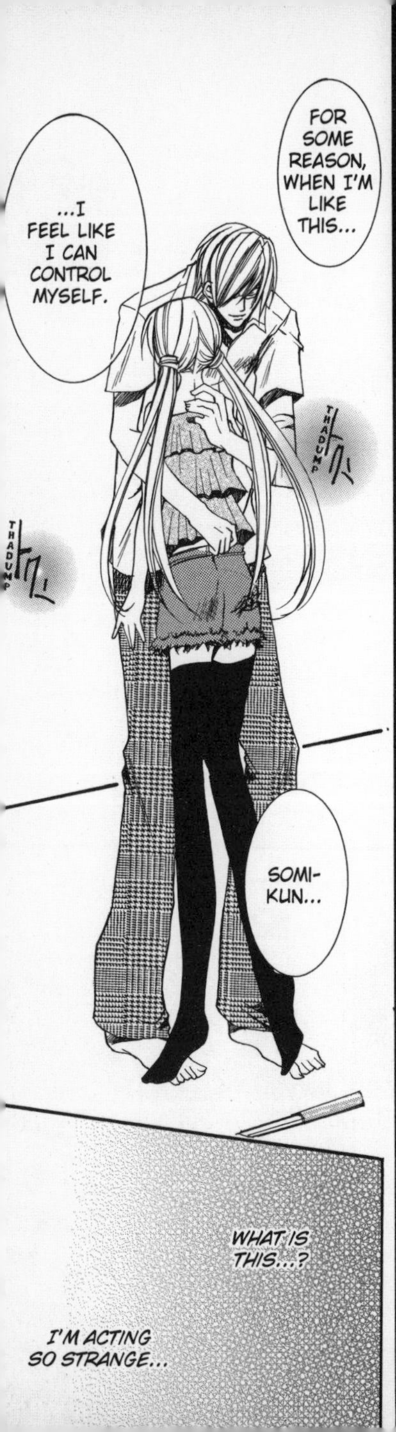
FOR SOME REASON, WHEN I'M LIKE THIS...
...I FEEL LIKE I CAN CONTROL MYSELF.
THADUMP
THADUMP
SOMI-KUN...
WHAT IS THIS...?
I'M ACTING SO STRANGE...

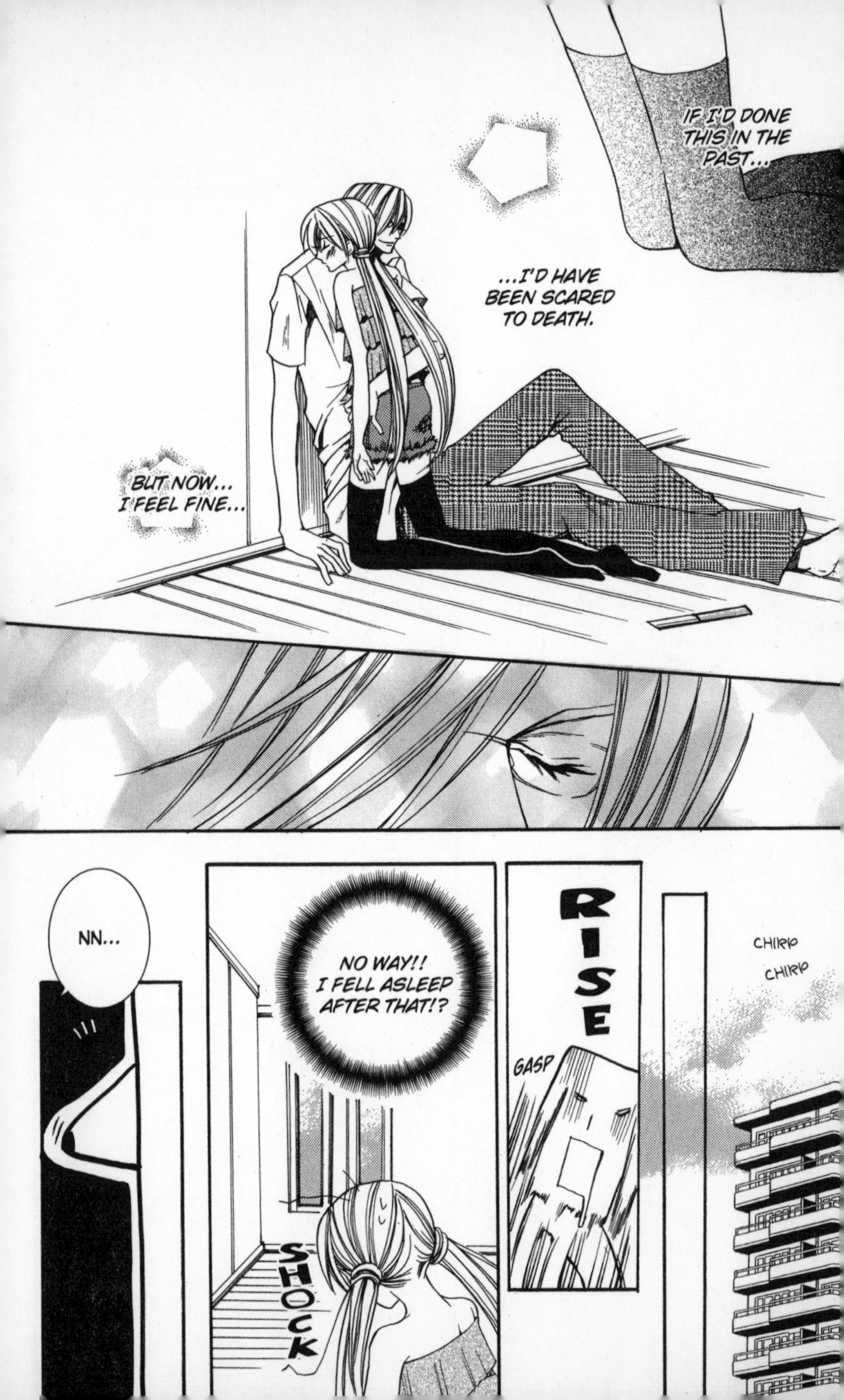
IF I'D DONE THIS IN THE PAST...
...I'D HAVE BEEN SCARED TO DEATH.
BUT NOW... I FEEL FINE...
CHIRP
CHIRP
RISE
GASP
NO WAY!! I FELL ASLEEP AFTER THAT!?
SHOCK
NN...

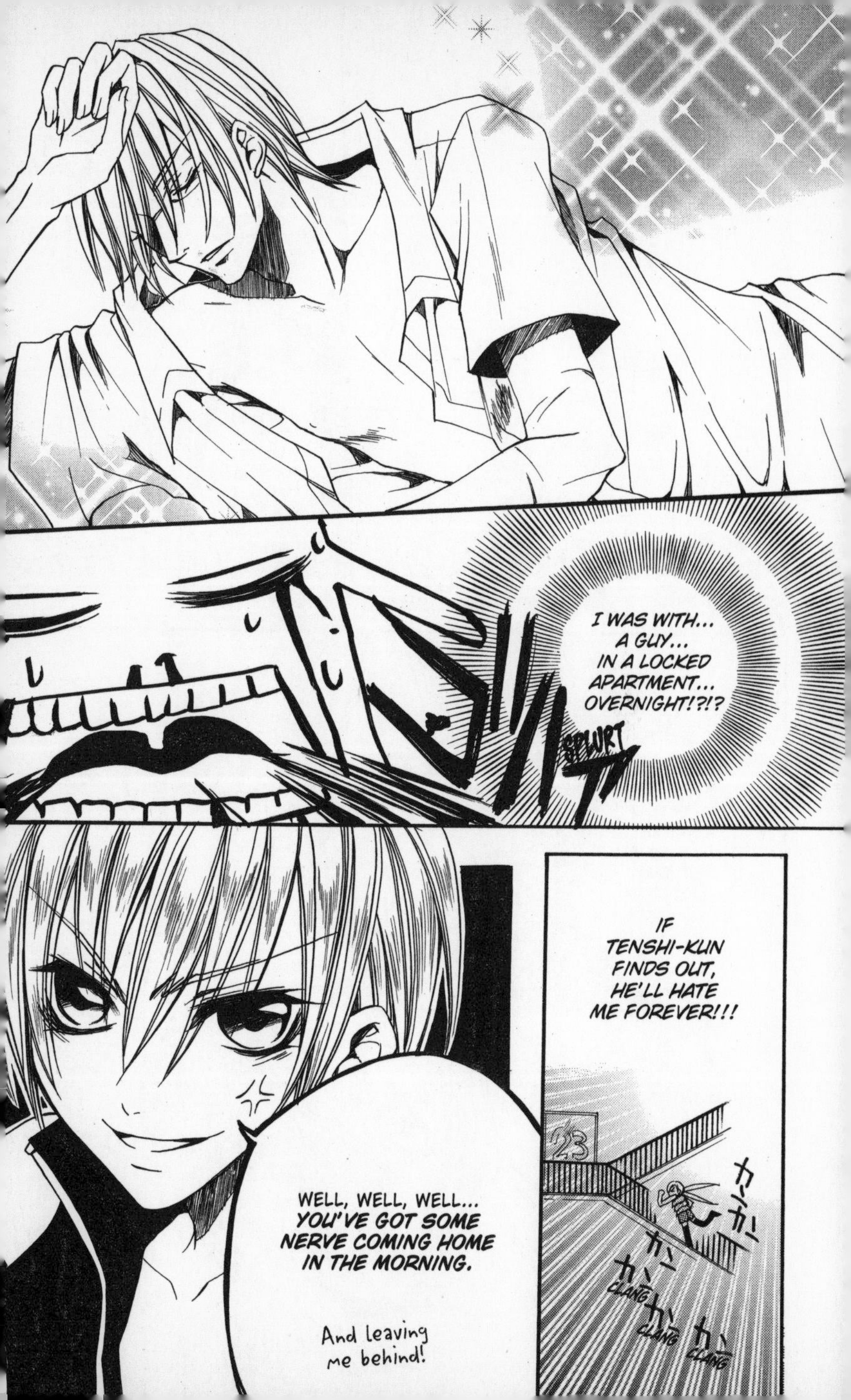
I WAS WITH... A GUY... IN A LOCKED APARTMENT... OVERNIGHT!?!?
SPLURT
IF TENSHI-KUN FINDS OUT, HE'LL HATE ME FOREVER!!!
CLANG
CLANG
CLANG
WELL, WELL, WELL... *YOU'VE GOT SOME NERVE COMING HOME IN THE MORNING.*
And leaving me behind!

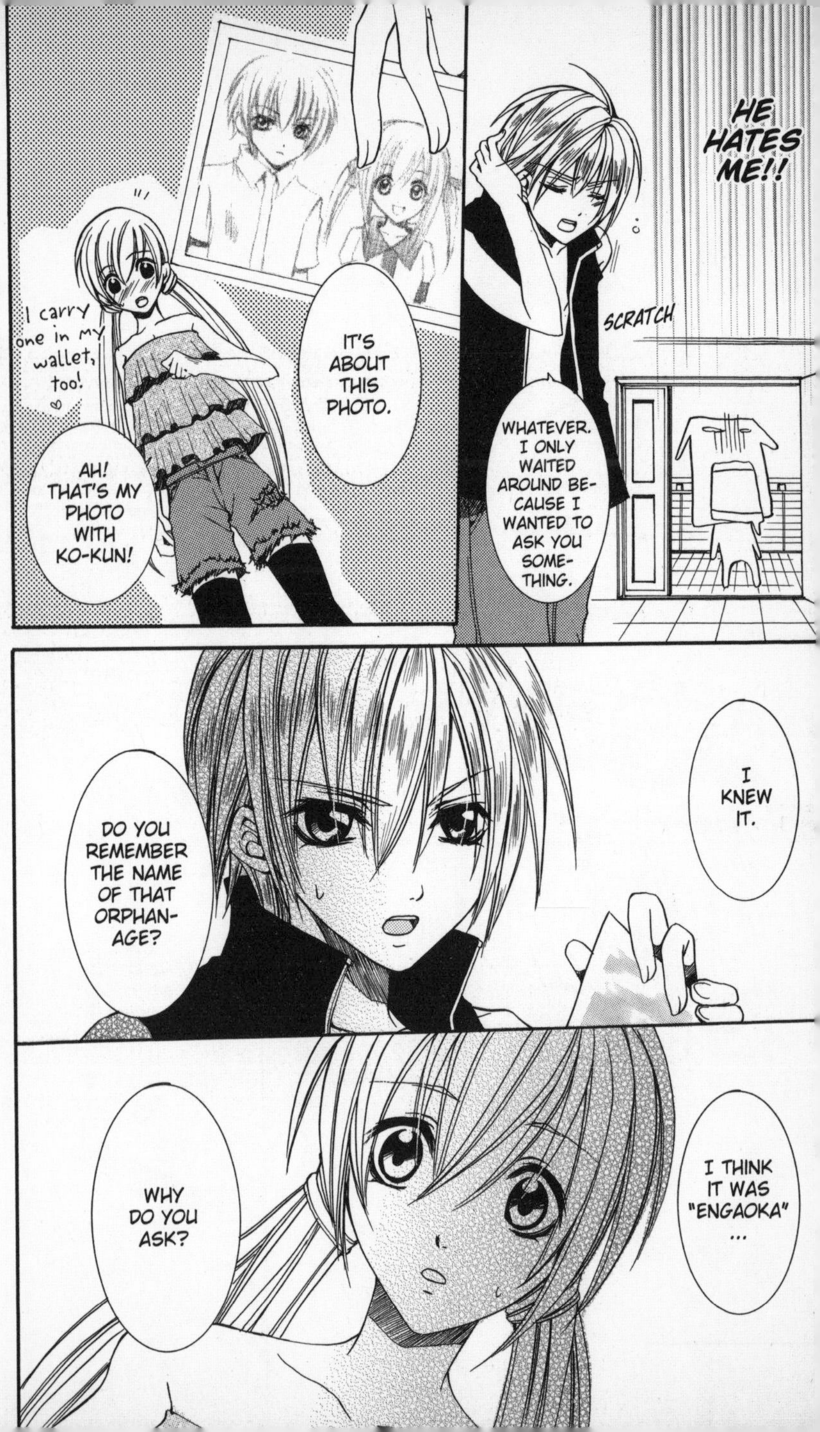
HE HATES ME!!
SCRATCH
WHATEVER. I ONLY WAITED AROUND BE-CAUSE I WANTED TO ASK YOU SOME-THING.
IT'S ABOUT THIS PHOTO.
AH! THAT'S MY PHOTO WITH KO-KUN!
I carry one in my wallet, too!
I KNEW IT.
DO YOU REMEMBER THE NAME OF THAT ORPHAN-AGE?
I THINK IT WAS "ENGAOKA" ...
WHY DO YOU ASK?

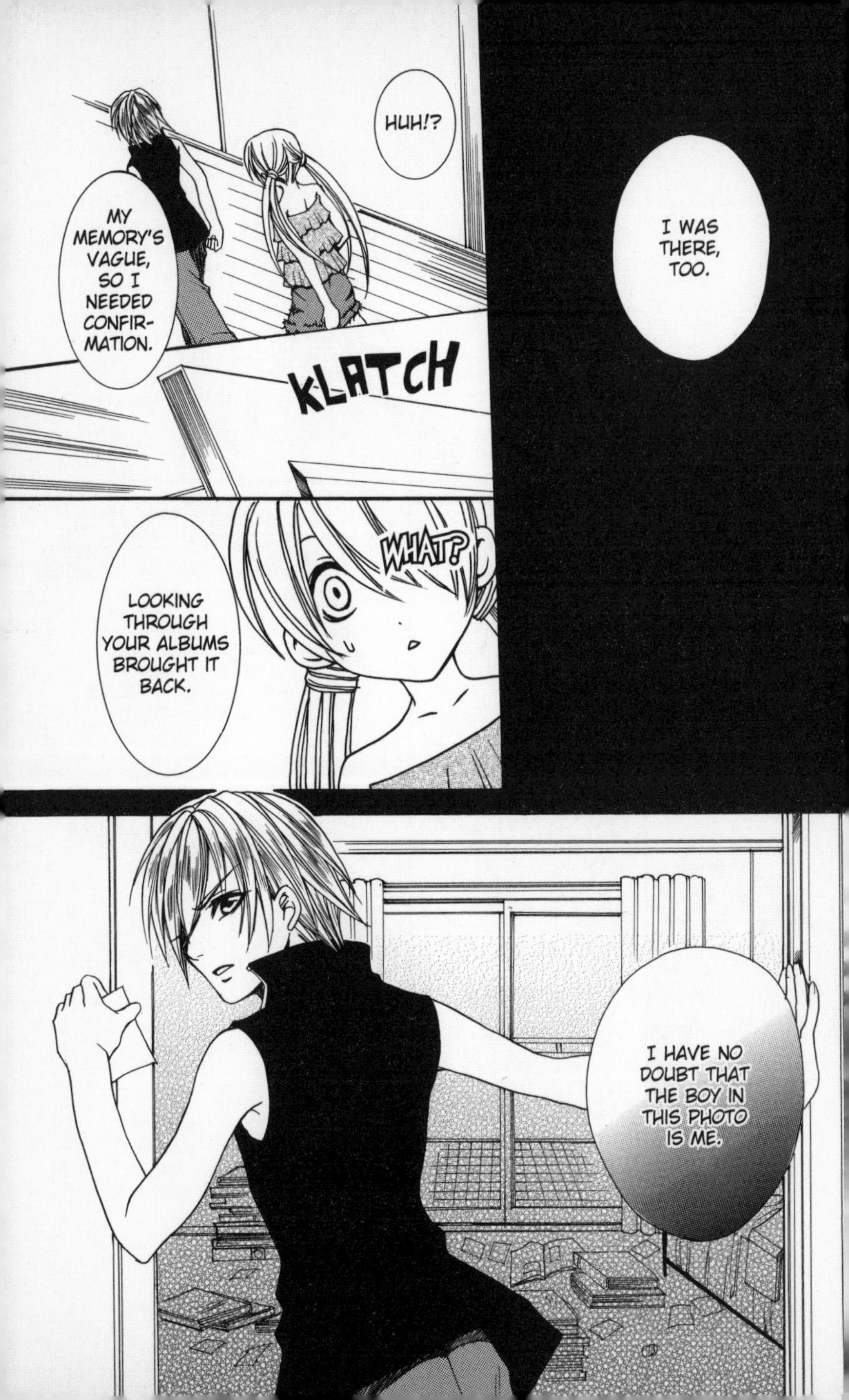
I WAS THERE, TOO.
HUH!?
MY MEMORY'S VAGUE, SO I NEEDED CONFIRMATION.
KLATCH
WHAT?
LOOKING THROUGH YOUR ALBUMS BROUGHT IT BACK.
I HAVE NO DOUBT THAT THE BOY IN THIS PHOTO IS ME.

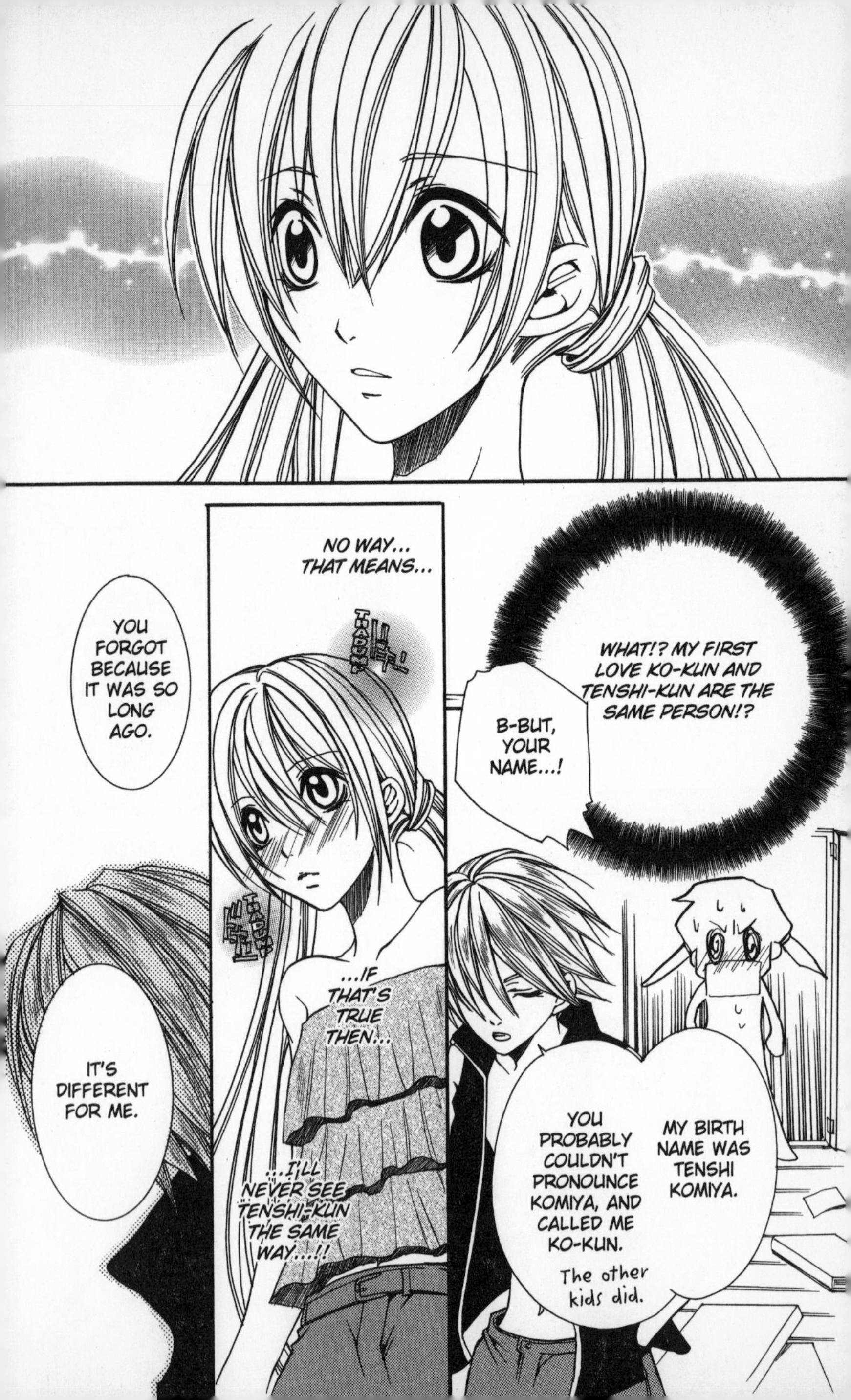
WHAT!? MY FIRST LOVE KO-KUN AND TENSHI-KUN ARE THE SAME PERSON!?
B-BUT, YOUR NAME...!
MY BIRTH NAME WAS TENSHI KOMIYA.
YOU PROBABLY COULDN'T PRONOUNCE KOMIYA, AND CALLED ME KO-KUN.
The other kids did.
NO WAY... THAT MEANS...
THADUMP
THADUMP
...IF THAT'S TRUE THEN...
...I'LL NEVER SEE TENSHI-KUN THE SAME WAY...!!
YOU FORGOT BECAUSE IT WAS SO LONG AGO.
IT'S DIFFERENT FOR ME.

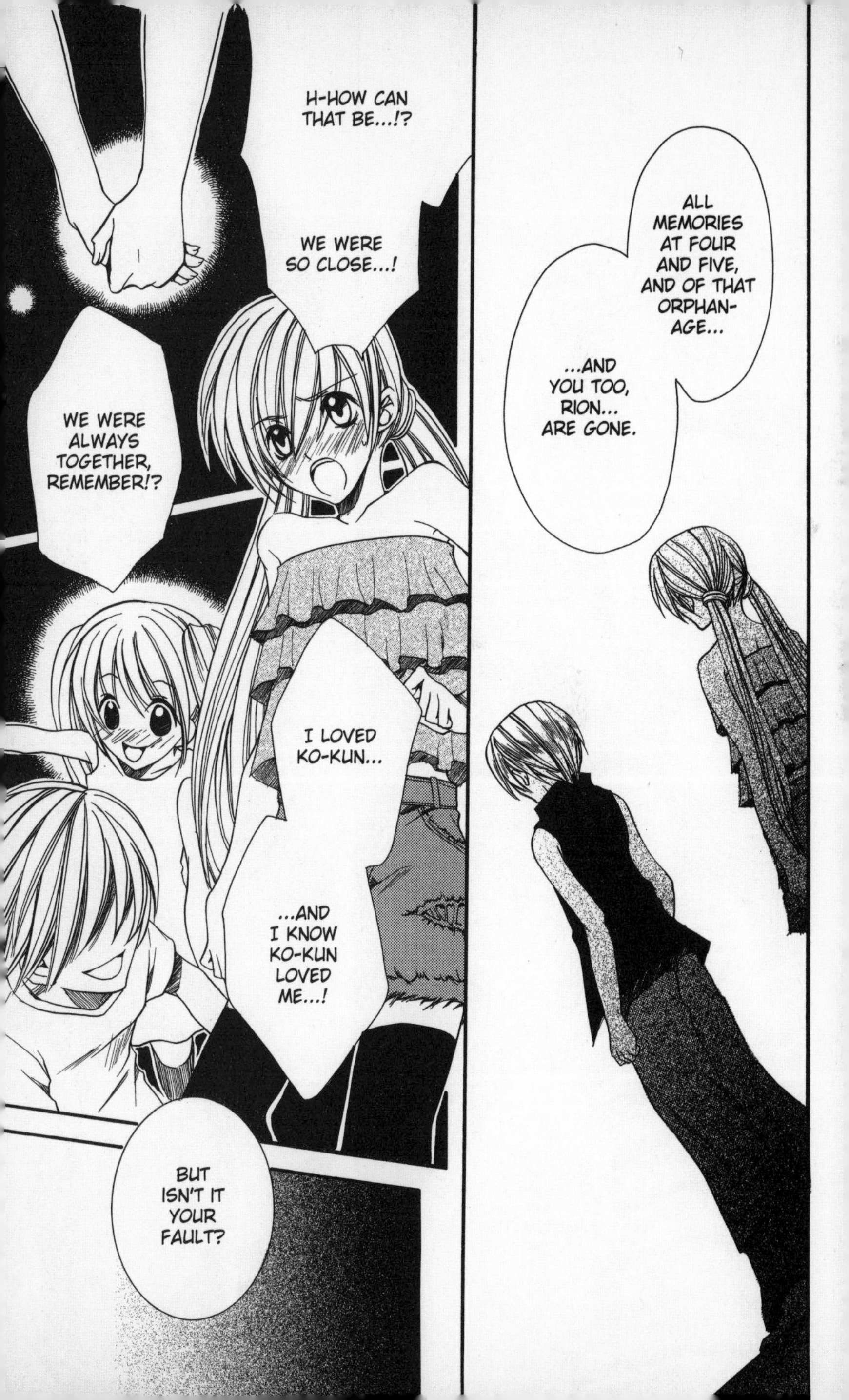
ALL MEMORIES AT FOUR AND FIVE, AND OF THAT ORPHAN-AGE...
...AND YOU TOO, RION... ARE GONE.
H-HOW CAN THAT BE...!?
WE WERE SO CLOSE...!
WE WERE ALWAYS TOGETHER, REMEMBER!?
I LOVED KO-KUN...
...AND I KNOW KO-KUN LOVED ME...!
BUT ISN'T IT YOUR FAULT?

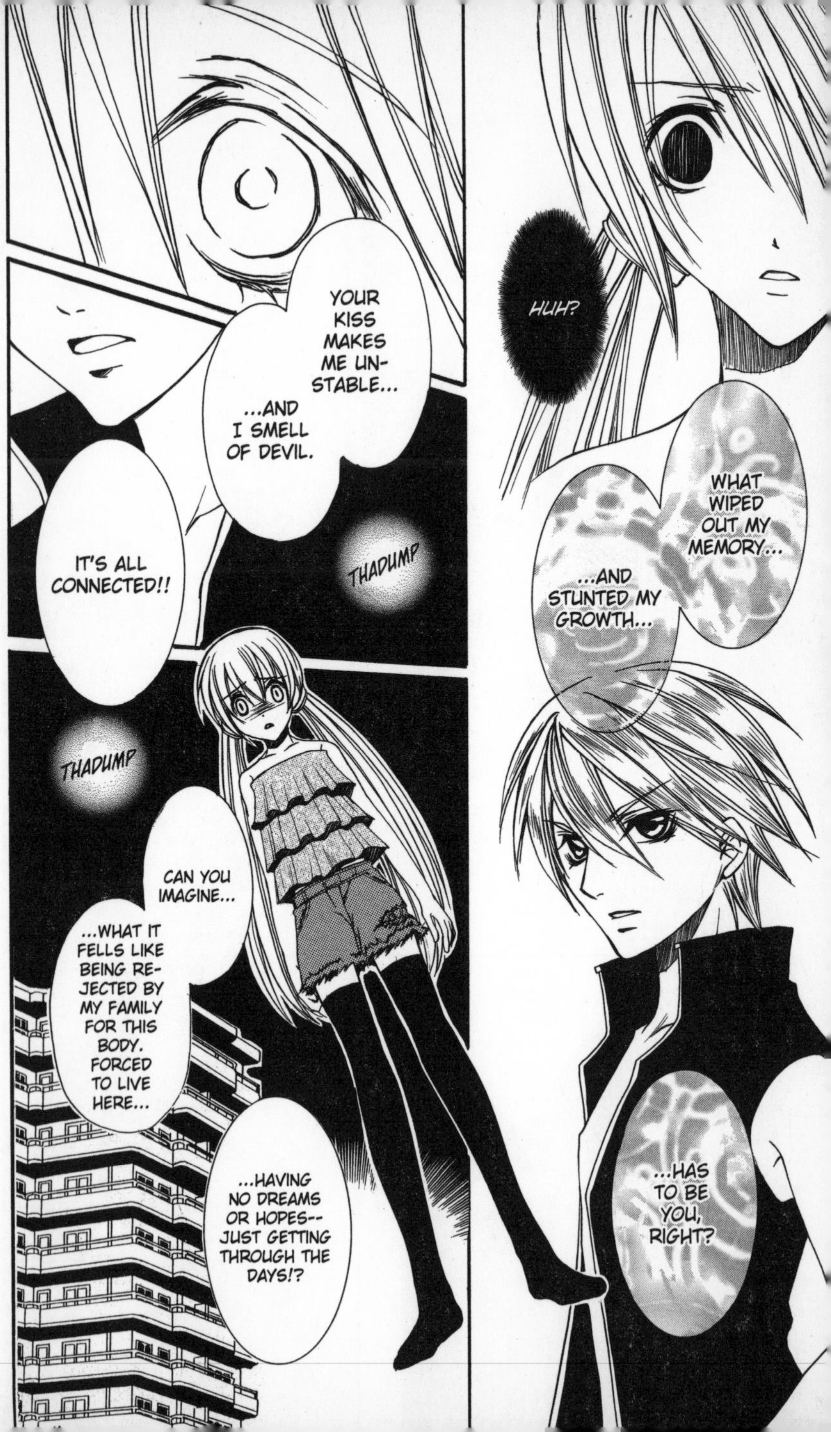
HUH?
WHAT WIPED OUT MY MEMORY...
...AND STUNTED MY GROWTH...
...HAS TO BE YOU, RIGHT?
YOUR KISS MAKES ME UN-STABLE...
...AND I SMELL OF DEVIL.
IT'S ALL CONNECTED!!
THADUMP
THADUMP
CAN YOU IMAGINE...
...WHAT IT FELLS LIKE BEING RE-JECTED BY MY FAMILY FOR THIS BODY. FORCED TO LIVE HERE...
...HAVING NO DREAMS OR HOPES--JUST GETTING THROUGH THE DAYS!?

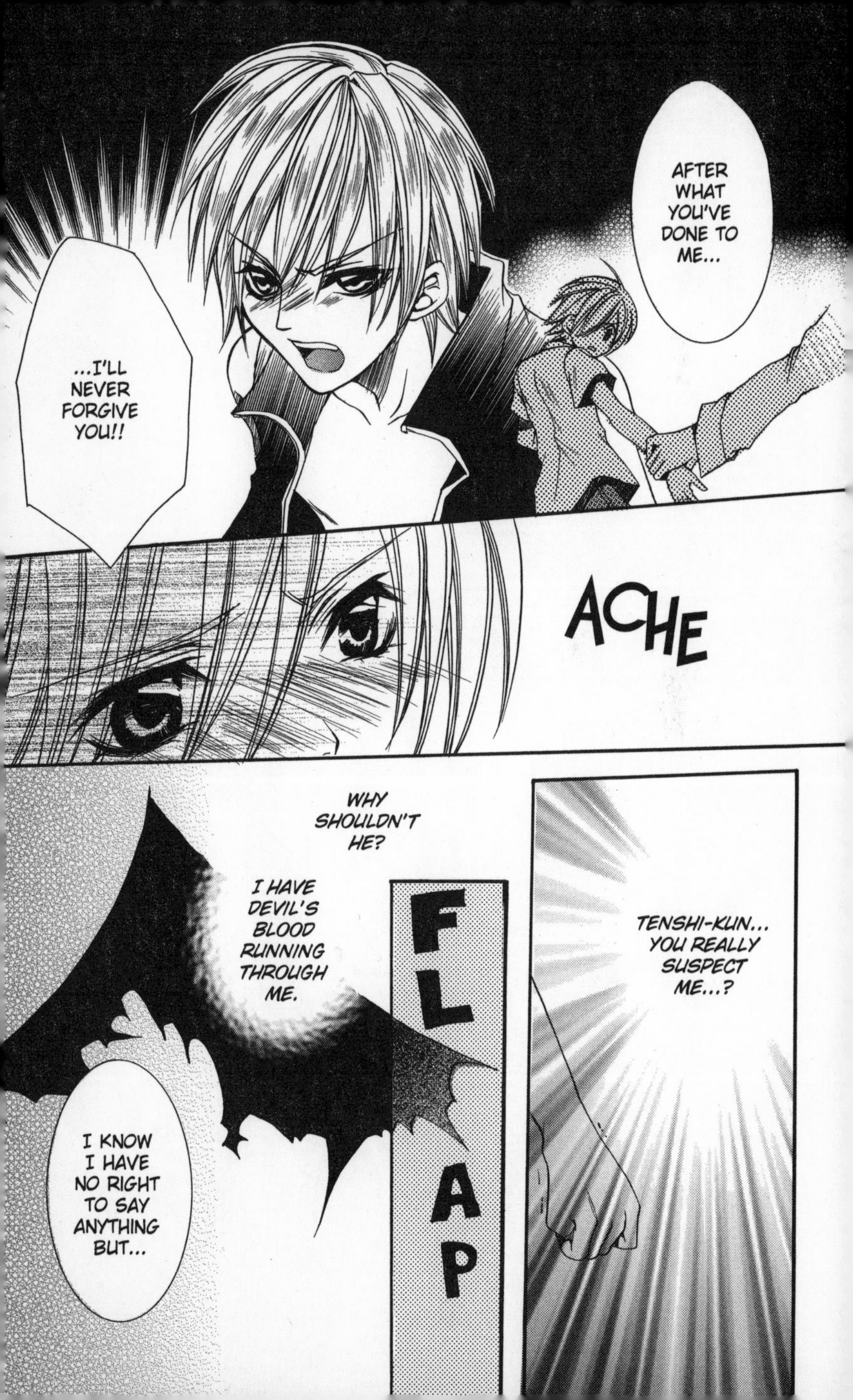
AFTER WHAT YOU'VE DONE TO ME...
...I'LL NEVER FORGIVE YOU!!
ACHE
TENSHI-KUN... YOU REALLY SUSPECT ME...?
FLAP
WHY SHOULDN'T HE?
I HAVE DEVIL'S BLOOD RUNNING THROUGH ME.
I KNOW I HAVE NO RIGHT TO SAY ANYTHING BUT...

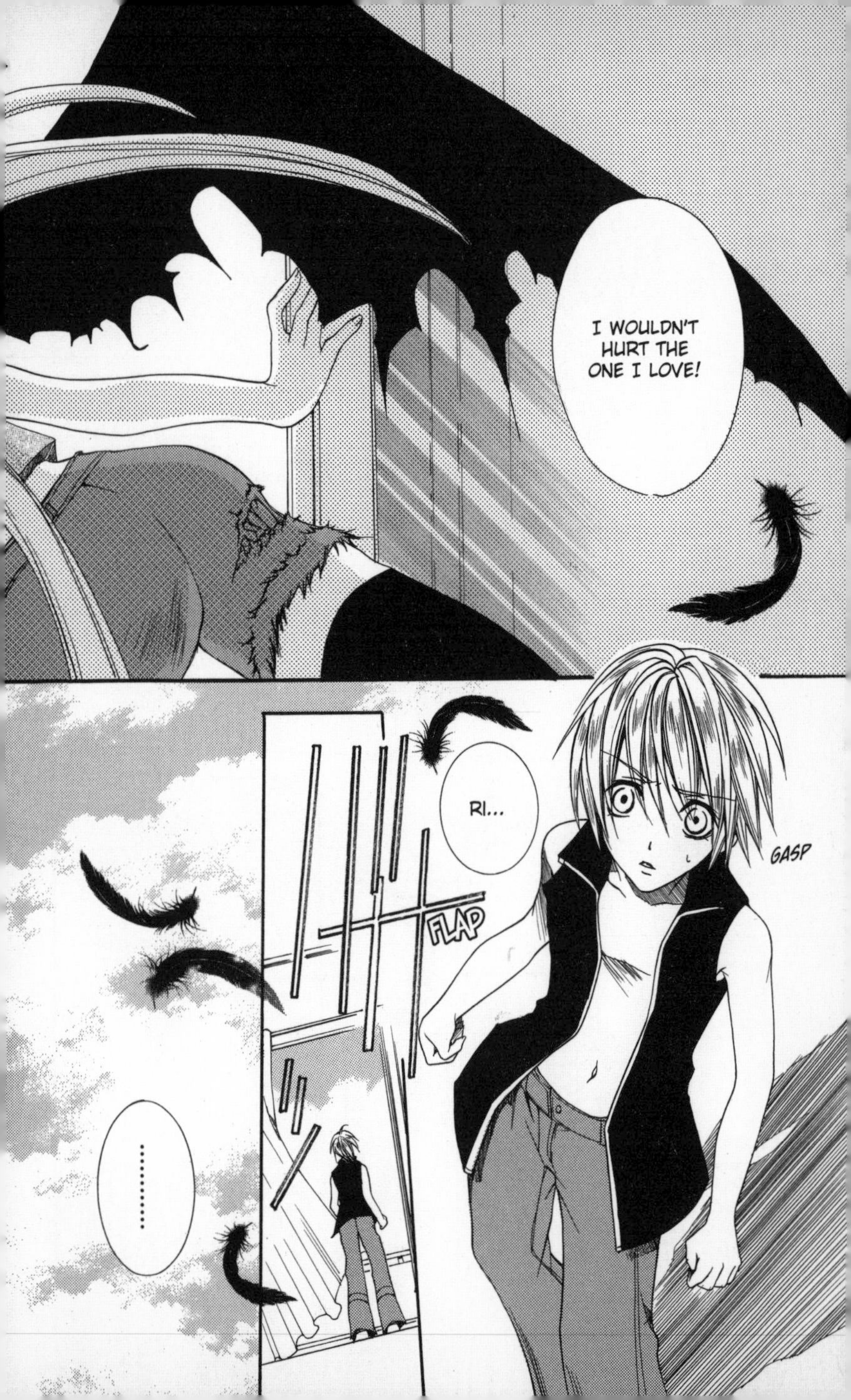
I WOULDN'T HURT THE ONE I LOVE!
RI...
GASP
FLAP
......

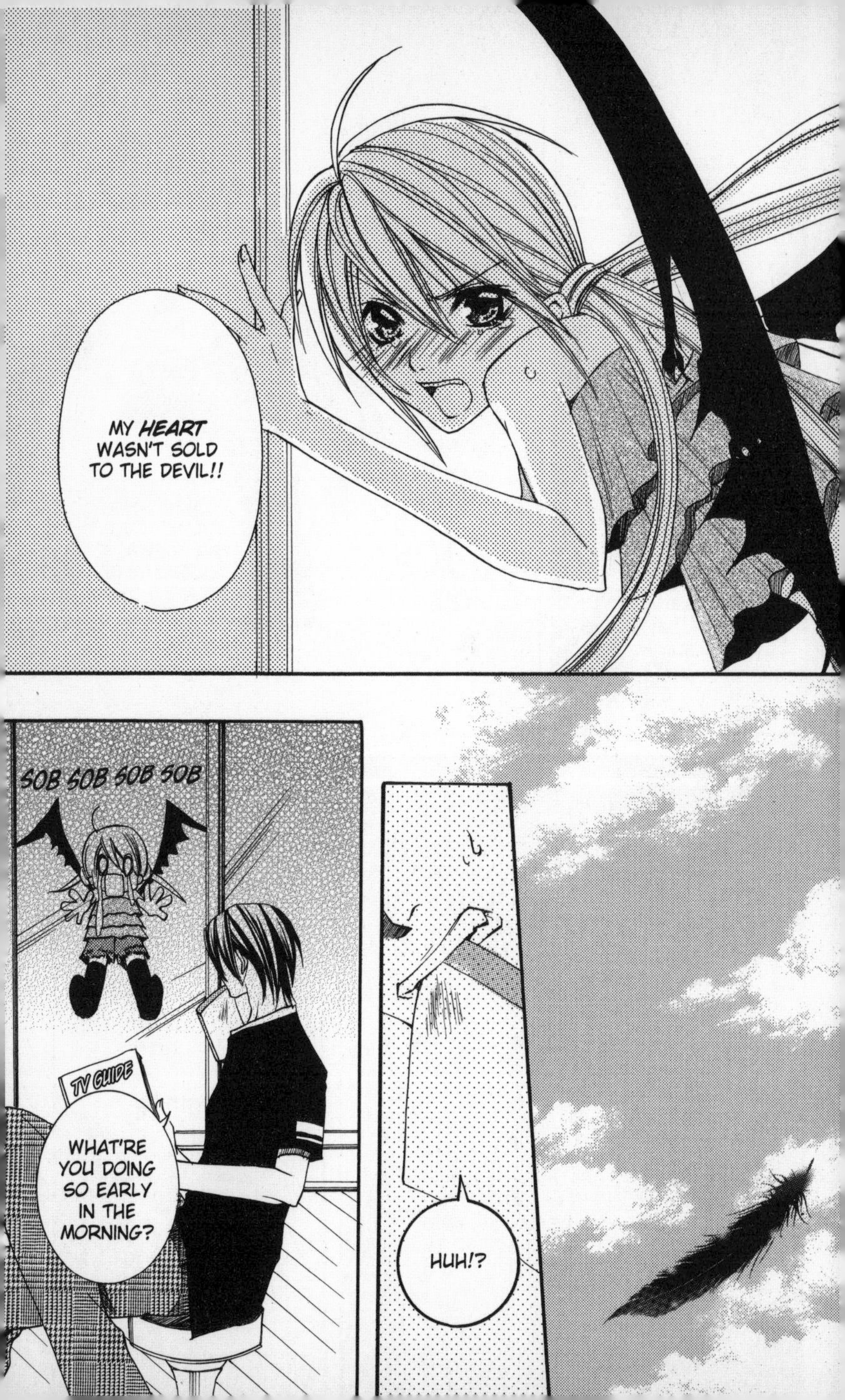
MY HEART WASN'T SOLD TO THE DEVIL!!
HUH!?
SOB SOB SOB SOB
TV GUIDE
WHAT'RE YOU DOING SO EARLY IN THE MORNING?

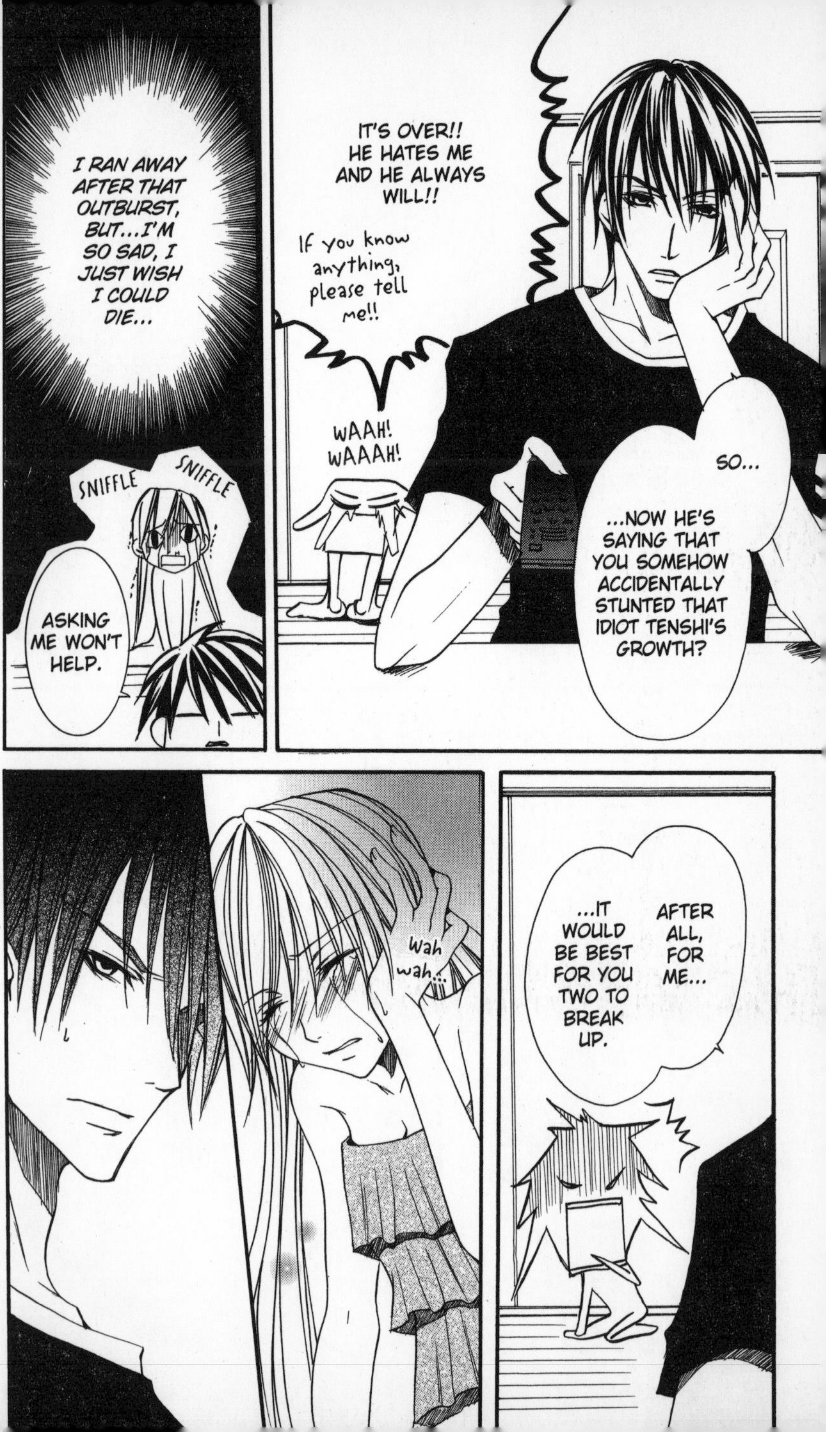
IT'S OVER!! HE HATES ME AND HE ALWAYS WILL!!
If you know anything, please tell me!!
WAAH! WAAAH!
SO...
...NOW HE'S SAYING THAT YOU SOMEHOW ACCIDENTALLY STUNTED THAT IDIOT TENSHI'S GROWTH?
I RAN AWAY AFTER THAT OUTBURST, BUT...I'M SO SAD, I JUST WISH I COULD DIE...
SNIFFLE
SNIFFLE
ASKING ME WON'T HELP.
AFTER ALL, FOR ME...
...IT WOULD BE BEST FOR YOU TWO TO BREAK UP.
Wah wah...

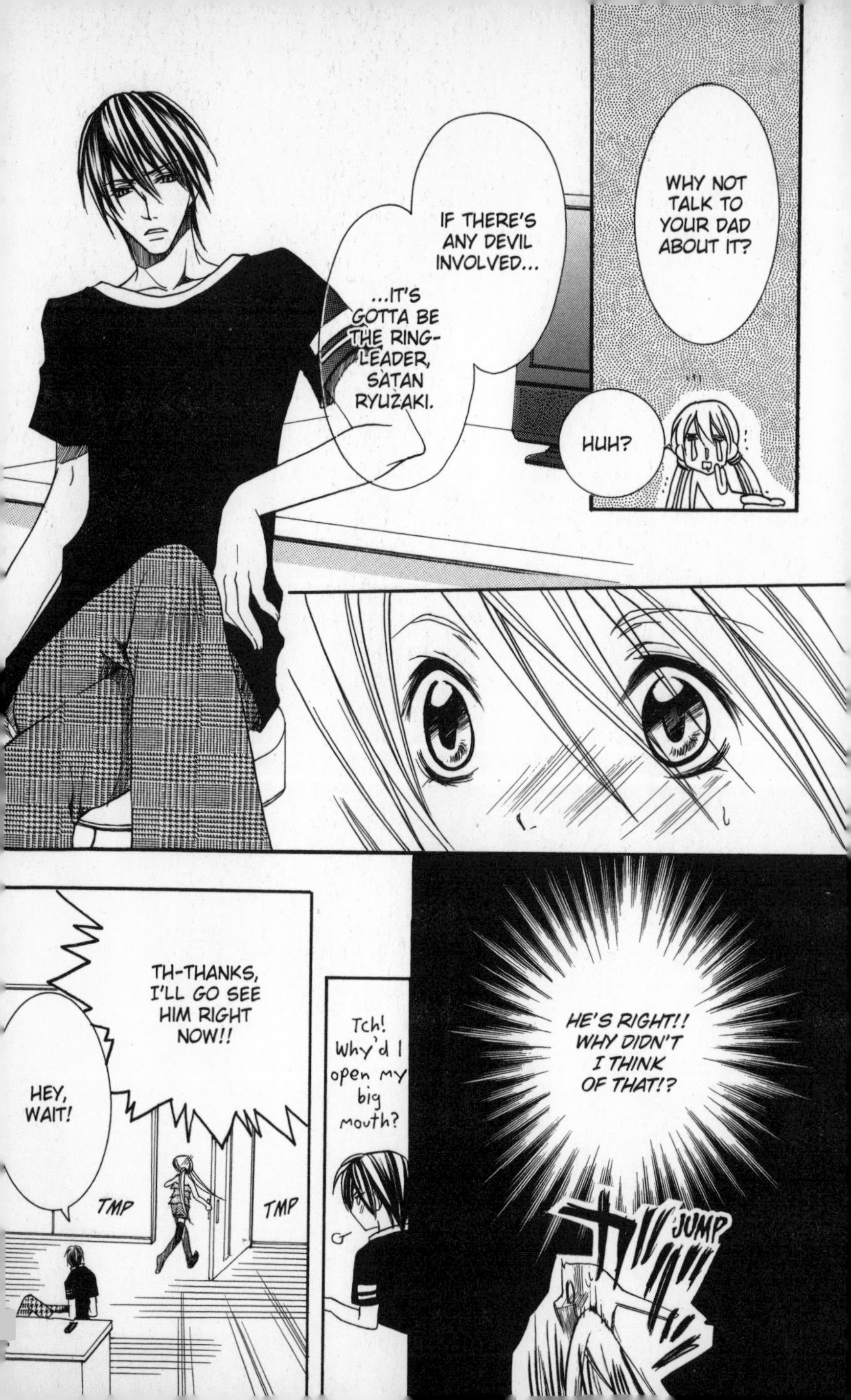
IF THERE'S ANY DEVIL INVOLVED...
...IT'S GOTTA BE THE RING-LEADER, SATAN RYUZAKI.
WHY NOT TALK TO YOUR DAD ABOUT IT?
HUH?
HE'S RIGHT!! WHY DIDN'T I THINK OF THAT!?
JUMP
Tch! Why'd I open my big mouth?
TH-THANKS, I'LL GO SEE HIM RIGHT NOW!!
HEY, WAIT!
TMP
TMP

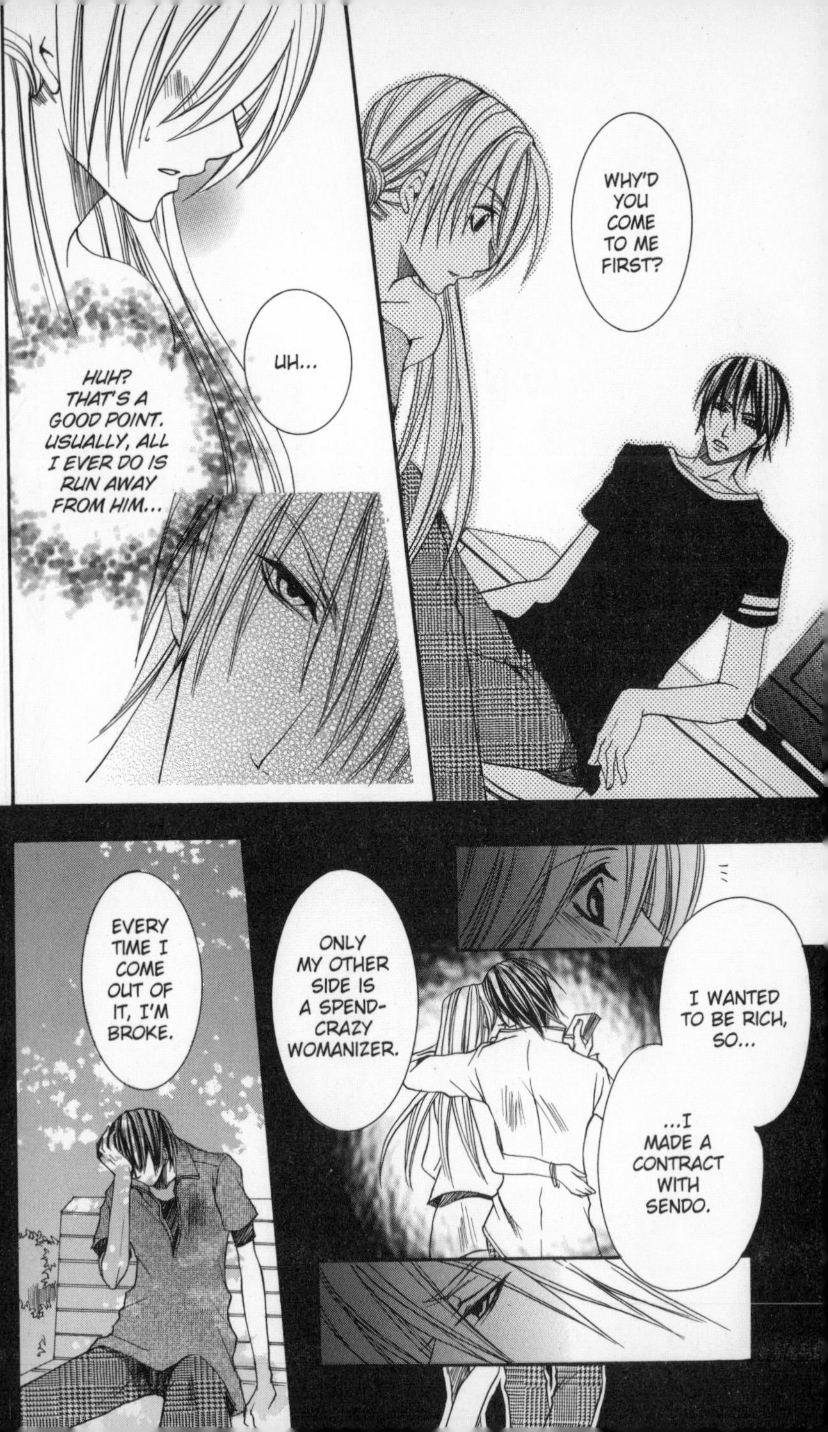
WHY'D YOU COME TO ME FIRST?
UH...
HUH? THAT'S A GOOD POINT. USUALLY, ALL I EVER DO IS RUN AWAY FROM HIM...
I WANTED TO BE RICH, SO...
...I MADE A CONTRACT WITH SENDO.
ONLY MY OTHER SIDE IS A SPEND-CRAZY WOMANIZER.
EVERY TIME I COME OUT OF IT, I'M BROKE.

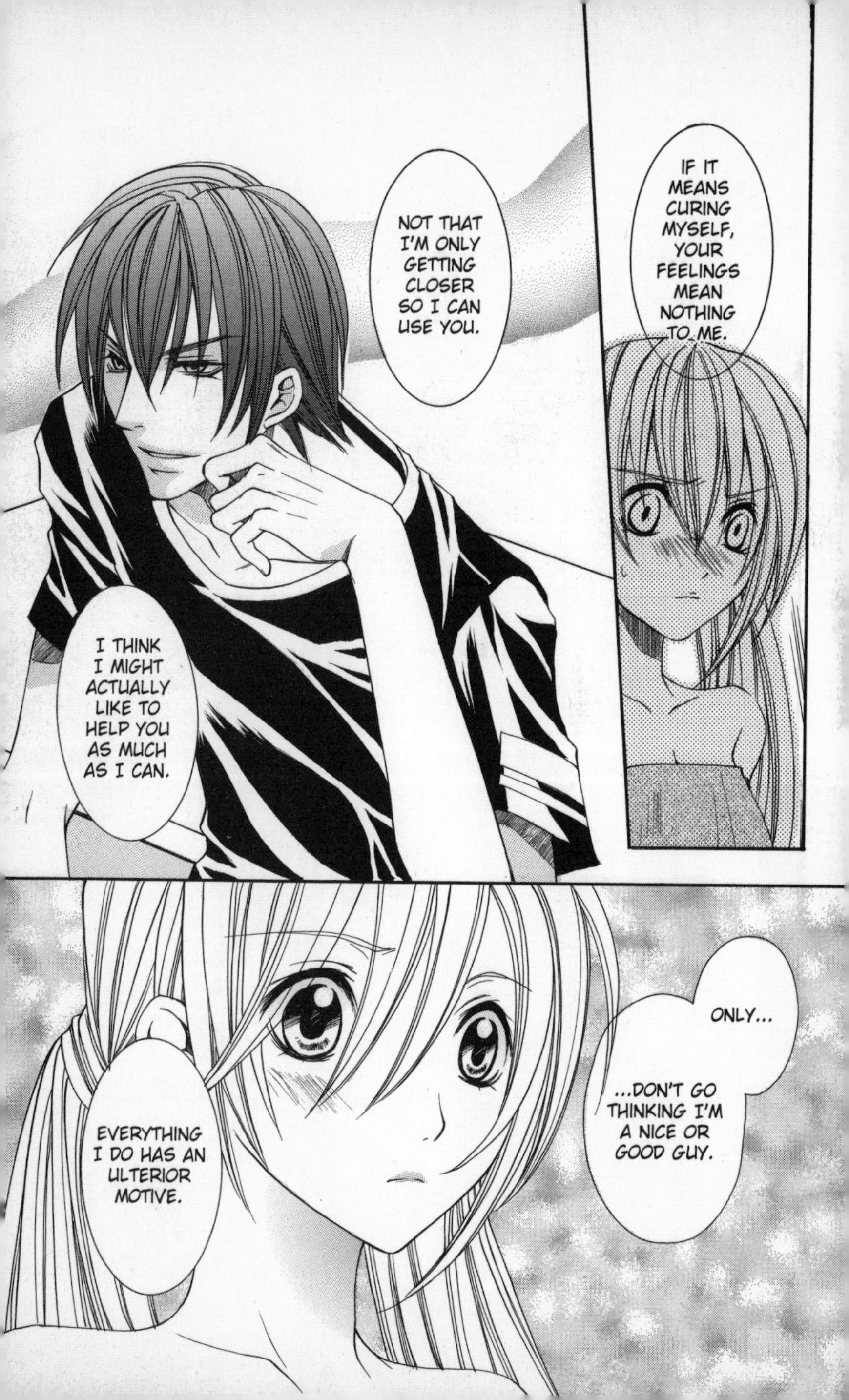

IF IT MEANS CURING MYSELF, YOUR FEELINGS MEAN NOTHING TO ME.
NOT THAT I'M ONLY GETTING CLOSER SO I CAN USE YOU.
I THINK I MIGHT ACTUALLY LIKE TO HELP YOU AS MUCH AS I CAN.
ONLY...
...DON'T GO THINKING I'M A NICE OR GOOD GUY.
EVERYTHING I DO HAS AN ULTERIOR MOTIVE.

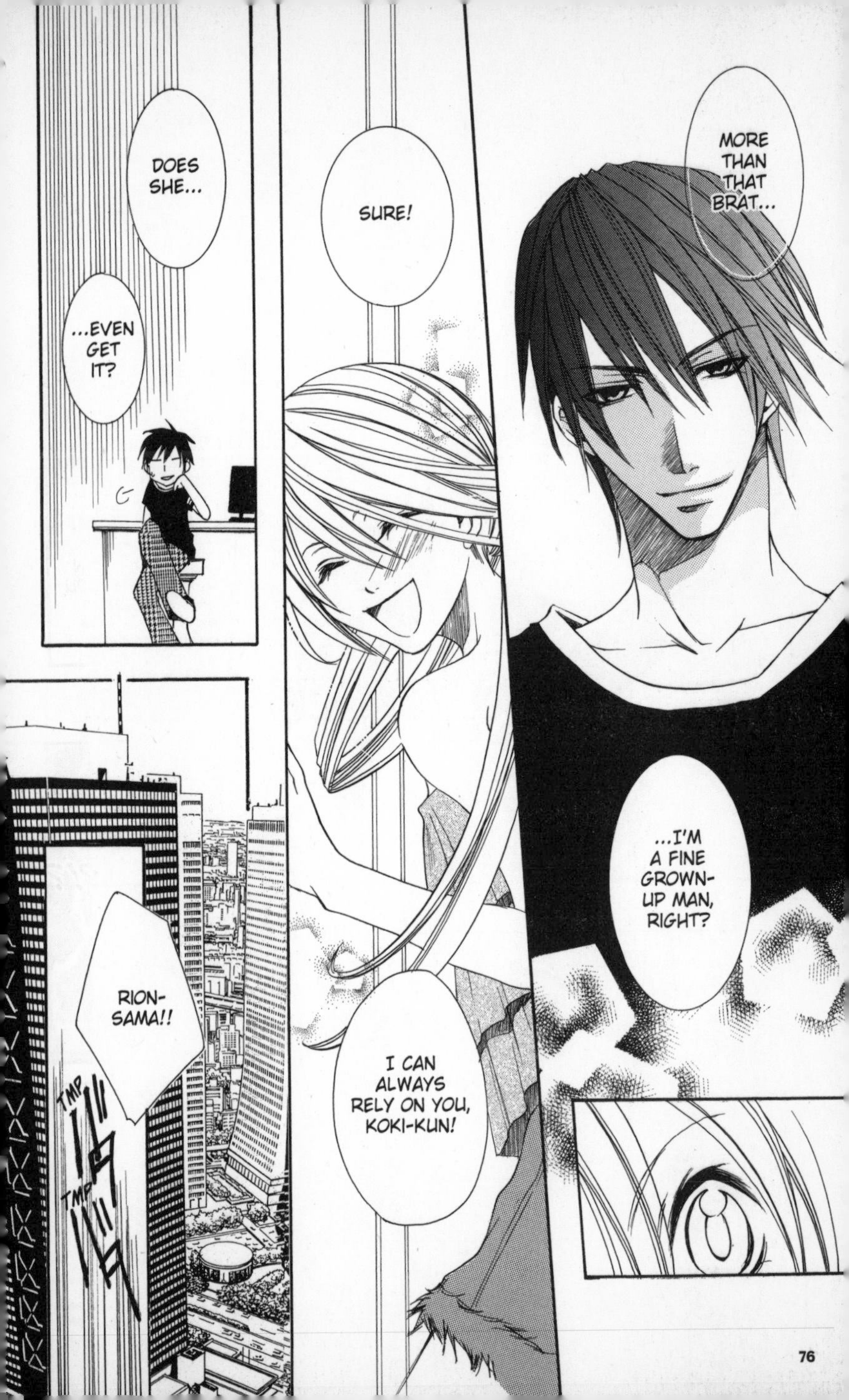
MORE THAN THAT BRAT...
...I'M A FINE GROWN-UP MAN, RIGHT?
SURE!
I CAN ALWAYS RELY ON YOU, KOKI-KUN!
DOES SHE...
...EVEN GET IT?
RION-SAMA!!
TMP
TMP

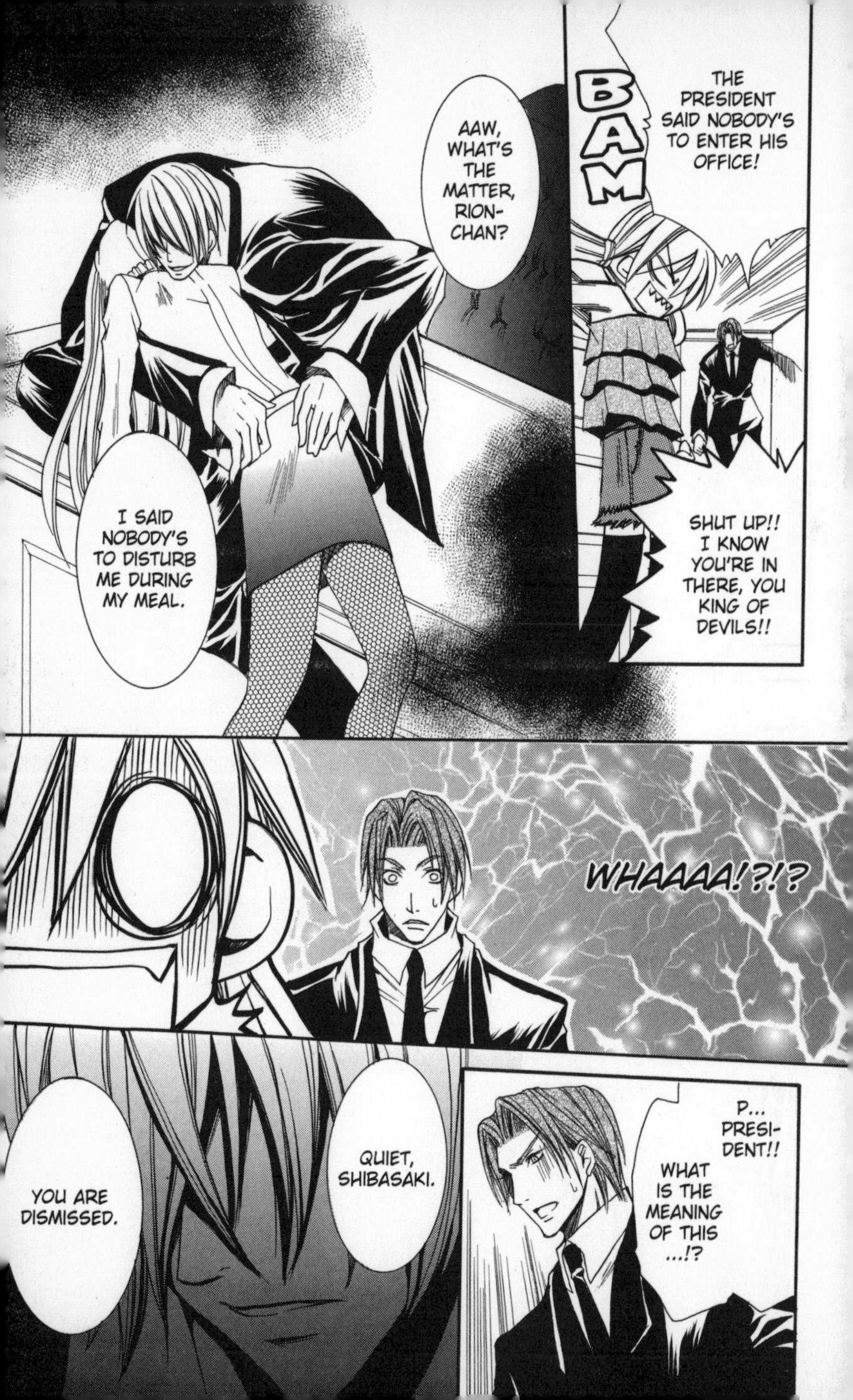
THE PRESIDENT SAID NOBODY'S TO ENTER HIS OFFICE!
BAM
SHUT UP!! I KNOW YOU'RE IN THERE, YOU KING OF DEVILS!!
AAW, WHAT'S THE MATTER, RION-CHAN?
I SAID NOBODY'S TO DISTURB ME DURING MY MEAL.
WHAAAA!?!?
P... PRESIDENT!!
WHAT IS THE MEANING OF THIS ...!?
QUIET, SHIBASAKI.
YOU ARE DISMISSED.

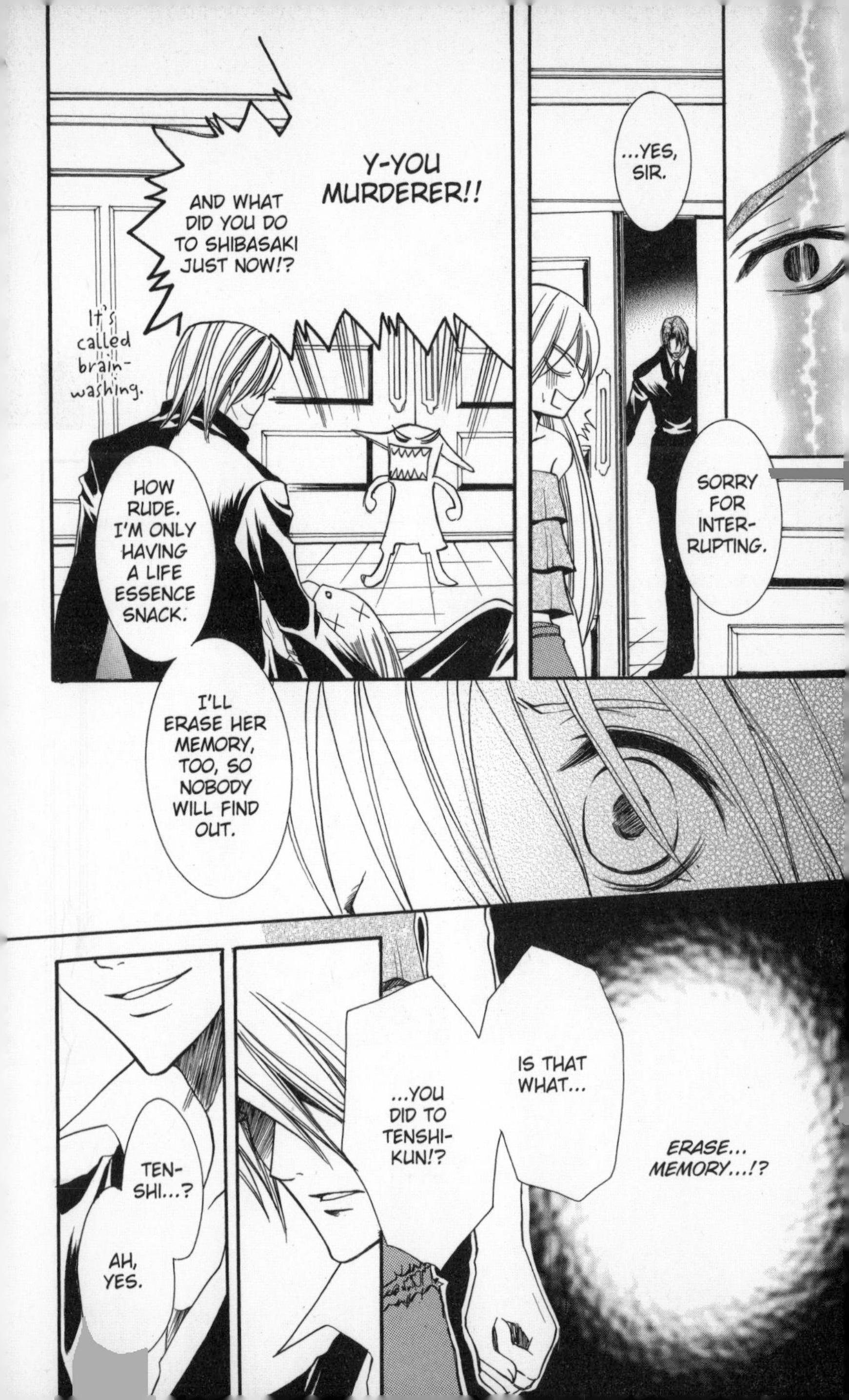

...YES, SIR.
SORRY FOR INTER-RUPTING.
Y-YOU MURDERER!!
AND WHAT DID YOU DO TO SHIBASAKI JUST NOW!?
HOW RUDE. I'M ONLY HAVING A LIFE ESSENCE SNACK.
It's called brain-washing.
I'LL ERASE HER MEMORY, TOO, SO NOBODY WILL FIND OUT.
ERASE... MEMORY...!?
IS THAT WHAT...
...YOU DID TO TENSHI-KUN!?
TEN-SHI...?
AH, YES.

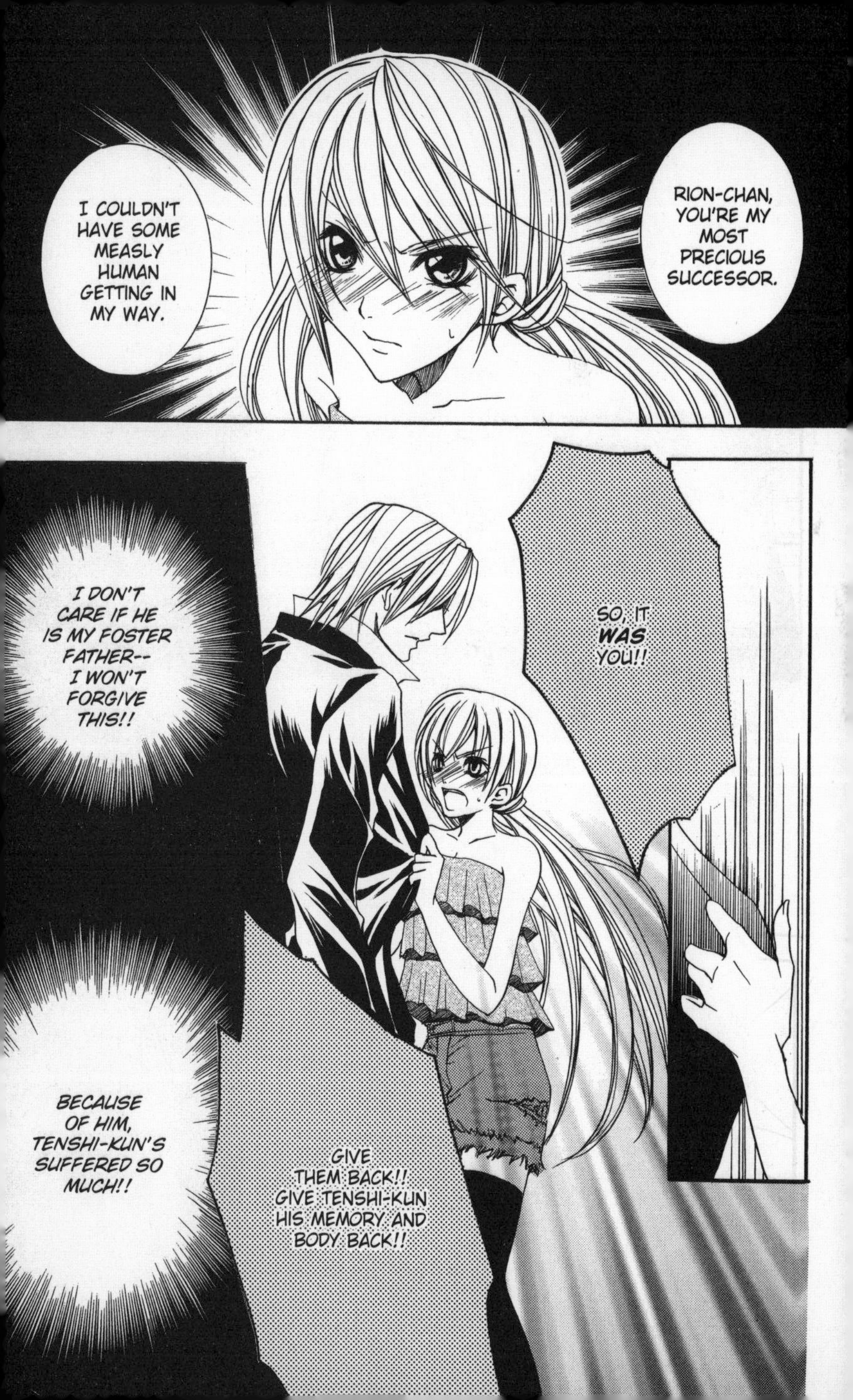
RION-CHAN, YOU'RE MY MOST PRECIOUS SUCCESSOR.
I COULDN'T HAVE SOME MEASLY HUMAN GETTING IN MY WAY.
SO, IT **WAS** YOU!!
*I DON'T CARE IF HE IS MY FOSTER FATHER-- I WON'T FORGIVE THIS!!*
GIVE THEM BACK!! GIVE TENSHI-KUN HIS MEMORY AND BODY BACK!!
*BECAUSE OF HIM, TENSHI-KUN'S SUFFERED SO MUCH!!*

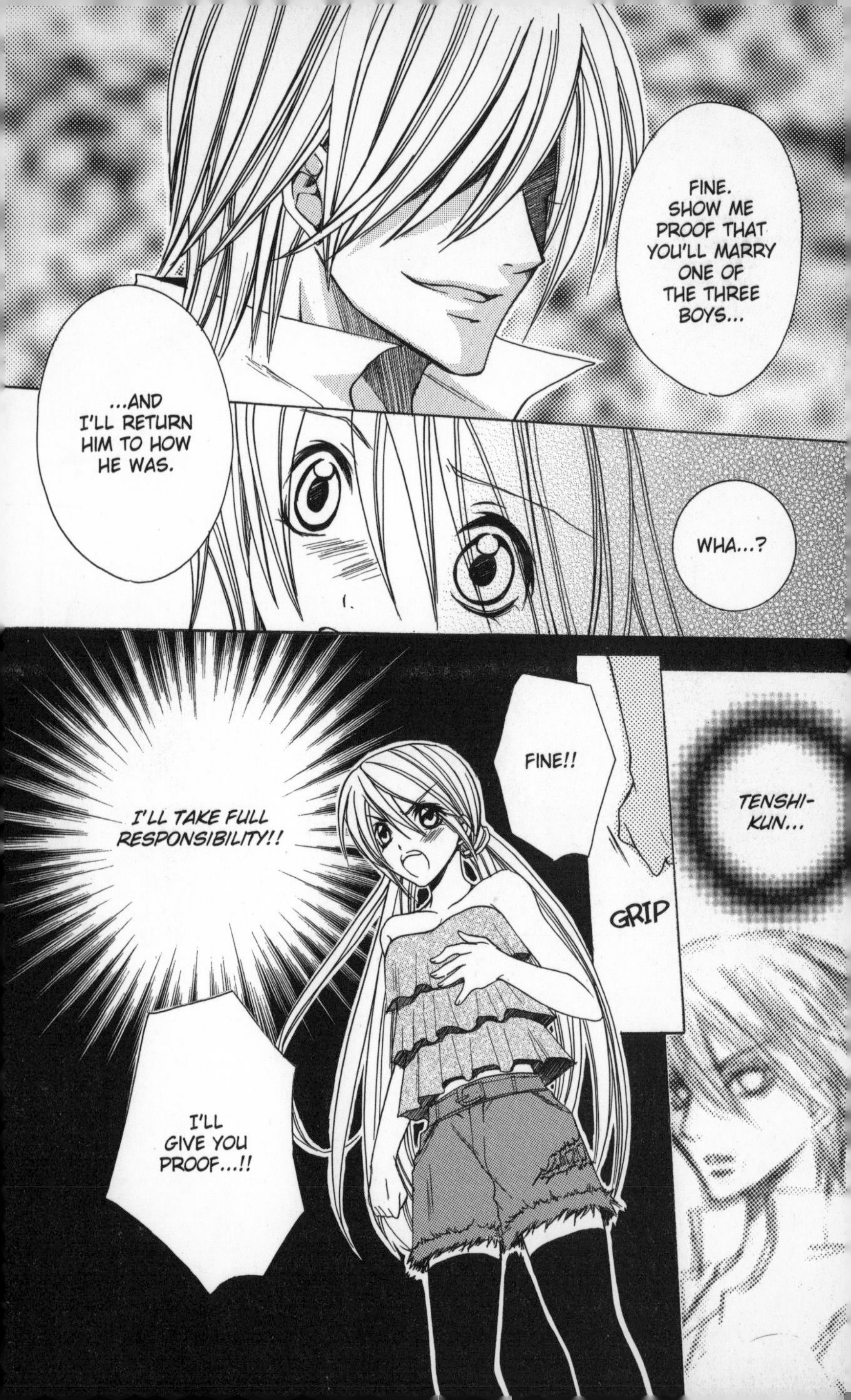
FINE. SHOW ME PROOF THAT YOU'LL MARRY ONE OF THE THREE BOYS...
...AND I'LL RETURN HIM TO HOW HE WAS.
WHA...?
TENSHI-KUN...
FINE!!
GRIP
I'LL TAKE FULL RESPONSIBILITY!!
I'LL GIVE YOU PROOF...!!

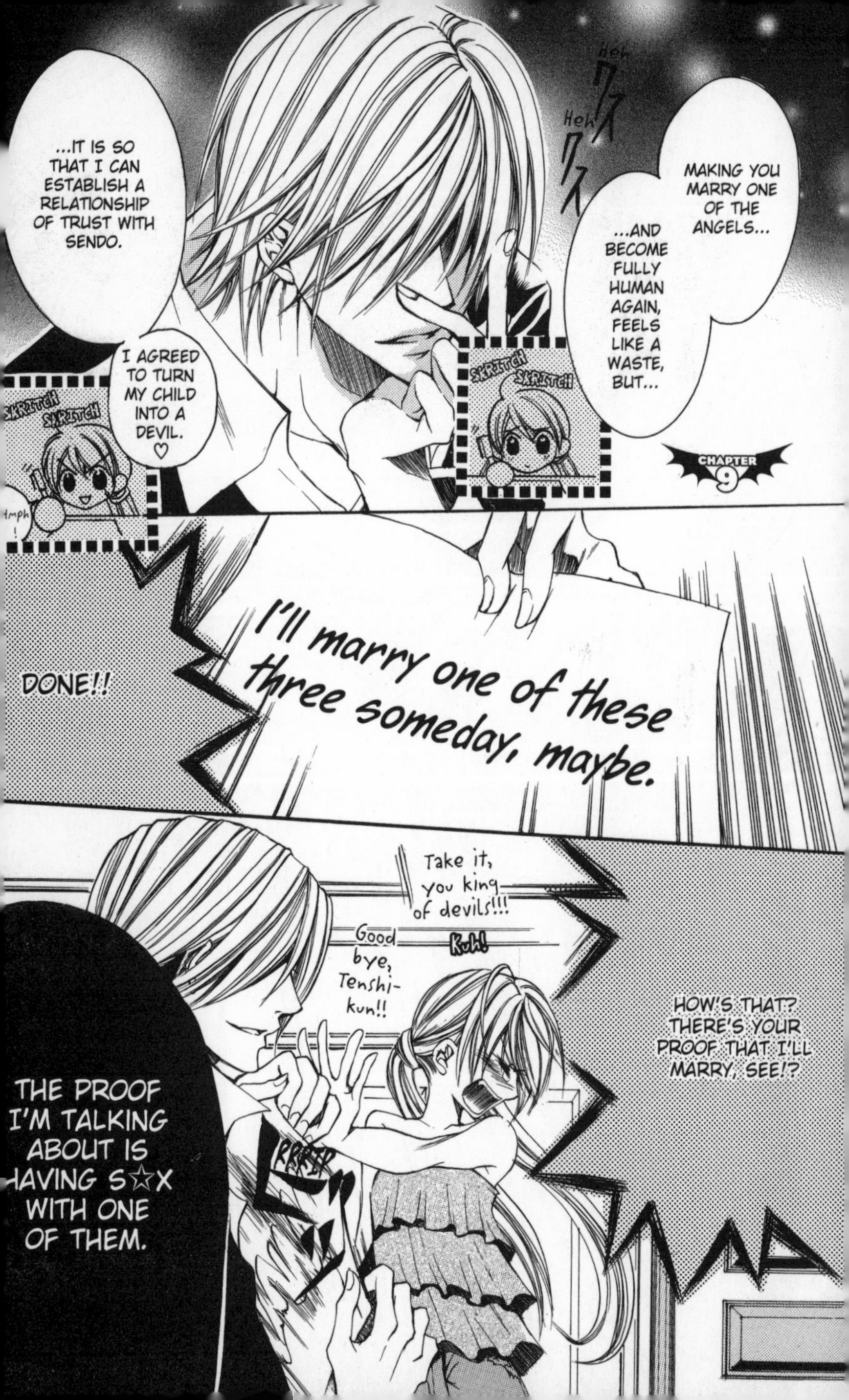
Heh
Heh
MAKING YOU MARRY ONE OF THE ANGELS...
...AND BECOME FULLY HUMAN AGAIN, FEELS LIKE A WASTE, BUT...
...IT IS SO THAT I CAN ESTABLISH A RELATIONSHIP OF TRUST WITH SENDO.
SKRITCH
SKRITCH
CHAPTER 9
I AGREED TO TURN MY CHILD INTO A DEVIL. ♡
SKRITCH
SKRITCH
mph !
I'll marry one of these three someday, maybe.
DONE!!
HOW'S THAT? THERE'S YOUR PROOF THAT I'LL MARRY, SEE!?
Take it, you king of devils!!!
Kuh!
Good bye, Tenshi-kun!!
RRRIP
THE PROOF I'M TALKING ABOUT IS HAVING S☆X WITH ONE OF THEM.

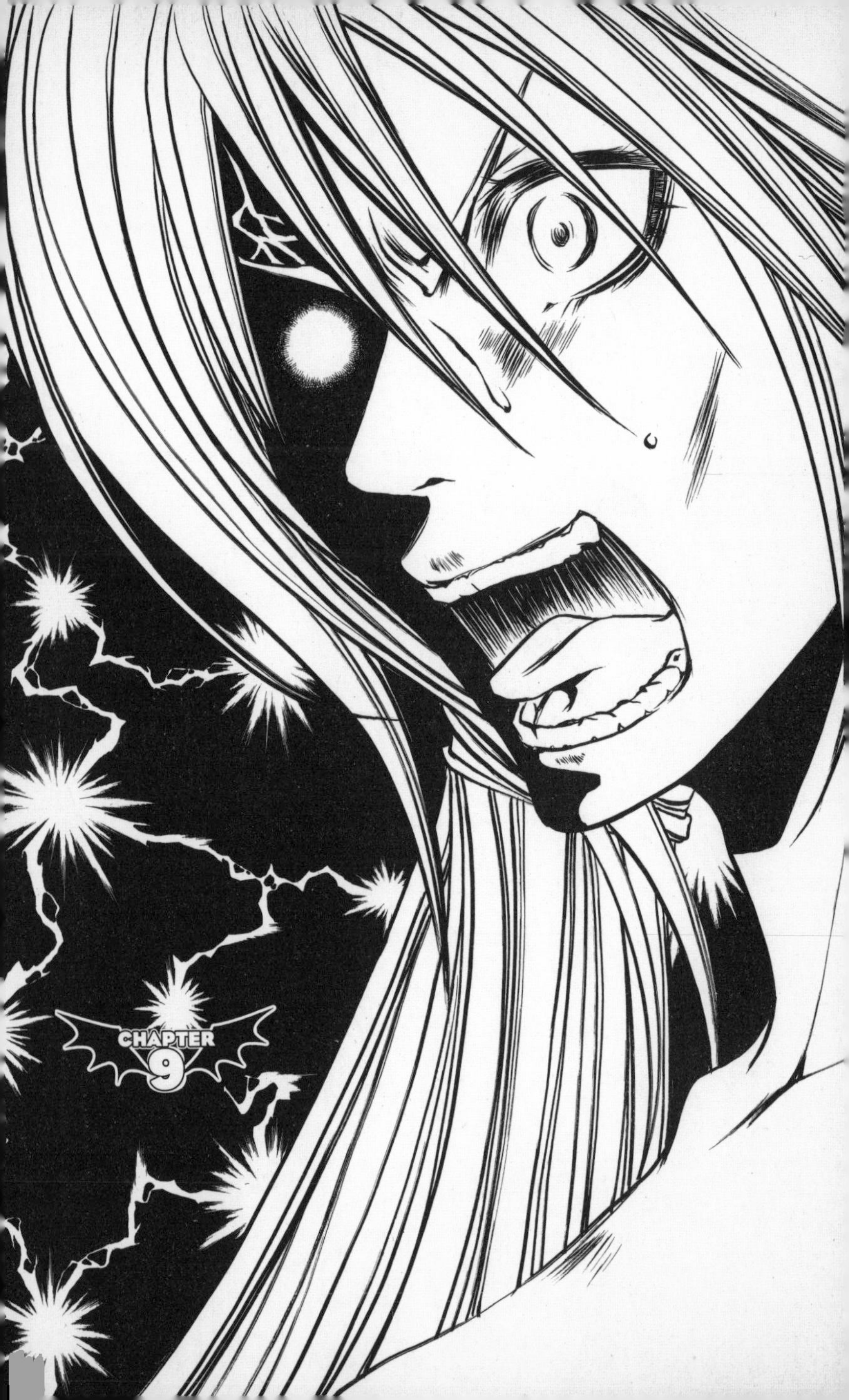
CHAPTER
9

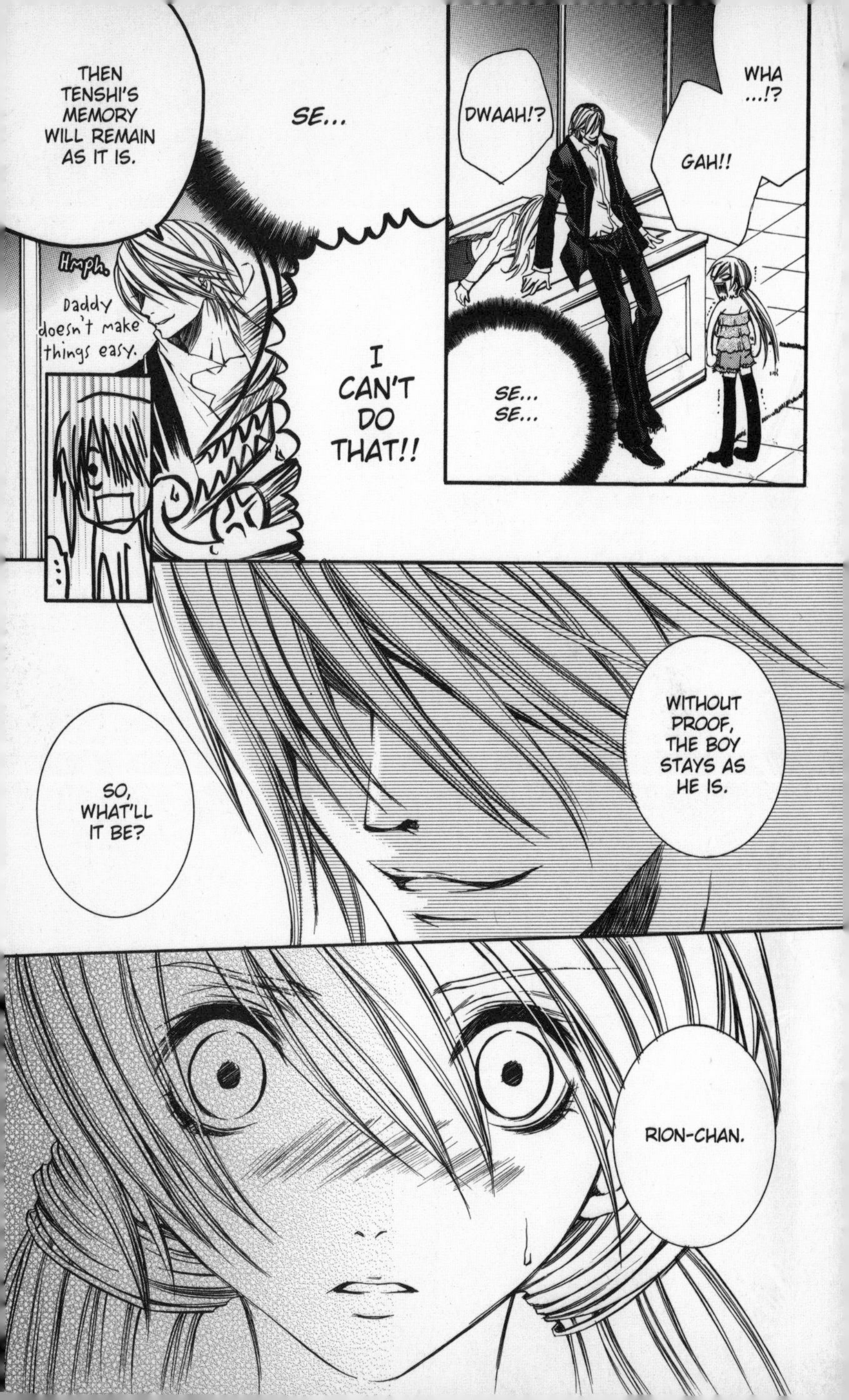
WHA ...!?
GAH!!
DWAAH!?
SE... SE...
THEN TENSHI'S MEMORY WILL REMAIN AS IT IS.
SE...
I CAN'T DO THAT!!
Hmph.
Daddy doesn't make things easy.
WITHOUT PROOF, THE BOY STAYS AS HE IS.
SO, WHAT'LL IT BE?
RION-CHAN.

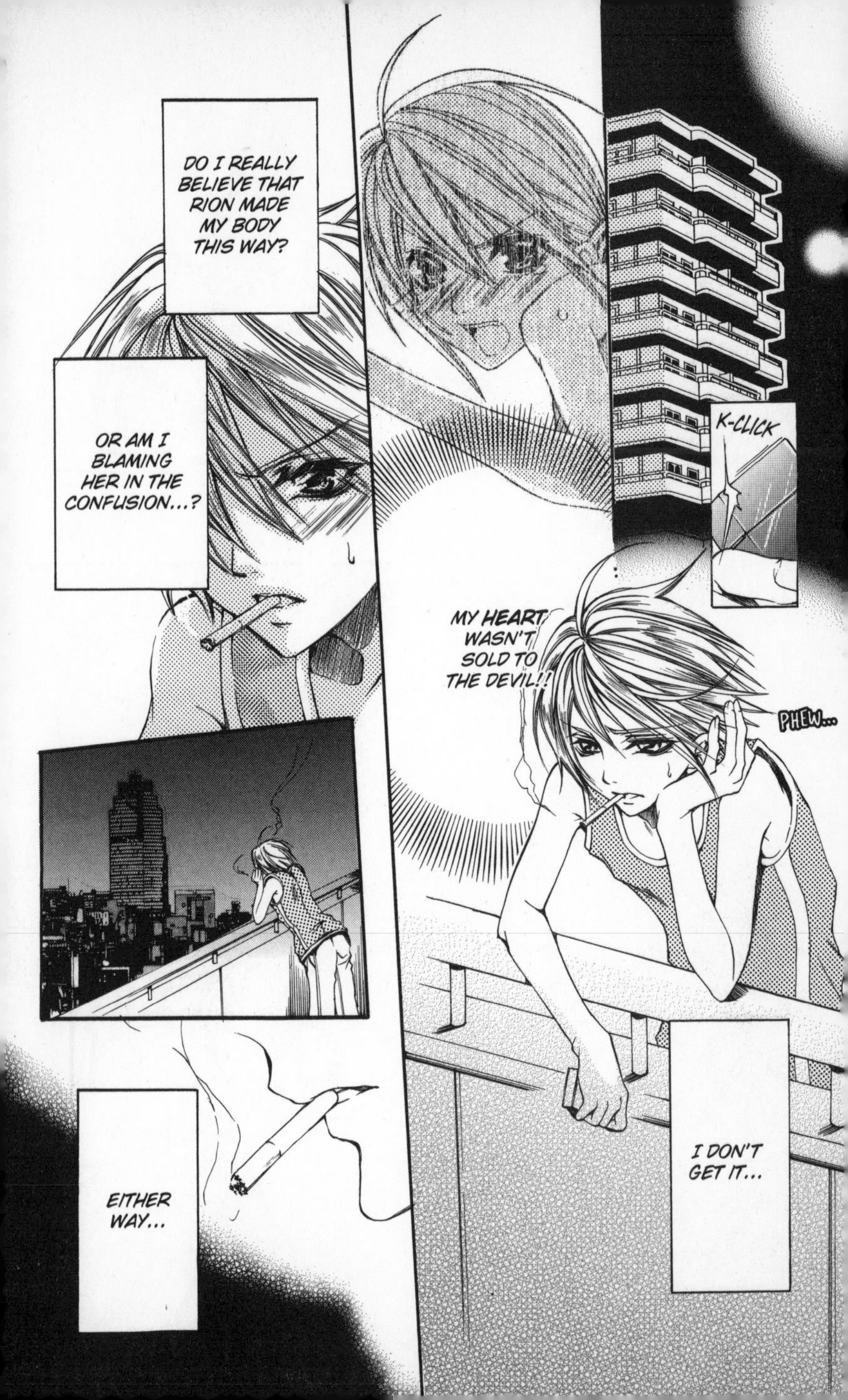
K-CLICK
MY HEART WASN'T SOLD TO THE DEVIL!!
PHEW...
I DON'T GET IT...
DO I REALLY BELIEVE THAT RION MADE MY BODY THIS WAY?
OR AM I BLAMING HER IN THE CONFUSION...?
EITHER WAY...

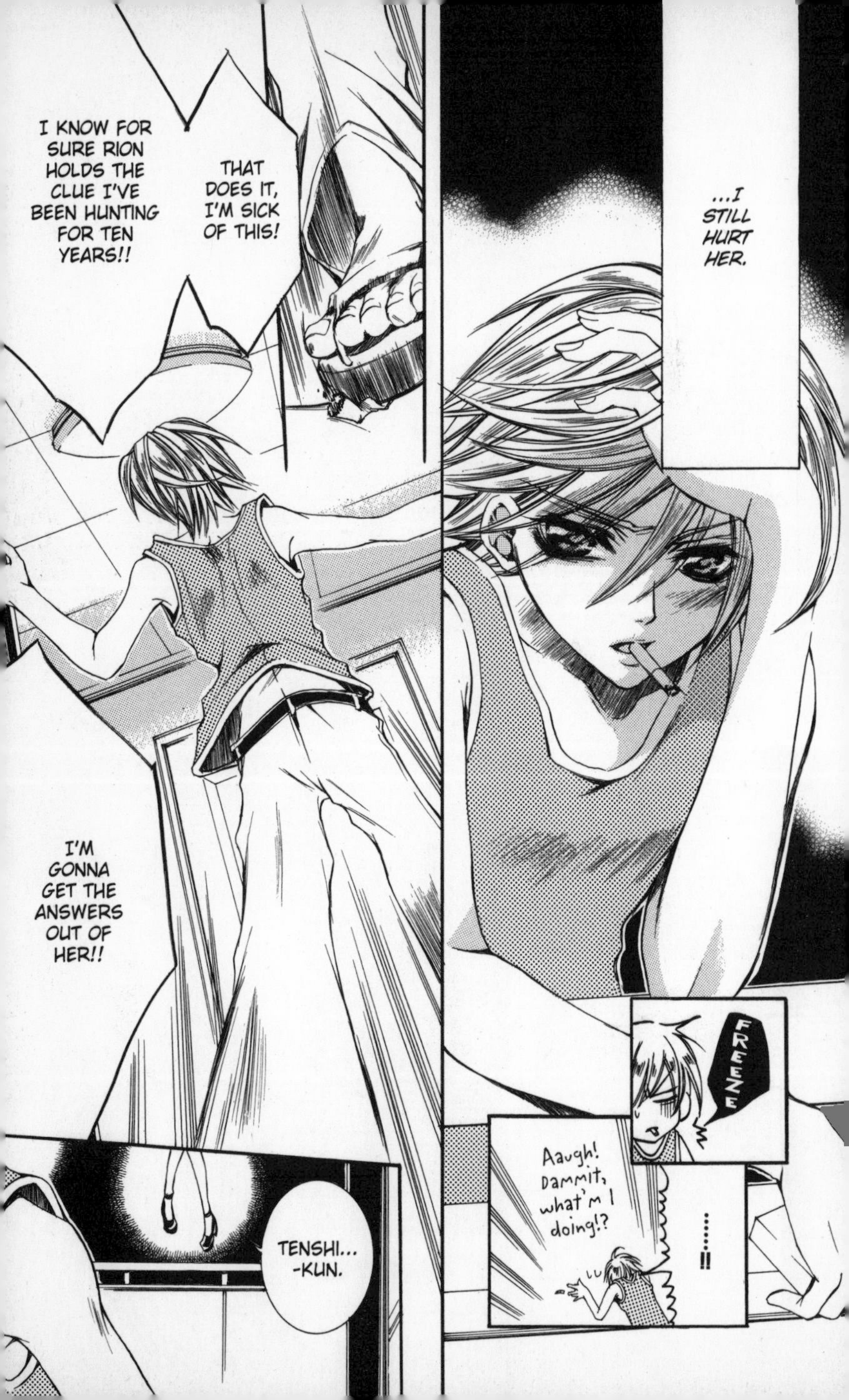
...I STILL HURT HER.
FREEZE
......!!
Aaugh! Dammit, what'm I doing!?
THAT DOES IT, I'M SICK OF THIS!
I KNOW FOR SURE RION HOLDS THE CLUE I'VE BEEN HUNTING FOR TEN YEARS!!
I'M GONNA GET THE ANSWERS OUT OF HER!!
TENSHI... -KUN.

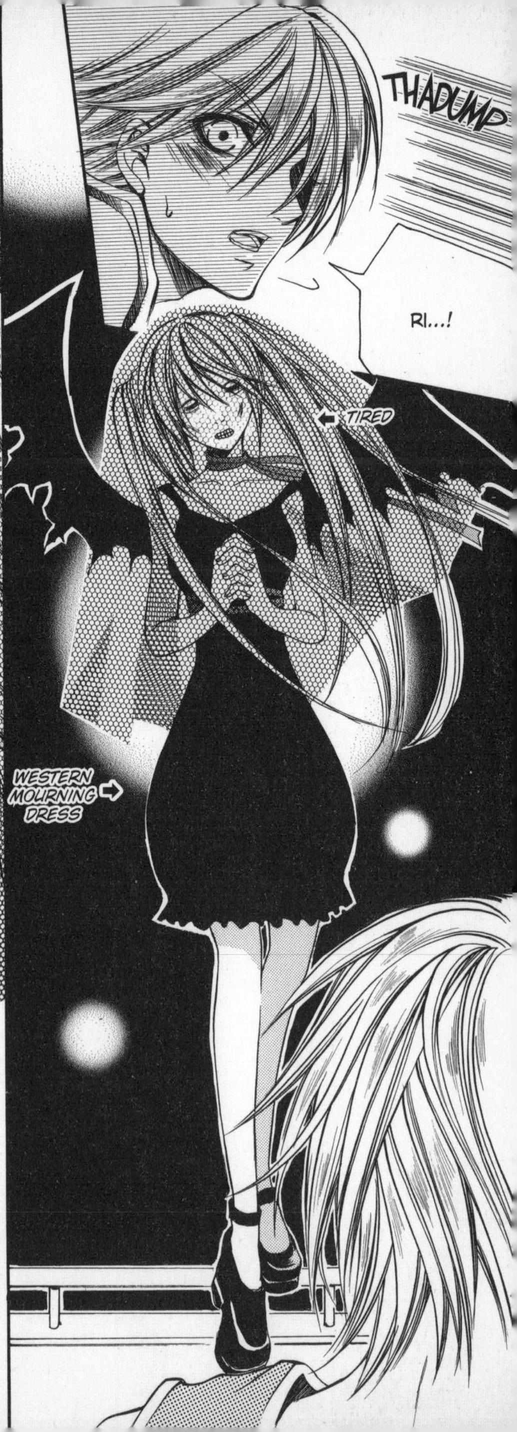
THADUMP
RI...!
TIRED
WESTERN MOURNING DRESS
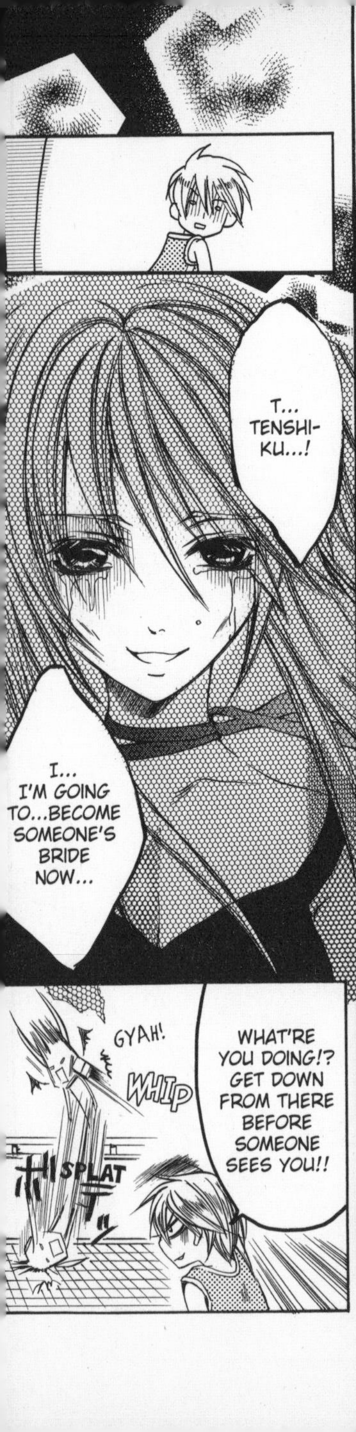
T... TENSHI-KU...!
I... I'M GOING TO...BECOME SOMEONE'S BRIDE NOW...
WHAT'RE YOU DOING!? GET DOWN FROM THERE BEFORE SOMEONE SEES YOU!!
WHIP
GYAH!
SPLAT

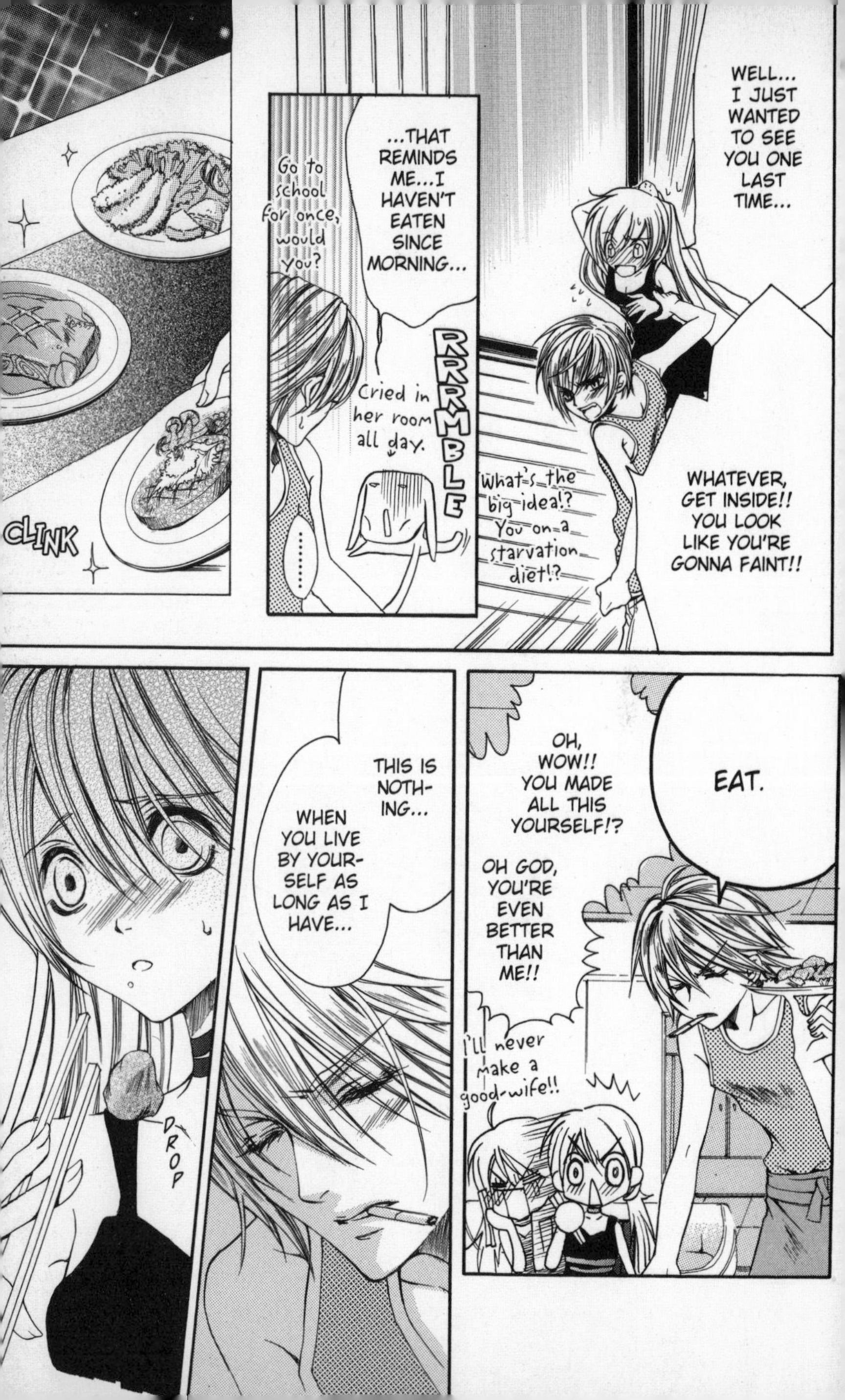
WELL... I JUST WANTED TO SEE YOU ONE LAST TIME...
WHATEVER, GET INSIDE!! YOU LOOK LIKE YOU'RE GONNA FAINT!!
What's the big idea!? You on a starvation diet!?
...THAT REMINDS ME...I HAVEN'T EATEN SINCE MORNING...
Go to school for once, would you?
RRRRMBLE
Cried in her room all day.
........
CLINK
EAT.
OH, WOW!! YOU MADE ALL THIS YOURSELF!?
OH GOD, YOU'RE EVEN BETTER THAN ME!!
I'll never make a good-wife!!
THIS IS NOTH-ING...
WHEN YOU LIVE BY YOUR-SELF AS LONG AS I HAVE...
DROP

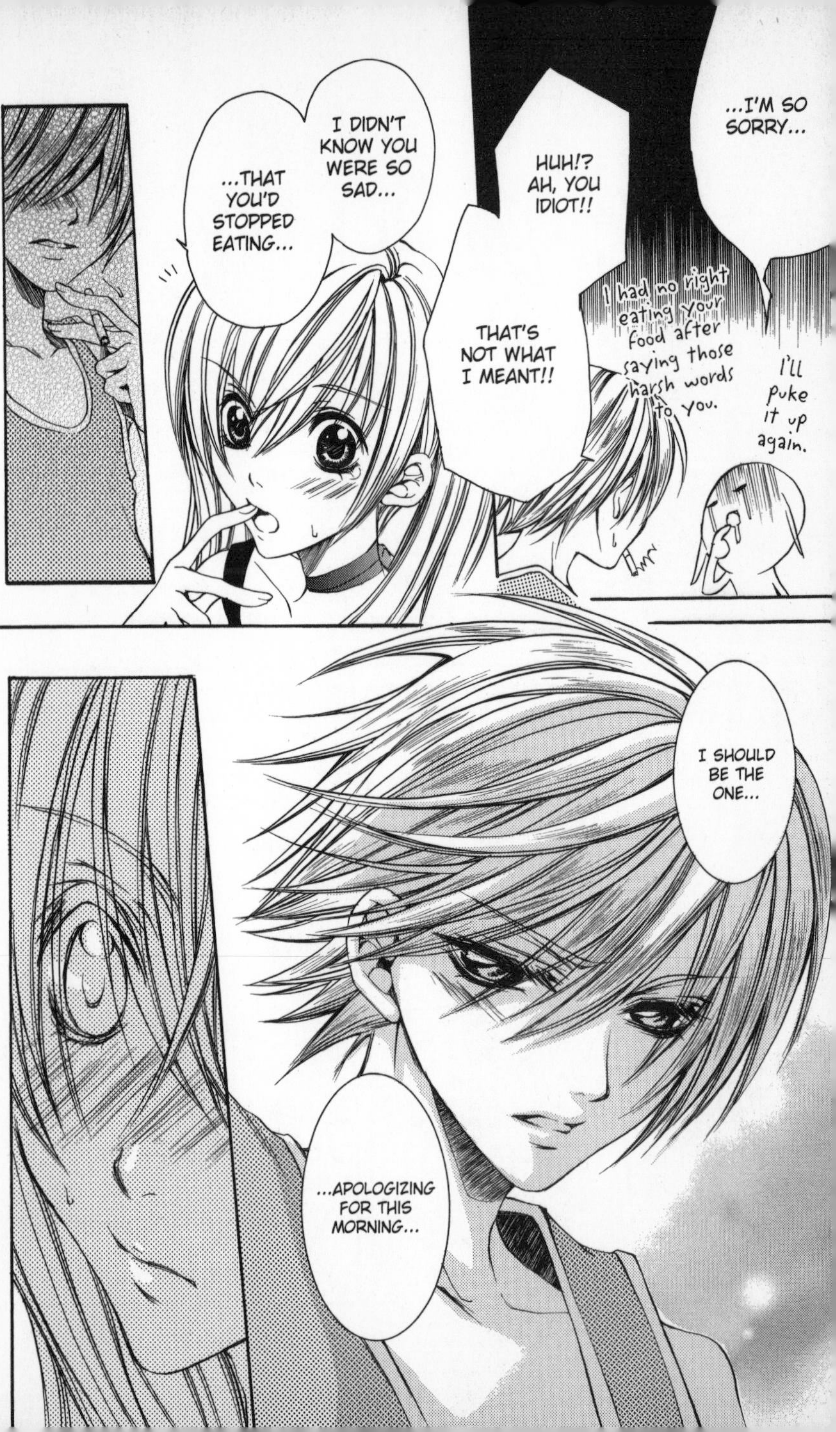

I DIDN'T KNOW YOU WERE SO SAD...
...THAT YOU'D STOPPED EATING...
HUH!? AH, YOU IDIOT!!
THAT'S NOT WHAT I MEANT!!
...I'M SO SORRY...
I had no right eating your food after saying those harsh words to you.
I'll puke it up again.
I SHOULD BE THE ONE...
...APOLOGIZING FOR THIS MORNING...

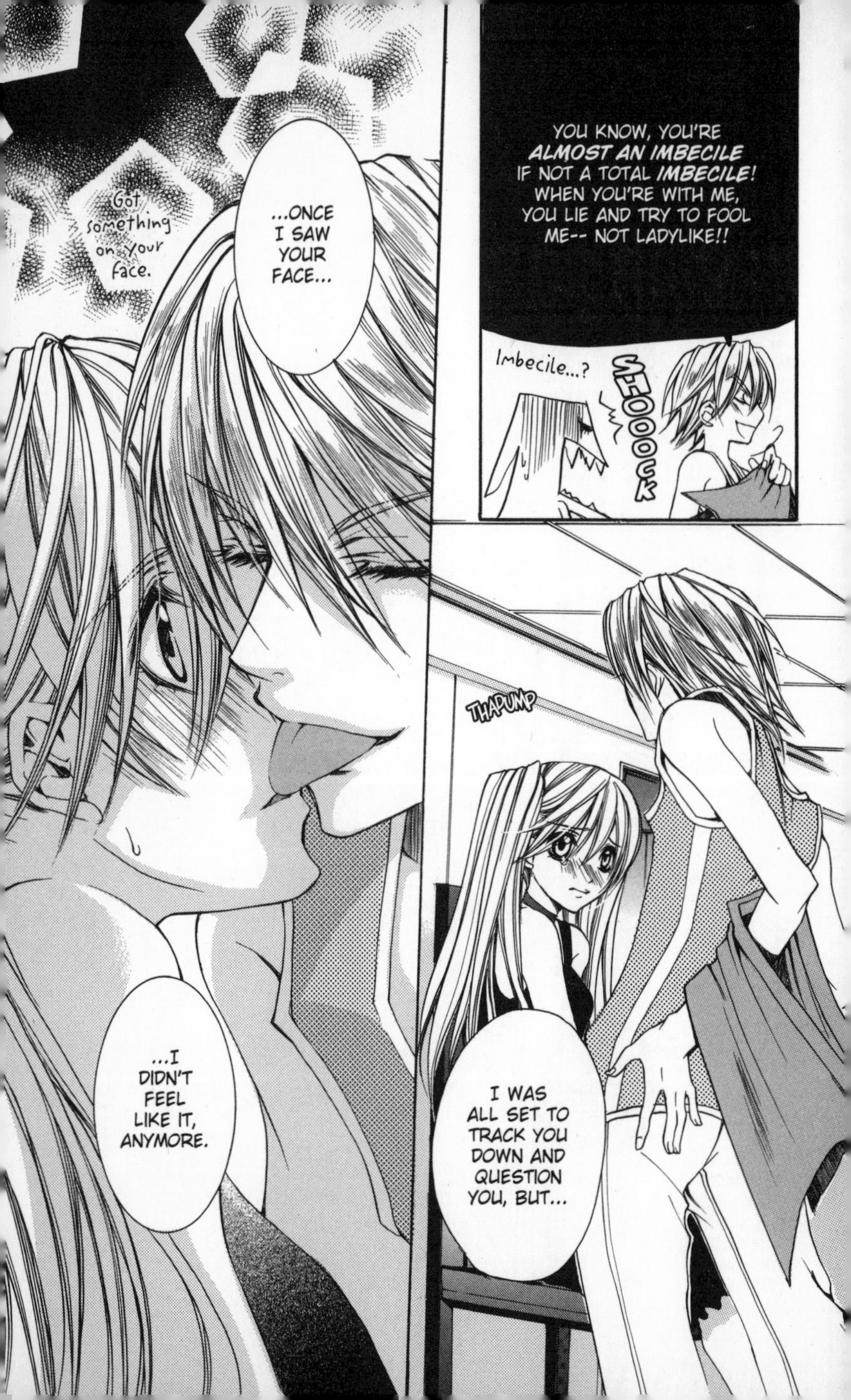
YOU KNOW, YOU'RE ALMOST AN IMBECILE IF NOT A TOTAL IMBECILE! WHEN YOU'RE WITH ME, YOU LIE AND TRY TO FOOL ME-- NOT LADYLIKE!!
SHOOOCK
Imbecile...?
THAPUMP
I WAS ALL SET TO TRACK YOU DOWN AND QUESTION YOU, BUT...
...ONCE I SAW YOUR FACE...
Got something on your face.
...I DIDN'T FEEL LIKE IT, ANYMORE.

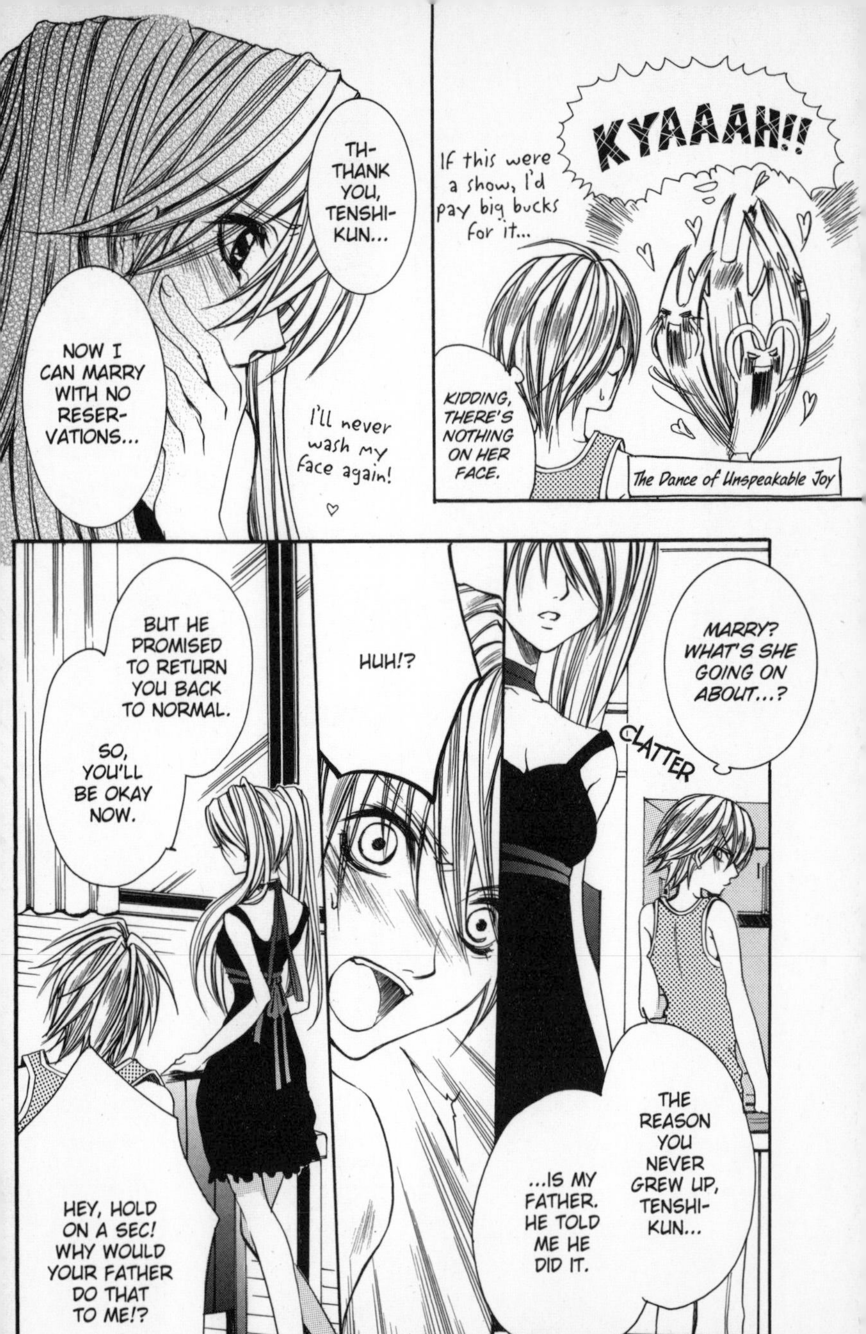
KYAAAH!!
If this were a show, I'd pay big bucks for it...
KIDDING, THERE'S NOTHING ON HER FACE.
The Dance of Unspeakable Joy
TH-THANK YOU, TENSHI-KUN...
NOW I CAN MARRY WITH NO RESERVATIONS...
I'll never wash my face again! ♡
MARRY? WHAT'S SHE GOING ON ABOUT...?
CLATTER
THE REASON YOU NEVER GREW UP, TENSHI-KUN...
...IS MY FATHER. HE TOLD ME HE DID IT.
HUH!?
BUT HE PROMISED TO RETURN YOU BACK TO NORMAL.
SO, YOU'LL BE OKAY NOW.
HEY, HOLD ON A SEC! WHY WOULD YOUR FATHER DO THAT TO ME!?

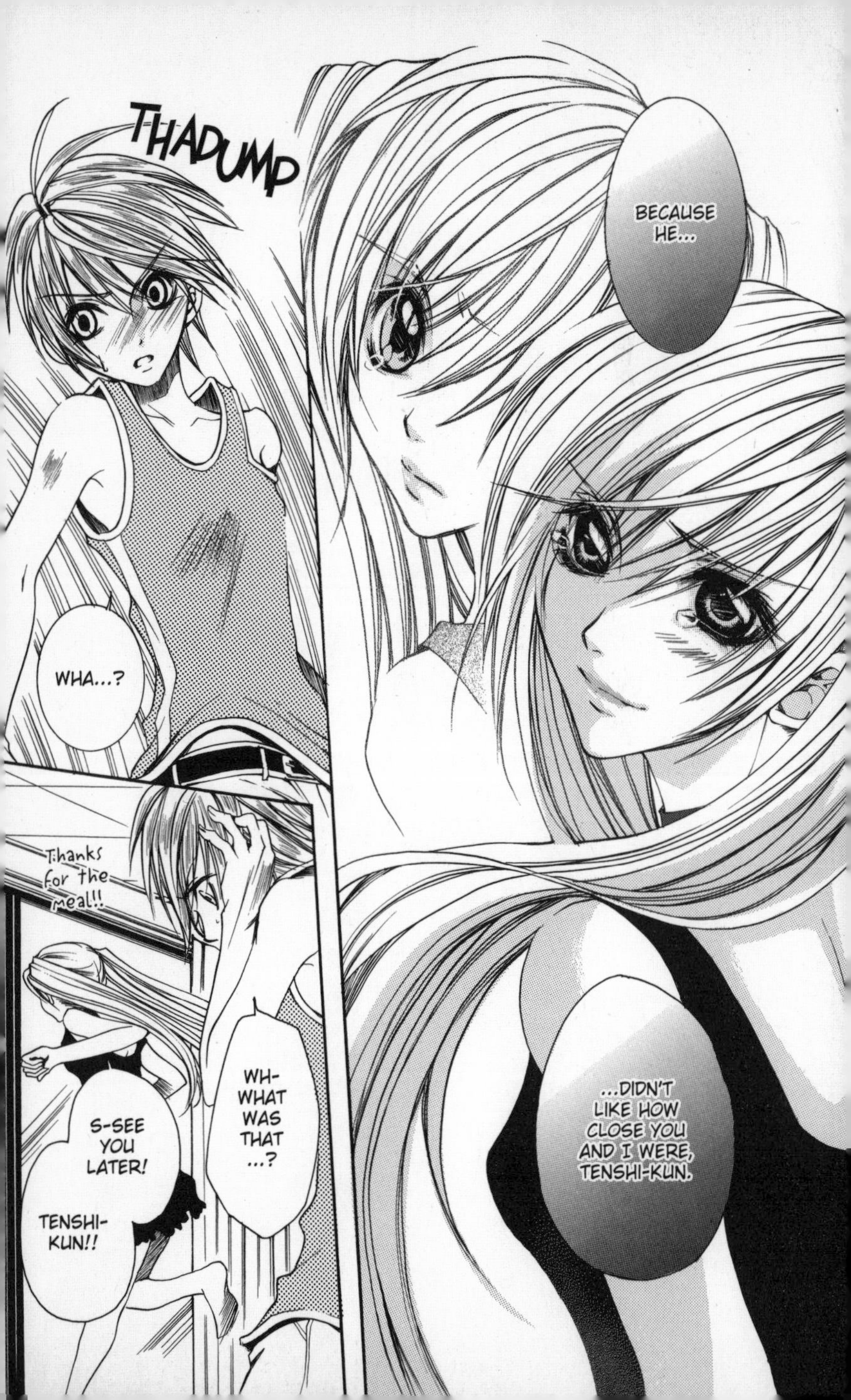
BECAUSE HE...
...DIDN'T LIKE HOW CLOSE YOU AND I WERE, TENSHI-KUN.
THADUMP
WHA...?
Thanks for the meal!!
WH-WHAT WAS THAT ...?
S-SEE YOU LATER!
TENSHI-KUN!!

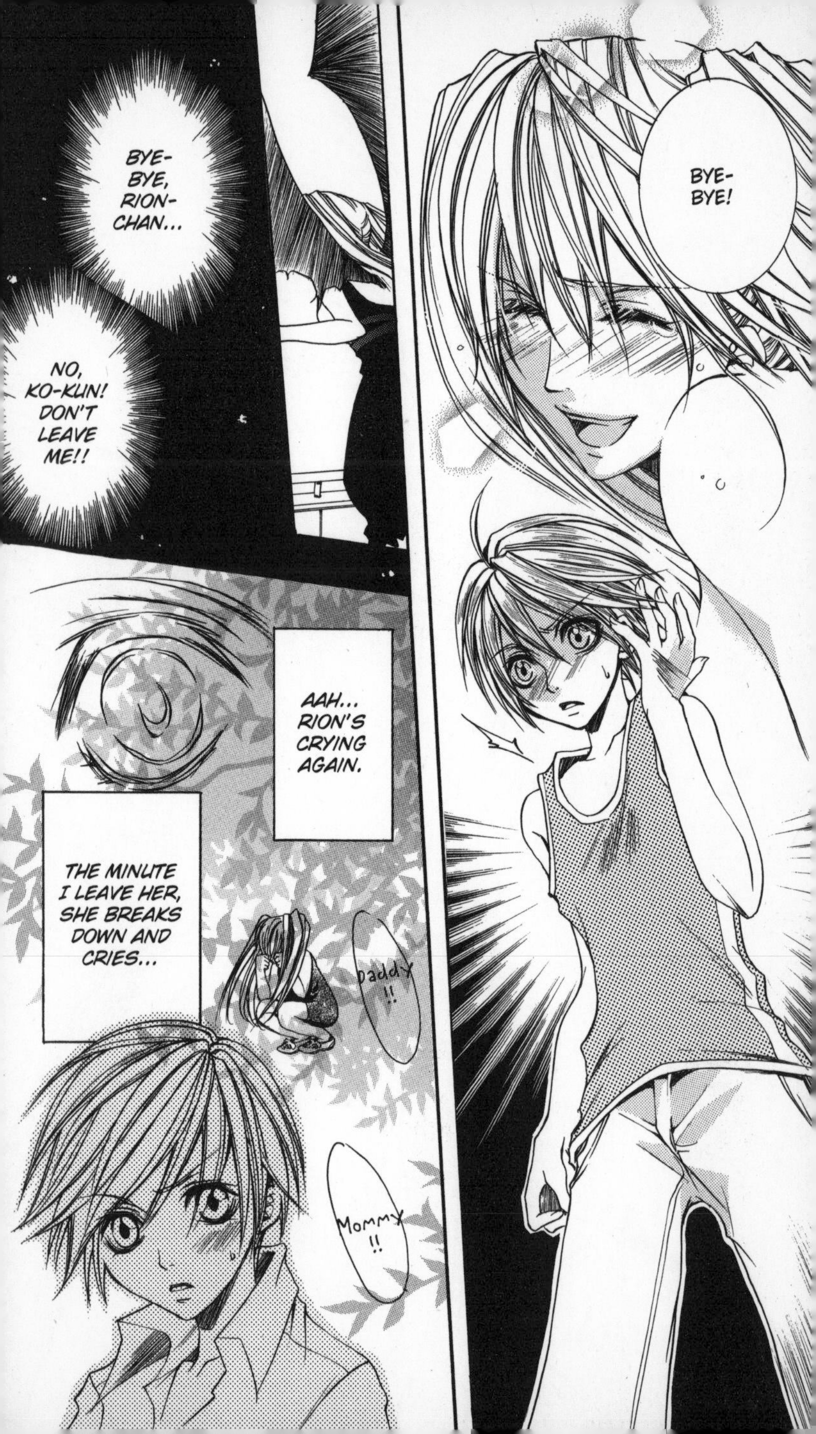
BYE-BYE!
BYE-BYE, RION-CHAN...
NO, KO-KUN! DON'T LEAVE ME!!
AAH... RION'S CRYING AGAIN.
THE MINUTE I LEAVE HER, SHE BREAKS DOWN AND CRIES...
Daddy !!
Mommy !!

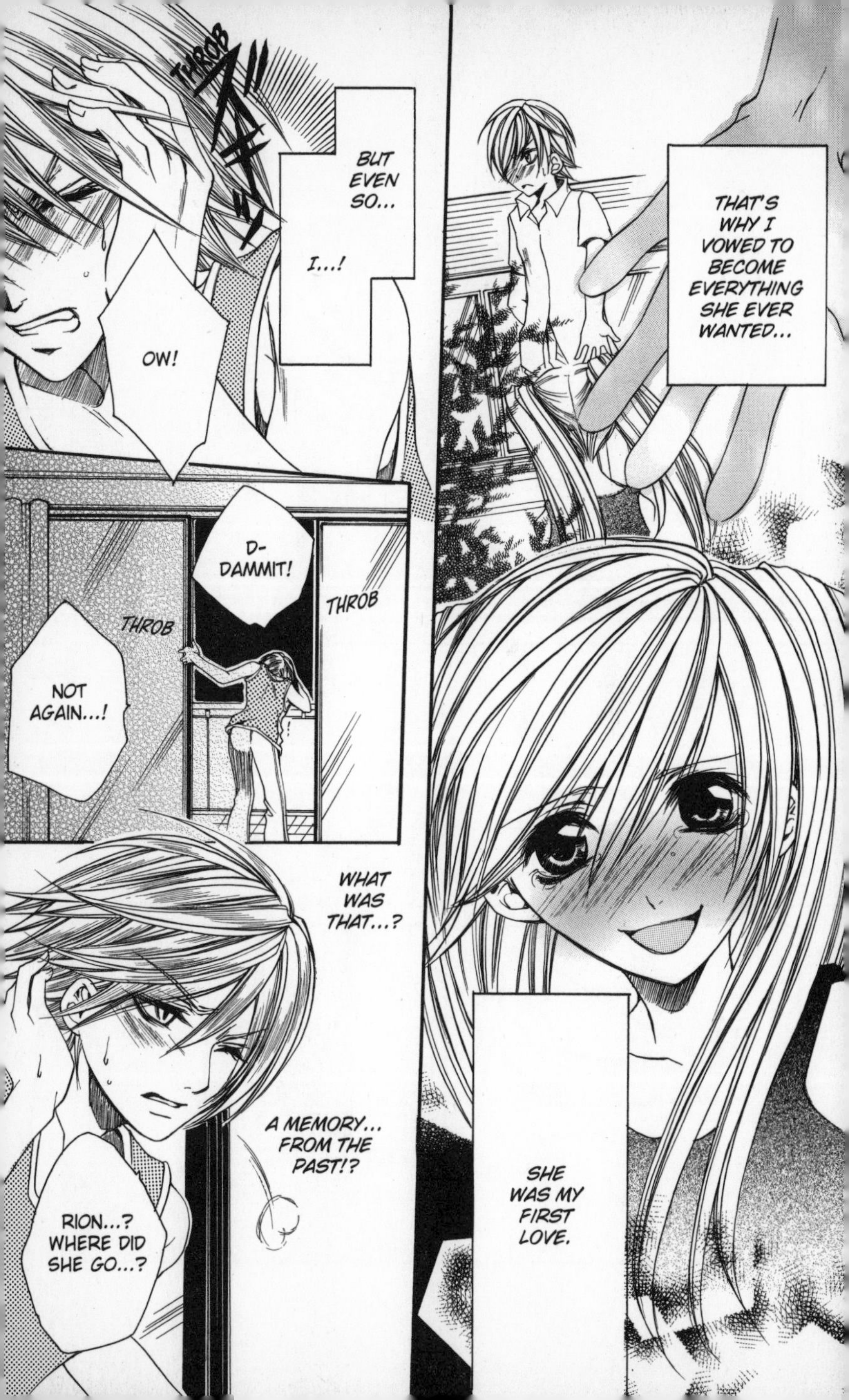
THAT'S WHY I VOWED TO BECOME EVERYTHING SHE EVER WANTED...
SHE WAS MY FIRST LOVE.
THROB
BUT EVEN SO...
I...!
OW!
D-DAMMIT!
THROB
THROB
NOT AGAIN...!
WHAT WAS THAT...?
A MEMORY... FROM THE PAST!?
RION...? WHERE DID SHE GO...?

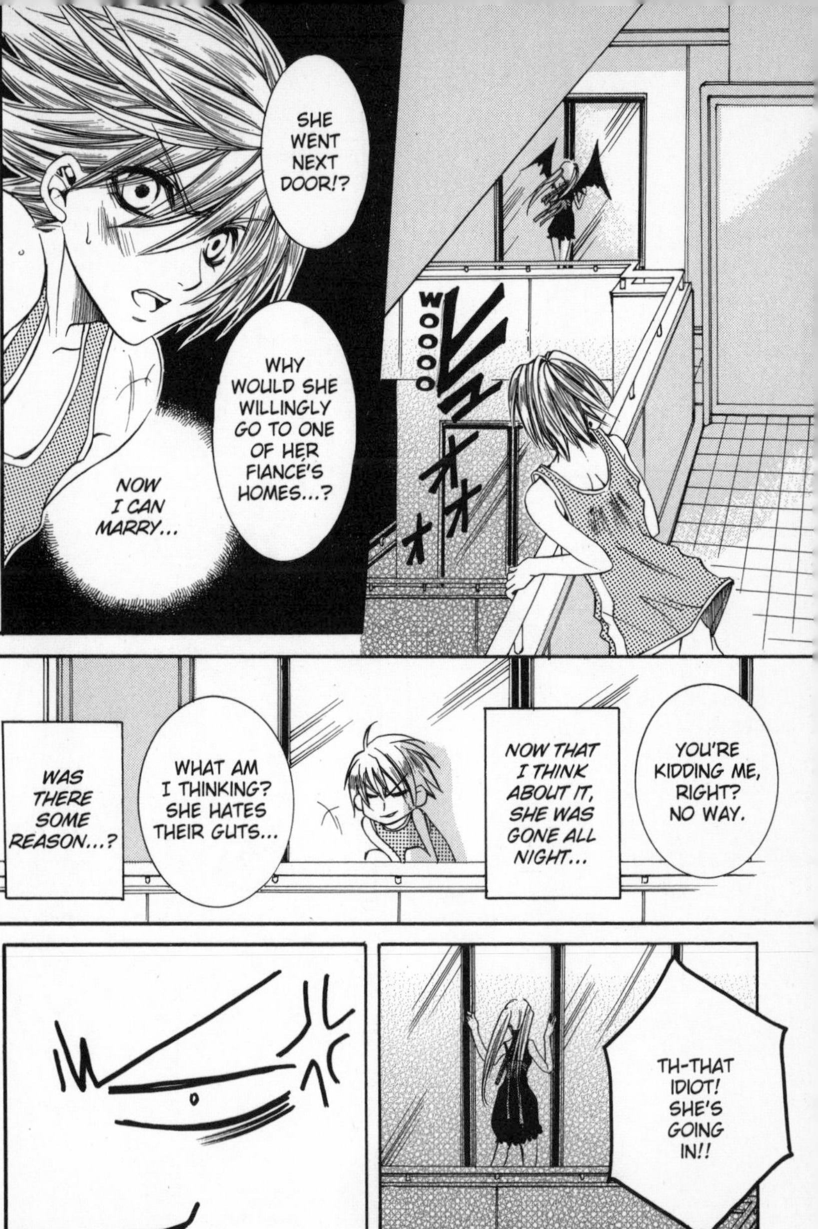
WOOOO
SHE WENT NEXT DOOR!?
WHY WOULD SHE WILLINGLY GO TO ONE OF HER FIANCÉ'S HOMES...?
NOW I CAN MARRY...
YOU'RE KIDDING ME, RIGHT? NO WAY.
NOW THAT I THINK ABOUT IT, SHE WAS GONE ALL NIGHT...
WHAT AM I THINKING? SHE HATES THEIR GUTS...
WAS THERE SOME REASON...?
TH-THAT IDIOT! SHE'S GOING IN!!

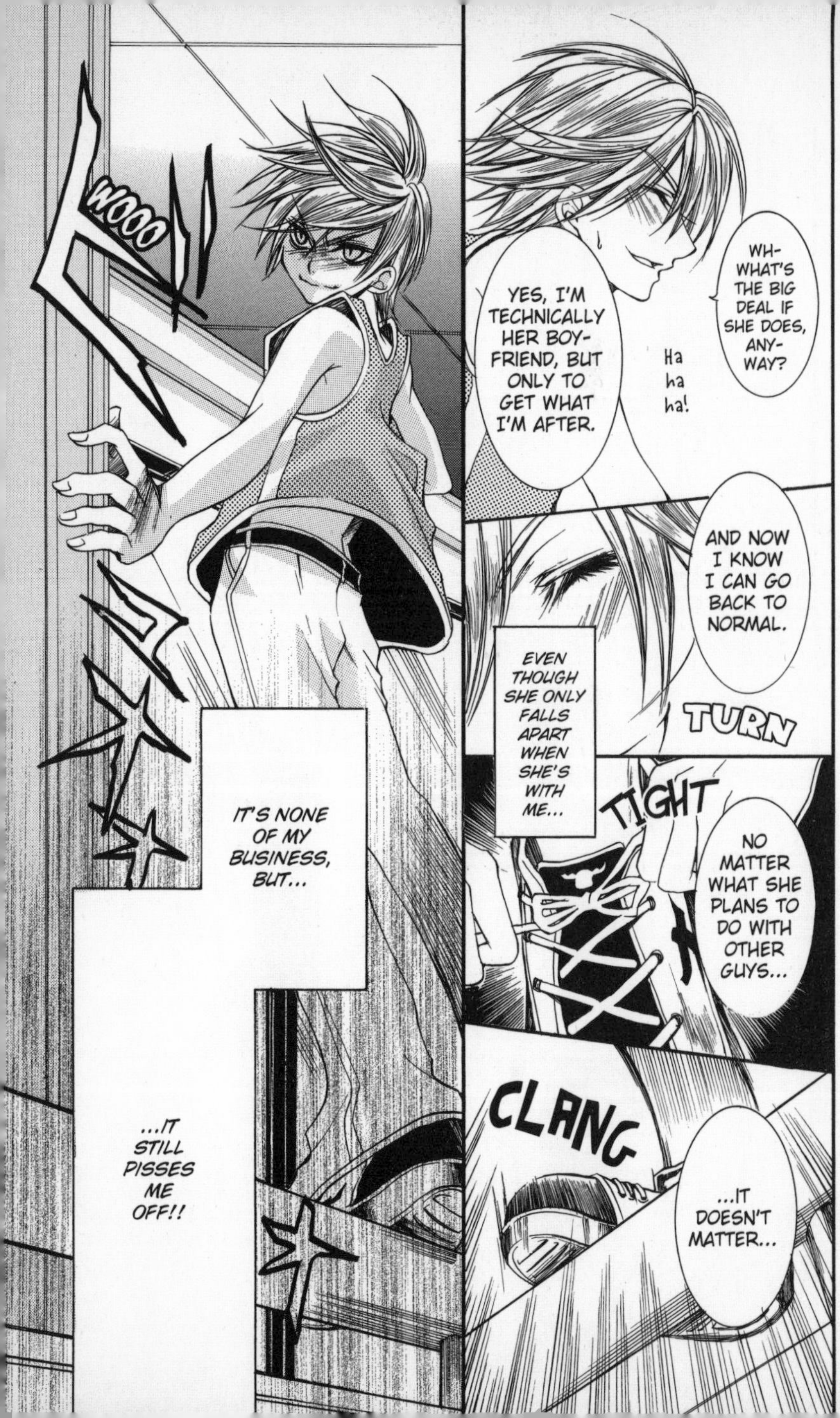
WH- WHAT'S THE BIG DEAL IF SHE DOES, ANY-WAY?
Ha ha ha!
YES, I'M TECHNICALLY HER BOY-FRIEND, BUT ONLY TO GET WHAT I'M AFTER.
AND NOW I KNOW I CAN GO BACK TO NORMAL.
TURN
EVEN THOUGH SHE ONLY FALLS APART WHEN SHE'S WITH ME...
NO MATTER WHAT SHE PLANS TO DO WITH OTHER GUYS...
TIGHT
CLANG
...IT DOESN'T MATTER...
WOOO
IT'S NONE OF MY BUSINESS, BUT...
...IT STILL PISSES ME OFF!!

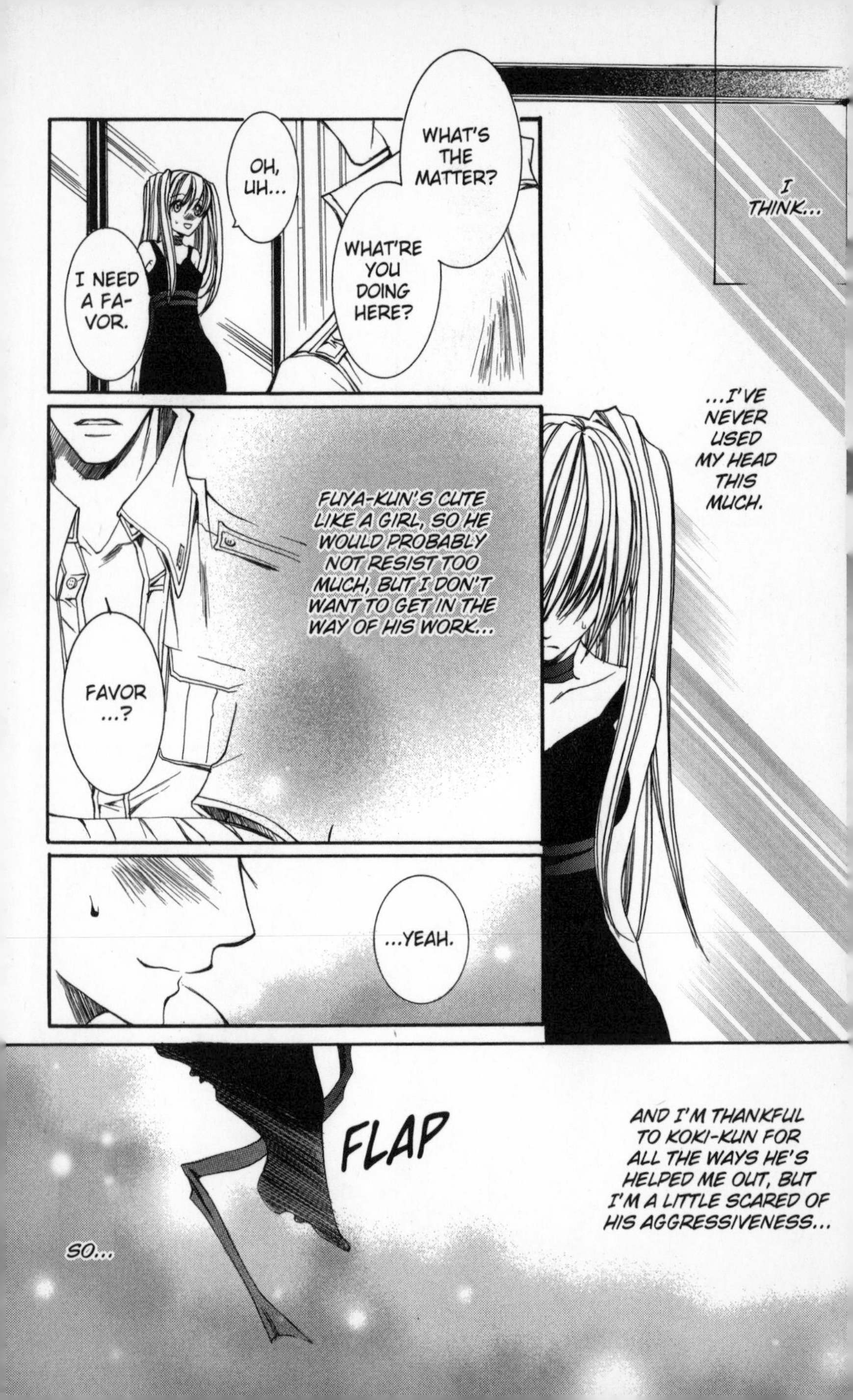
I THINK...
...I'VE NEVER USED MY HEAD THIS MUCH.
WHAT'S THE MATTER?
WHAT'RE YOU DOING HERE?
OH, UH...
I NEED A FA-VOR.
FUYA-KUN'S CUTE LIKE A GIRL, SO HE WOULD PROBABLY NOT RESIST TOO MUCH, BUT I DON'T WANT TO GET IN THE WAY OF HIS WORK...
FAVOR ...?
...YEAH.
AND I'M THANKFUL TO KOKI-KUN FOR ALL THE WAYS HE'S HELPED ME OUT, BUT I'M A LITTLE SCARED OF HIS AGGRESSIVENESS...
FLAP
SO...

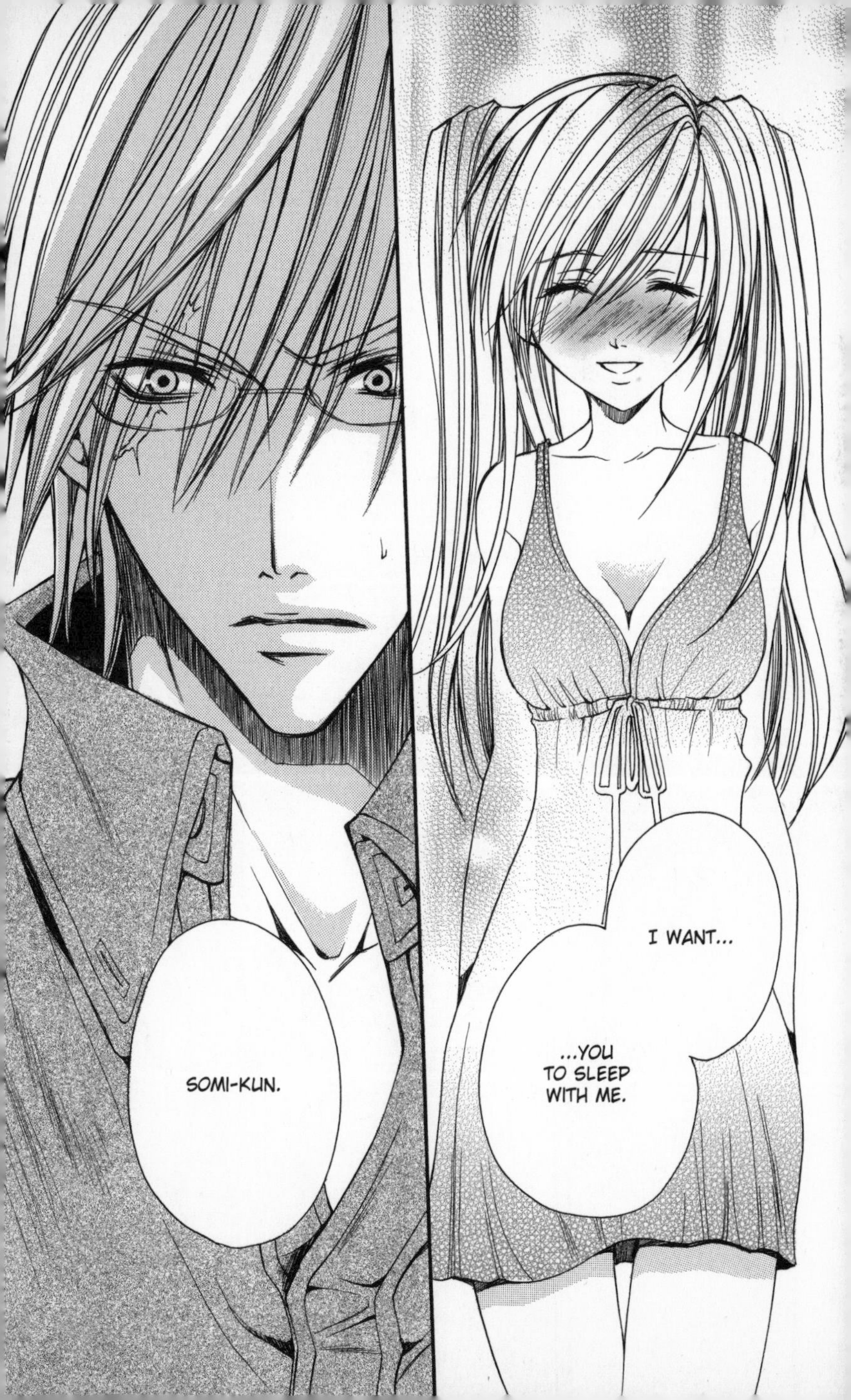
I WANT...
...YOU TO SLEEP WITH ME.
SOMI-KUN.

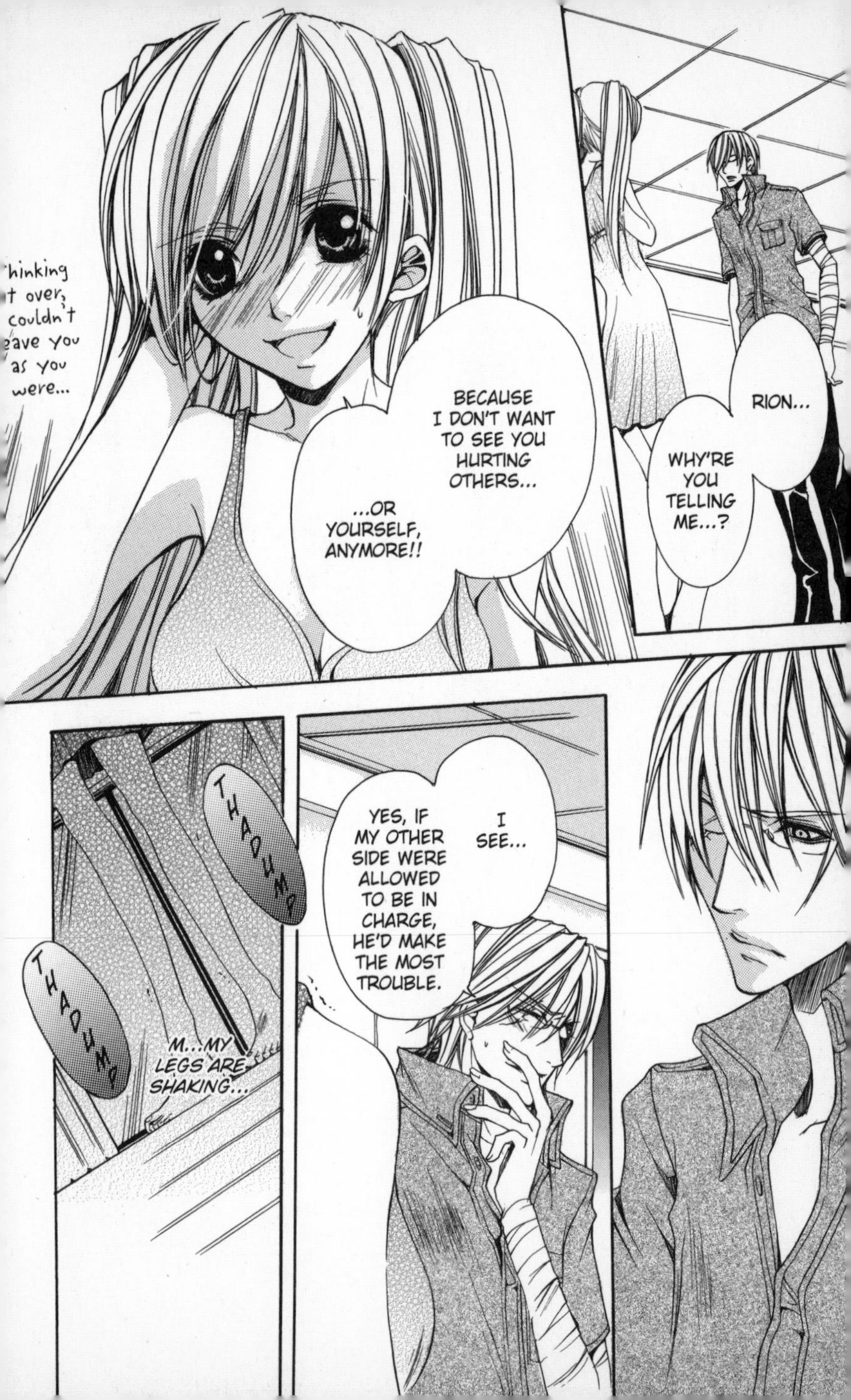
RION...
WHY'RE YOU TELLING ME...?
BECAUSE I DON'T WANT TO SEE YOU HURTING OTHERS...
...OR YOURSELF, ANYMORE!!
hinking t over, couldn't eave you as you were...
I SEE...
YES, IF MY OTHER SIDE WERE ALLOWED TO BE IN CHARGE, HE'D MAKE THE MOST TROUBLE.
THADUMP
THADUMP
M...MY LEGS ARE SHAKING...

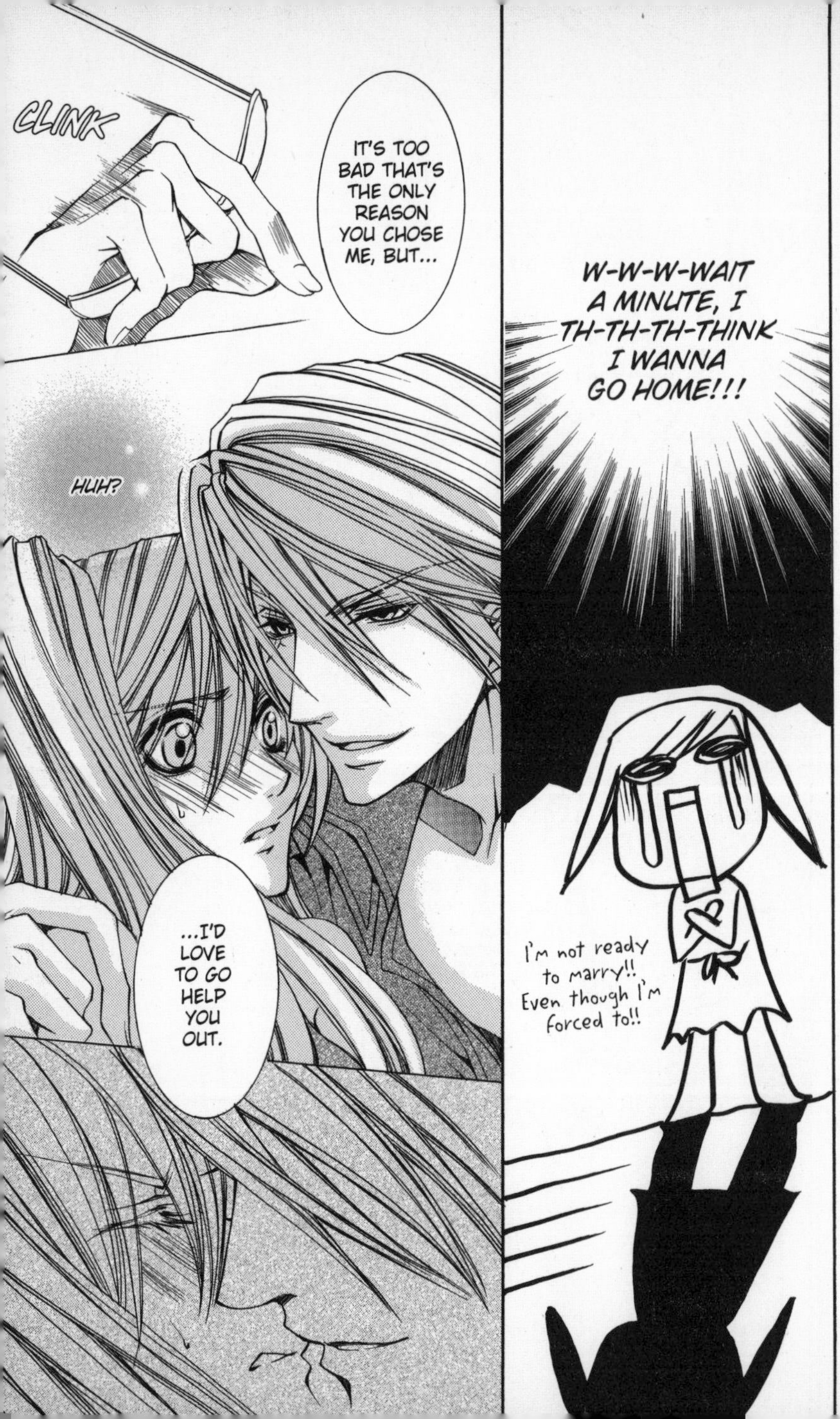
W-W-W-WAIT A MINUTE, I TH-TH-TH-THINK I WANNA GO HOME!!!
I'm not ready to marry!! Even though I'm forced to!!
IT'S TOO BAD THAT'S THE ONLY REASON YOU CHOSE ME, BUT...
CLINK
HUH?
...I'D LOVE TO GO HELP YOU OUT.

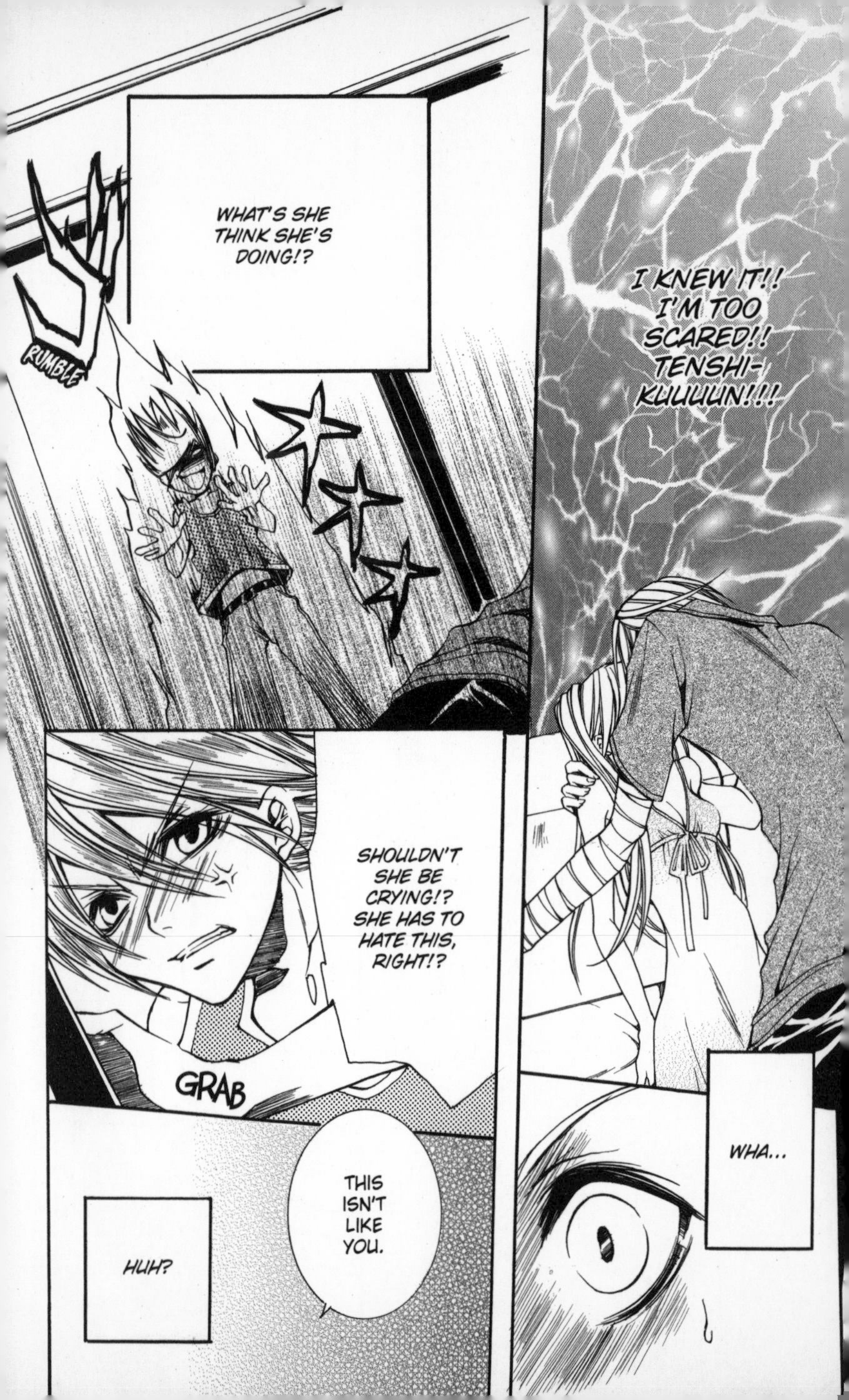
I KNEW IT!! I'M TOO SCARED!! TENSHI-KUUUUN!!!
WHAT'S SHE THINK SHE'S DOING!?
RUMBLE
SHOULDN'T SHE BE CRYING!? SHE HAS TO HATE THIS, RIGHT!?
GRAB
WHA...
THIS ISN'T LIKE YOU.
HUH?

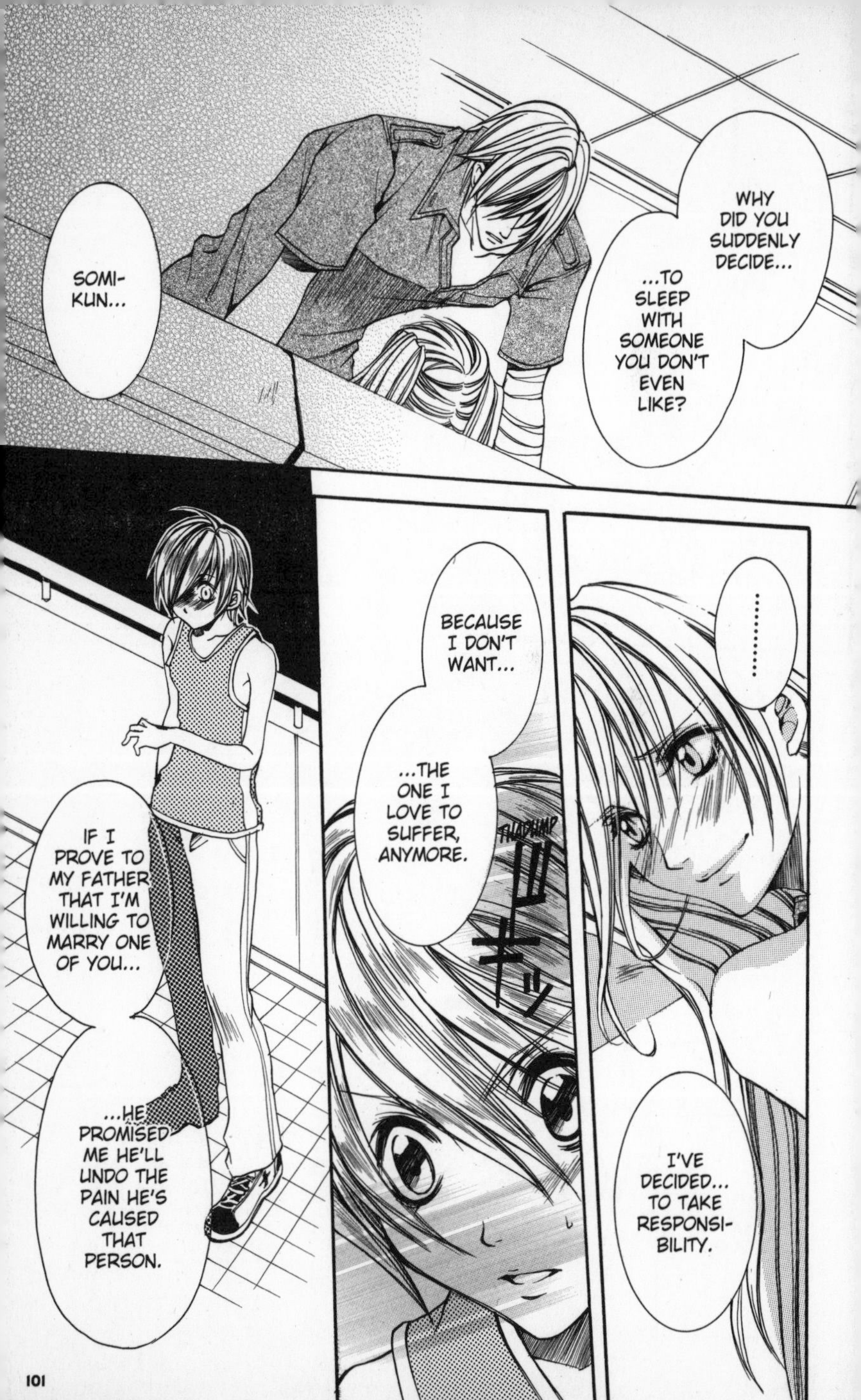
WHY DID YOU SUDDENLY DECIDE...
...TO SLEEP WITH SOMEONE YOU DON'T EVEN LIKE?
SOMI-KUN...
......
I'VE DECIDED... TO TAKE RESPONSI-BILITY.
BECAUSE I DON'T WANT...
...THE ONE I LOVE TO SUFFER, ANYMORE.
THADUMP
ギッ
IF I PROVE TO MY FATHER THAT I'M WILLING TO MARRY ONE OF YOU...
...HE PROMISED ME HE'LL UNDO THE PAIN HE'S CAUSED THAT PERSON.

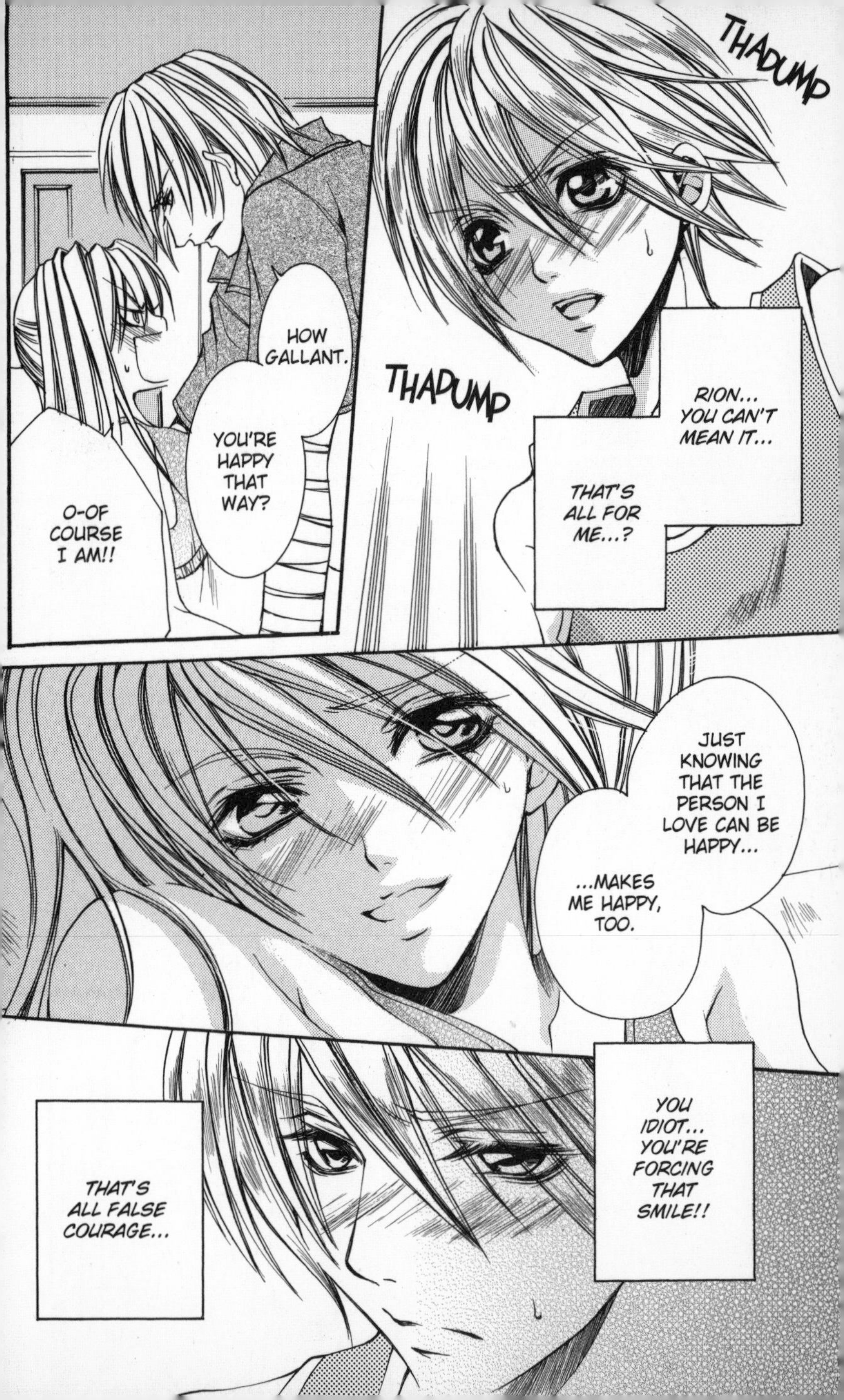
THADUMP
THADUMP
RION... YOU CAN'T MEAN IT...
THAT'S ALL FOR ME...?
HOW GALLANT.
YOU'RE HAPPY THAT WAY?
O-OF COURSE I AM!!
JUST KNOWING THAT THE PERSON I LOVE CAN BE HAPPY...
...MAKES ME HAPPY, TOO.
YOU IDIOT... YOU'RE FORCING THAT SMILE!!
THAT'S ALL FALSE COURAGE...

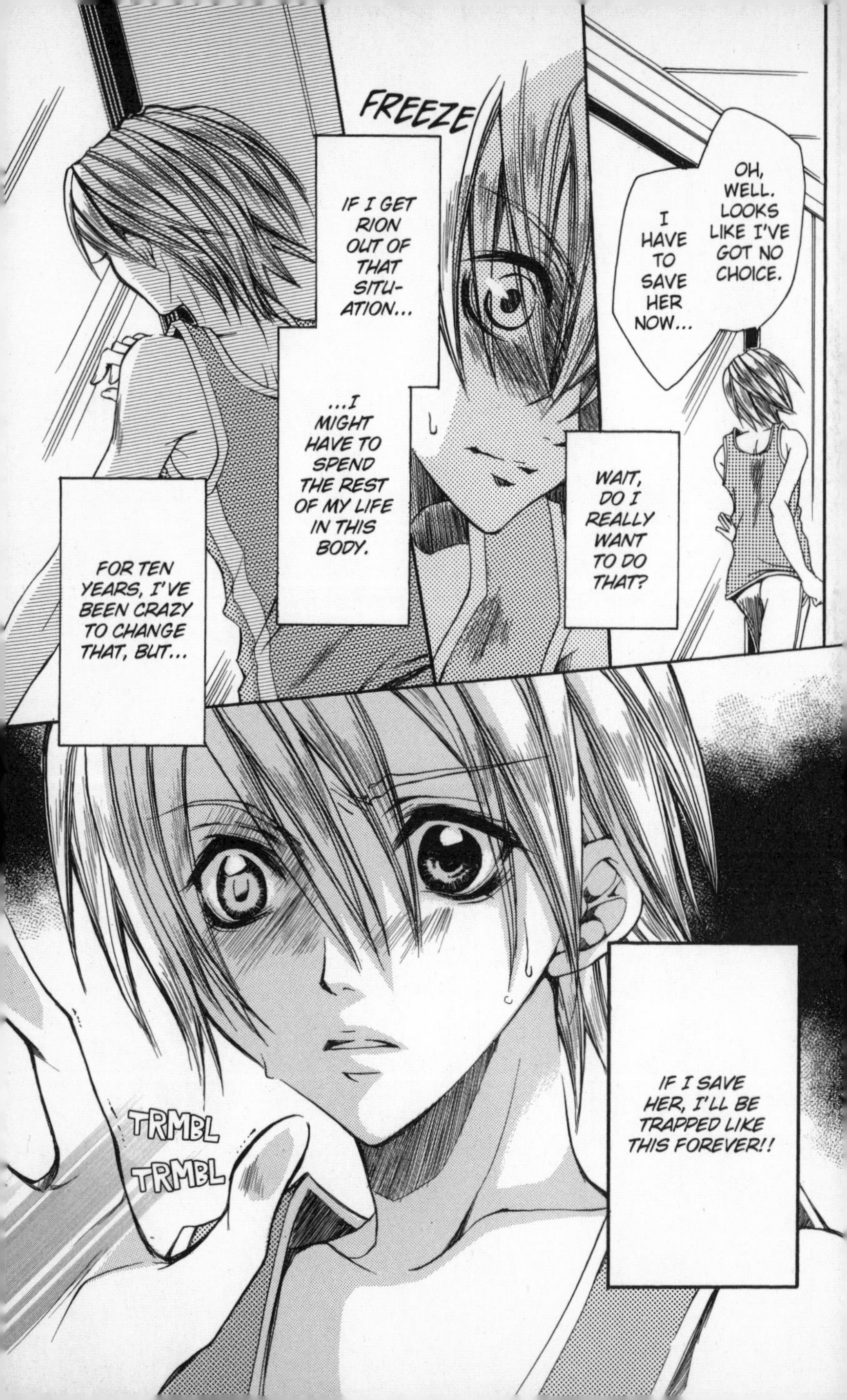
OH, WELL. LOOKS LIKE I'VE GOT NO CHOICE.
I HAVE TO SAVE HER NOW...
WAIT, DO I REALLY WANT TO DO THAT?
FREEZE
IF I GET RION OUT OF THAT SITU-ATION...
...I MIGHT HAVE TO SPEND THE REST OF MY LIFE IN THIS BODY.
FOR TEN YEARS, I'VE BEEN CRAZY TO CHANGE THAT, BUT...
IF I SAVE HER, I'LL BE TRAPPED LIKE THIS FOREVER!!
TRMBL
TRMBL

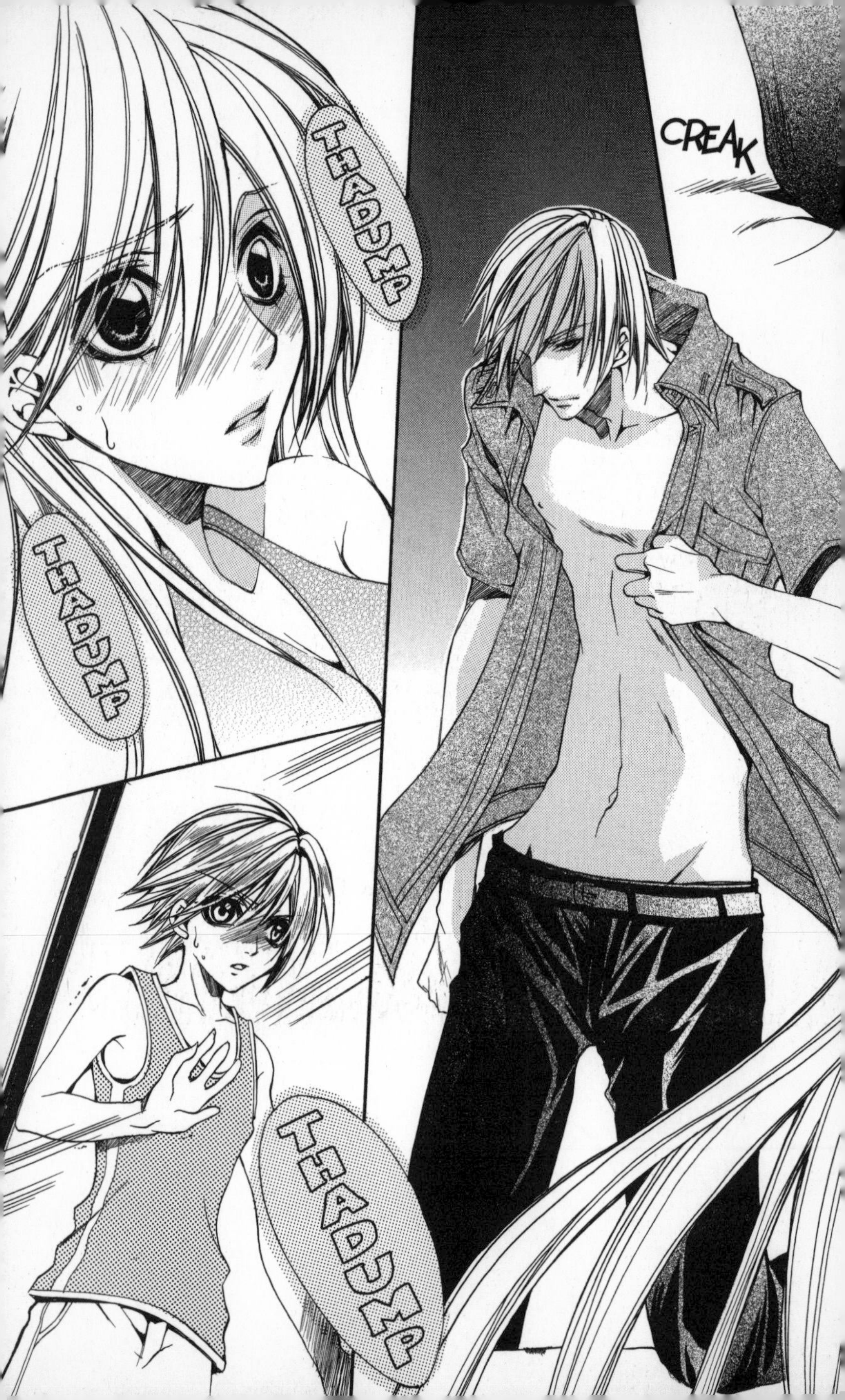
CREAK
THADUMP
THADUMP
THADUMP

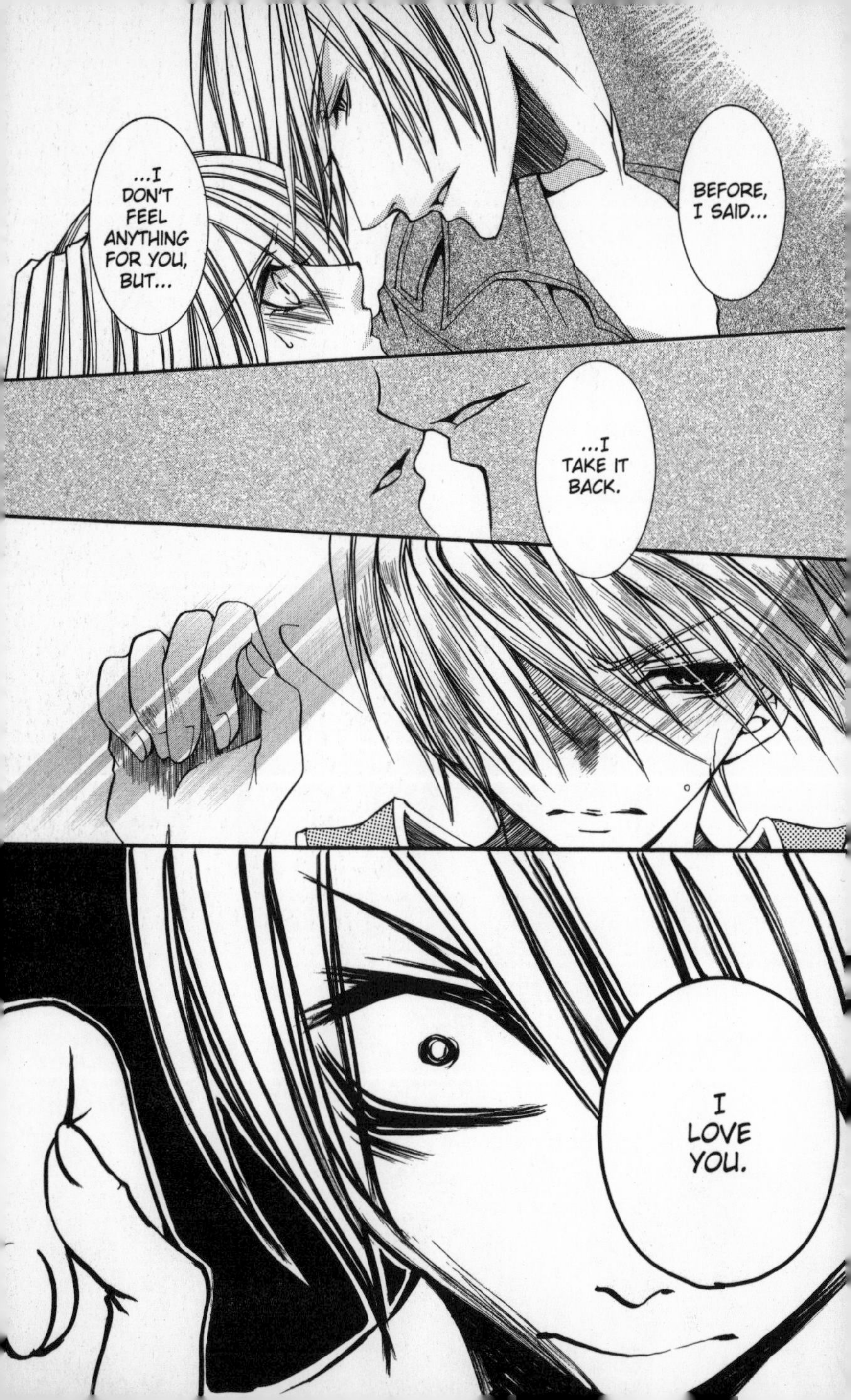
BEFORE, I SAID...
...I DON'T FEEL ANYTHING FOR YOU, BUT...
...I TAKE IT BACK.
I LOVE YOU.

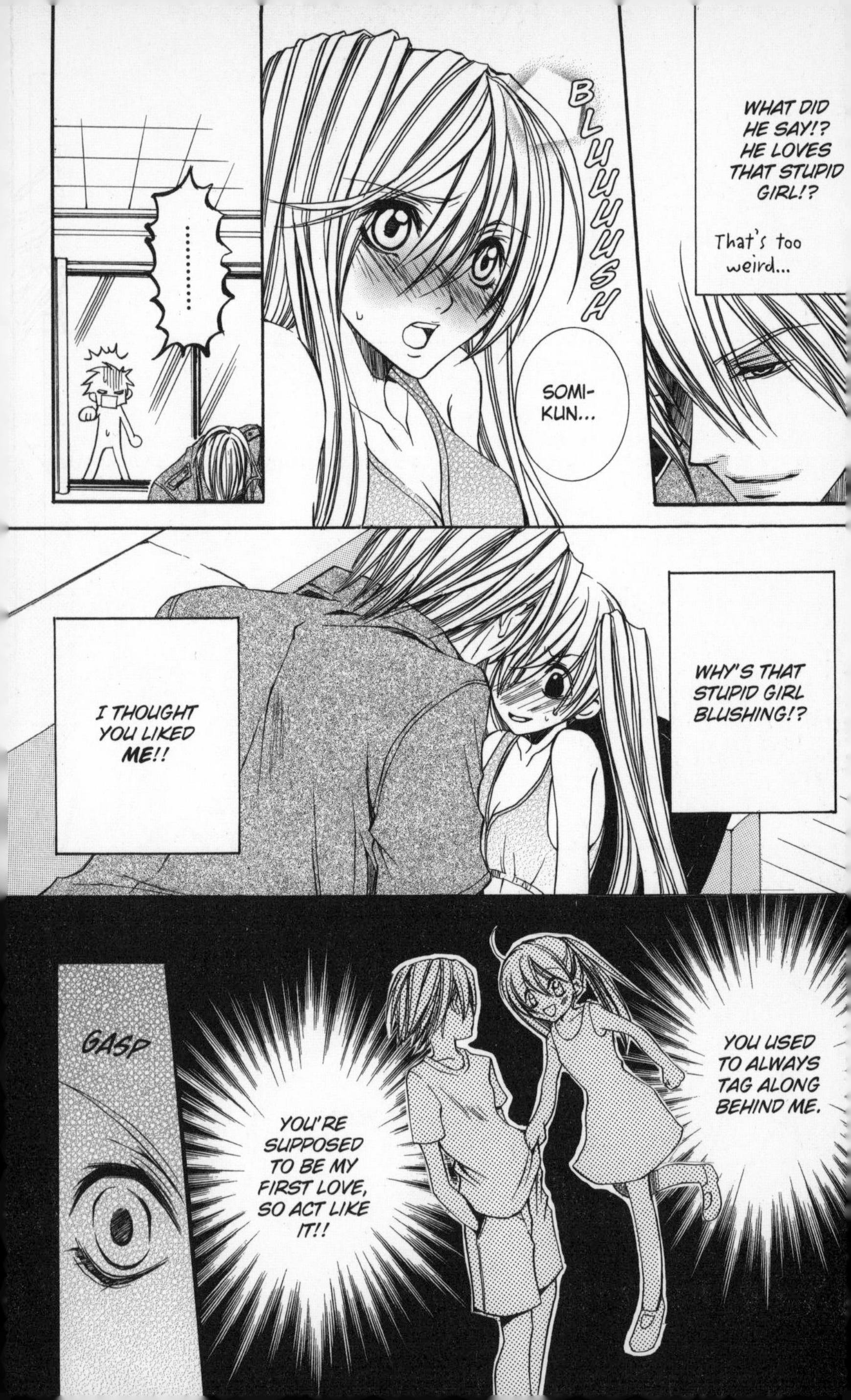
WHAT DID HE SAY!? HE LOVES THAT STUPID GIRL!?
That's too weird...
BLUUUUSH
SOMI-KUN...
......
WHY'S THAT STUPID GIRL BLUSHING!?
I THOUGHT YOU LIKED ME!!
YOU USED TO ALWAYS TAG ALONG BEHIND ME.
YOU'RE SUPPOSED TO BE MY FIRST LOVE, SO ACT LIKE IT!!
GASP

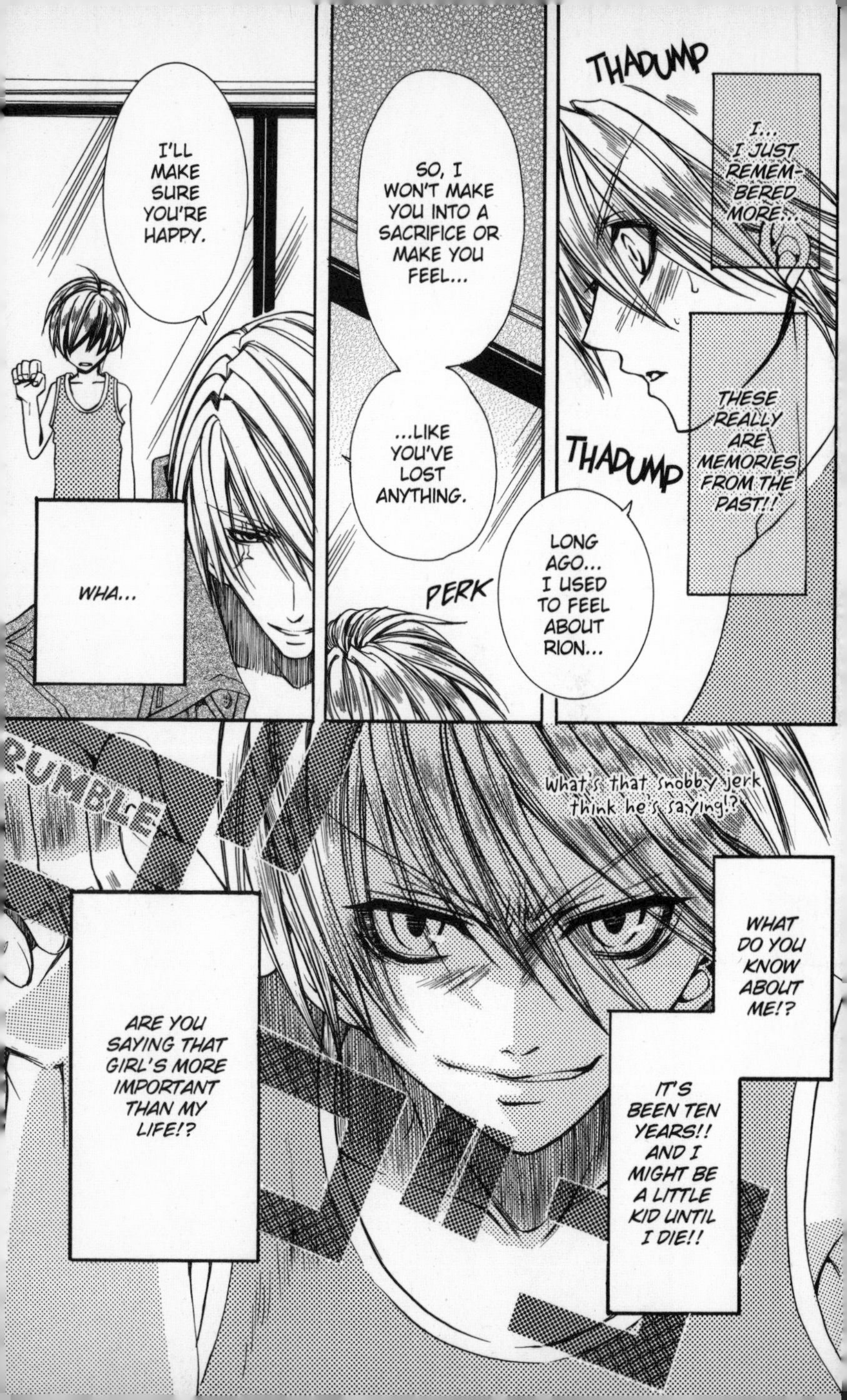
THADUMP
I... I JUST REMEM-BERED MORE...
THESE REALLY ARE MEMORIES FROM THE PAST!!
THADUMP
LONG AGO... I USED TO FEEL ABOUT RION...
SO, I WON'T MAKE YOU INTO A SACRIFICE OR MAKE YOU FEEL...
...LIKE YOU'VE LOST ANYTHING.
PERK
I'LL MAKE SURE YOU'RE HAPPY.
WHA...
What's that snobby jerk think he's saying!?
WHAT DO YOU KNOW ABOUT ME!?
IT'S BEEN TEN YEARS!! AND I MIGHT BE A LITTLE KID UNTIL I DIE!!
RUMBLE
ARE YOU SAYING THAT GIRL'S MORE IMPORTANT THAN MY LIFE!?

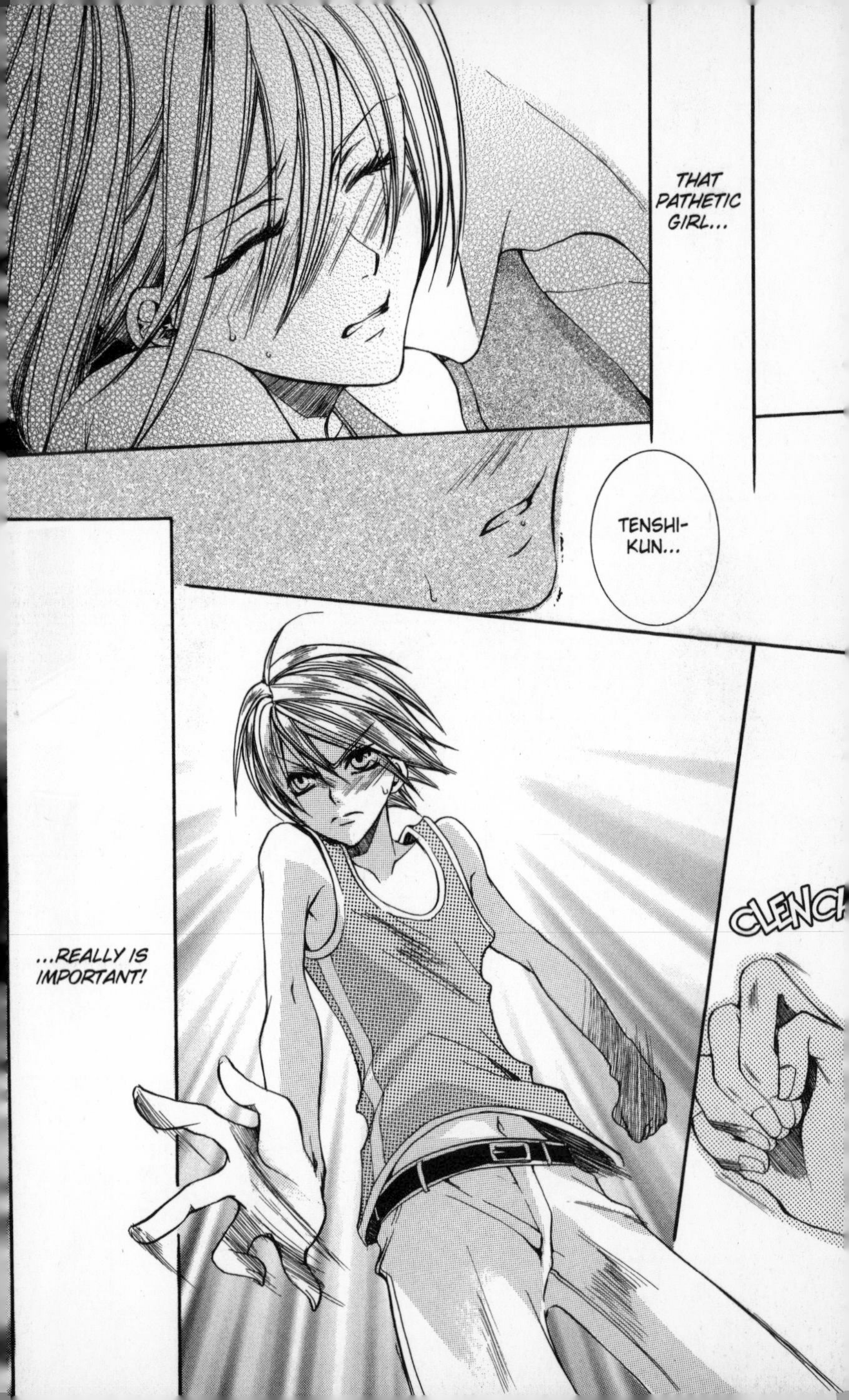
THAT PATHETIC GIRL...
TENSHI-KUN...
CLENC
...REALLY IS IMPORTANT!

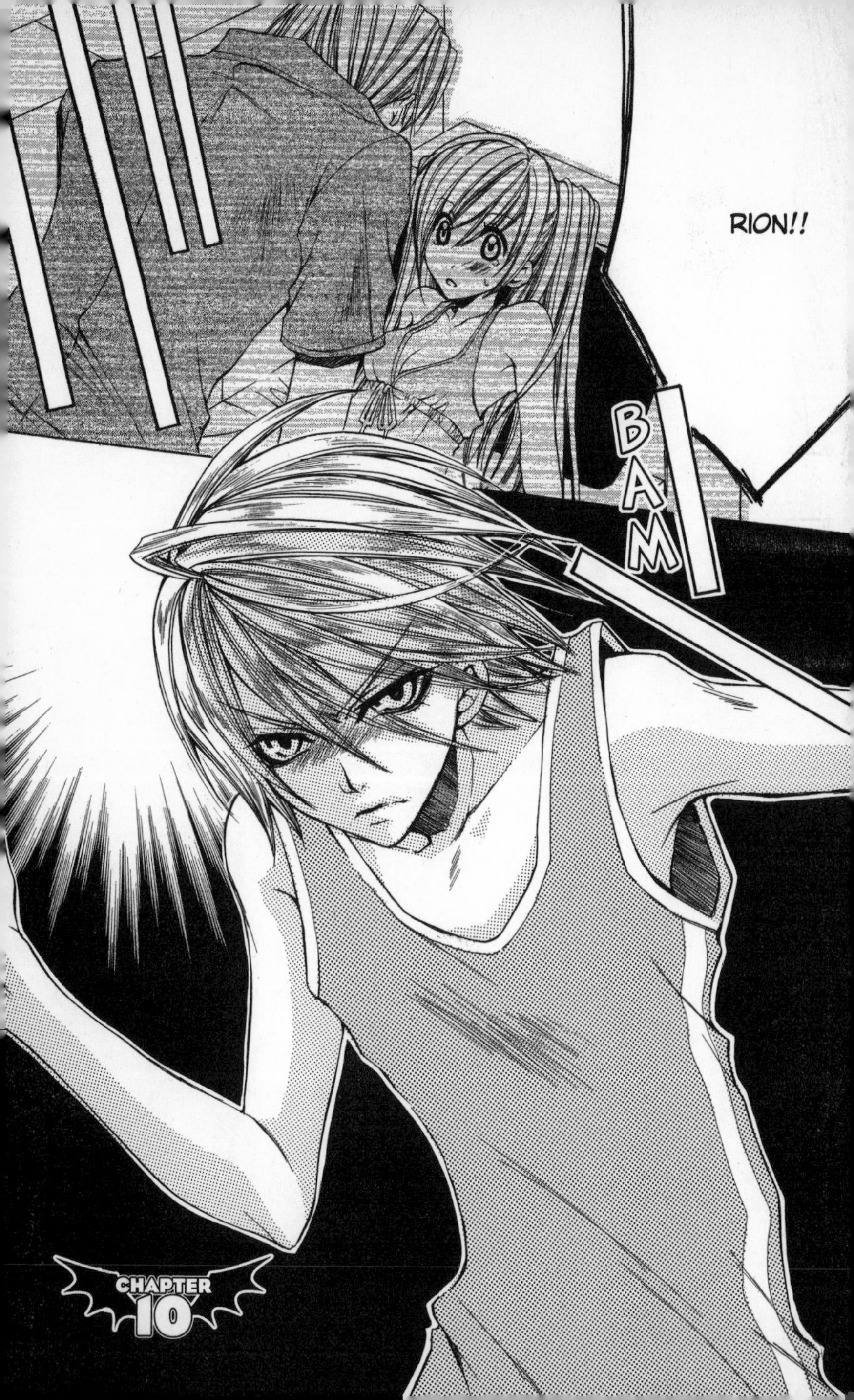
RION!!
BAM
CHAPTER 10

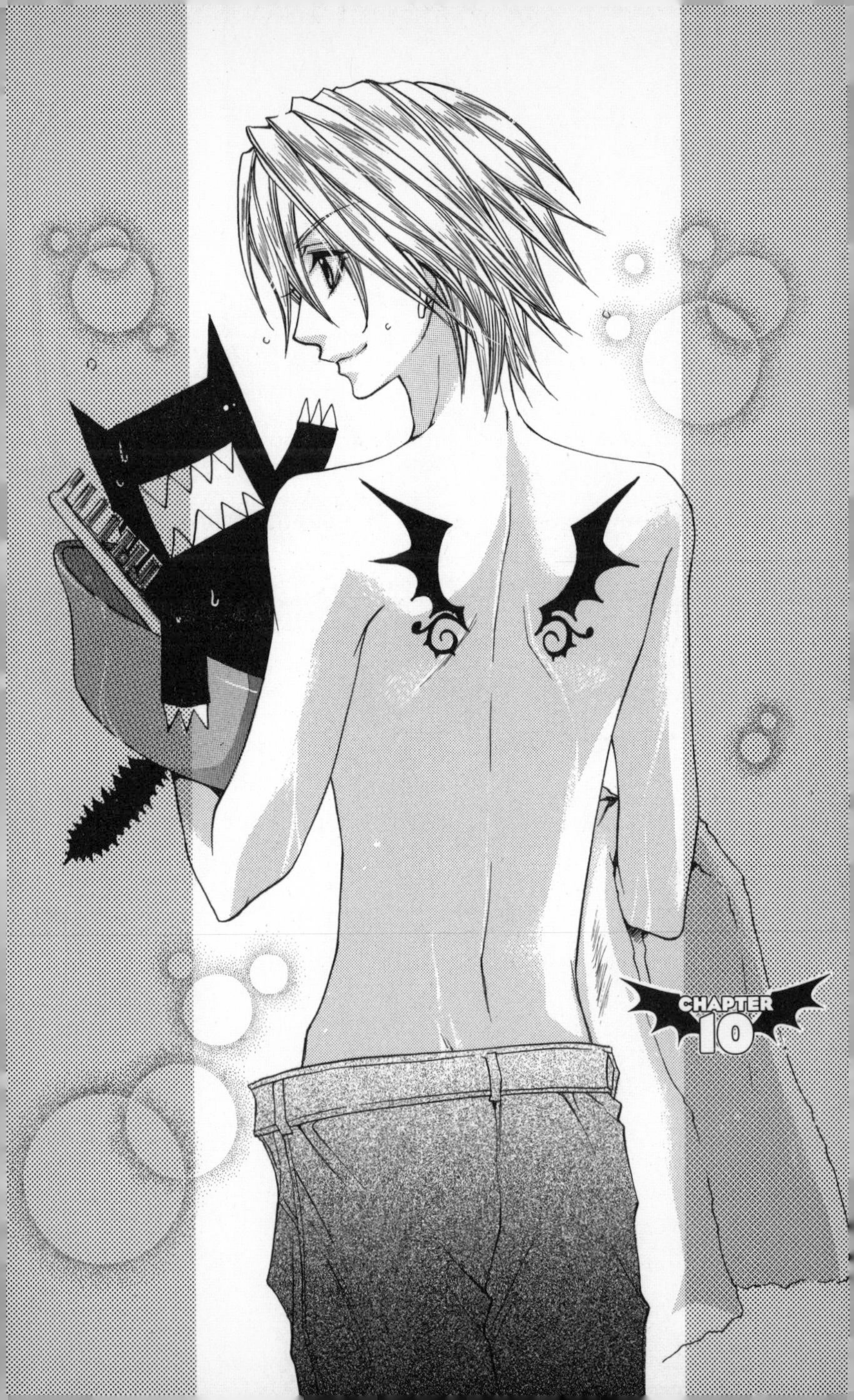
CHAPTER
10

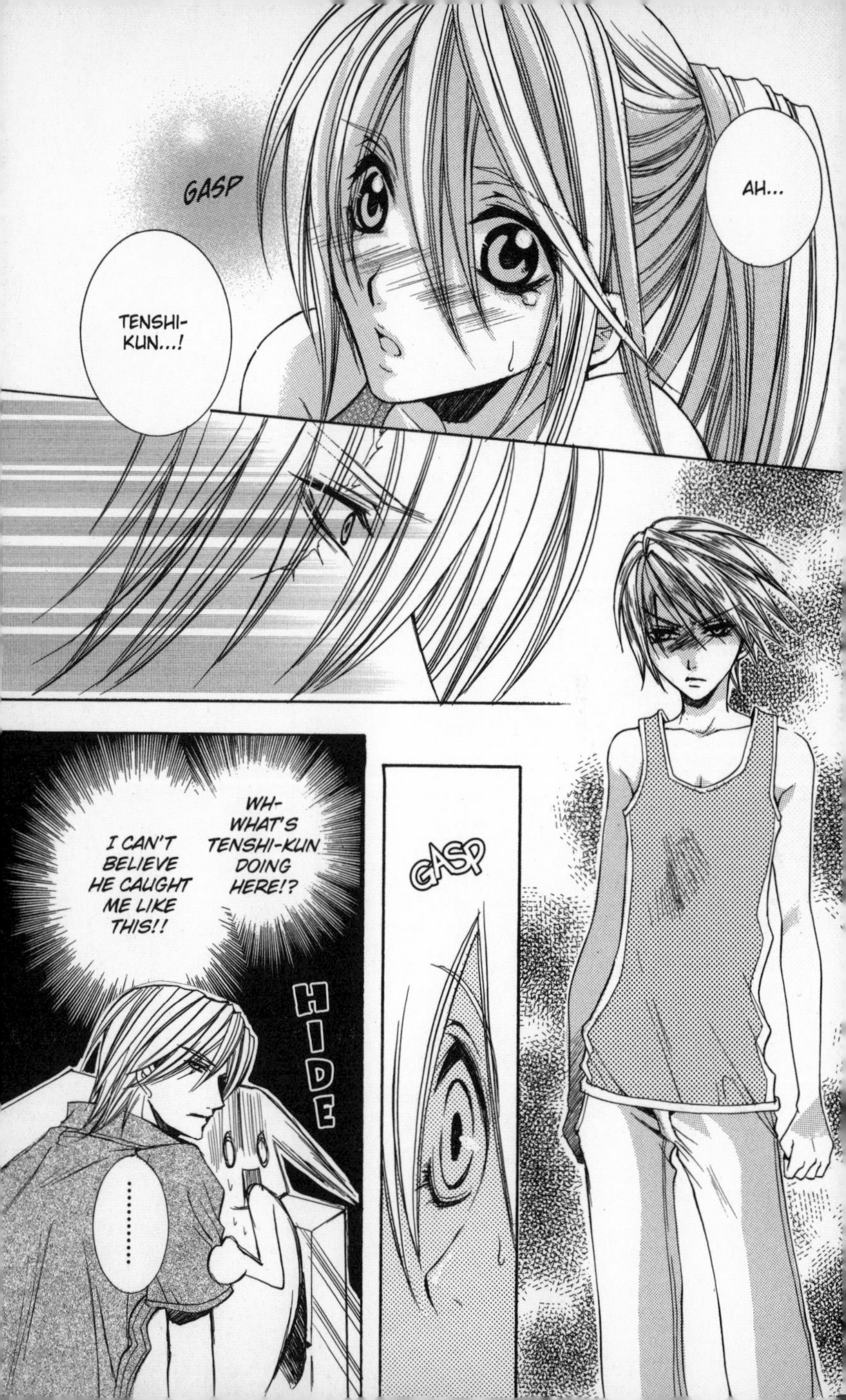
AH...
GASP
TENSHI-KUN...!
GASP
WH- WHAT'S TENSHI-KUN DOING HERE!?
I CAN'T BELIEVE HE CAUGHT ME LIKE THIS!!
HIDE
........

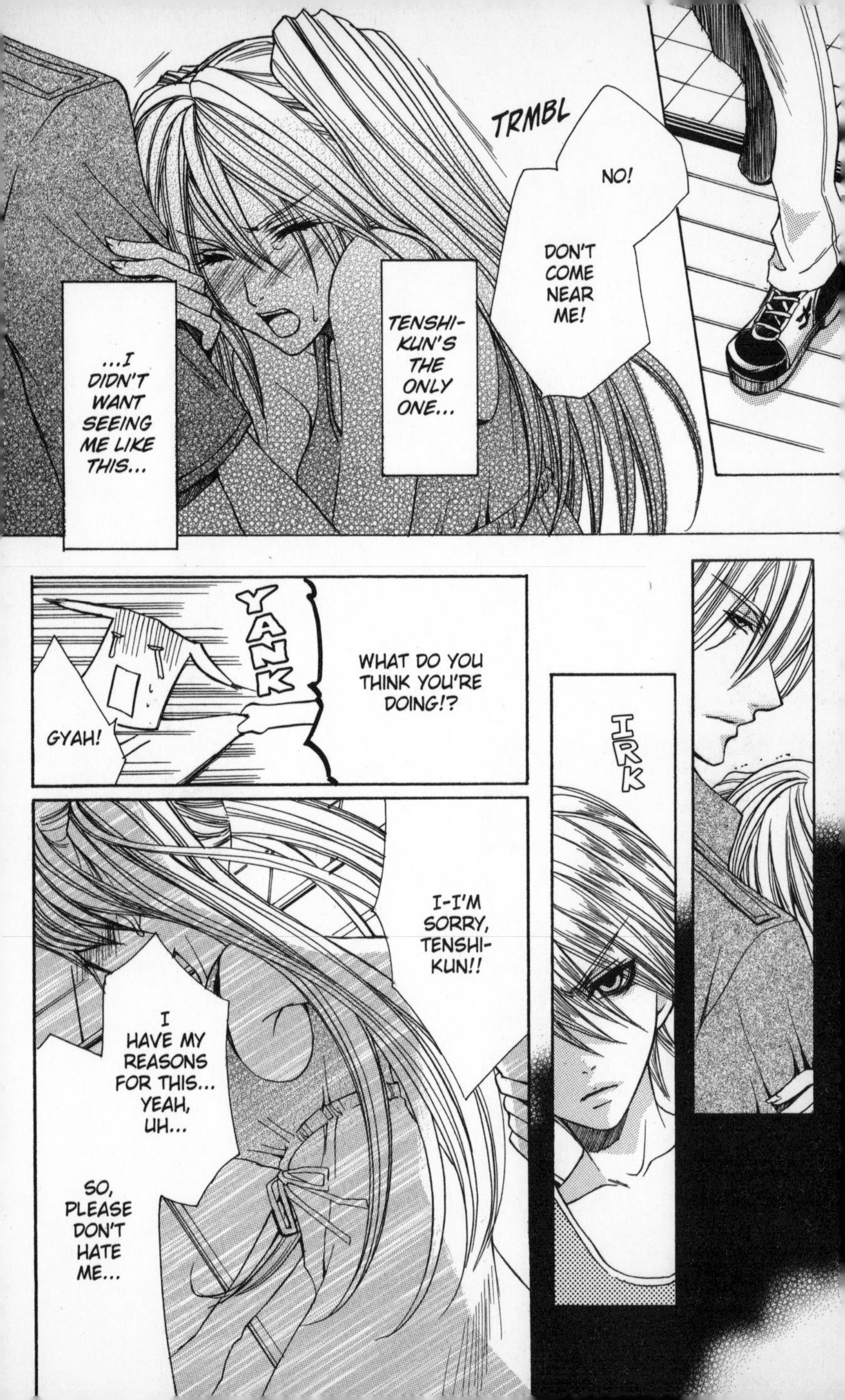
TRMBL
NO!
DON'T COME NEAR ME!
TENSHI-KUN'S THE ONLY ONE...
...I DIDN'T WANT SEEING ME LIKE THIS...
IRK
WHAT DO YOU THINK YOU'RE DOING!?
YANK
GYAH!
I-I'M SORRY, TENSHI-KUN!!
I HAVE MY REASONS FOR THIS... YEAH, UH...
SO, PLEASE DON'T HATE ME...

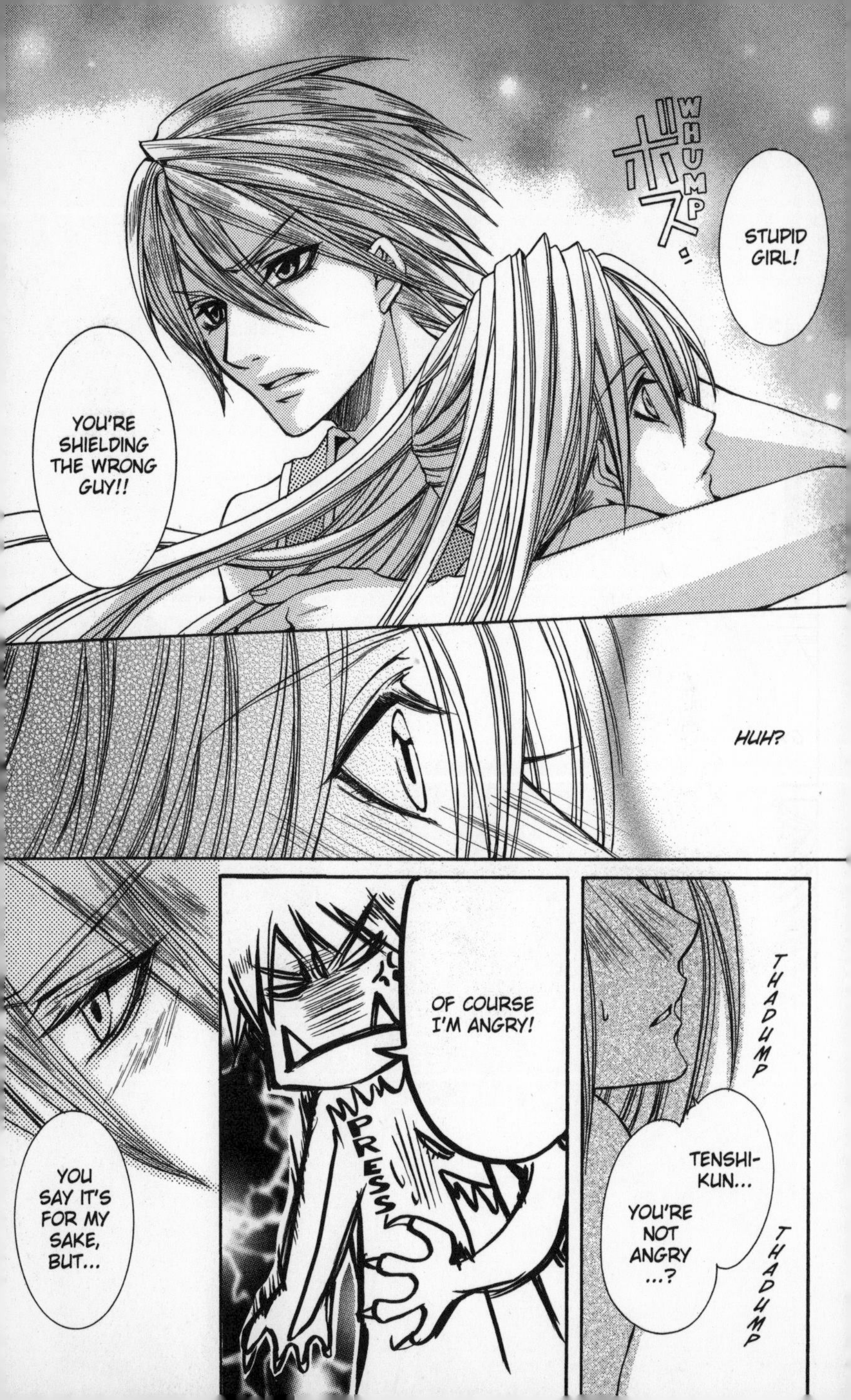
WHUMP
STUPID GIRL!
YOU'RE SHIELDING THE WRONG GUY!!
HUH?
THADUMP
TENSHI-KUN...
YOU'RE NOT ANGRY ...?
THADUMP
OF COURSE I'M ANGRY!
PRESS
YOU SAY IT'S FOR MY SAKE, BUT...

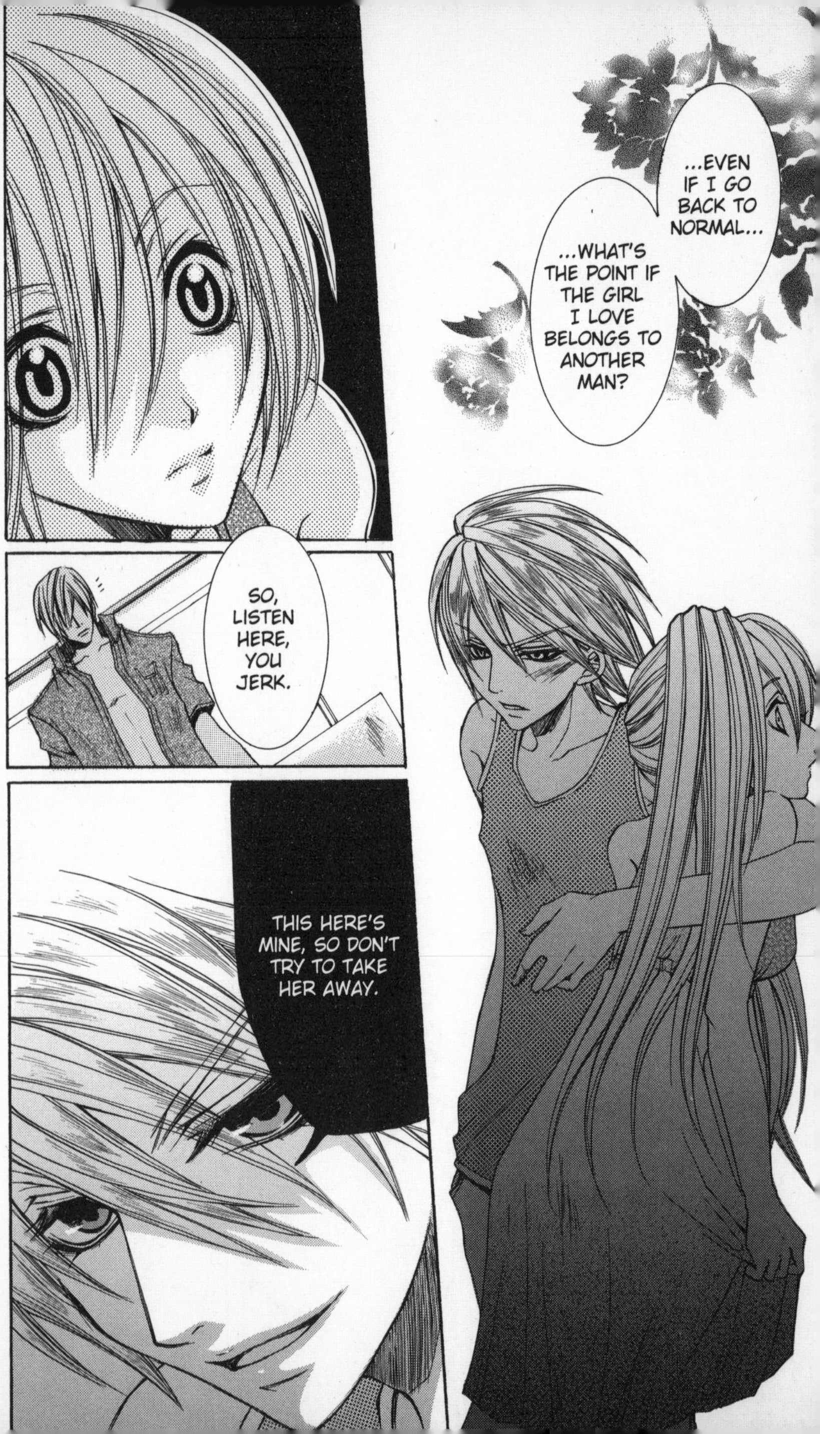
...EVEN IF I GO BACK TO NORMAL...
...WHAT'S THE POINT IF THE GIRL I LOVE BELONGS TO ANOTHER MAN?
SO, LISTEN HERE, YOU JERK.
THIS HERE'S MINE, SO DON'T TRY TO TAKE HER AWAY.

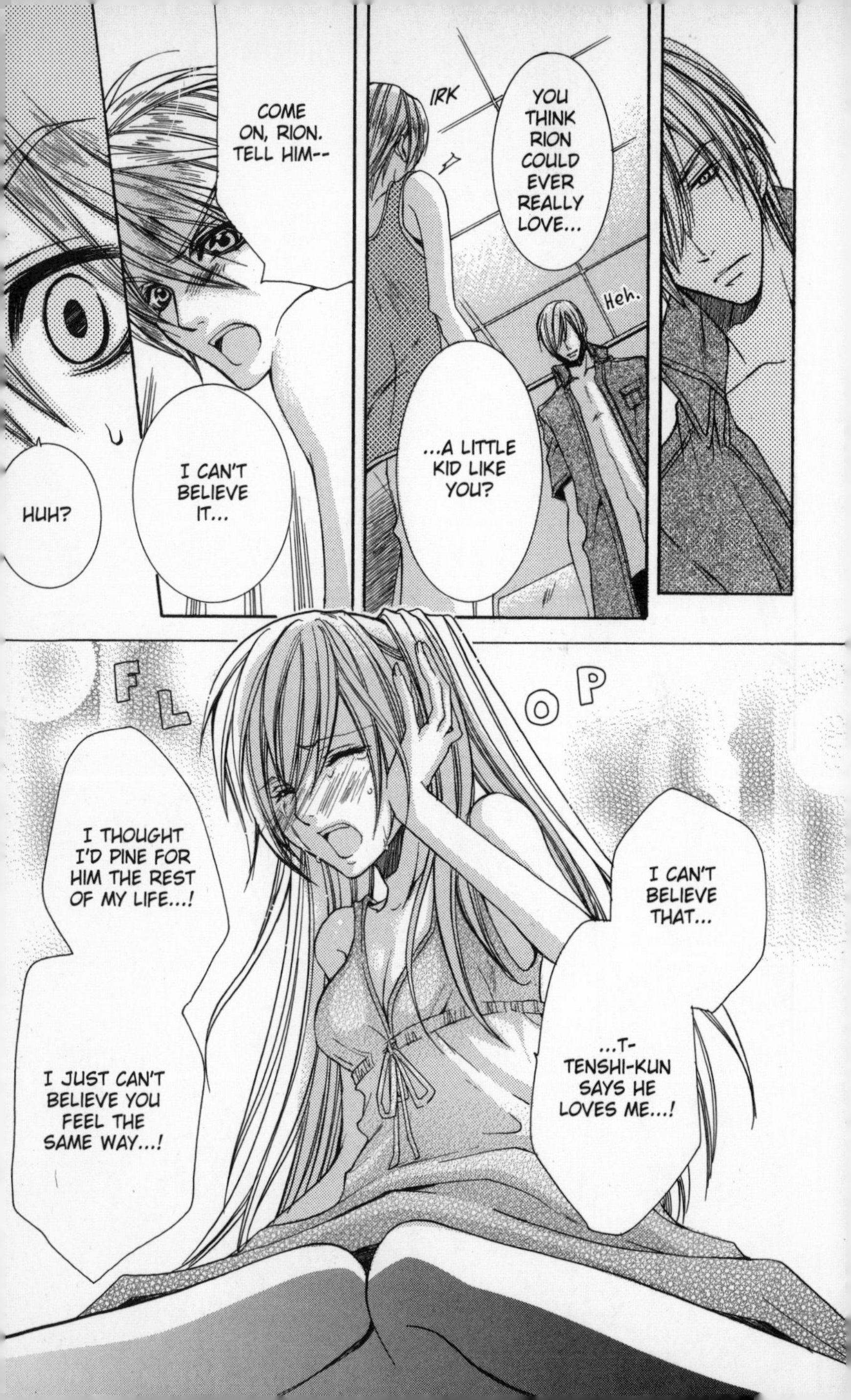
YOU THINK RION COULD EVER REALLY LOVE...
IRK
Heh.
...A LITTLE KID LIKE YOU?
COME ON, RION. TELL HIM--
I CAN'T BELIEVE IT...
HUH?
FLOP
I CAN'T BELIEVE THAT...
...T-TENSHI-KUN SAYS HE LOVES ME...!
I THOUGHT I'D PINE FOR HIM THE REST OF MY LIFE...!
I JUST CAN'T BELIEVE YOU FEEL THE SAME WAY...!

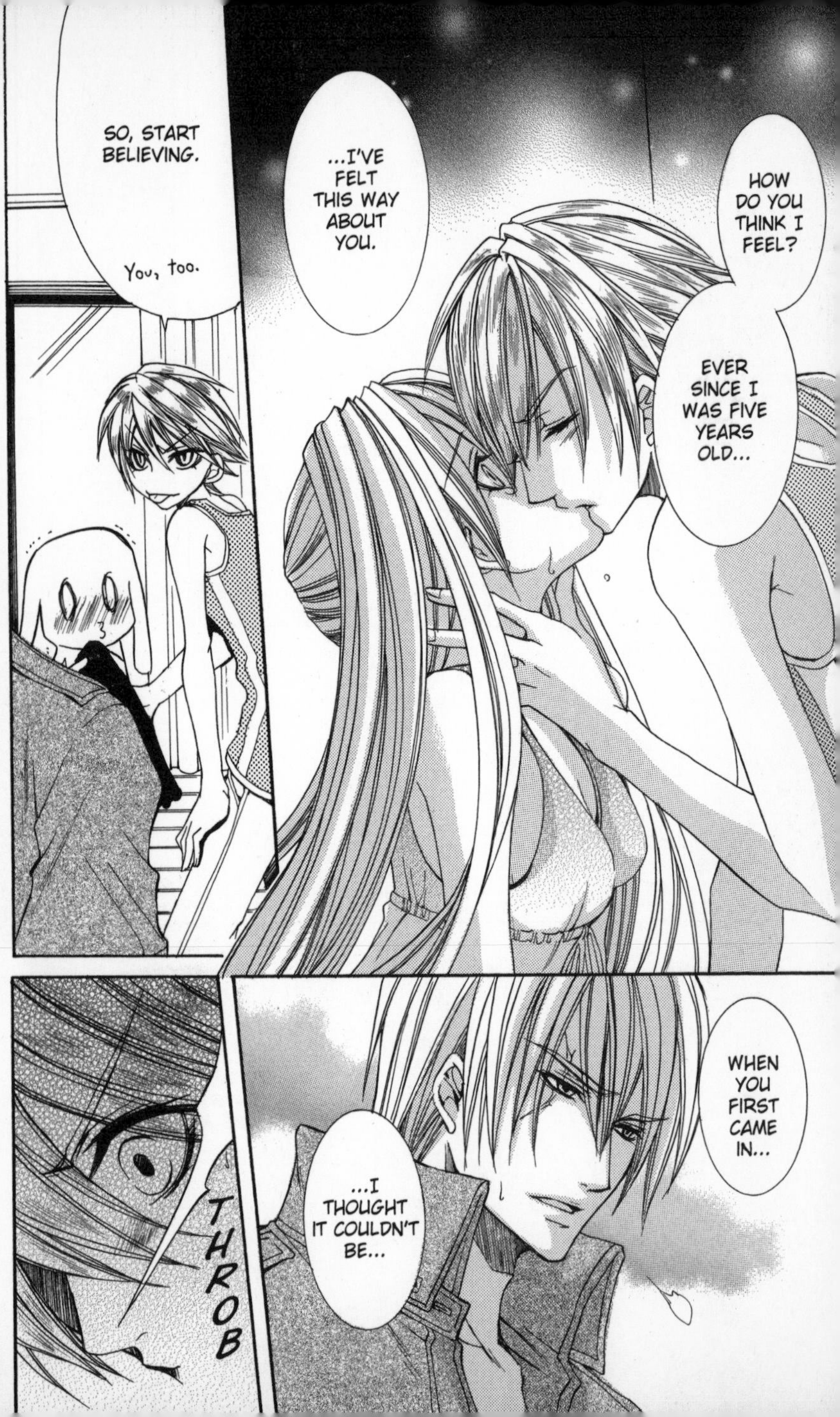
HOW DO YOU THINK I FEEL?
EVER SINCE I WAS FIVE YEARS OLD...
...I'VE FELT THIS WAY ABOUT YOU.
SO, START BELIEVING.
You, too.
WHEN YOU FIRST CAME IN...
...I THOUGHT IT COULDN'T BE...
THROB

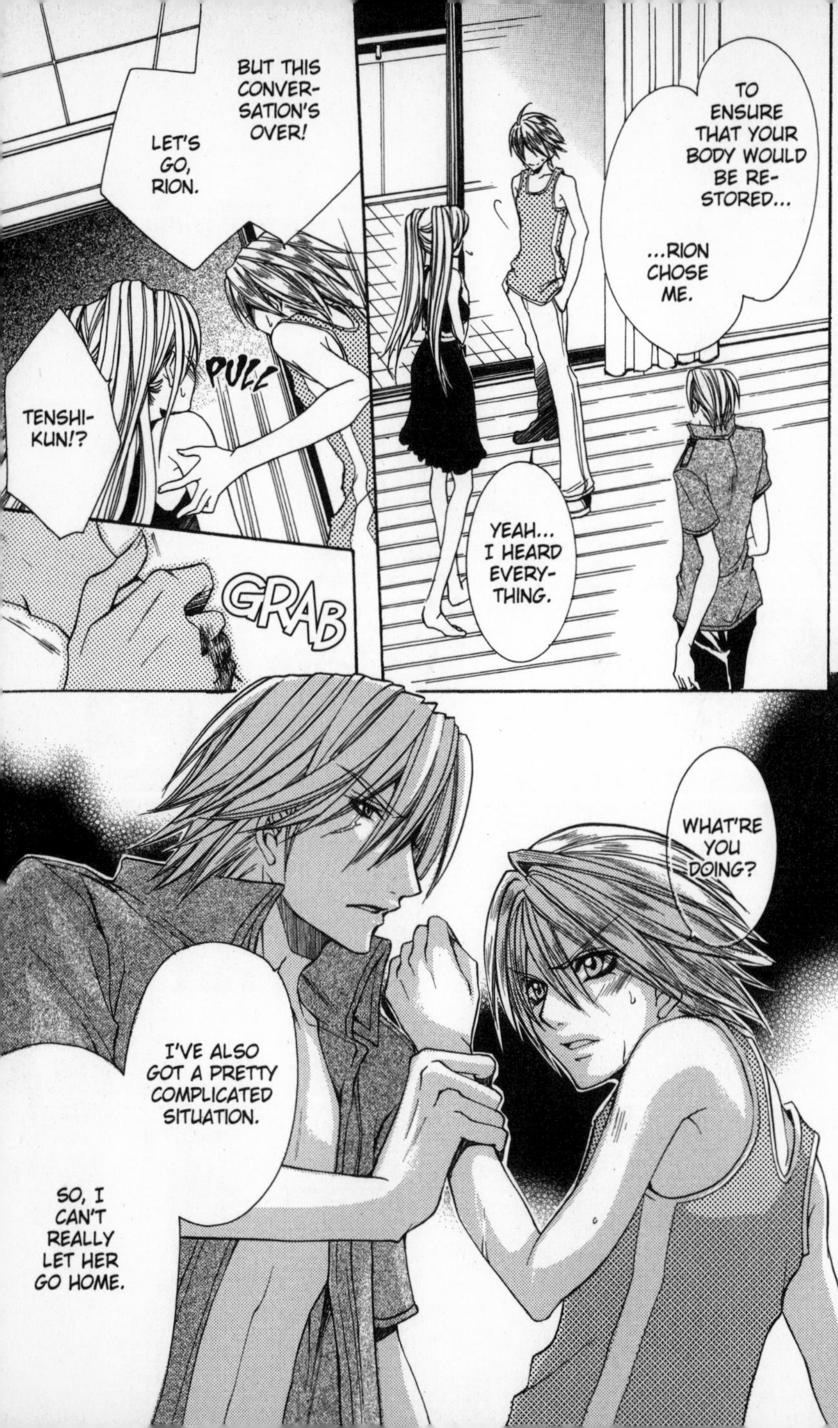
TO ENSURE THAT YOUR BODY WOULD BE RE-STORED...
...RION CHOSE ME.
YEAH... I HEARD EVERY-THING.
BUT THIS CONVER-SATION'S OVER!
LET'S GO, RION.
PULL
TENSHI-KUN!?
GRAB
WHAT'RE YOU DOING?
I'VE ALSO GOT A PRETTY COMPLICATED SITUATION.
SO, I CAN'T REALLY LET HER GO HOME.

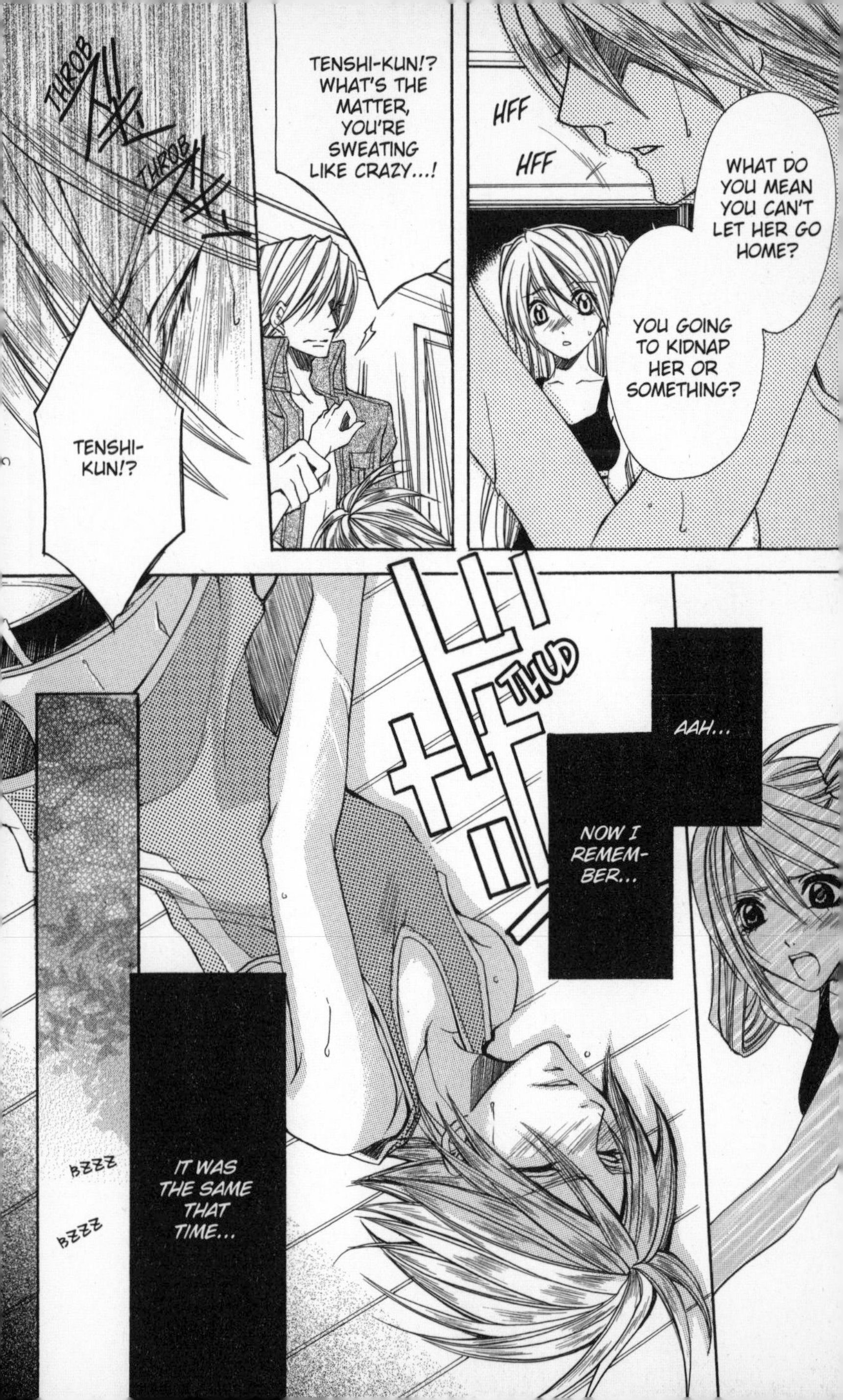
HFF
HFF
WHAT DO YOU MEAN YOU CAN'T LET HER GO HOME?
YOU GOING TO KIDNAP HER OR SOMETHING?
TENSHI-KUN!? WHAT'S THE MATTER, YOU'RE SWEATING LIKE CRAZY...!
THROB
THROB
TENSHI-KUN!?
AAH...
NOW I REMEMBER...
THUD
IT WAS THE SAME THAT TIME...
BZZZ
BZZZ

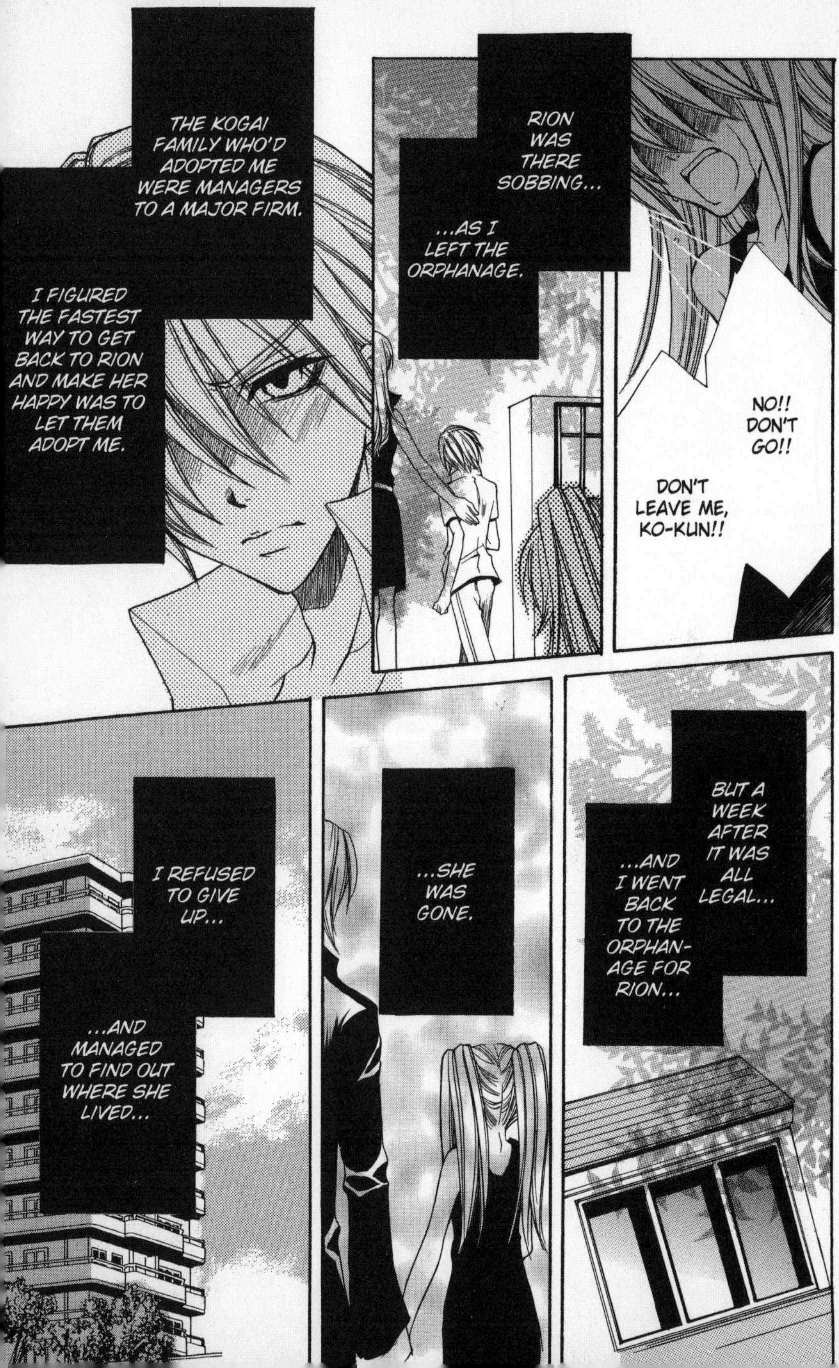
NO!! DON'T GO!!
DON'T LEAVE ME, KO-KUN!!
RION WAS THERE SOBBING...
...AS I LEFT THE ORPHANAGE.
THE KOGAI FAMILY WHO'D ADOPTED ME WERE MANAGERS TO A MAJOR FIRM.
I FIGURED THE FASTEST WAY TO GET BACK TO RION AND MAKE HER HAPPY WAS TO LET THEM ADOPT ME.
BUT A WEEK AFTER IT WAS ALL LEGAL...
...AND I WENT BACK TO THE ORPHANAGE FOR RION...
...SHE WAS GONE.
I REFUSED TO GIVE UP...
...AND MANAGED TO FIND OUT WHERE SHE LIVED...

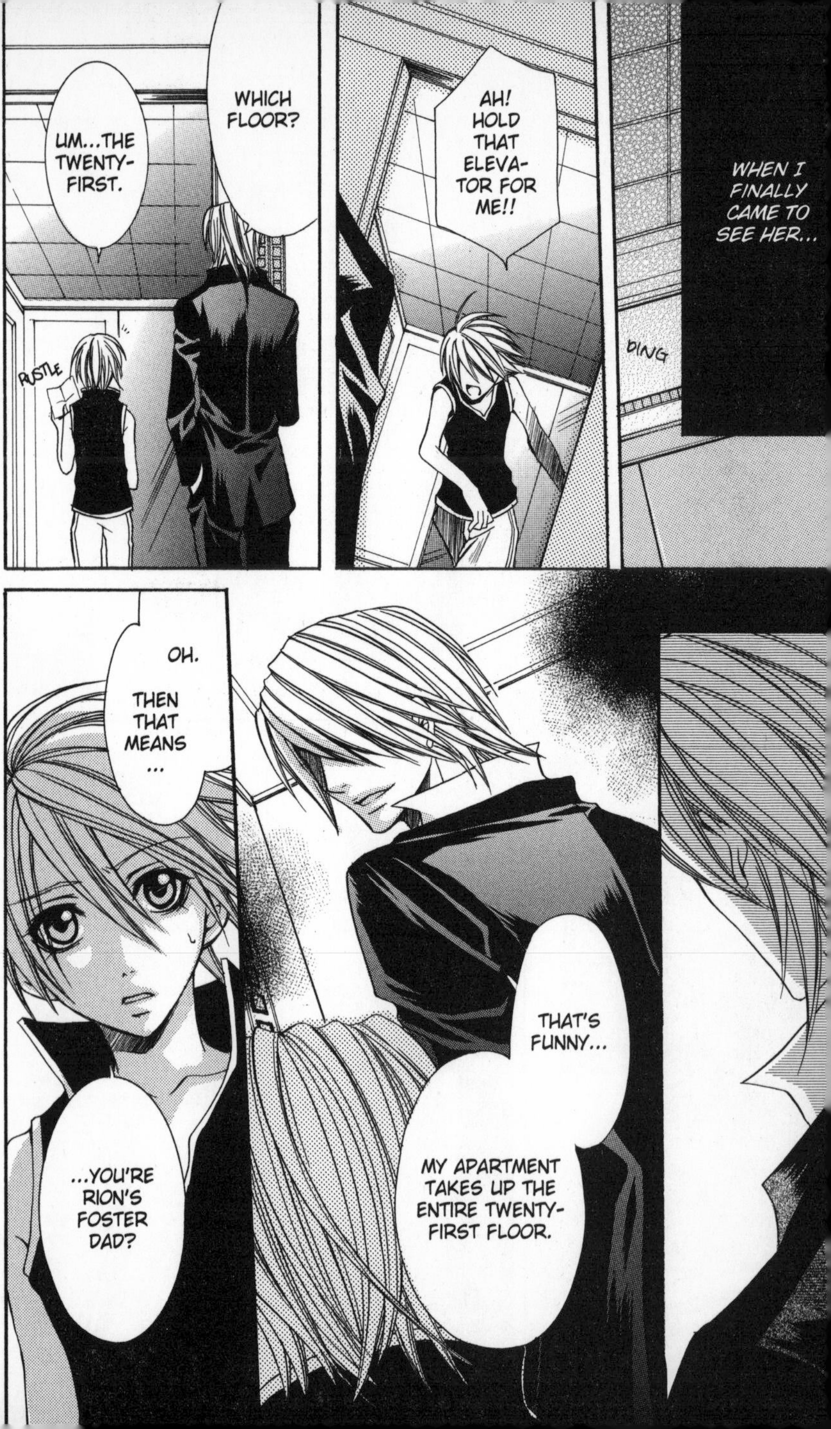
WHEN I FINALLY CAME TO SEE HER...
DING
AH! HOLD THAT ELEVATOR FOR ME!!
WHICH FLOOR?
UM...THE TWENTY-FIRST.
RUSTLE
THAT'S FUNNY...
MY APARTMENT TAKES UP THE ENTIRE TWENTY-FIRST FLOOR.
OH.
THEN THAT MEANS ...
...YOU'RE RION'S FOSTER DAD?

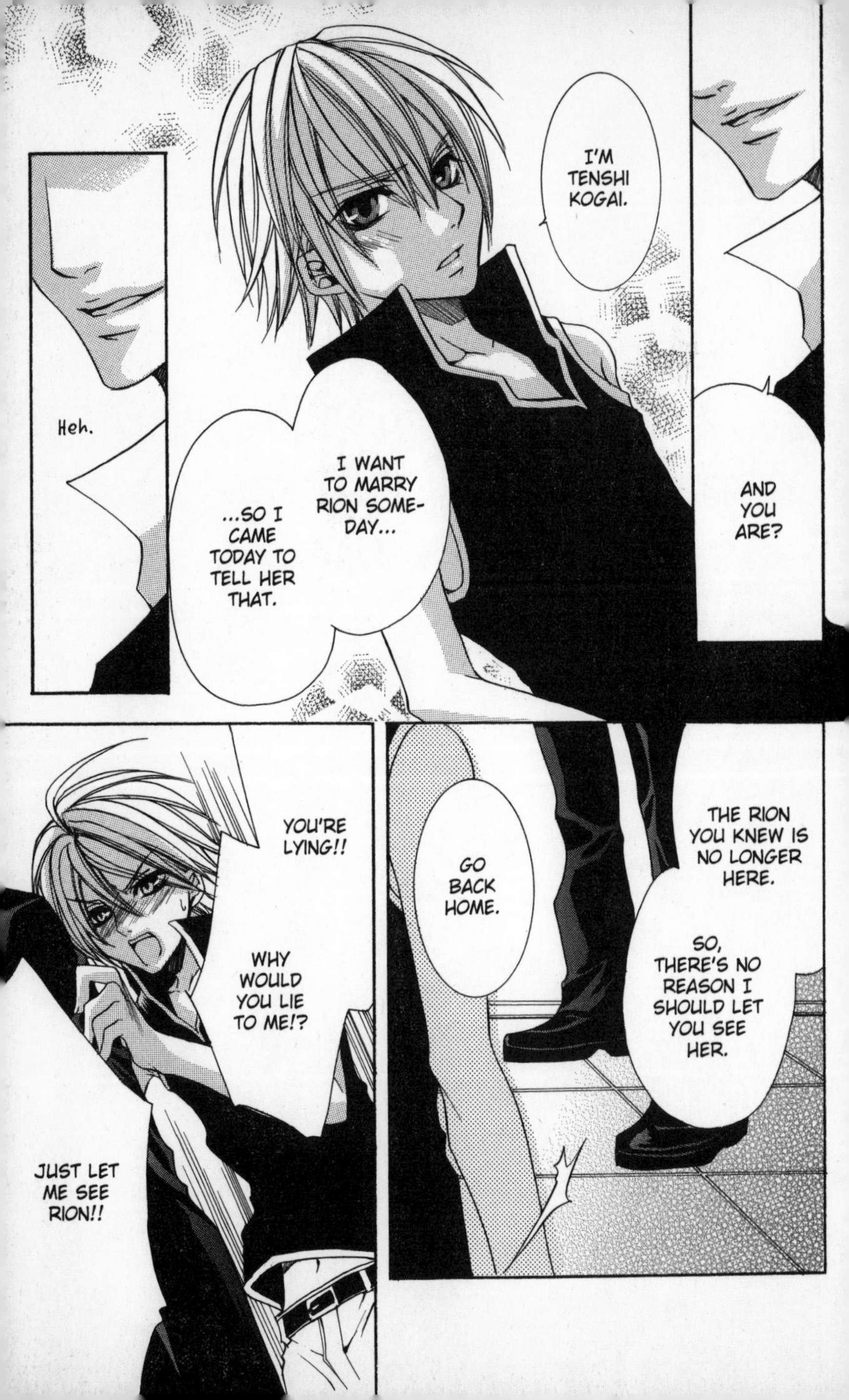
AND YOU ARE?
I'M TENSHI KOGAI.
I WANT TO MARRY RION SOME-DAY...
...SO I CAME TODAY TO TELL HER THAT.
Heh.
THE RION YOU KNEW IS NO LONGER HERE.
SO, THERE'S NO REASON I SHOULD LET YOU SEE HER.
GO BACK HOME.
YOU'RE LYING!!
WHY WOULD YOU LIE TO ME!?
JUST LET ME SEE RION!!

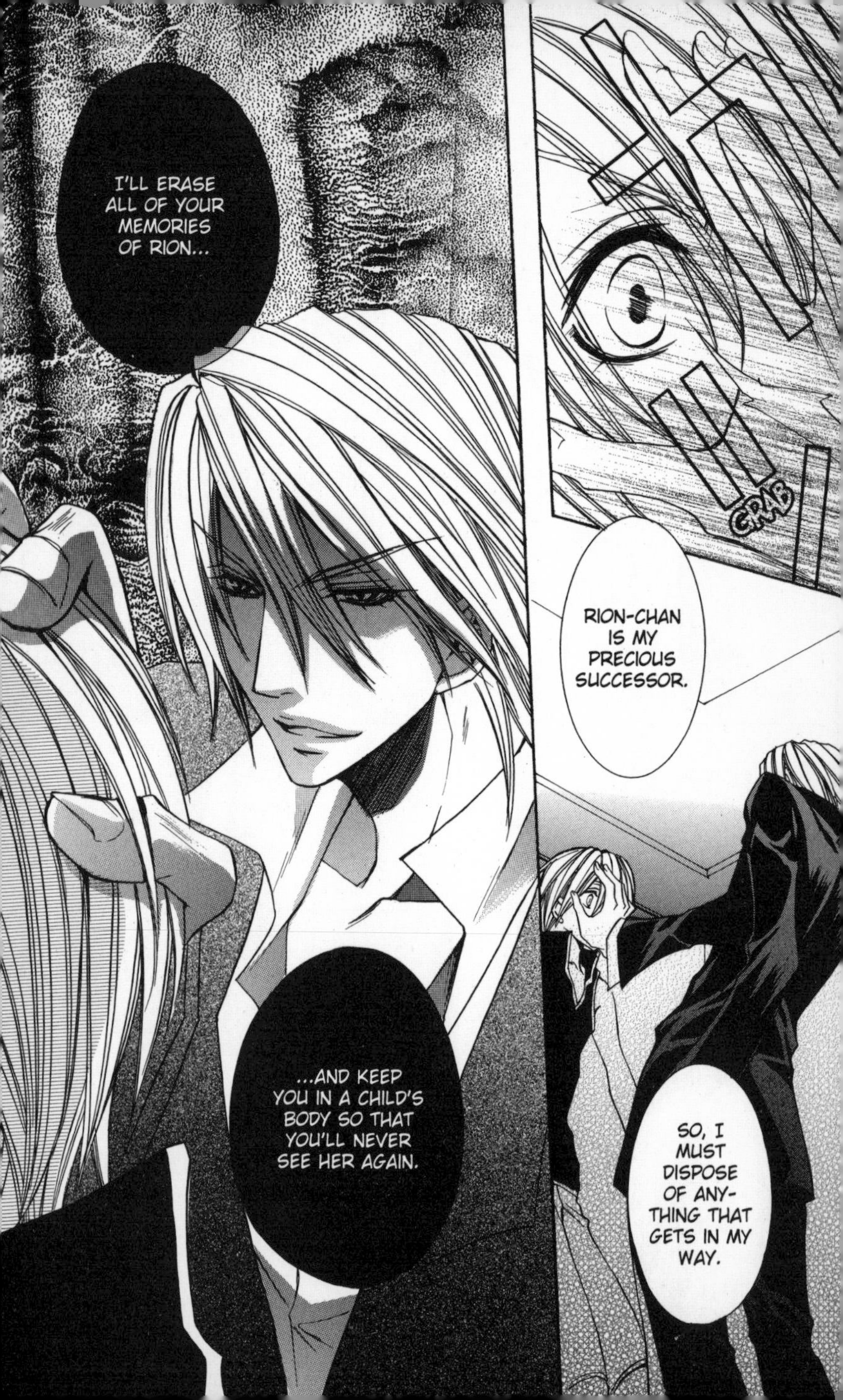
GRAB
RION-CHAN IS MY PRECIOUS SUCCESSOR.
SO, I MUST DISPOSE OF ANY-THING THAT GETS IN MY WAY.
I'LL ERASE ALL OF YOUR MEMORIES OF RION...
...AND KEEP YOU IN A CHILD'S BODY SO THAT YOU'LL NEVER SEE HER AGAIN.

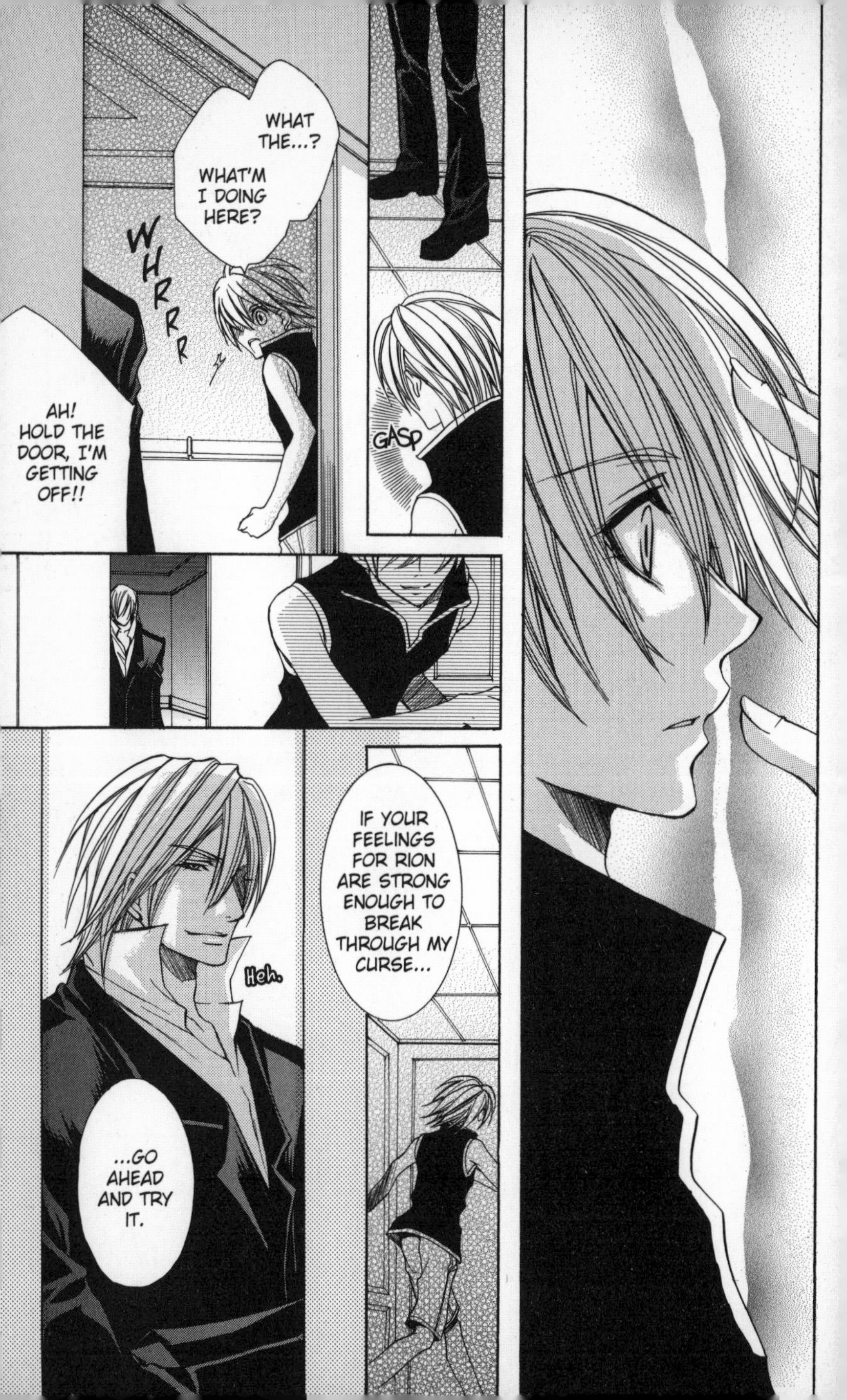
GASP
WHAT THE...?
WHAT'M I DOING HERE?
WHRRR
AH! HOLD THE DOOR, I'M GETTING OFF!!
IF YOUR FEELINGS FOR RION ARE STRONG ENOUGH TO BREAK THROUGH MY CURSE...
Heh.
...GO AHEAD AND TRY IT.

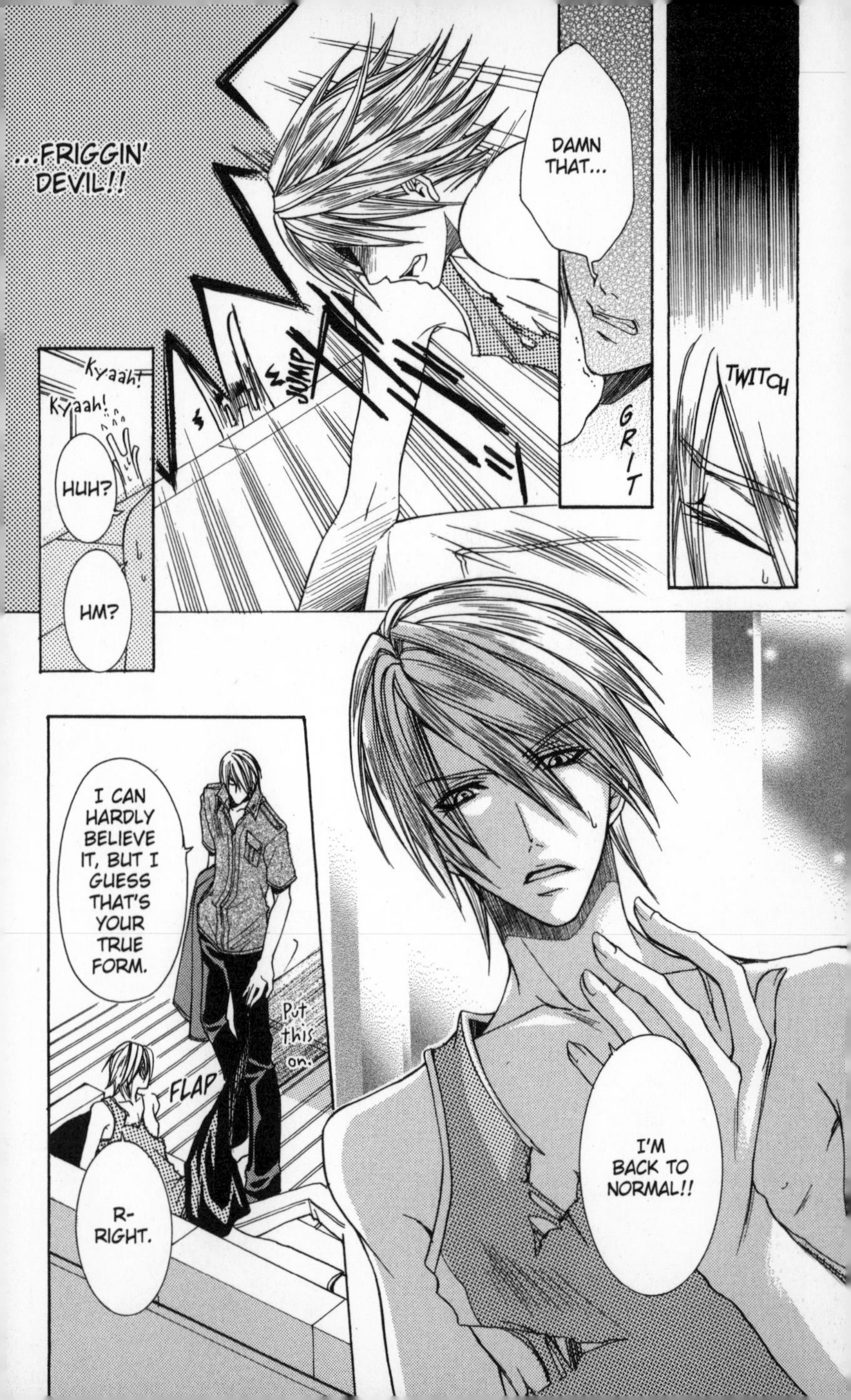

TWITCH
DAMN THAT...
GRIT
...FRIGGIN' DEVIL!!
JUMP
Kyaah! Kyaah!
HUH?
HM?
I'M BACK TO NORMAL!!
I CAN HARDLY BELIEVE IT, BUT I GUESS THAT'S YOUR TRUE FORM.
Put this on.
FLAP
R-RIGHT.

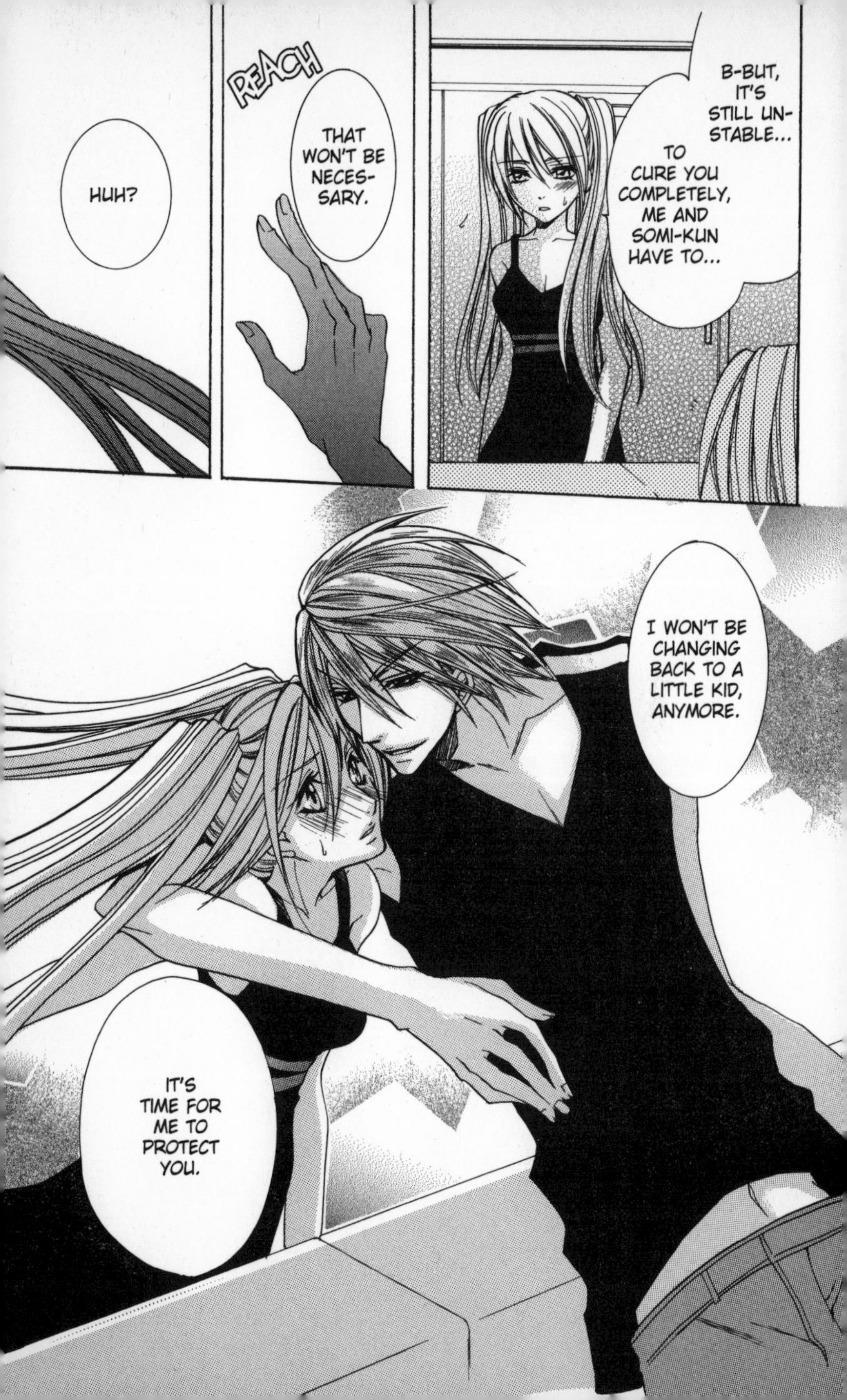
B-BUT, IT'S STILL UN-STABLE...
TO CURE YOU COMPLETELY, ME AND SOMI-KUN HAVE TO...
REACH
THAT WON'T BE NECES-SARY.
HUH?
I WON'T BE CHANGING BACK TO A LITTLE KID, ANYMORE.
IT'S TIME FOR ME TO PROTECT YOU.

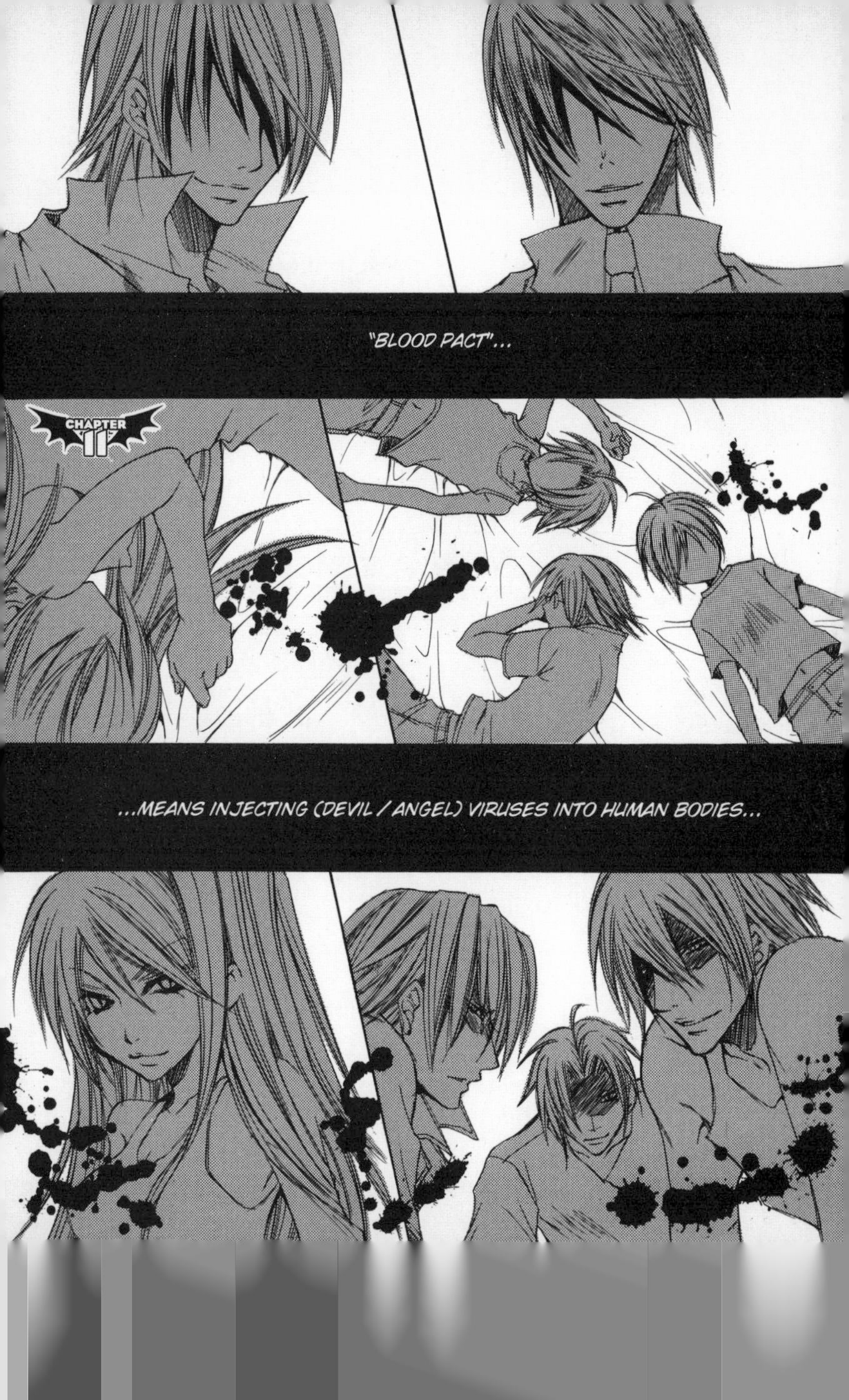
"BLOOD PACT"...
CHAPTER 11
...MEANS INJECTING (DEVIL / ANGEL) VIRUSES INTO HUMAN BODIES...

CHAPTER
11

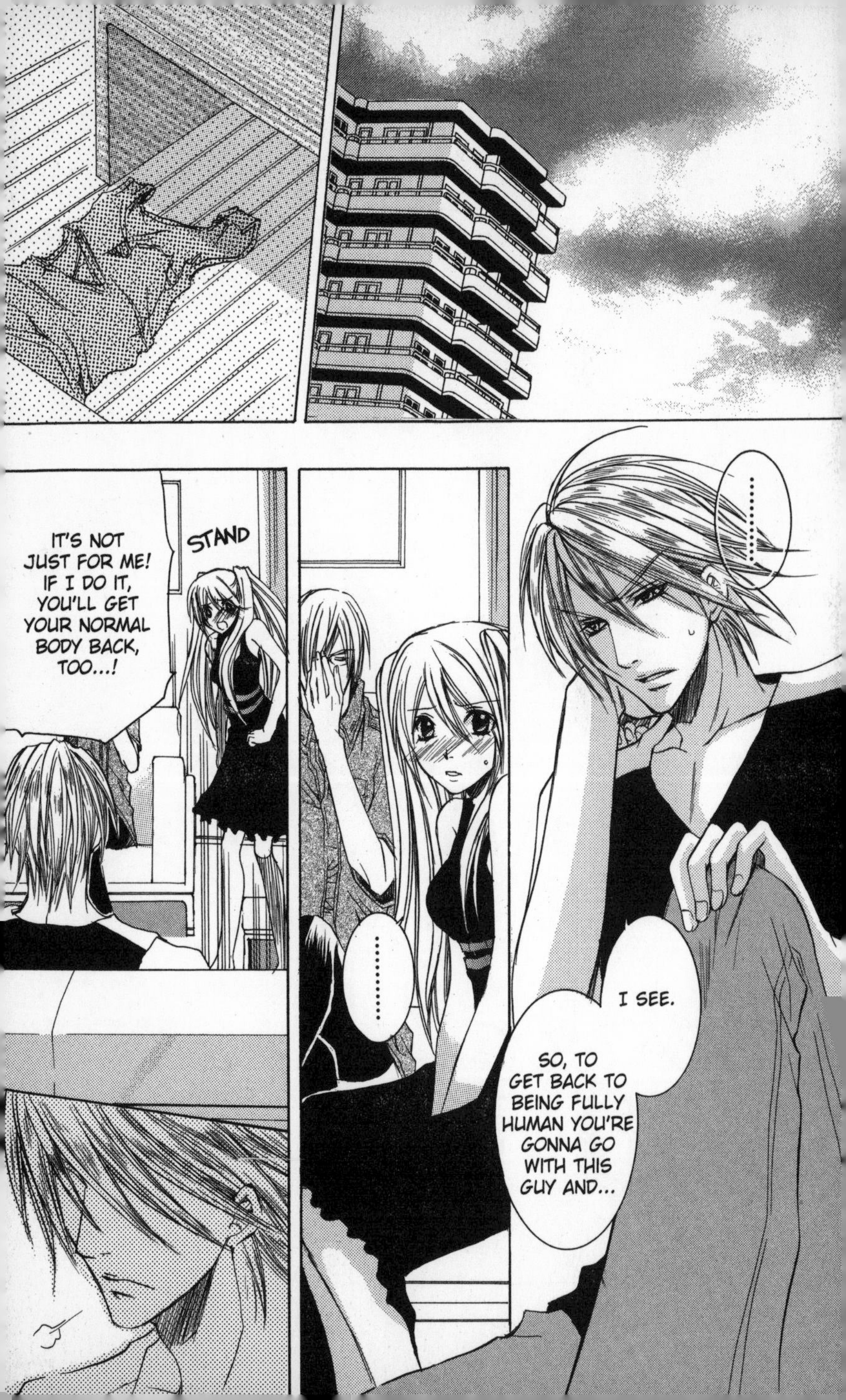
......
I SEE.
SO, TO GET BACK TO BEING FULLY HUMAN YOU'RE GONNA GO WITH THIS GUY AND...
......
IT'S NOT JUST FOR ME! IF I DO IT, YOU'LL GET YOUR NORMAL BODY BACK, TOO...!
STAND

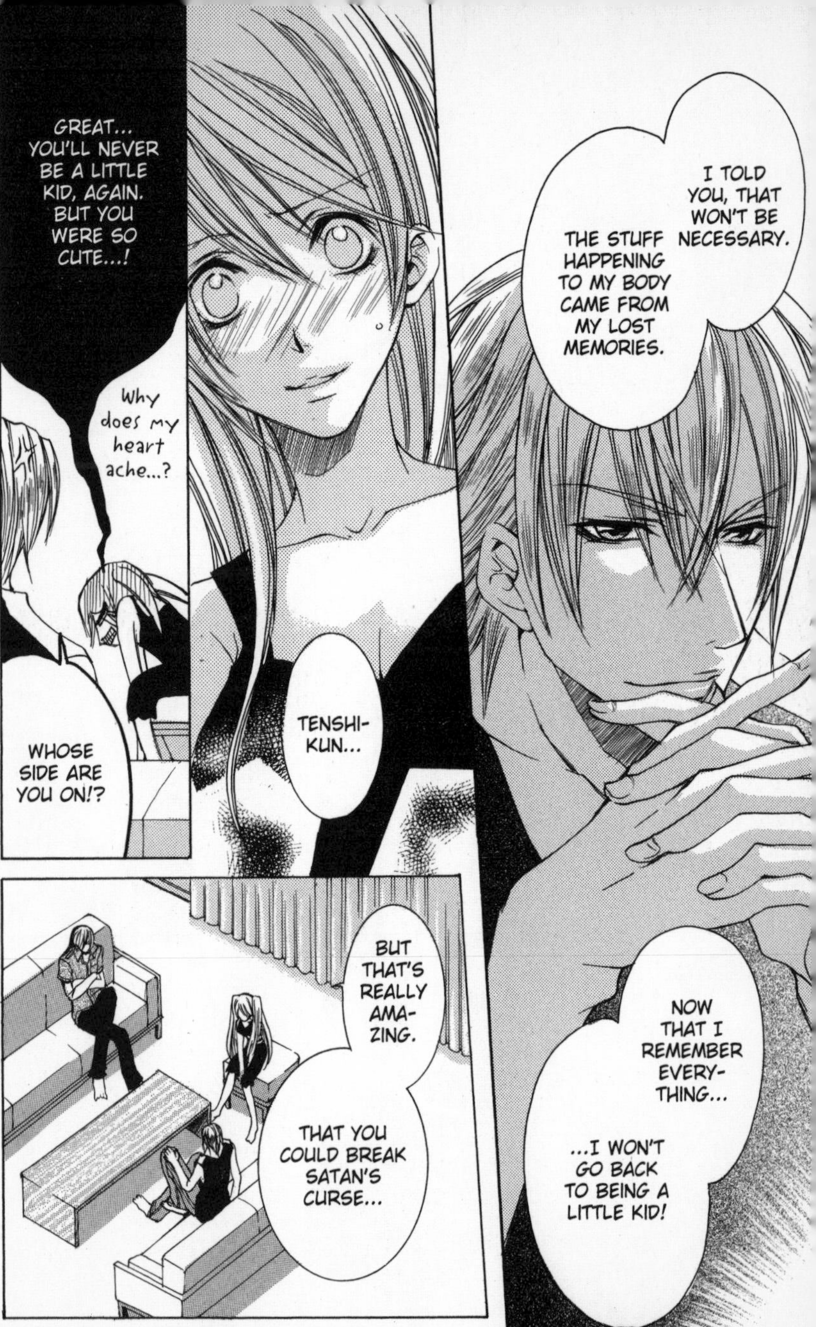
I TOLD YOU, THAT WON'T BE NECESSARY.
THE STUFF HAPPENING TO MY BODY CAME FROM MY LOST MEMORIES.
NOW THAT I REMEMBER EVERY-THING...
...I WON'T GO BACK TO BEING A LITTLE KID!
TENSHI-KUN...
GREAT... YOU'LL NEVER BE A LITTLE KID, AGAIN. BUT YOU WERE SO CUTE...!
Why does my heart ache...?
WHOSE SIDE ARE YOU ON!?
BUT THAT'S REALLY AMA-ZING.
THAT YOU COULD BREAK SATAN'S CURSE...

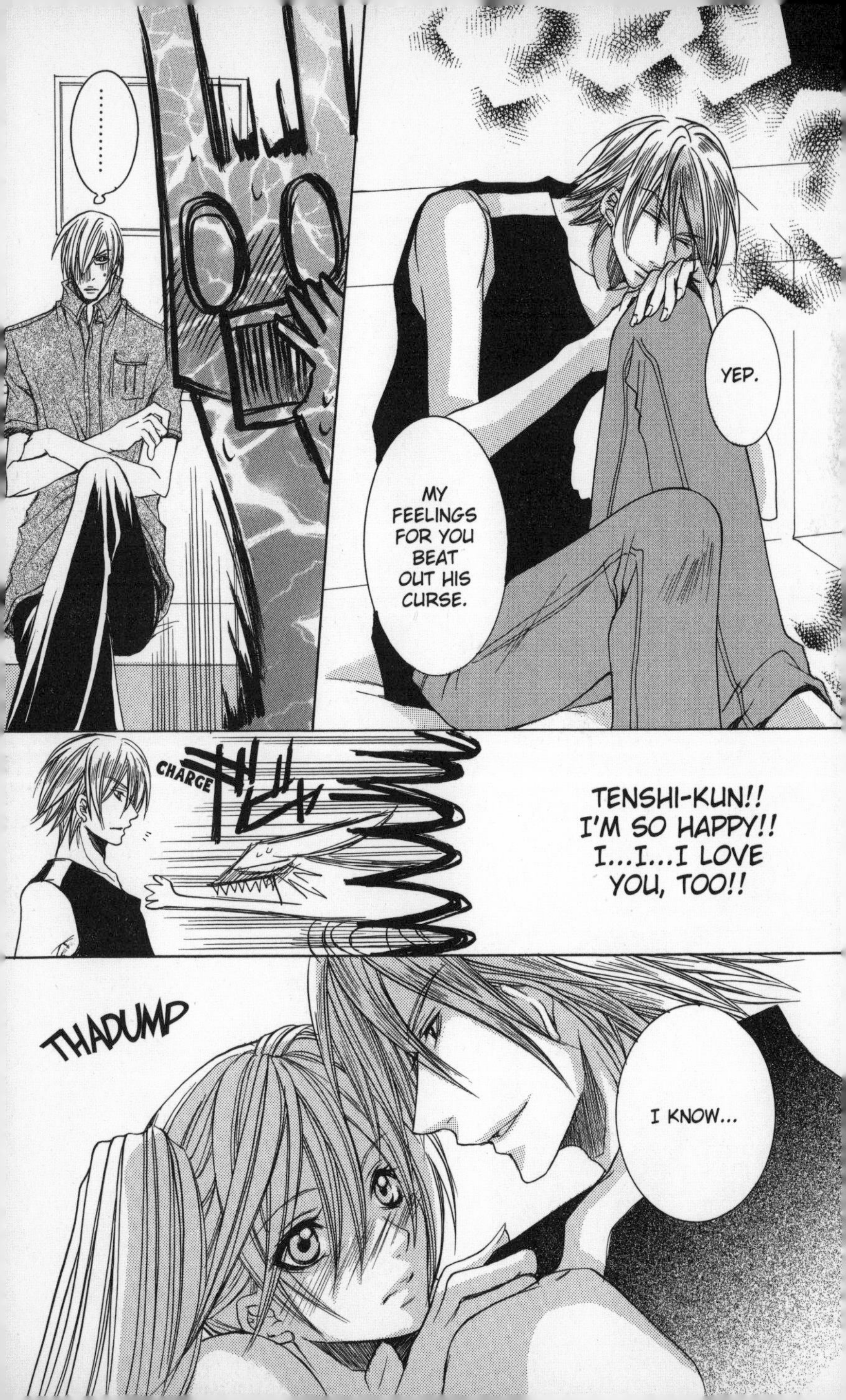
YEP.
MY FEELINGS FOR YOU BEAT OUT HIS CURSE.
......
TENSHI-KUN!! I'M SO HAPPY!! I...I...I LOVE YOU, TOO!!
CHARGE
I KNOW...
THADUMP

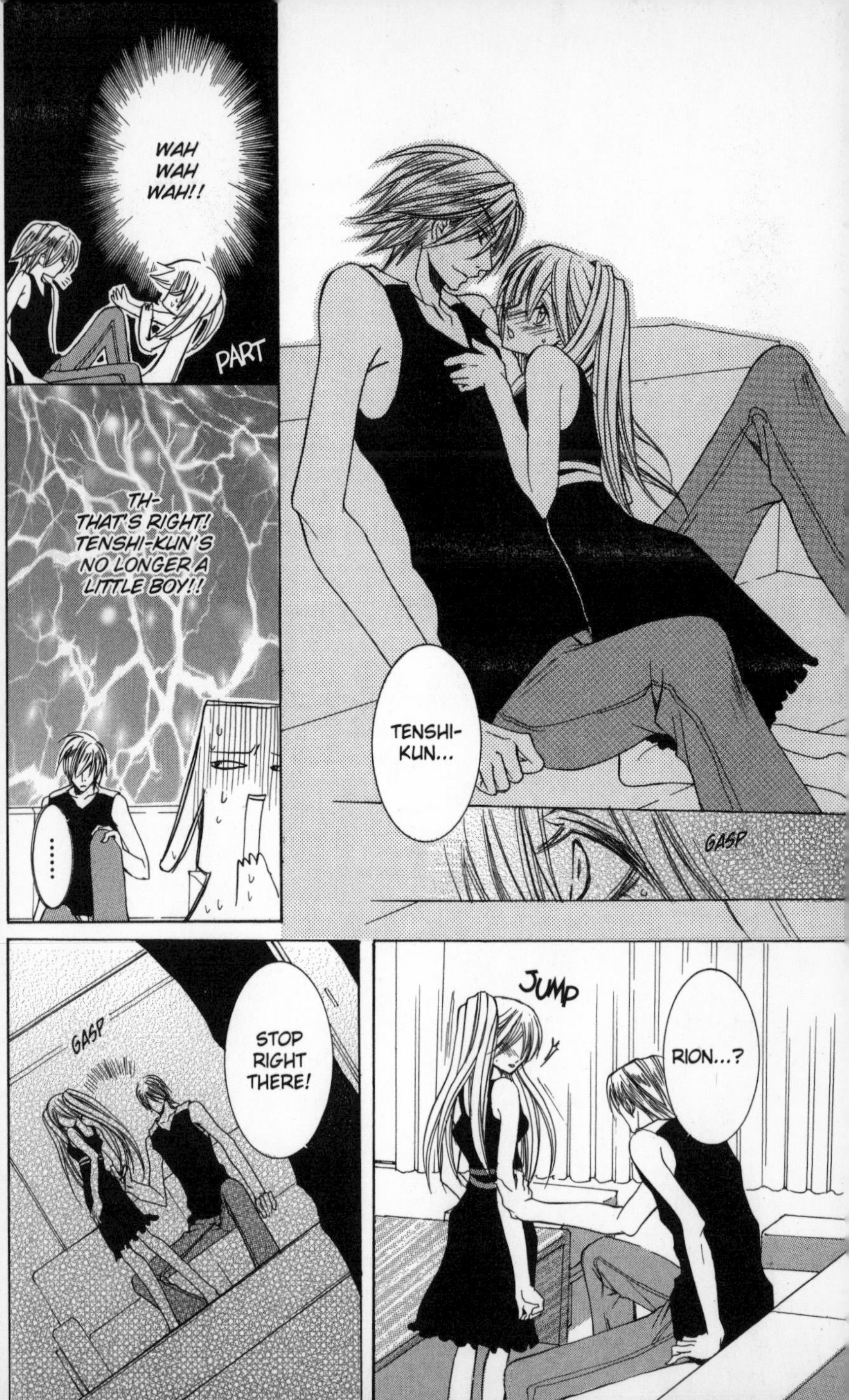

TENSHI-KUN...
GASP
WAH WAH WAH!!
PART
TH- THAT'S RIGHT! TENSHI-KUN'S NO LONGER A LITTLE BOY!!
......
JUMP
RION...?
STOP RIGHT THERE!
GASP

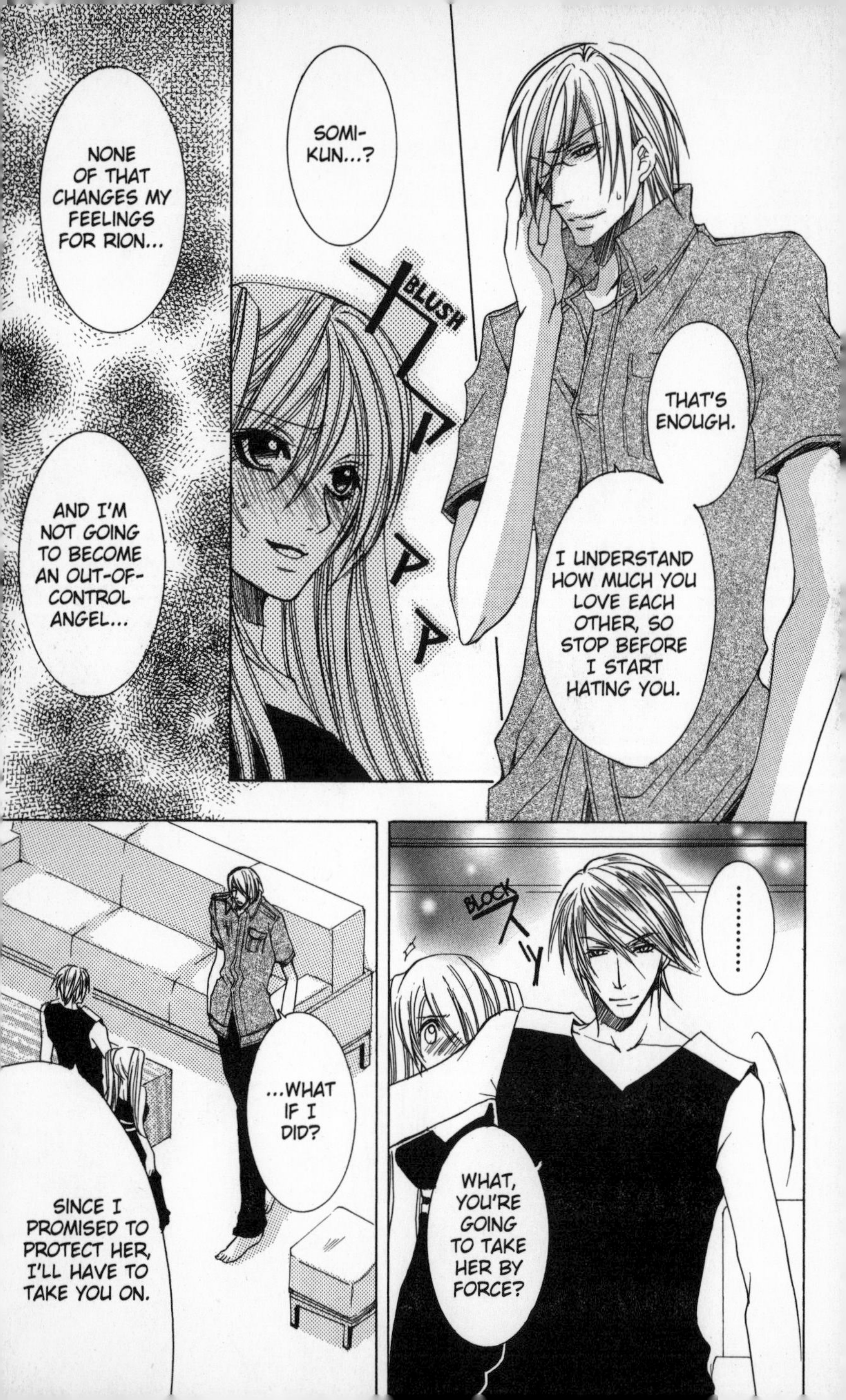
THAT'S ENOUGH.
I UNDERSTAND HOW MUCH YOU LOVE EACH OTHER, SO STOP BEFORE I START HATING YOU.
BLUSH
SOMI-KUN...?
NONE OF THAT CHANGES MY FEELINGS FOR RION...
AND I'M NOT GOING TO BECOME AN OUT-OF-CONTROL ANGEL...
.........
BLOCK
WHAT, YOU'RE GOING TO TAKE HER BY FORCE?
...WHAT IF I DID?
SINCE I PROMISED TO PROTECT HER, I'LL HAVE TO TAKE YOU ON.

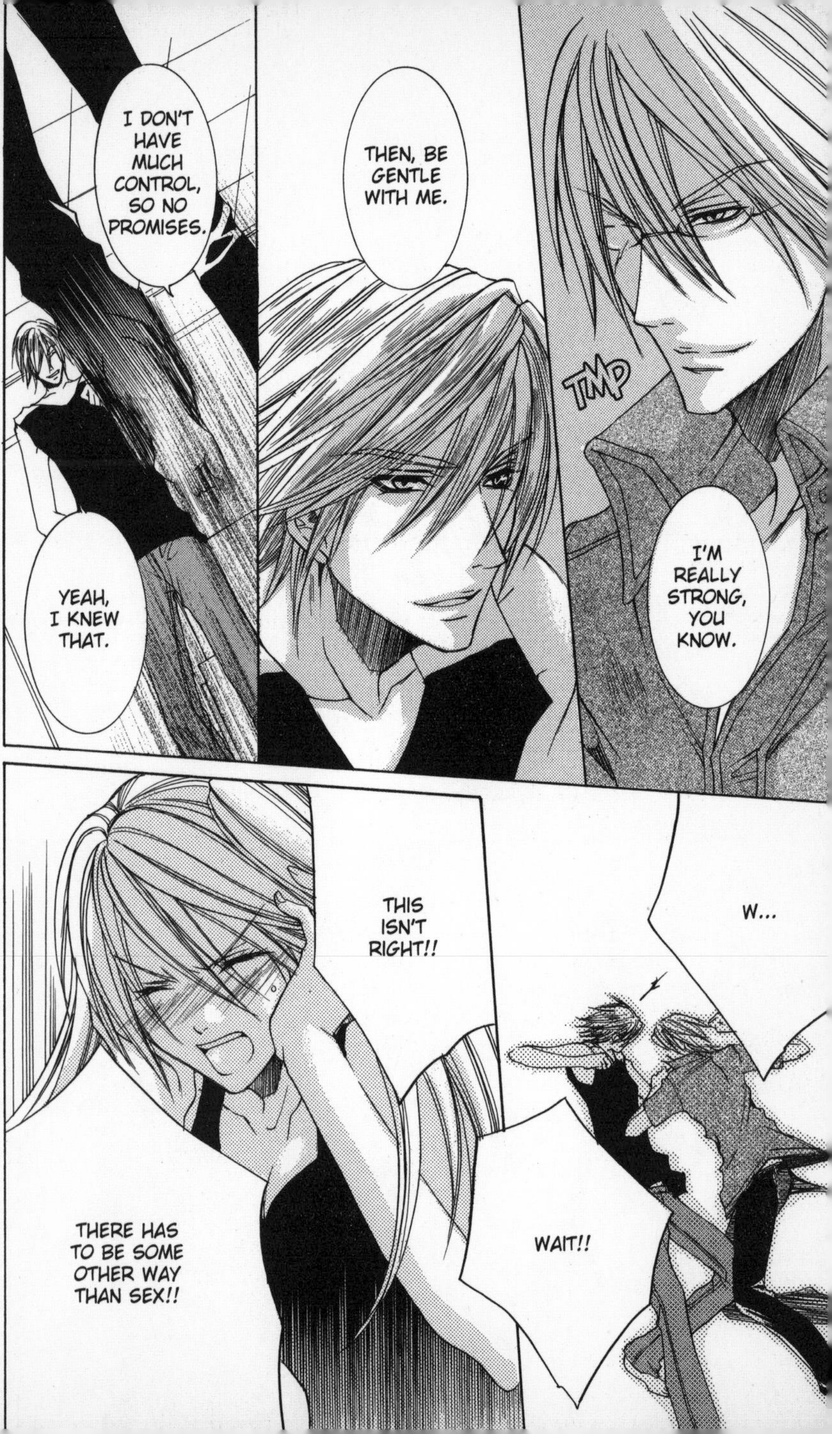
TMP
I'M REALLY STRONG, YOU KNOW.
THEN, BE GENTLE WITH ME.
I DON'T HAVE MUCH CONTROL, SO NO PROMISES.
YEAH, I KNEW THAT.
W...
WAIT!!
THIS ISN'T RIGHT!!
THERE HAS TO BE SOME OTHER WAY THAN SEX!!

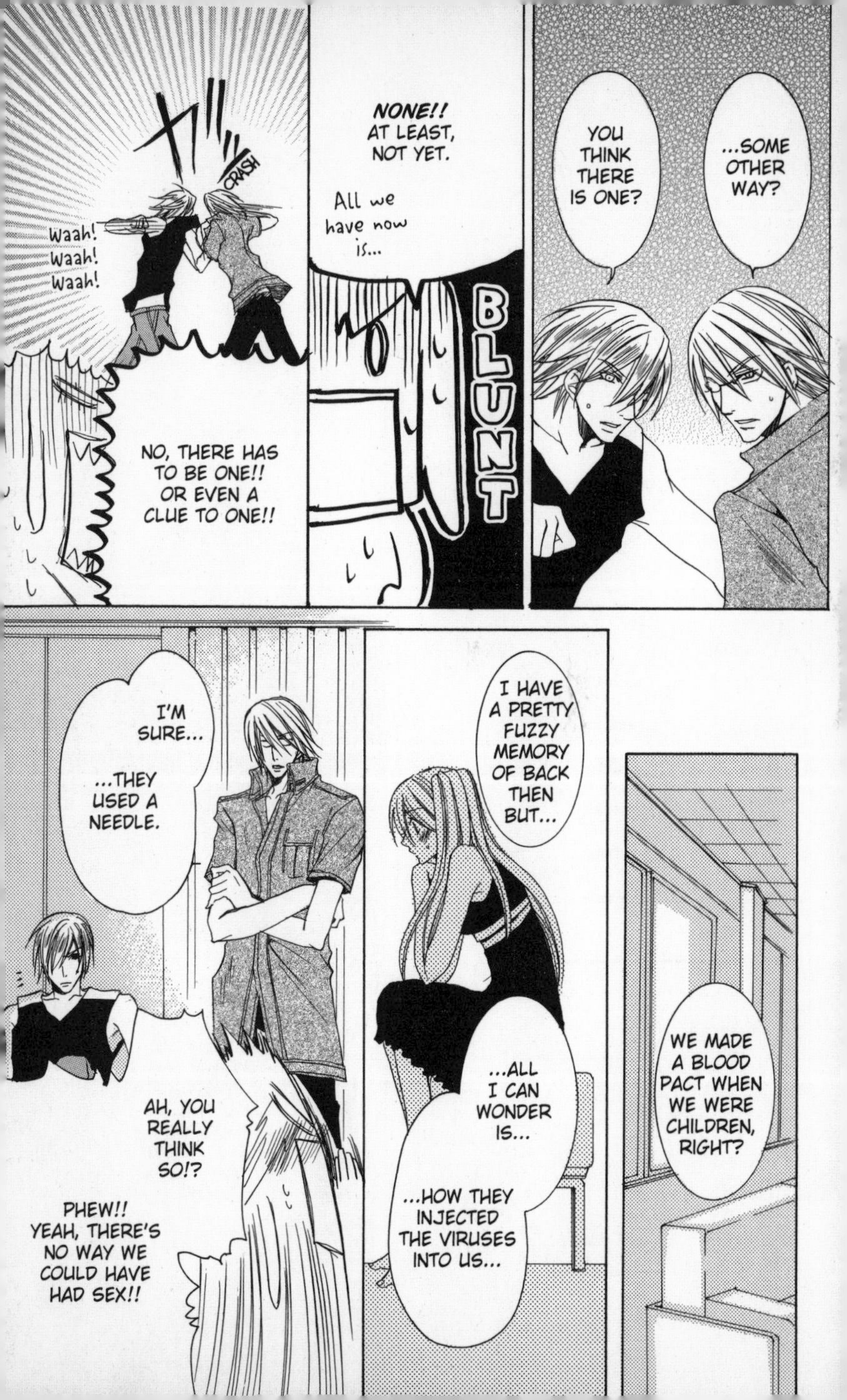
...SOME OTHER WAY?
YOU THINK THERE IS ONE?
NONE!! AT LEAST, NOT YET.
All we have now is...
BLUNT
CRASH
Waah! Waah! Waah!
NO, THERE HAS TO BE ONE!! OR EVEN A CLUE TO ONE!!
WE MADE A BLOOD PACT WHEN WE WERE CHILDREN, RIGHT?
I HAVE A PRETTY FUZZY MEMORY OF BACK THEN BUT...
...ALL I CAN WONDER IS...
...HOW THEY INJECTED THE VIRUSES INTO US...
I'M SURE...
...THEY USED A NEEDLE.
AH, YOU REALLY THINK SO!?
PHEW!! YEAH, THERE'S NO WAY WE COULD HAVE HAD SEX!!

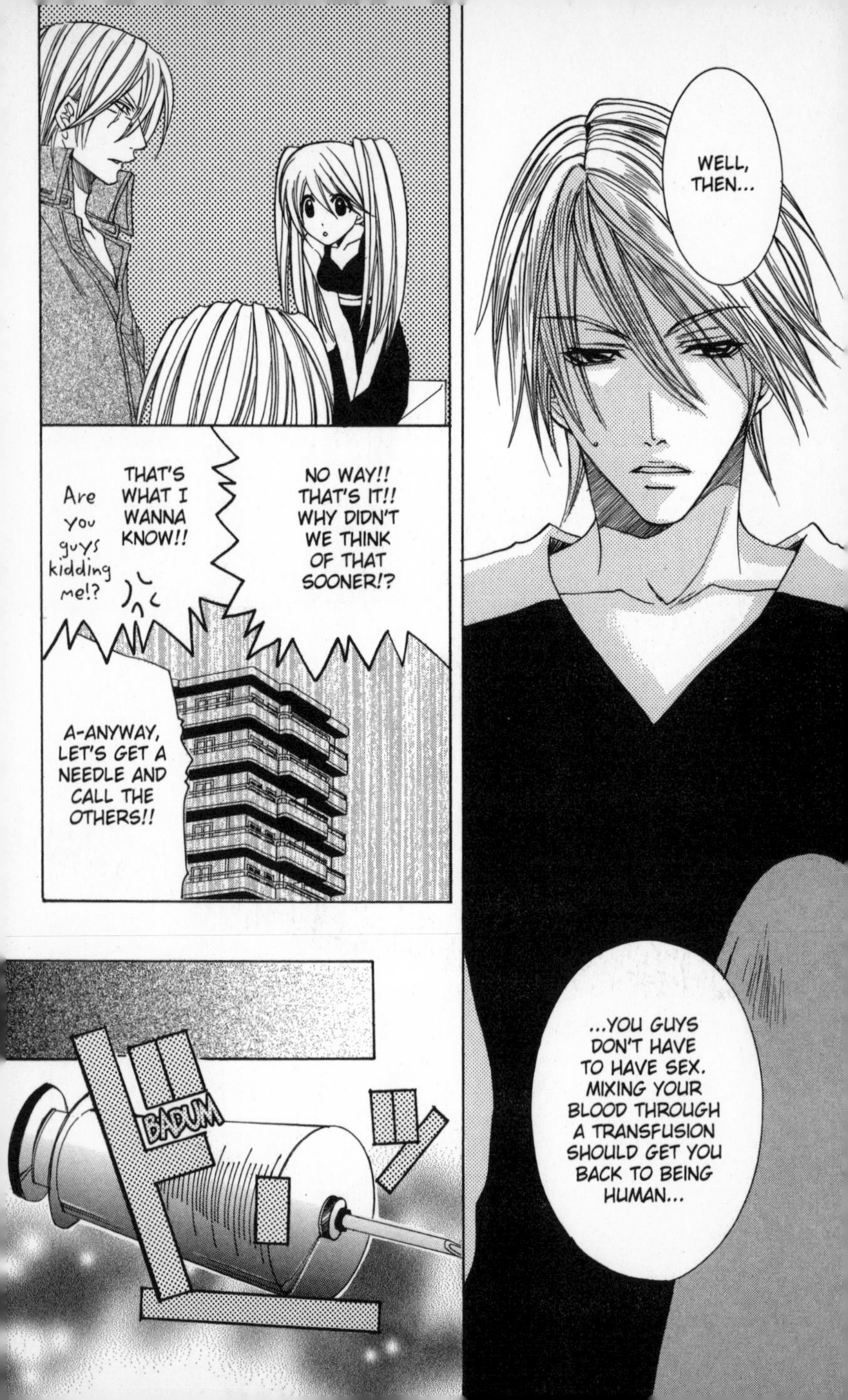
WELL, THEN...
...YOU GUYS DON'T HAVE TO HAVE SEX. MIXING YOUR BLOOD THROUGH A TRANSFUSION SHOULD GET YOU BACK TO BEING HUMAN...
NO WAY!! THAT'S IT!! WHY DIDN'T WE THINK OF THAT SOONER!?
THAT'S WHAT I WANNA KNOW!!
Are you guys kidding me!?
A-ANYWAY, LET'S GET A NEEDLE AND CALL THE OTHERS!!
BADUM

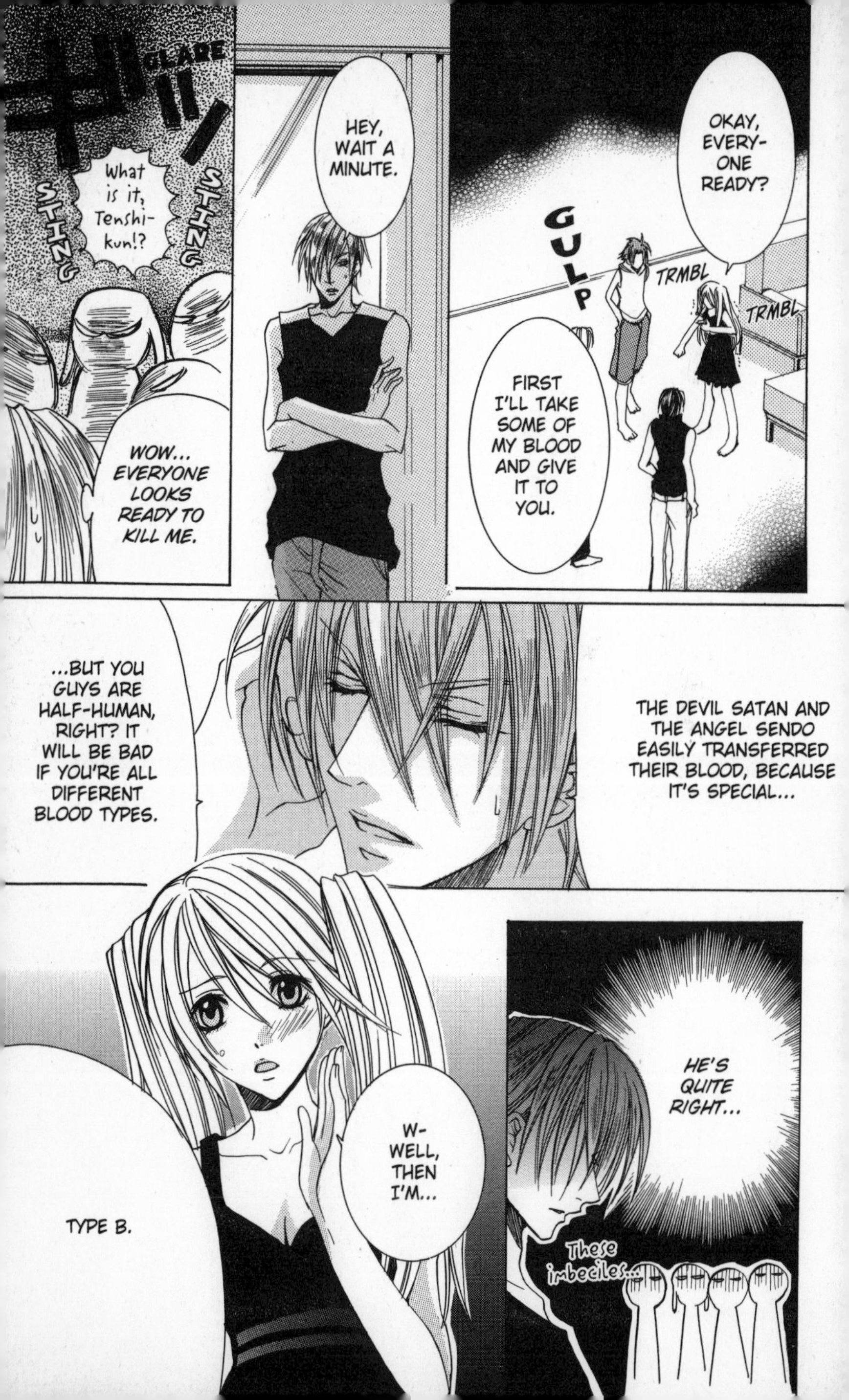
OKAY, EVERYONE READY?
GULP
TRMBL
TRMBL
FIRST I'LL TAKE SOME OF MY BLOOD AND GIVE IT TO YOU.
HEY, WAIT A MINUTE.
CLARE
What is it, Tenshi-kun!?
STING
STING
WOW... EVERYONE LOOKS READY TO KILL ME.
THE DEVIL SATAN AND THE ANGEL SENDO EASILY TRANSFERRED THEIR BLOOD, BECAUSE IT'S SPECIAL...
...BUT YOU GUYS ARE HALF-HUMAN, RIGHT? IT WILL BE BAD IF YOU'RE ALL DIFFERENT BLOOD TYPES.
HE'S QUITE RIGHT...
These imbeciles...
W-WELL, THEN I'M...
TYPE B.

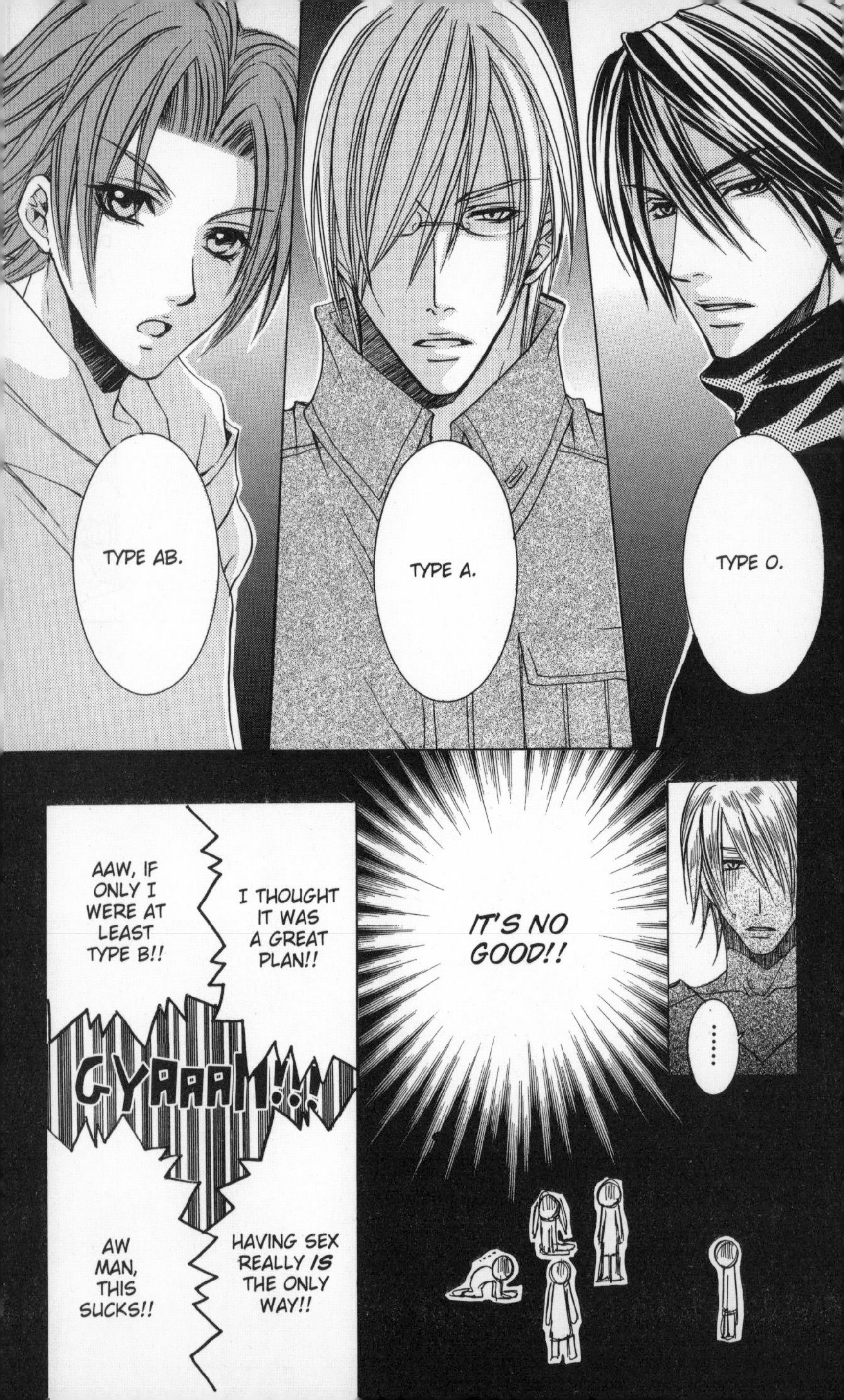
TYPE O.
TYPE A.
TYPE AB.
……
IT'S NO GOOD!!
I THOUGHT IT WAS A GREAT PLAN!!
AAW, IF ONLY I WERE AT LEAST TYPE B!!
GYAAAH!!!
HAVING SEX REALLY *IS* THE ONLY WAY!!
AW MAN, THIS SUCKS!!

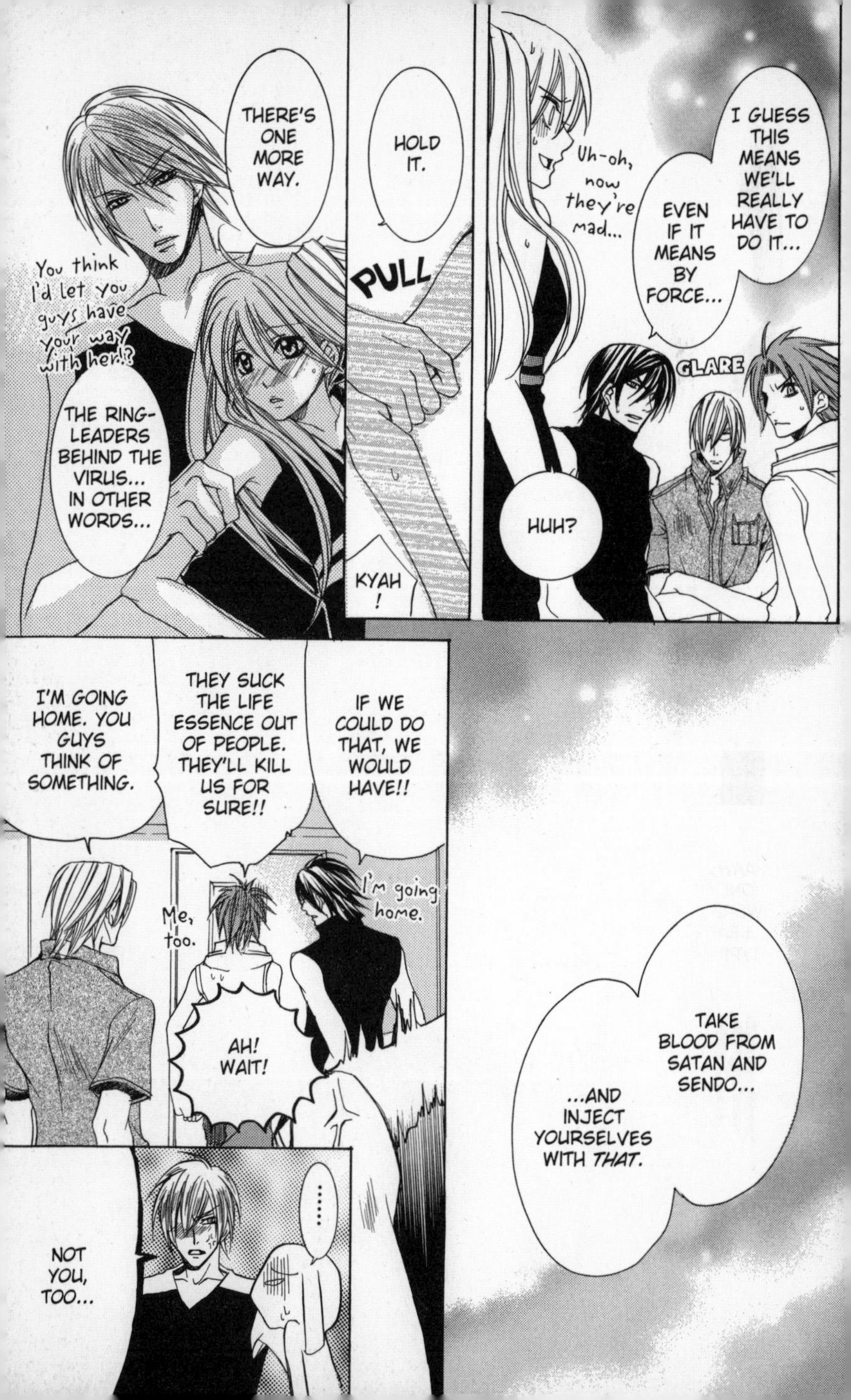
I GUESS THIS MEANS WE'LL REALLY HAVE TO DO IT...
EVEN IF IT MEANS BY FORCE...
Uh-oh, now they're mad...
GLARE
HUH?
HOLD IT.
PULL
KYAH!
THERE'S ONE MORE WAY.
You think I'd let you guys have your way with her!?
THE RING-LEADERS BEHIND THE VIRUS... IN OTHER WORDS...
TAKE BLOOD FROM SATAN AND SENDO...
...AND INJECT YOURSELVES WITH *THAT*.
IF WE COULD DO THAT, WE WOULD HAVE!!
THEY SUCK THE LIFE ESSENCE OUT OF PEOPLE. THEY'LL KILL US FOR SURE!!
I'M GOING HOME. YOU GUYS THINK OF SOMETHING.
I'm going home.
Me, too.
AH! WAIT!
......
NOT YOU, TOO...

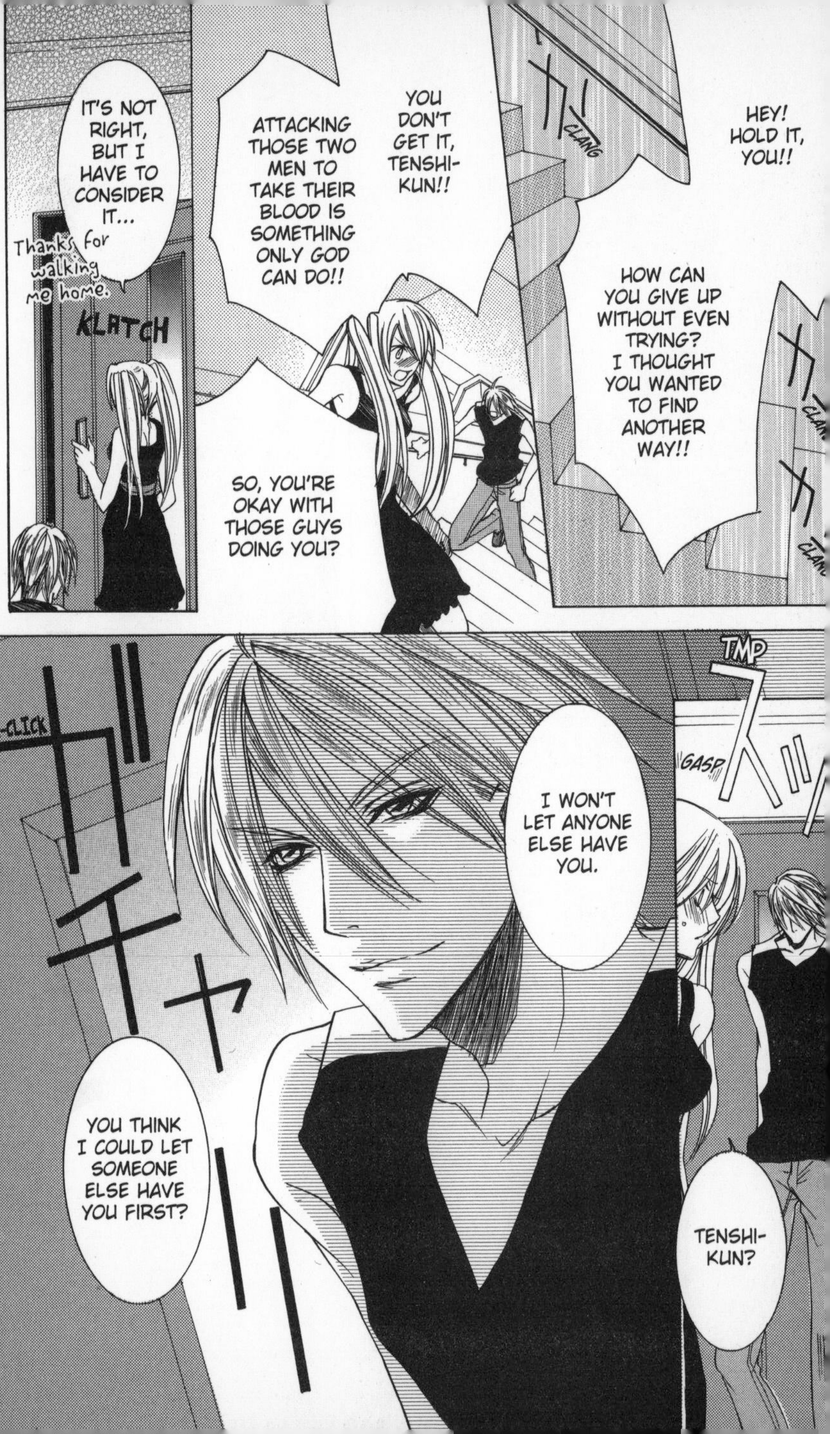
HEY! HOLD IT, YOU!!
CLANG
CLANG
HOW CAN YOU GIVE UP WITHOUT EVEN TRYING? I THOUGHT YOU WANTED TO FIND ANOTHER WAY!!
CLANG
YOU DON'T GET IT, TENSHI-KUN!!
ATTACKING THOSE TWO MEN TO TAKE THEIR BLOOD IS SOMETHING ONLY GOD CAN DO!!
SO, YOU'RE OKAY WITH THOSE GUYS DOING YOU?
IT'S NOT RIGHT, BUT I HAVE TO CONSIDER IT...
Thanks for walking me home.
KLATCH
TMP
GASP
I WON'T LET ANYONE ELSE HAVE YOU.
TENSHI-KUN?
YOU THINK I COULD LET SOMEONE ELSE HAVE YOU FIRST?
K-CLICK

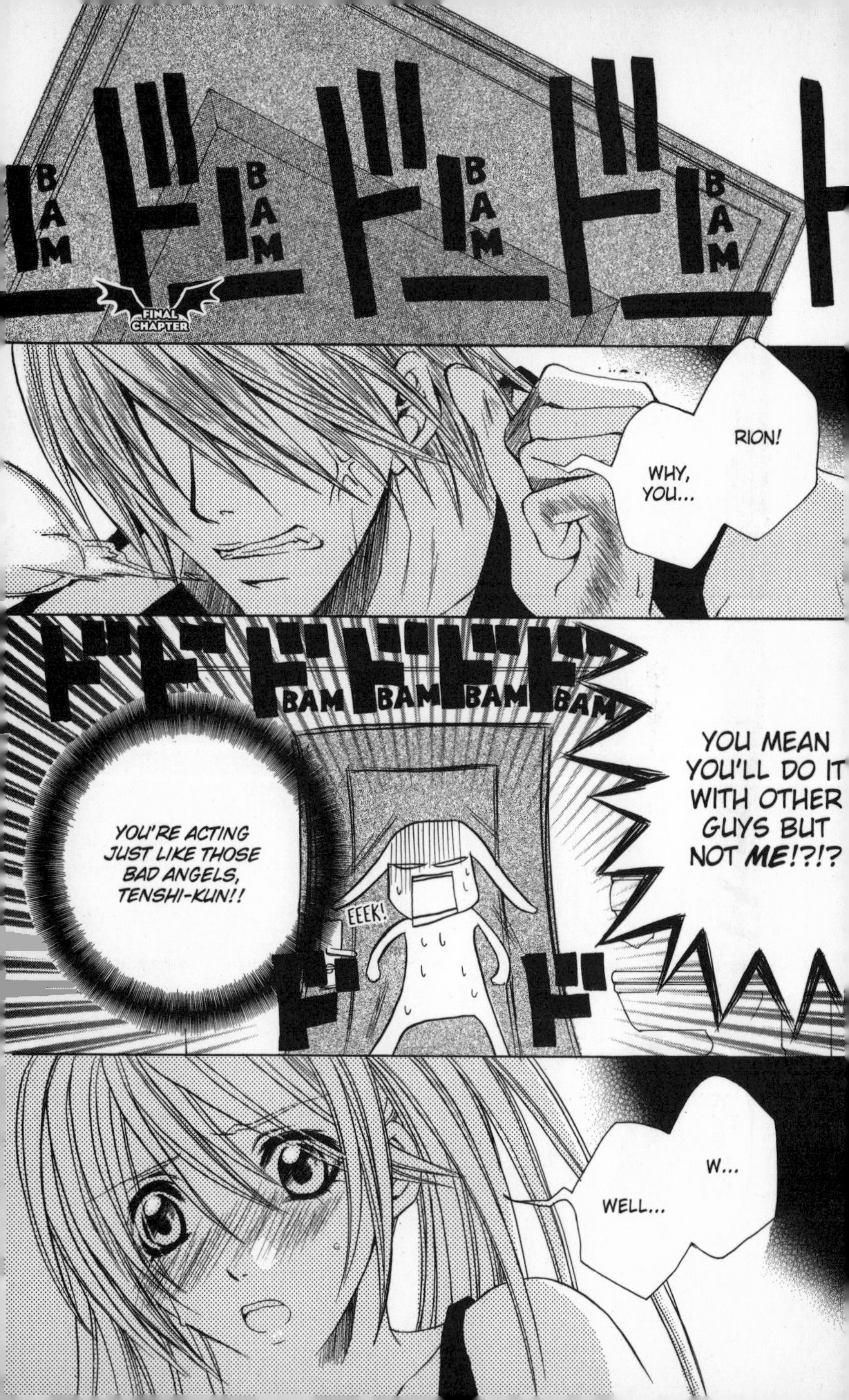
BAM
BAM
BAM
BAM
FINAL CHAPTER
RION!
WHY, YOU...
YOU MEAN YOU'LL DO IT WITH OTHER GUYS BUT NOT *ME*!?!?
BAM BAM BAM BAM
YOU'RE ACTING JUST LIKE THOSE BAD ANGELS, TENSHI-KUN!!
EEEK!
W...
WELL...

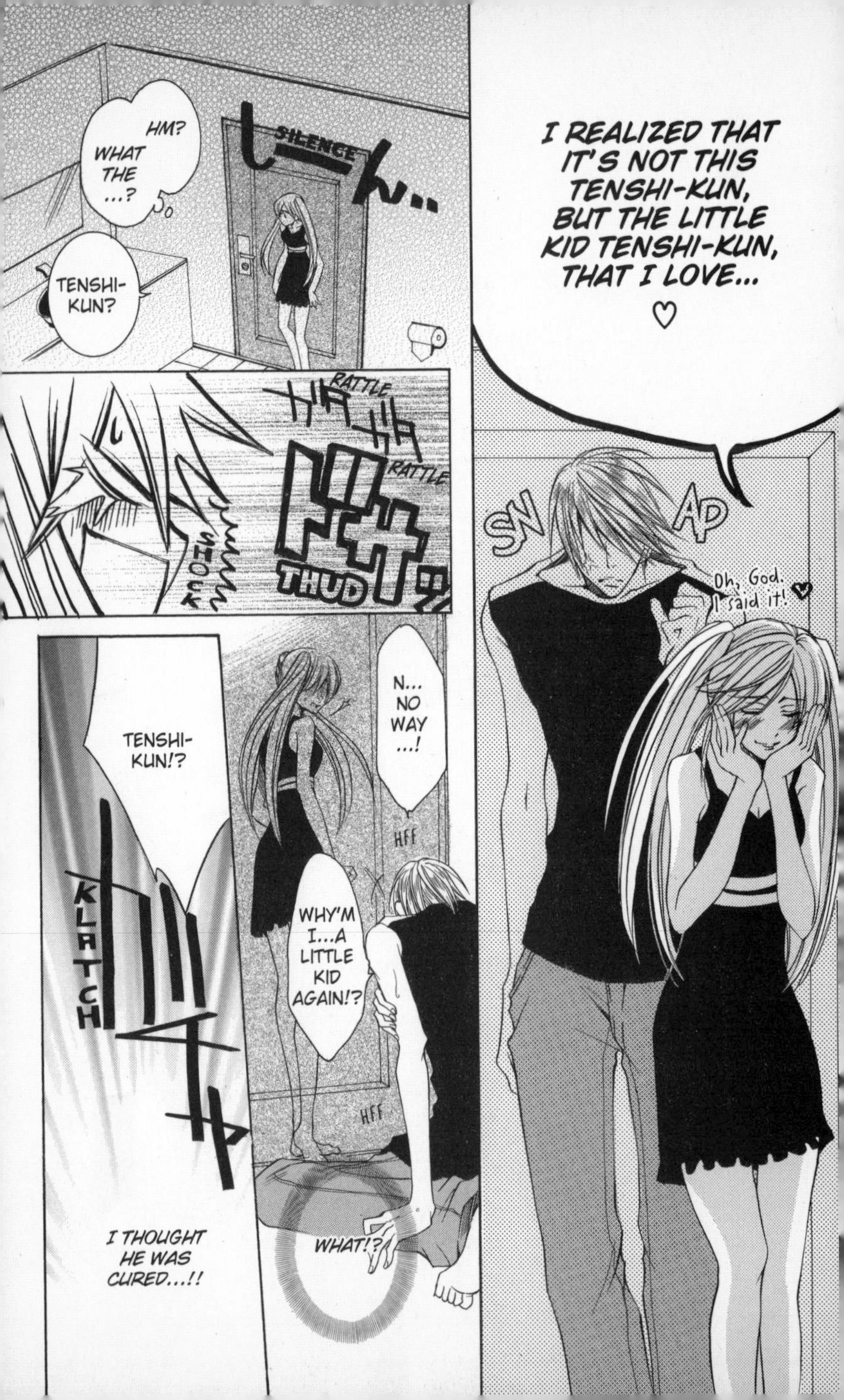
I REALIZED THAT IT'S NOT THIS TENSHI-KUN, BUT THE LITTLE KID TENSHI-KUN, THAT I LOVE... ♡
SNAP
Oh, God. I said it! ♥
SILENCE
HM? WHAT THE ...?
TENSHI-KUN?
RATTLE
RATTLE
THUD
SHOCK
N... NO WAY ...!
HFF
WHY'M I...A LITTLE KID AGAIN!?
HFF
WHAT!?
TENSHI-KUN!?
KLATCH
I THOUGHT HE WAS CURED...!!

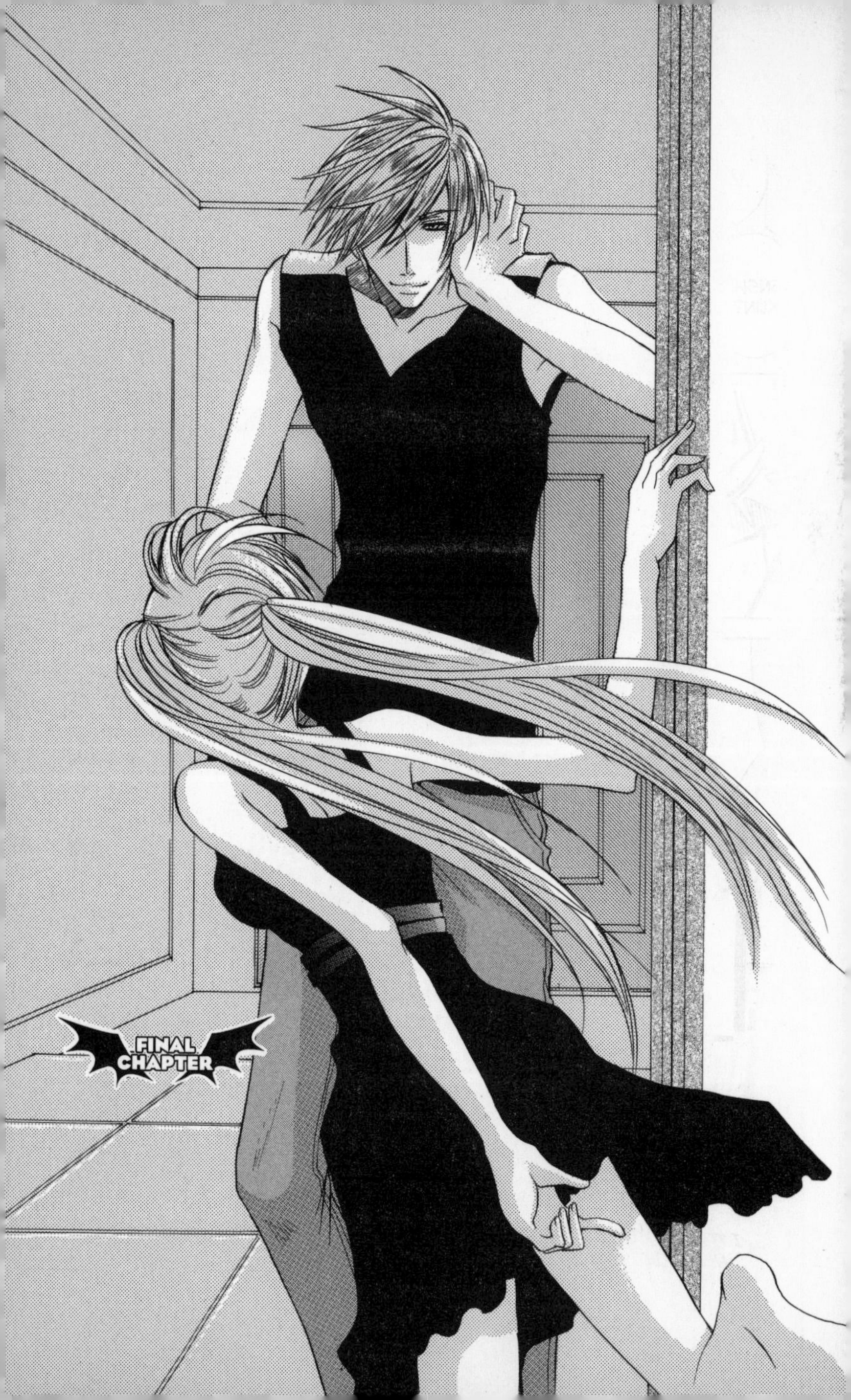
FINAL CHAPTER

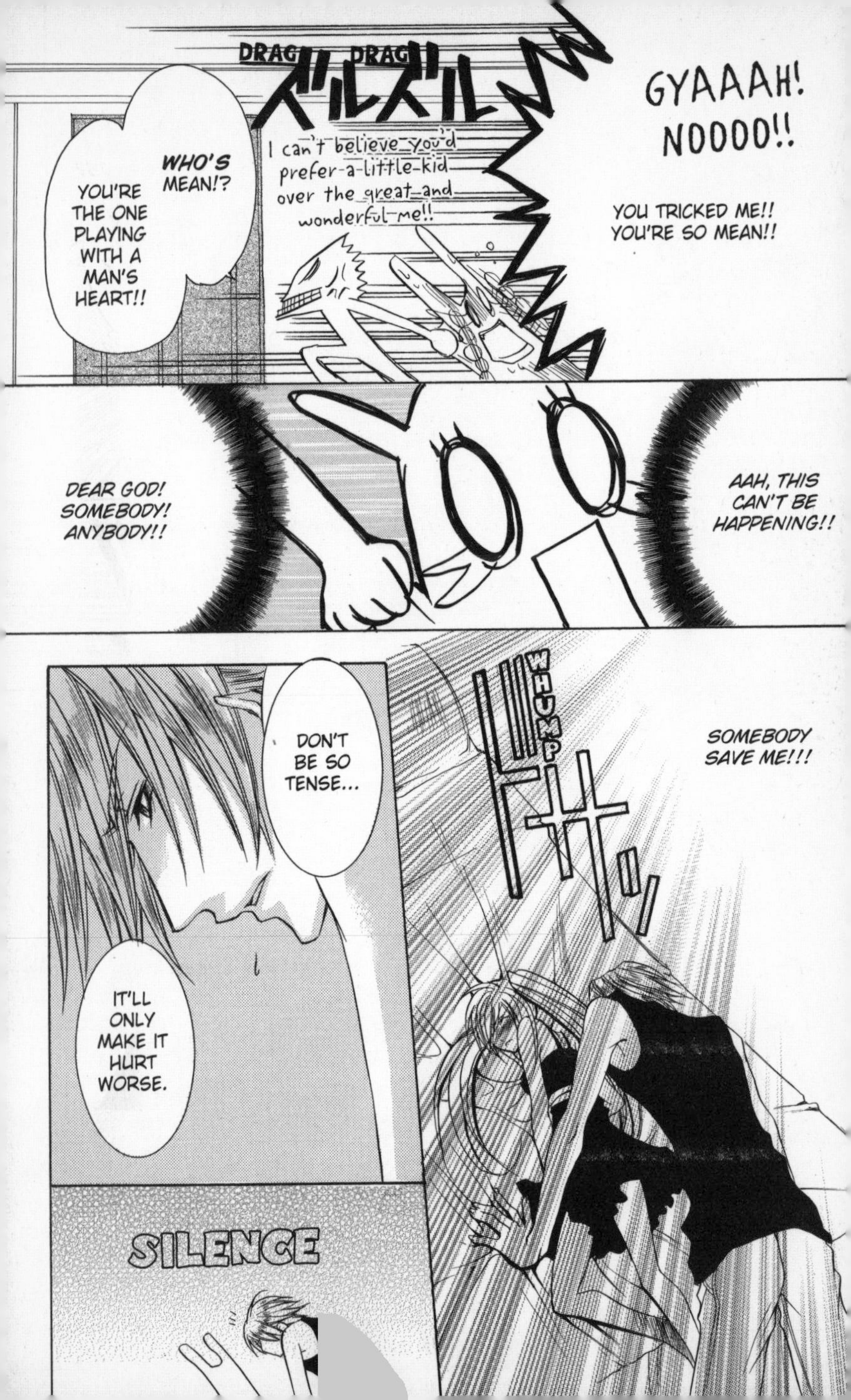
GYAAAH! NOOOO!!
YOU TRICKED ME!! YOU'RE SO MEAN!!
DRAG DRAG
ズルズル
I can't believe you'd prefer a little kid over the great and wonderful me!!
WHO'S MEAN!?
YOU'RE THE ONE PLAYING WITH A MAN'S HEART!!
AAH, THIS CAN'T BE HAPPENING!!
DEAR GOD! SOMEBODY! ANYBODY!!
SOMEBODY SAVE ME!!!
WHUMP
DON'T BE SO TENSE...
IT'LL ONLY MAKE IT HURT WORSE.
SILENCE

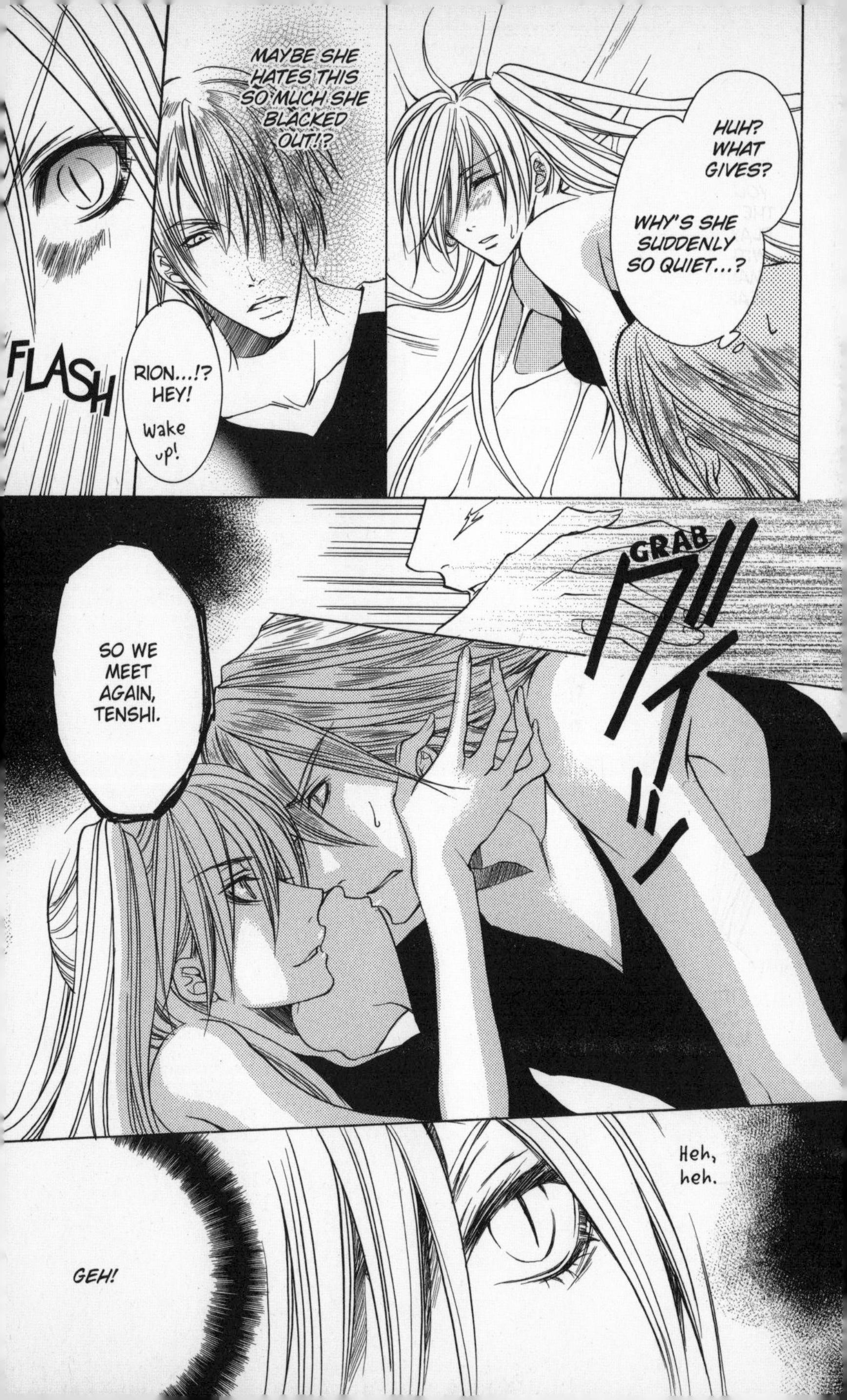
HUH? WHAT GIVES?
WHY'S SHE SUDDENLY SO QUIET...?
MAYBE SHE HATES THIS SO MUCH SHE BLACKED OUT!?
RION...!? HEY!
Wake up!
FLASH
GRAB
SO WE MEET AGAIN, TENSHI.
Heh, heh.
GEH!

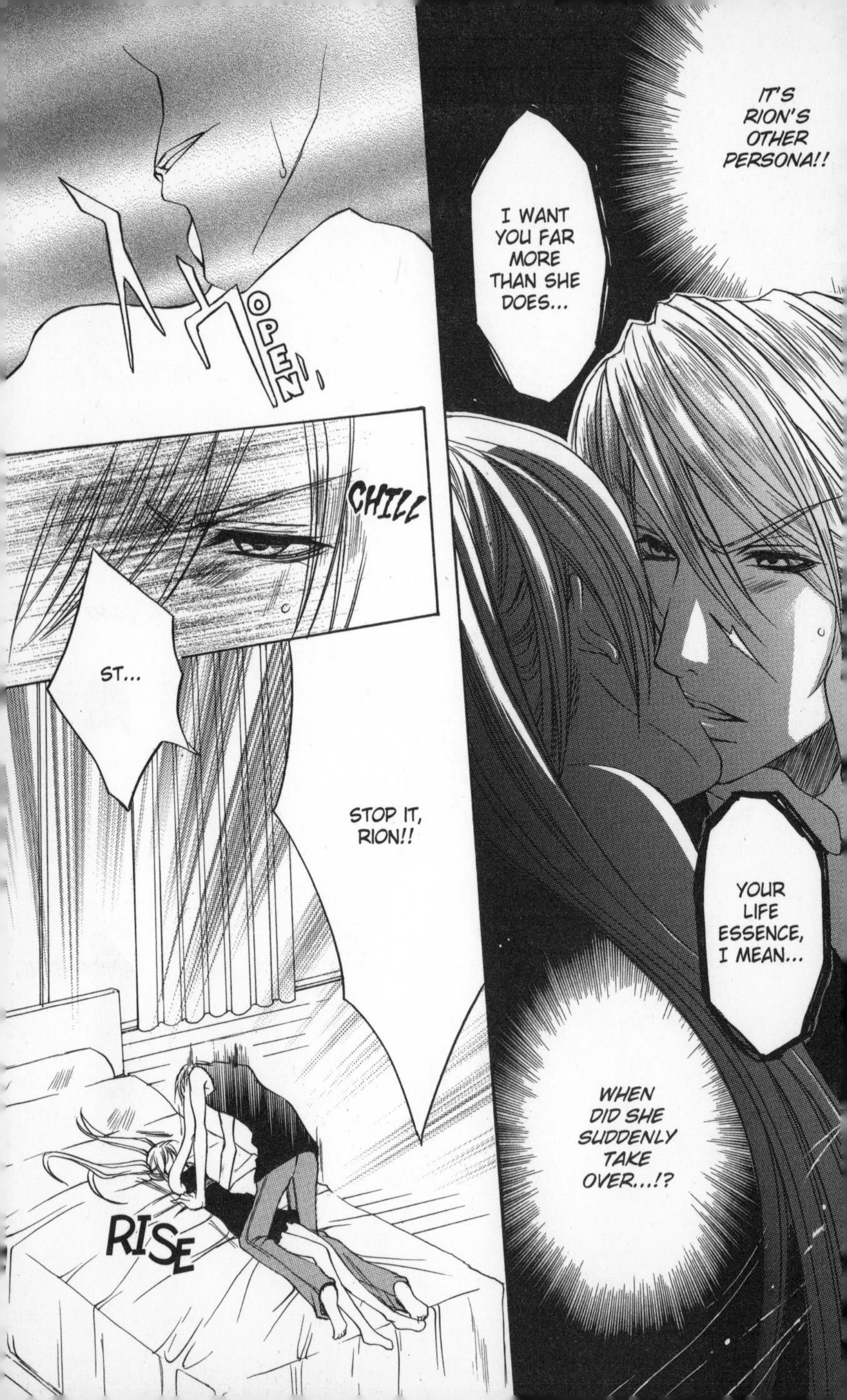
IT'S RION'S OTHER PERSONA!!
I WANT YOU FAR MORE THAN SHE DOES...
YOUR LIFE ESSENCE, I MEAN...
WHEN DID SHE SUDDENLY TAKE OVER...!?
OPEN
CHILL
ST...
STOP IT, RION!!
RISE

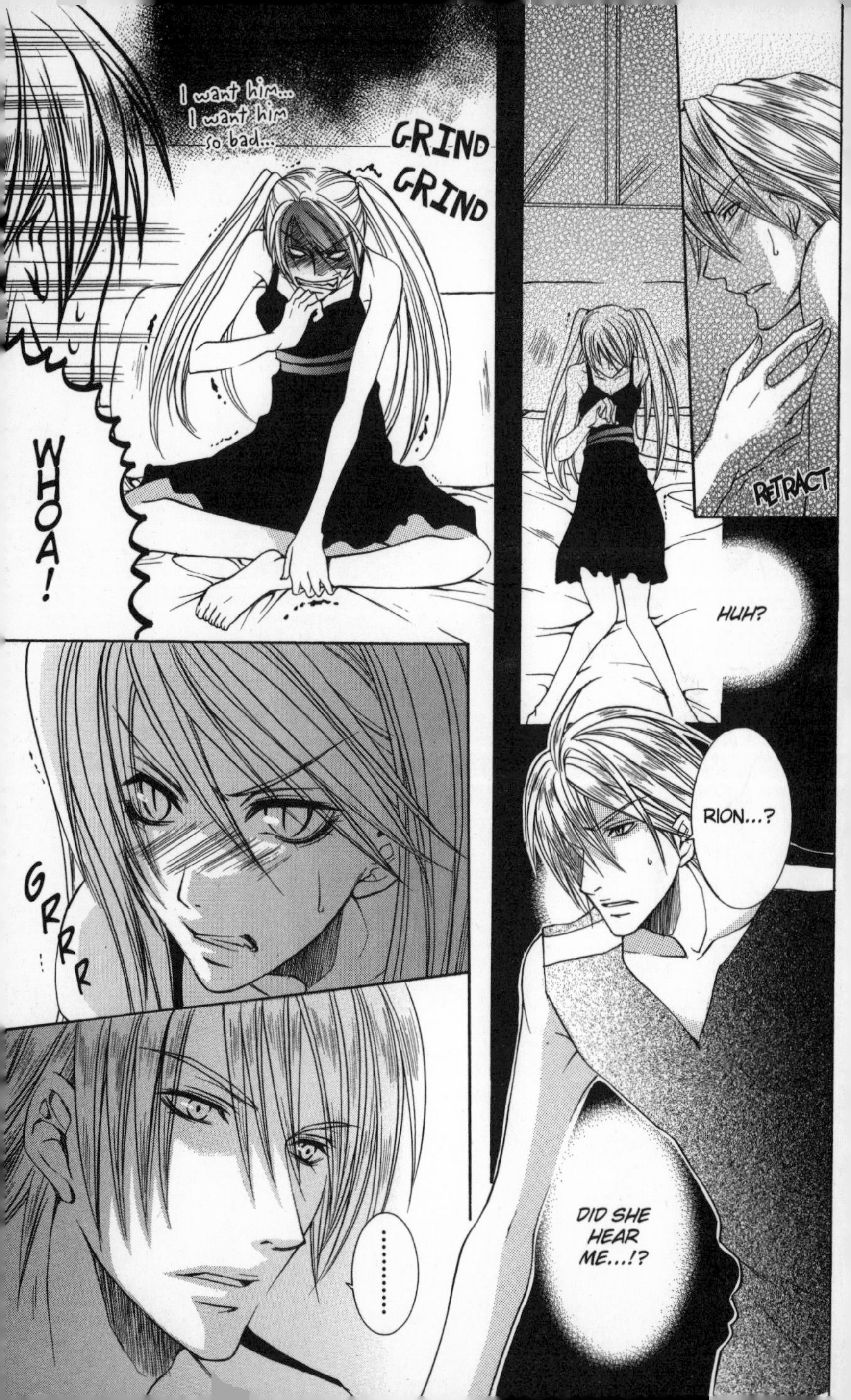
RETRACT
HUH?
RION...?
DID SHE HEAR ME...!?
GRIND GRIND
I want him... I want him so bad...
WHOA!
GRRR
.........

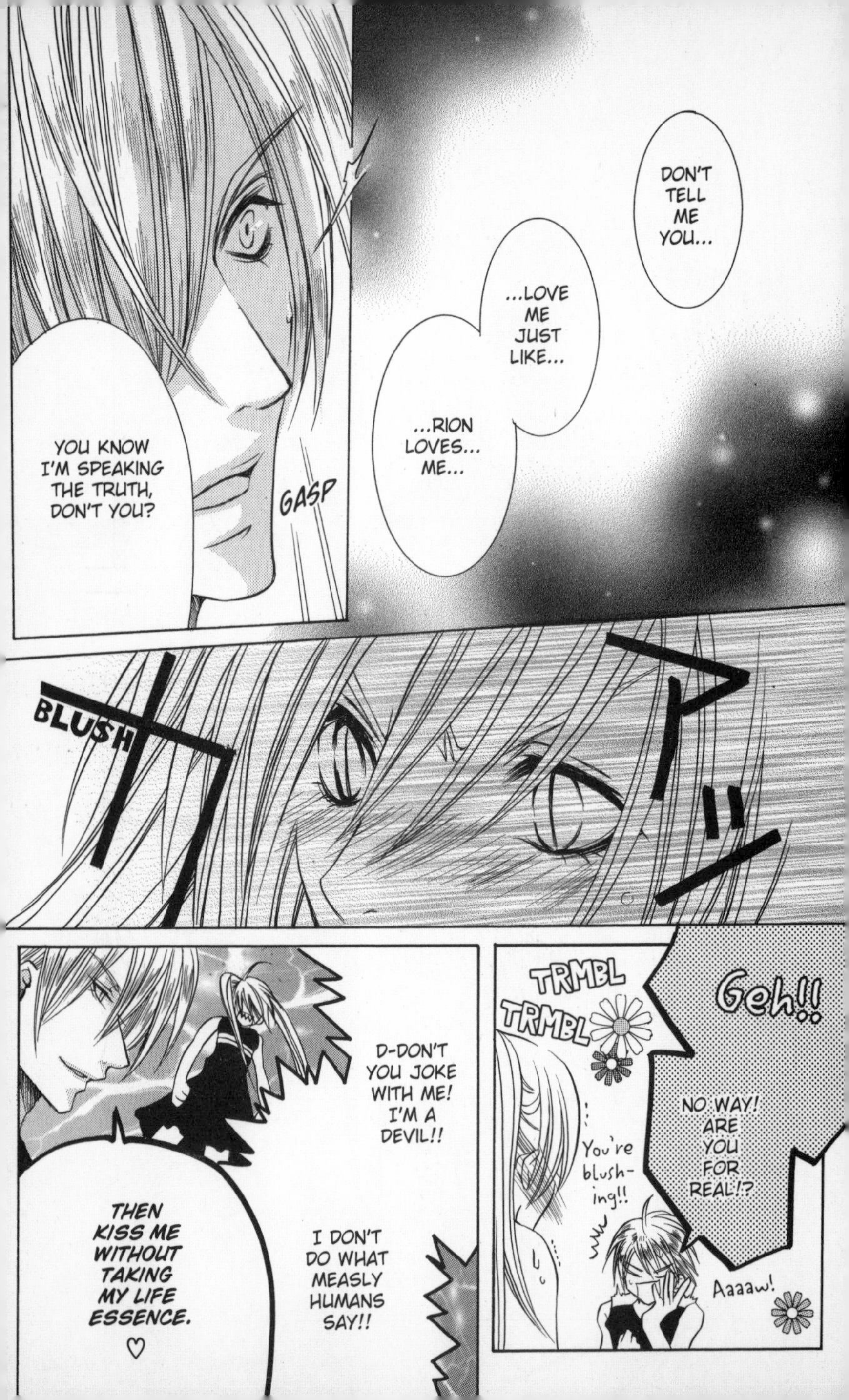
DON'T TELL ME YOU...
...LOVE ME JUST LIKE...
...RION LOVES... ME...
GASP
YOU KNOW I'M SPEAKING THE TRUTH, DON'T YOU?
BLUSH
Geh!!
TRMBL TRMBL
NO WAY! ARE YOU FOR REAL!?
You're blush-ing!!
Aaaaw!
D-DON'T YOU JOKE WITH ME! I'M A DEVIL!!
I DON'T DO WHAT MEASLY HUMANS SAY!!
THEN KISS ME WITHOUT TAKING MY LIFE ESSENCE. ♡

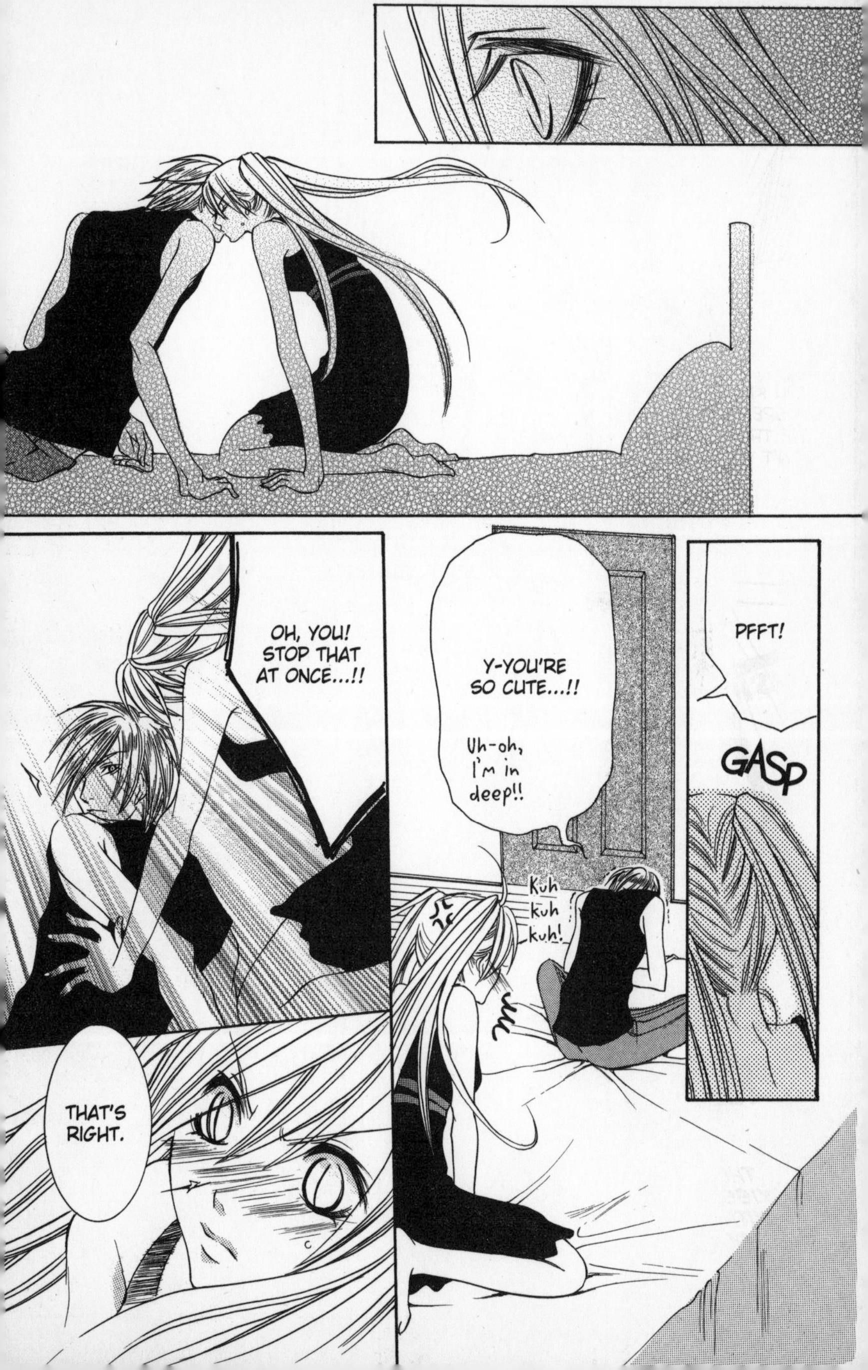
PFFT!
GASP
Y-YOU'RE SO CUTE...!!
Uh-oh, I'm in deep!!
Kuh kuh kuh!
OH, YOU! STOP THAT AT ONCE...!!
THAT'S RIGHT.

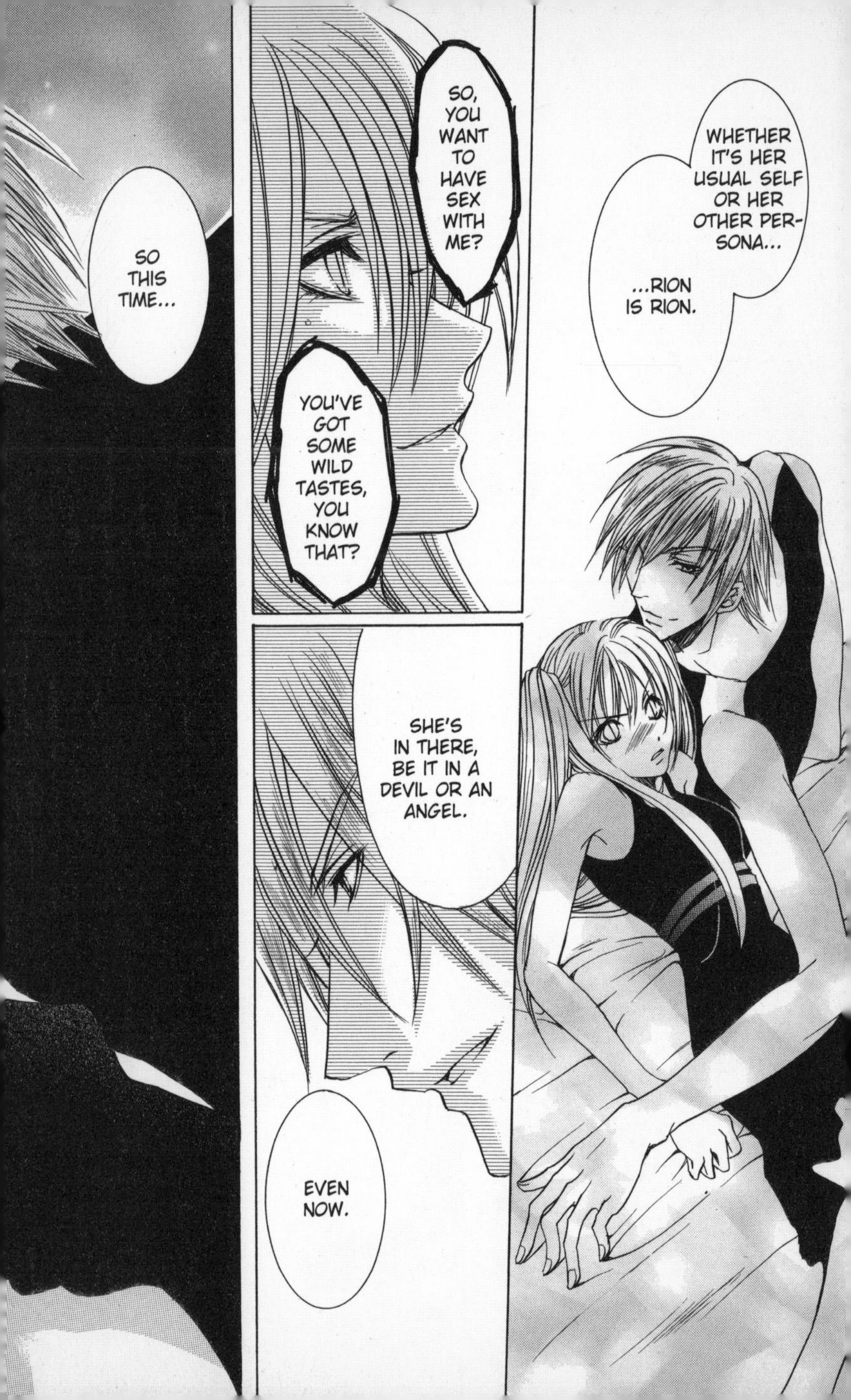
WHETHER IT'S HER USUAL SELF OR HER OTHER PER-SONA...
...RION IS RION.
SO, YOU WANT TO HAVE SEX WITH ME?
YOU'VE GOT SOME WILD TASTES, YOU KNOW THAT?
SHE'S IN THERE, BE IT IN A DEVIL OR AN ANGEL.
EVEN NOW.
SO THIS TIME...

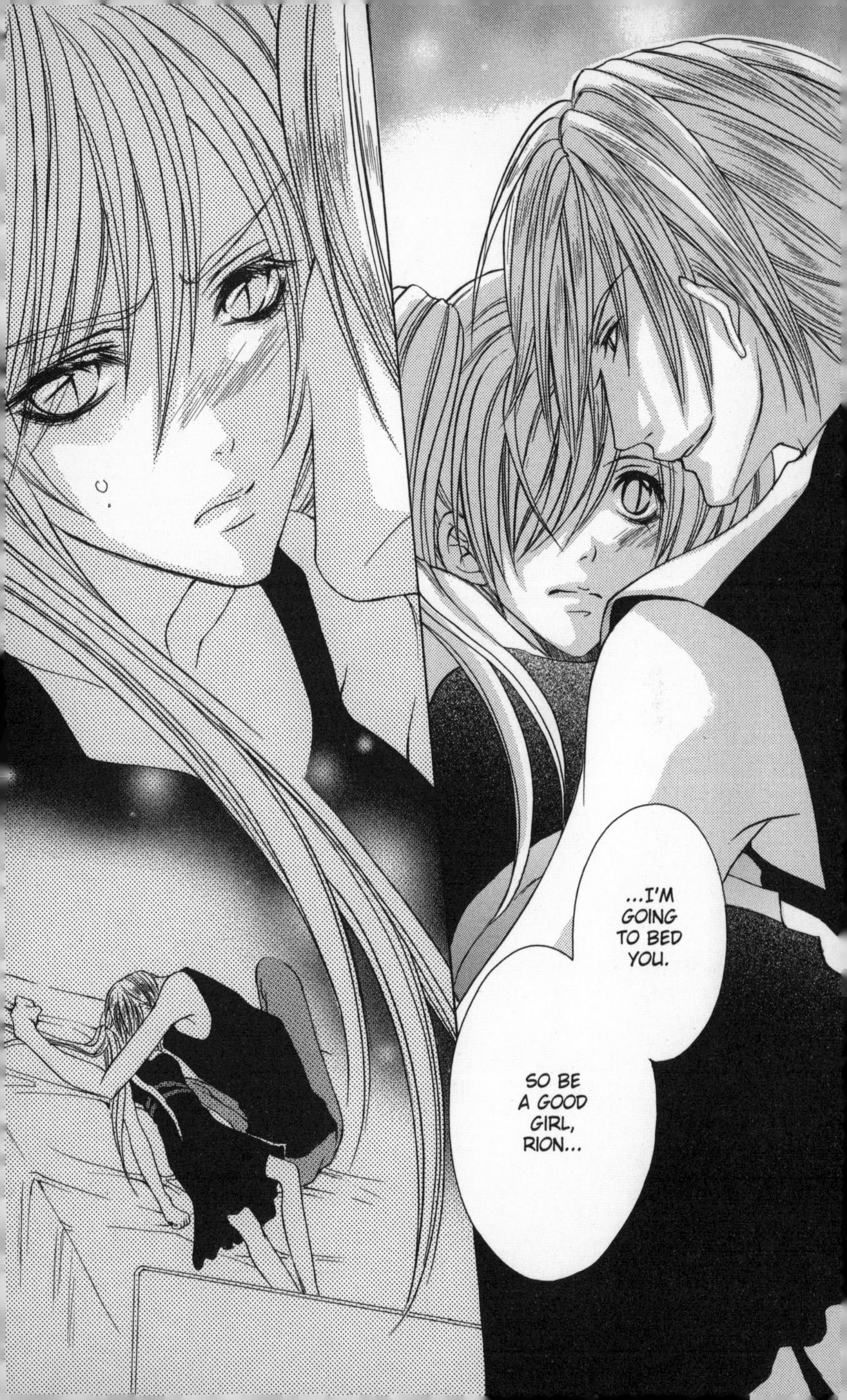
...I'M GOING TO BED YOU.
SO BE A GOOD GIRL, RION...

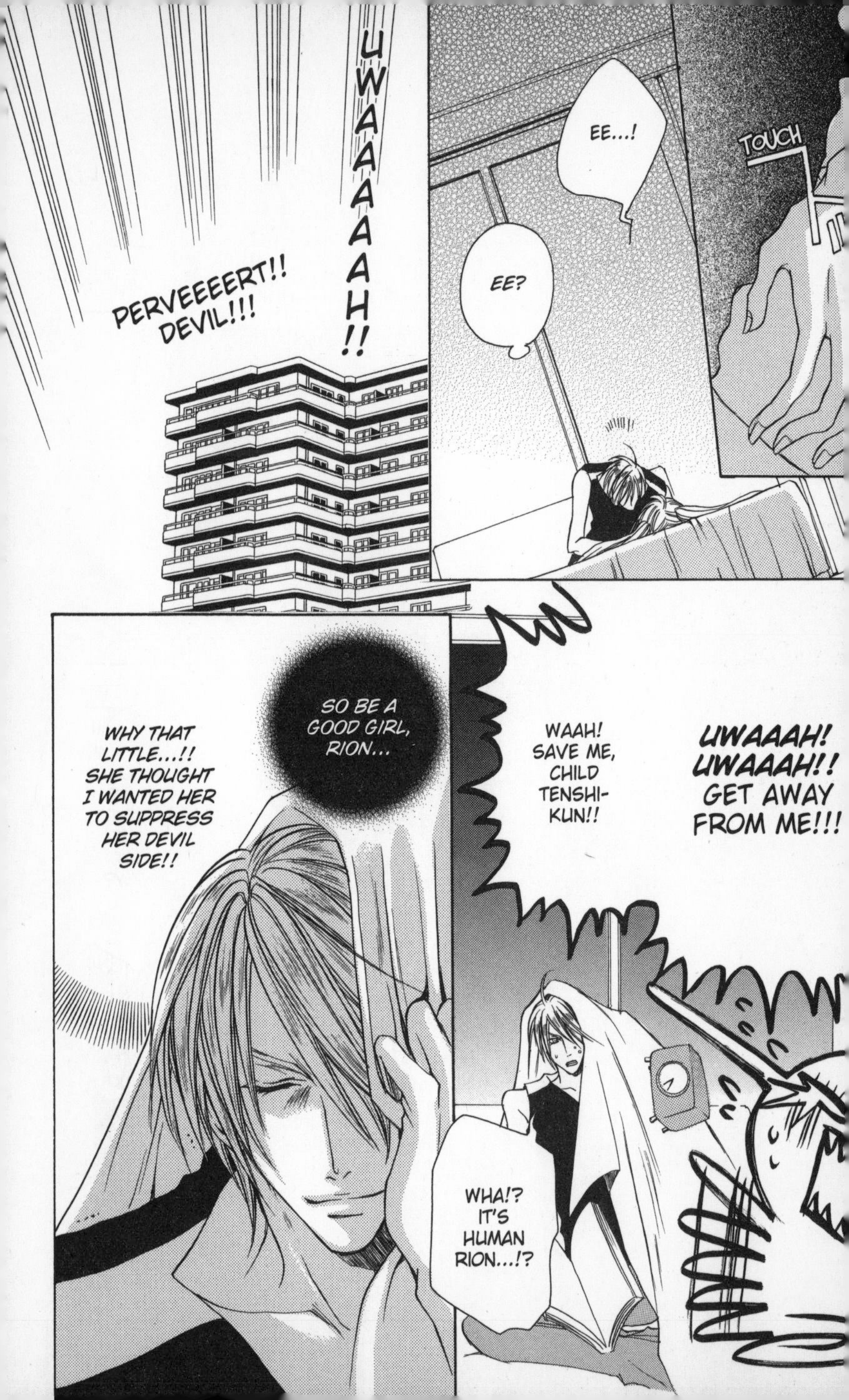
TOUCH
EE...!
EE?
UWAAAAAAAH!!
PERVEEEERT!! DEVIL!!!
UWAAAH! UWAAAH!! GET AWAY FROM ME!!!
WAAH! SAVE ME, CHILD TENSHI-KUN!!
WHA!? IT'S HUMAN RION...!?
SO BE A GOOD GIRL, RION...
WHY THAT LITTLE...!! SHE THOUGHT I WANTED HER TO SUPPRESS HER DEVIL SIDE!!

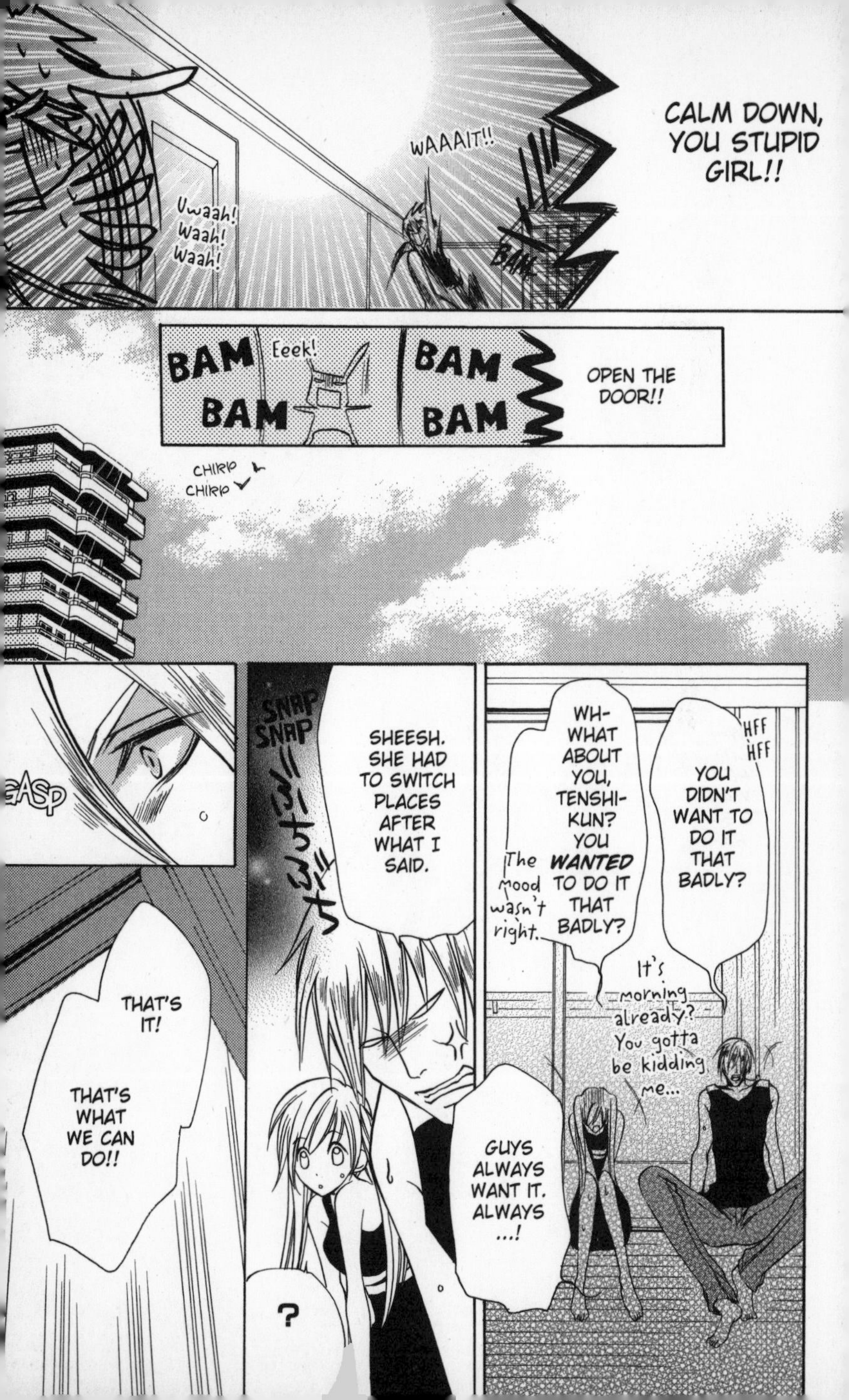

CALM DOWN, YOU STUPID GIRL!!
WAAAIT!!
BAM
Uwaah! Waah! Waah!
OPEN THE DOOR!!
BAM BAM
Eeek!
BAM BAM
CHIRP CHIRP
HFF HFF
YOU DIDN'T WANT TO DO IT THAT BADLY?
WH- WHAT ABOUT YOU, TENSHI-KUN? YOU *WANTED* TO DO IT THAT BADLY?
The mood wasn't right.
It's morning already? You gotta be kidding me...
SHEESH. SHE HAD TO SWITCH PLACES AFTER WHAT I SAID.
SNAP SNAP
GUYS ALWAYS WANT IT. ALWAYS ...!
?
GASP
THAT'S IT!
THAT'S WHAT WE CAN DO!!

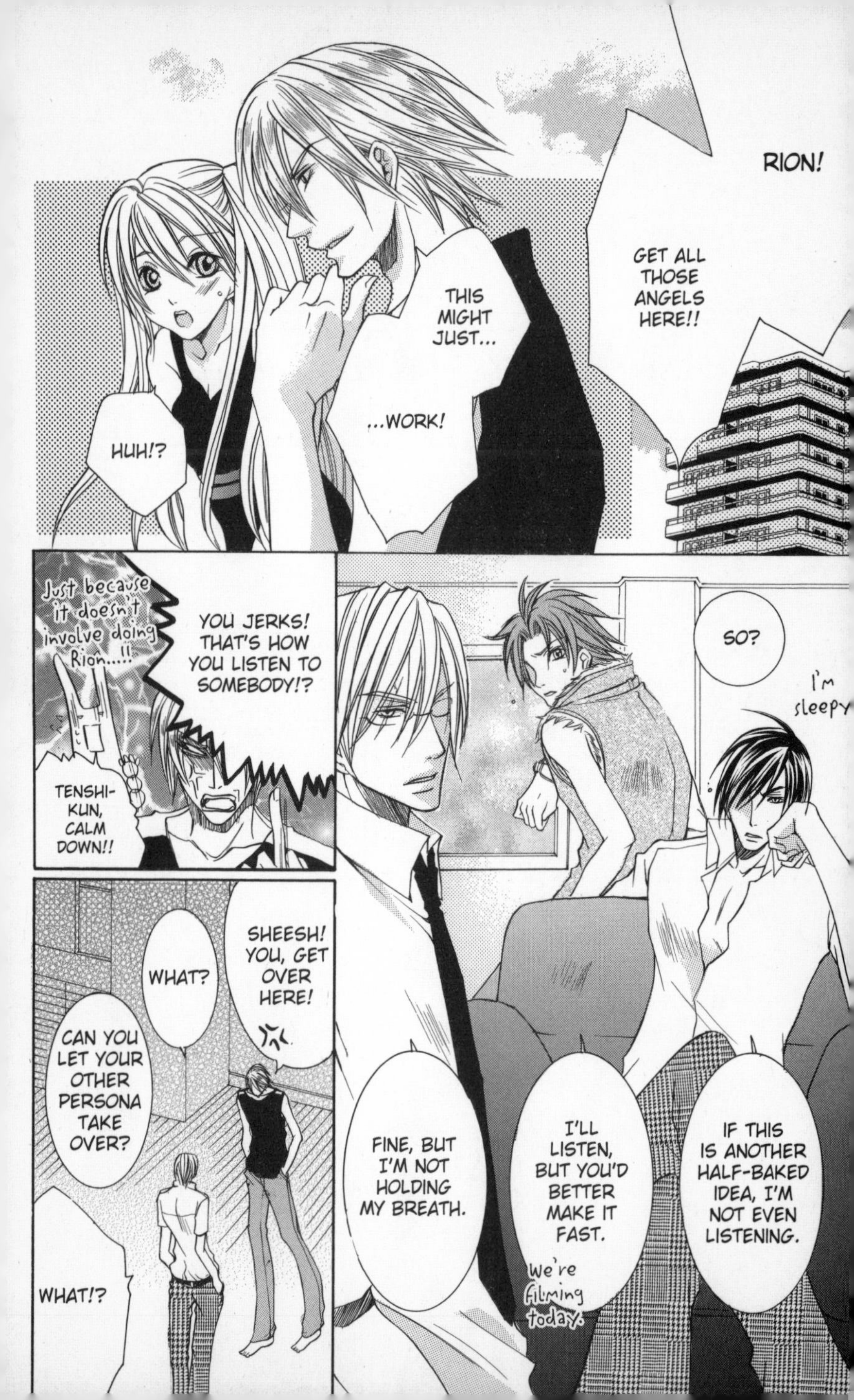
RION!
GET ALL THOSE ANGELS HERE!!
THIS MIGHT JUST...
...WORK!
HUH!?
SO?
I'm sleepy
IF THIS IS ANOTHER HALF-BAKED IDEA, I'M NOT EVEN LISTENING.
I'LL LISTEN, BUT YOU'D BETTER MAKE IT FAST.
We're filming today.
FINE, BUT I'M NOT HOLDING MY BREATH.
YOU JERKS! THAT'S HOW YOU LISTEN TO SOMEBODY!?
Just because it doesn't involve doing Rion....!!
TENSHI-KUN, CALM DOWN!!
SHEESH! YOU, GET OVER HERE!
WHAT?
CAN YOU LET YOUR OTHER PERSONA TAKE OVER?
WHAT!?

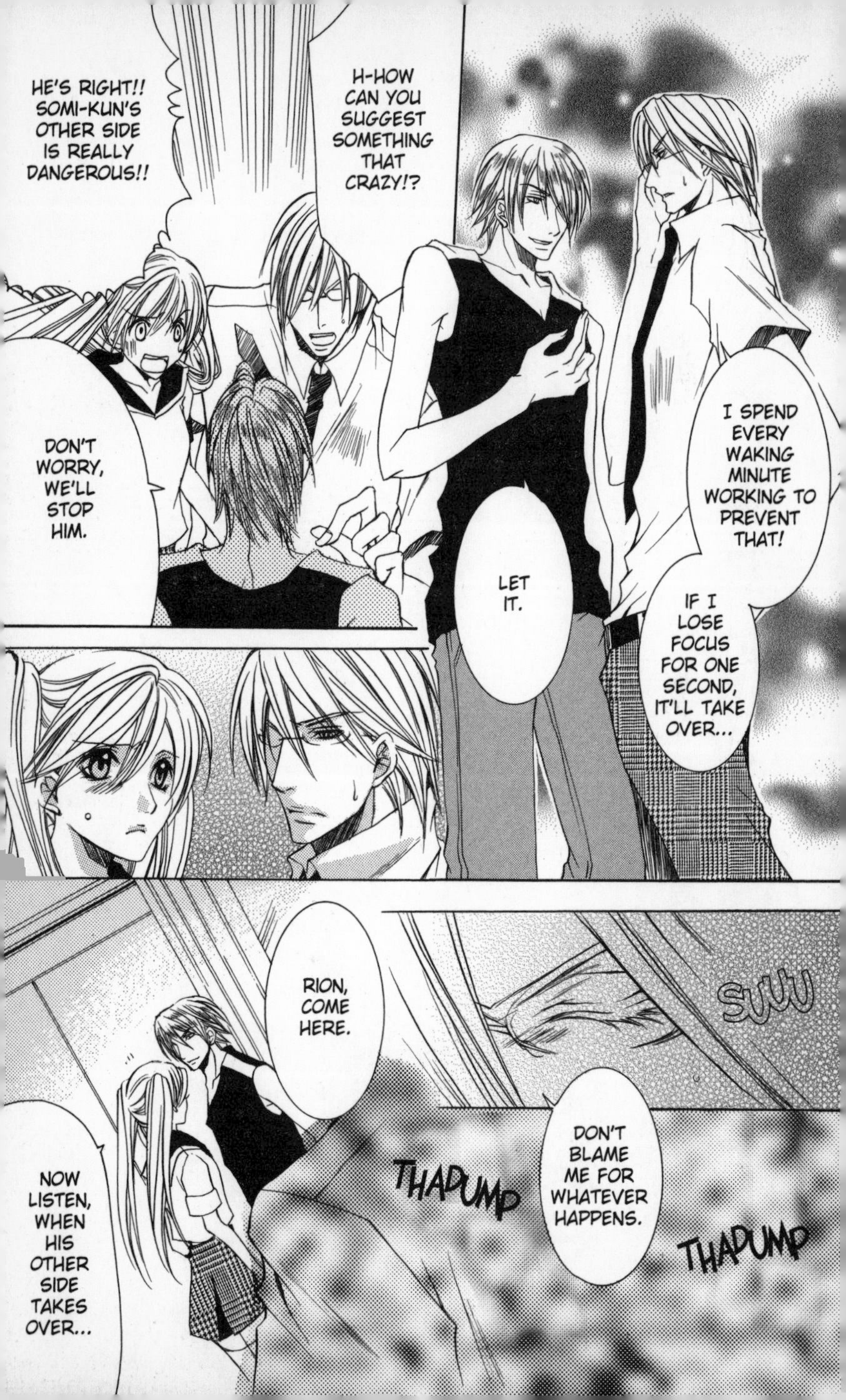
I SPEND EVERY WAKING MINUTE WORKING TO PREVENT THAT!
IF I LOSE FOCUS FOR ONE SECOND, IT'LL TAKE OVER...
LET IT.
H-HOW CAN YOU SUGGEST SOMETHING THAT CRAZY!?
HE'S RIGHT!! SOMI-KUN'S OTHER SIDE IS REALLY DANGEROUS!!
DON'T WORRY, WE'LL STOP HIM.
SUUU
DON'T BLAME ME FOR WHATEVER HAPPENS.
THADUMP
THADUMP
RION, COME HERE.
NOW LISTEN, WHEN HIS OTHER SIDE TAKES OVER...

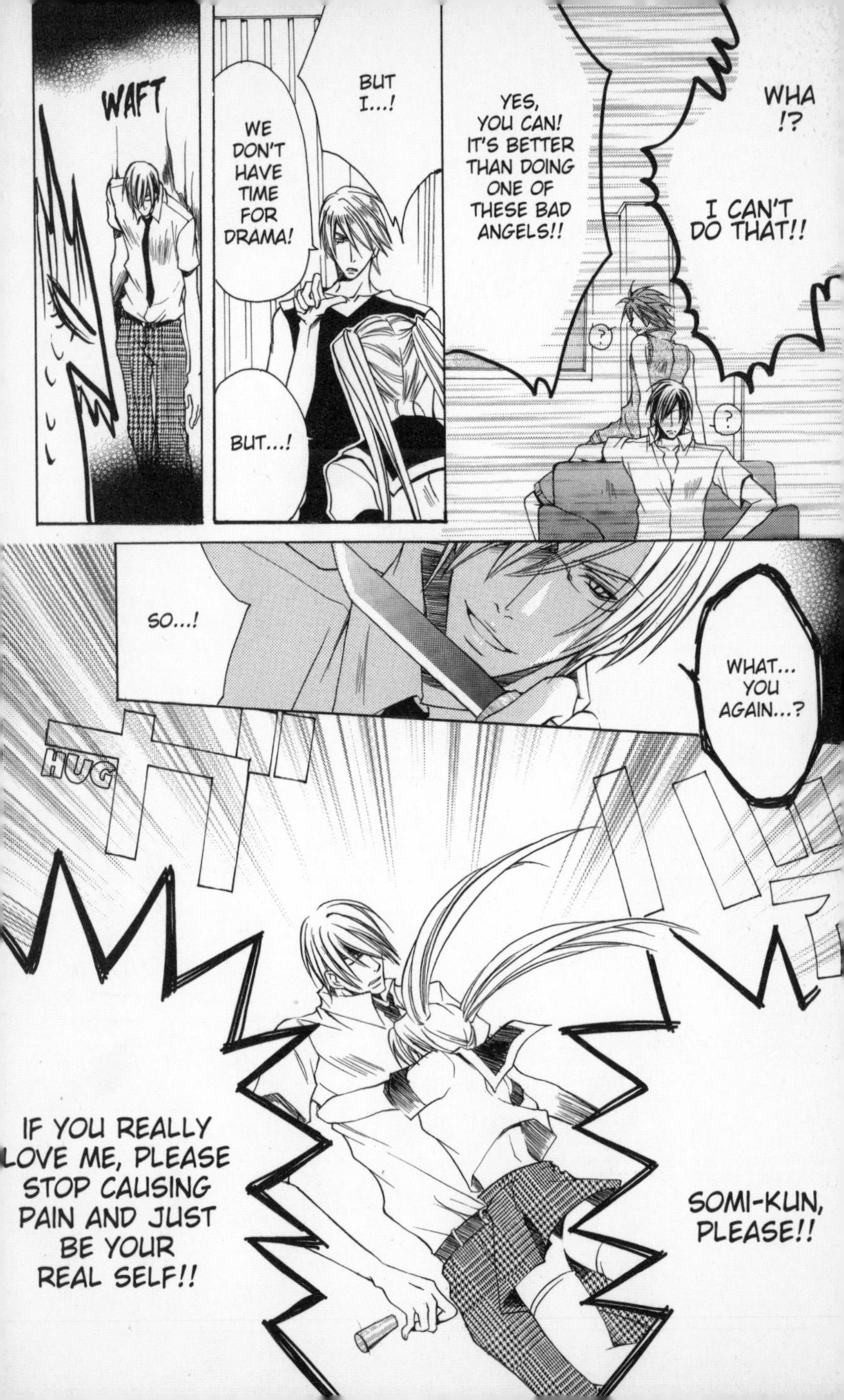
WHA !?
I CAN'T DO THAT!!
YES, YOU CAN! IT'S BETTER THAN DOING ONE OF THESE BAD ANGELS!!
BUT I...!
WE DON'T HAVE TIME FOR DRAMA!
BUT...!
WAFT
WHAT... YOU AGAIN...?
SO...!
HUG
SOMI-KUN, PLEASE!!
IF YOU REALLY LOVE ME, PLEASE STOP CAUSING PAIN AND JUST BE YOUR REAL SELF!!

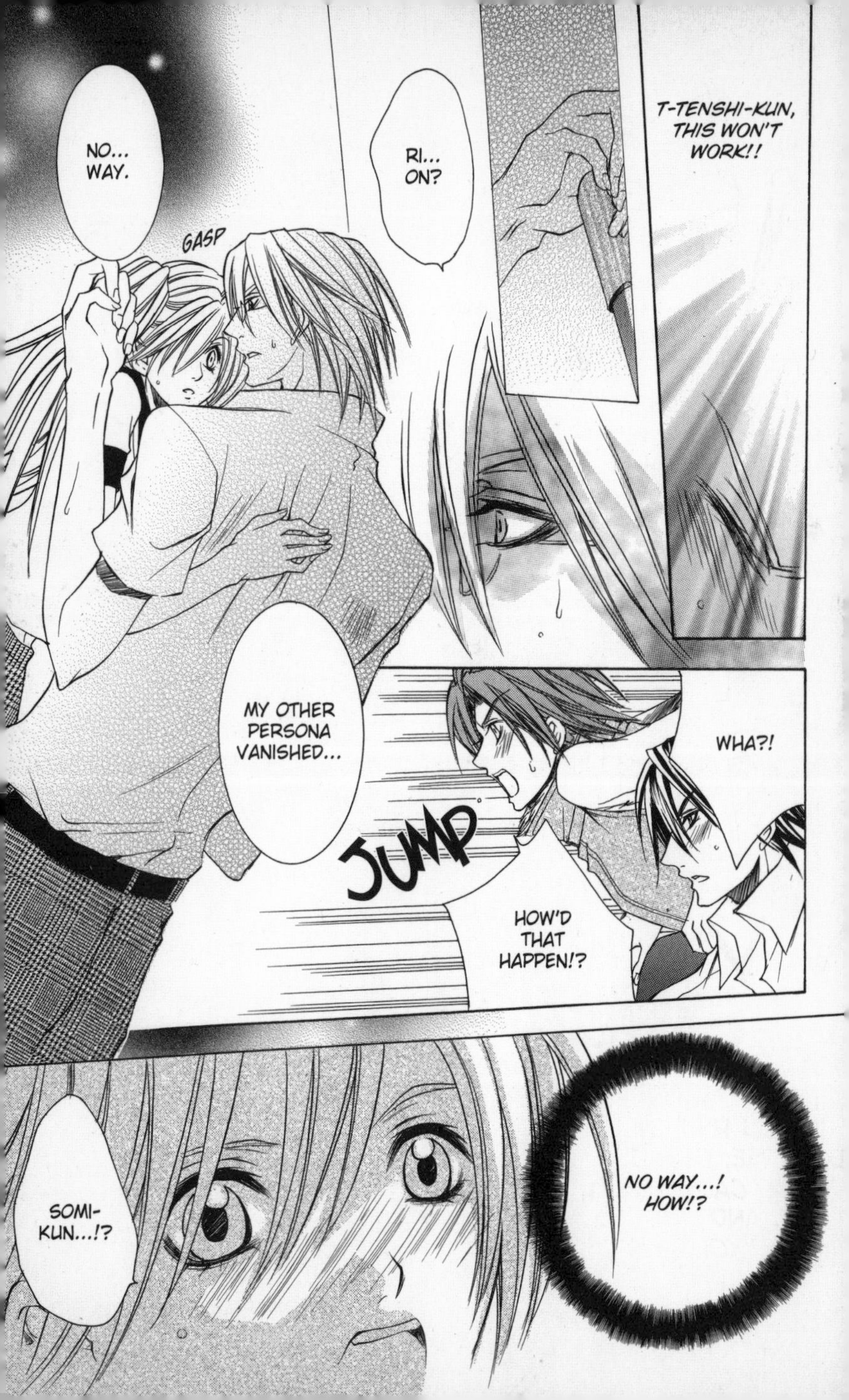
T-TENSHI-KUN, THIS WON'T WORK!!
RI... ON?
WHA?!
JUMP
HOW'D THAT HAPPEN!?
NO... WAY.
GASP
MY OTHER PERSONA VANISHED...
NO WAY...! HOW!?
SOMI-KUN...!?

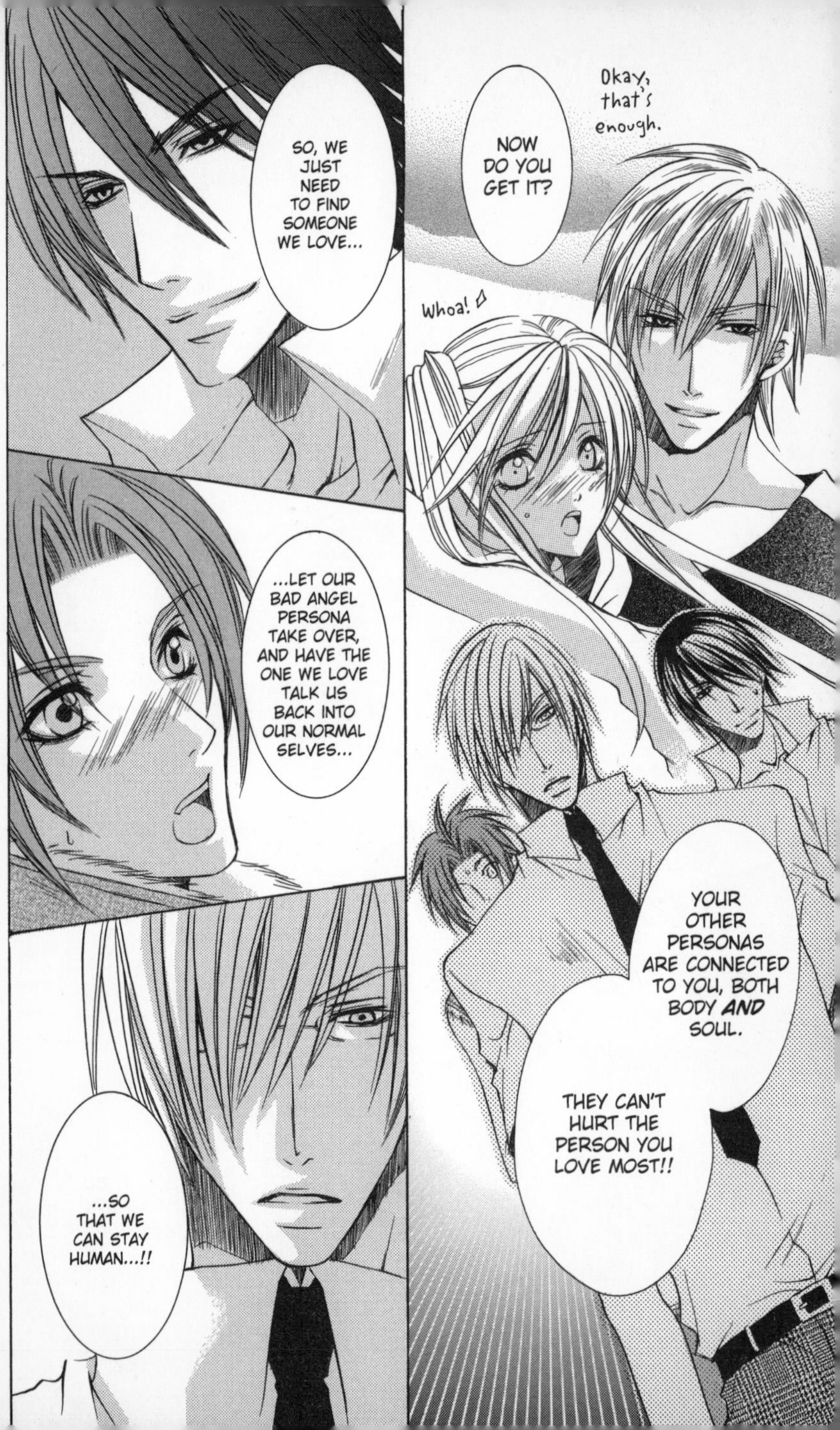

NOW DO YOU GET IT?
Okay, that's enough.
Whoa!
YOUR OTHER PERSONAS ARE CONNECTED TO YOU, BOTH BODY AND SOUL.
THEY CAN'T HURT THE PERSON YOU LOVE MOST!!
SO, WE JUST NEED TO FIND SOMEONE WE LOVE...
...LET OUR BAD ANGEL PERSONA TAKE OVER, AND HAVE THE ONE WE LOVE TALK US BACK INTO OUR NORMAL SELVES...
...SO THAT WE CAN STAY HUMAN...!!

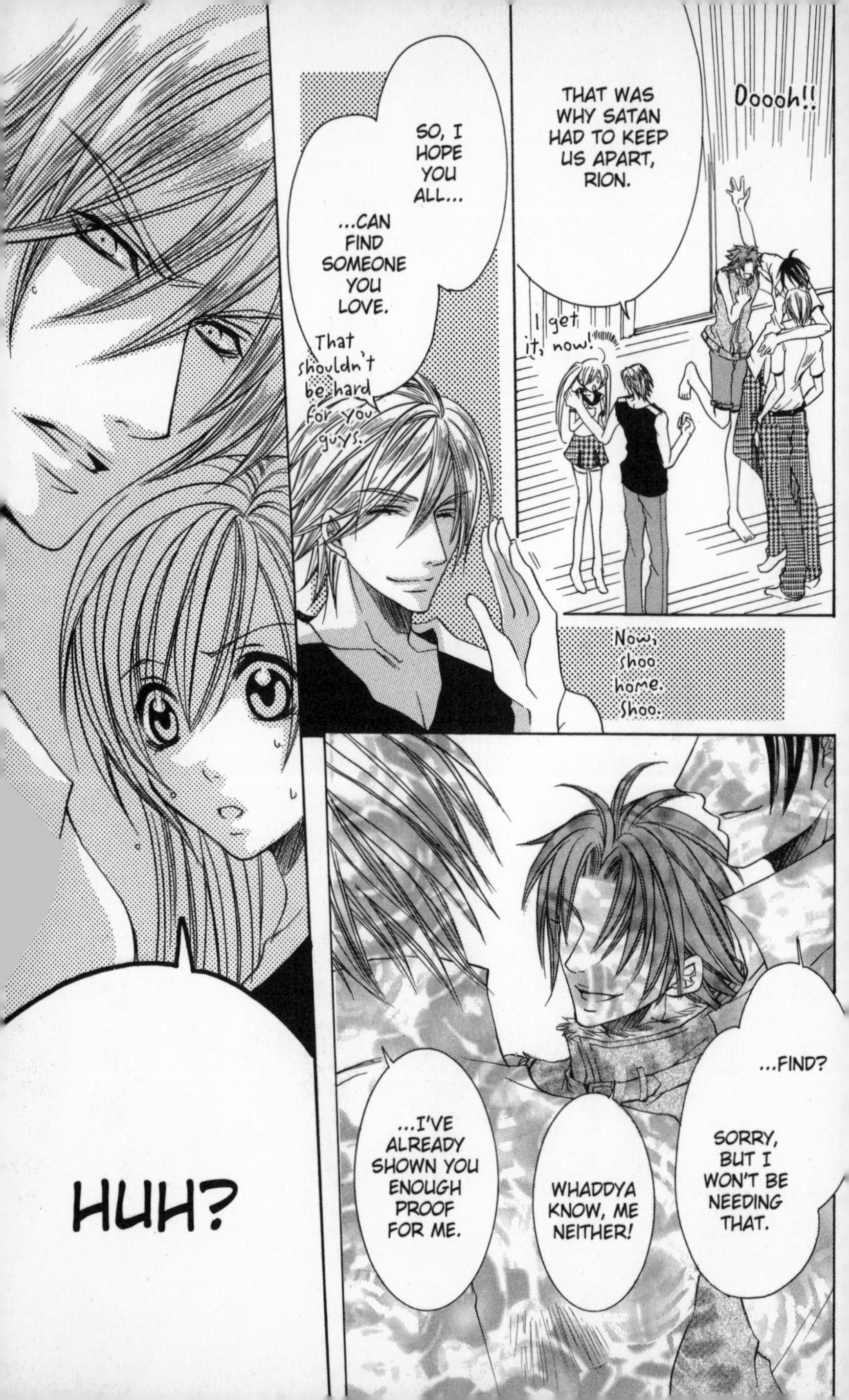
Ooooh!!
THAT WAS WHY SATAN HAD TO KEEP US APART, RION.
I get it, now!
SO, I HOPE YOU ALL...
...CAN FIND SOMEONE YOU LOVE.
That shouldn't be hard for you guys.
Now, shoo home. Shoo.
...FIND?
SORRY, BUT I WON'T BE NEEDING THAT.
WHADDYA KNOW, ME NEITHER!
...I'VE ALREADY SHOWN YOU ENOUGH PROOF FOR ME.
HUH?

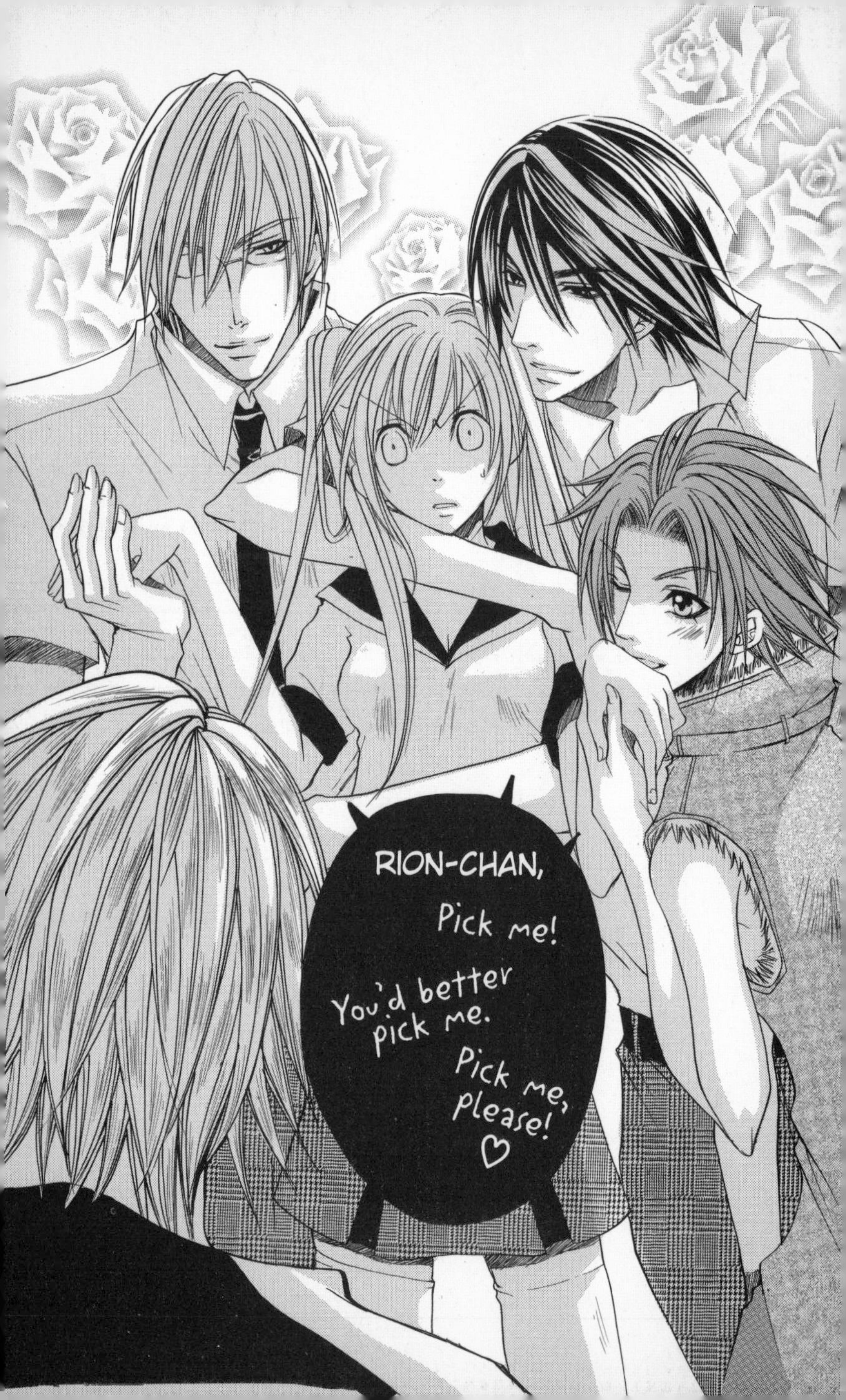
RION-CHAN,
Pick me!
You'd better pick me.
Pick me, please! ♡

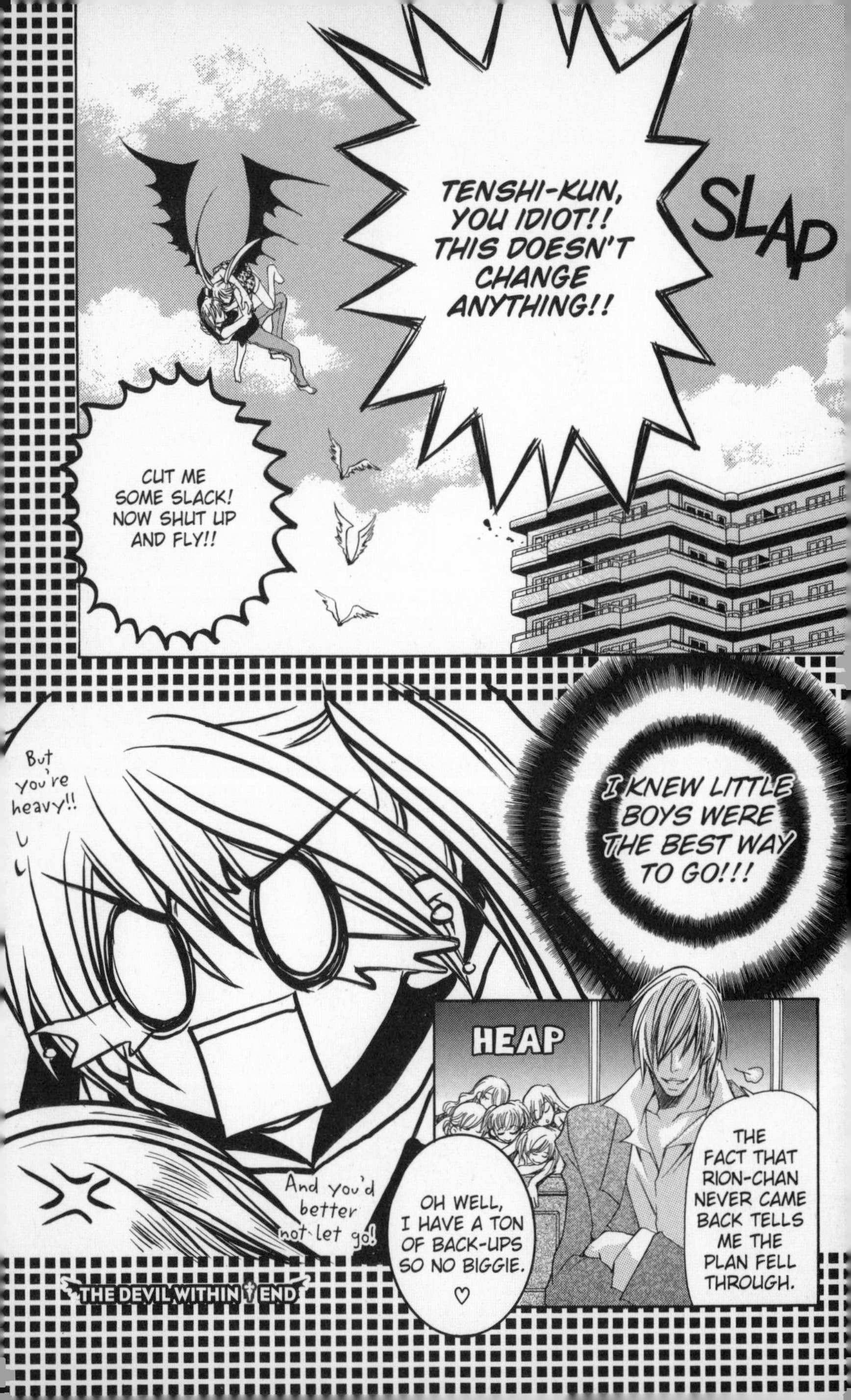
SLAP
TENSHI-KUN, YOU IDIOT!! THIS DOESN'T CHANGE ANYTHING!!
CUT ME SOME SLACK! NOW SHUT UP AND FLY!!
I KNEW LITTLE BOYS WERE THE BEST WAY TO GO!!!
HEAP
THE FACT THAT RION-CHAN NEVER CAME BACK TELLS ME THE PLAN FELL THROUGH.
OH WELL, I HAVE A TON OF BACK-UPS SO NO BIGGIE. ♡
But you're heavy!!
And you'd better not let go!
THE DEVIL WITHIN END

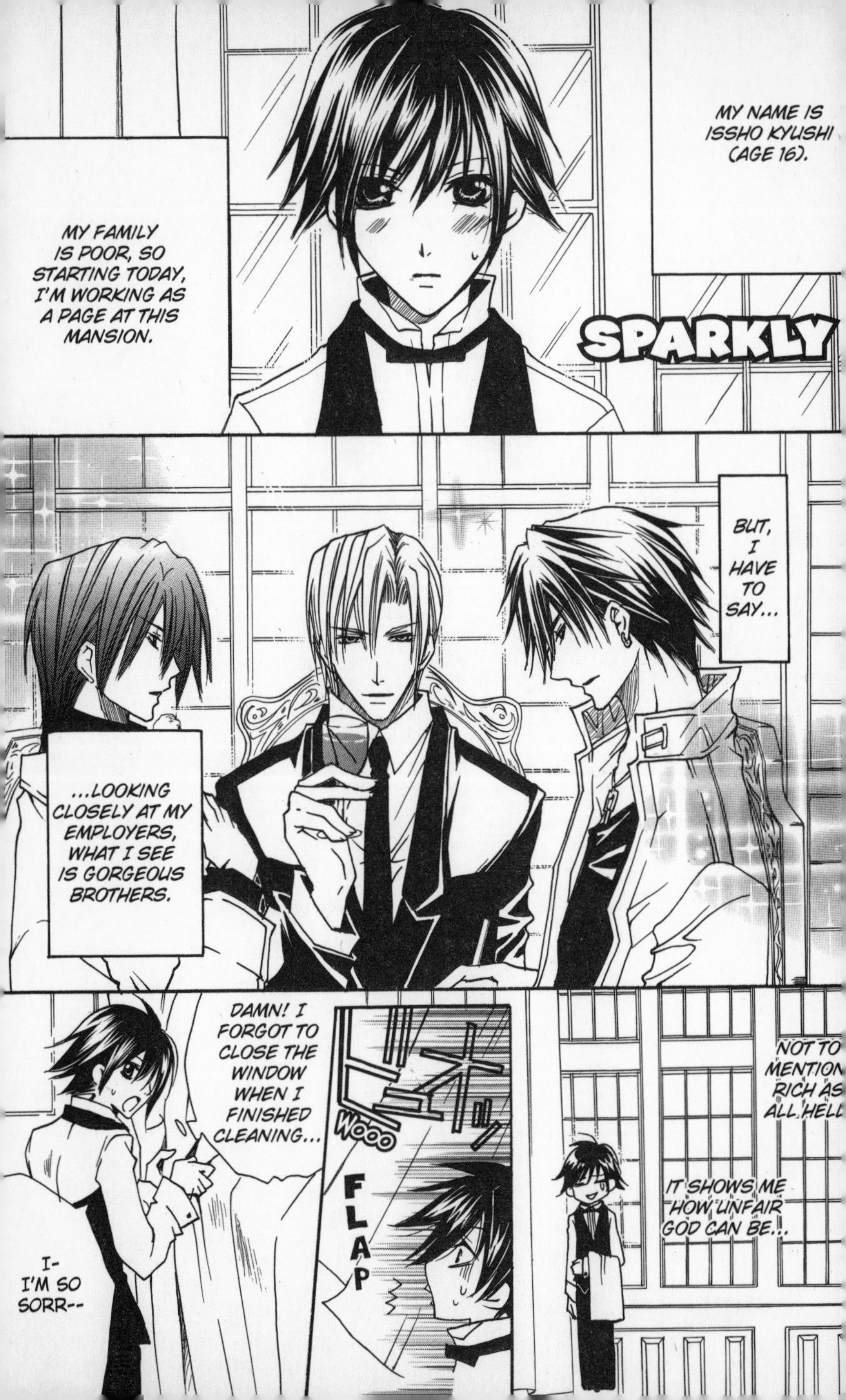
MY NAME IS ISSHO KYUSHI (AGE 16).
MY FAMILY IS POOR, SO STARTING TODAY, I'M WORKING AS A PAGE AT THIS MANSION.
SPARKLY
BUT, I HAVE TO SAY...
...LOOKING CLOSELY AT MY EMPLOYERS, WHAT I SEE IS GORGEOUS BROTHERS.
NOT TO MENTION RICH AS ALL HELL.
IT SHOWS ME HOW UNFAIR GOD CAN BE...
WOOO
FLAP
DAMN! I FORGOT TO CLOSE THE WINDOW WHEN I FINISHED CLEANING...
I- I'M SO SORR--

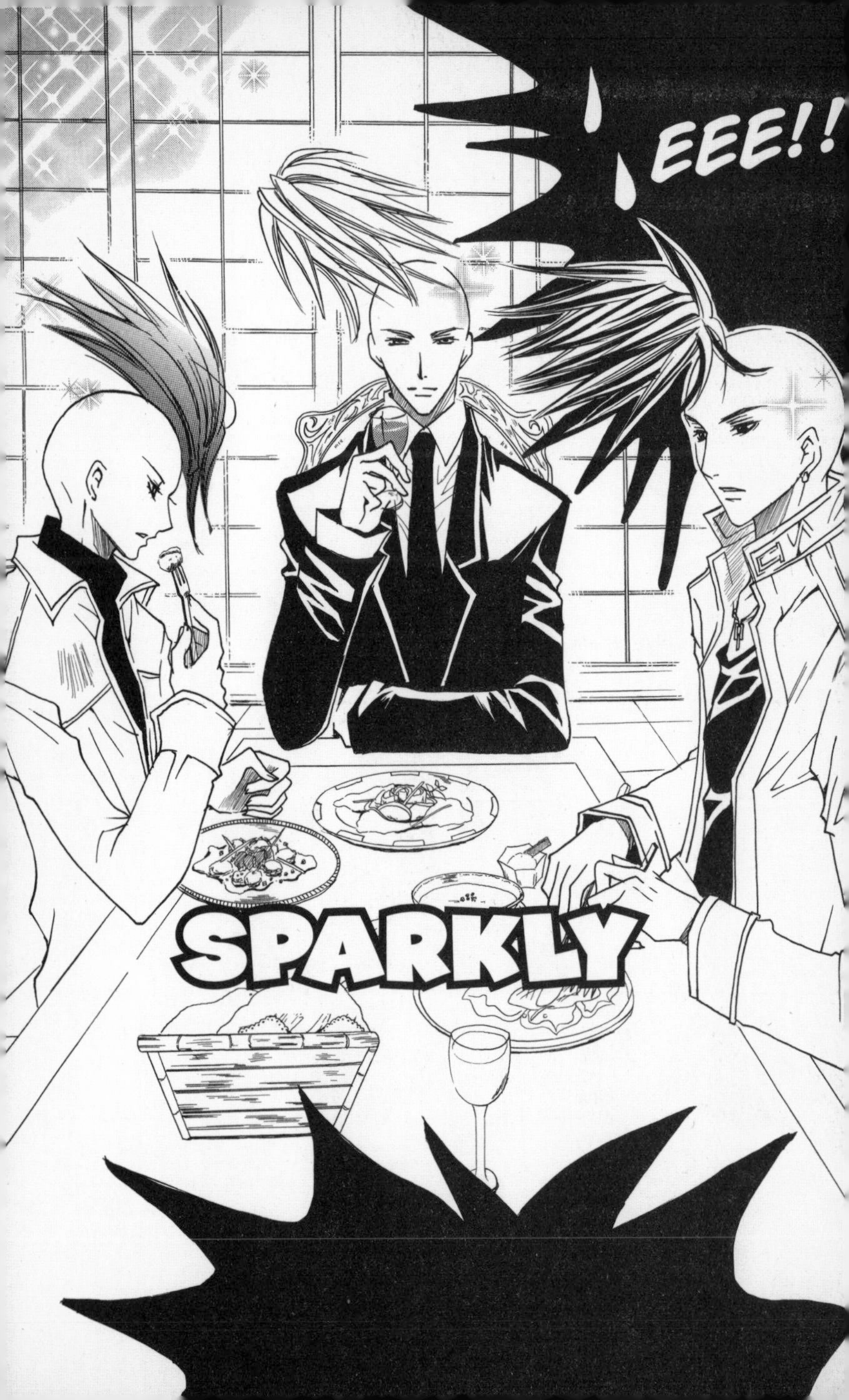
EEE!!
SPARKLY

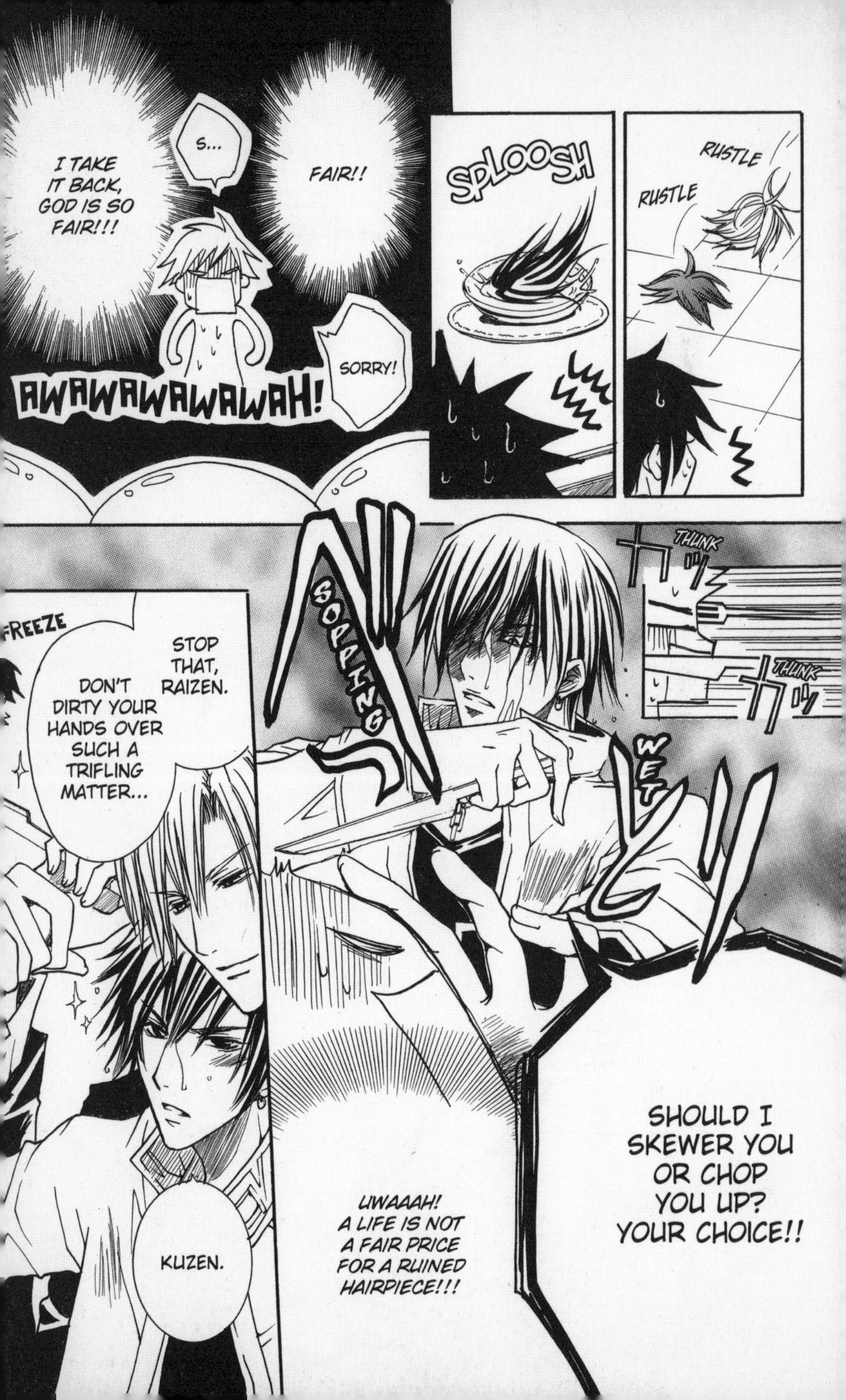
RUSTLE
RUSTLE
SPLOOSH
S...
FAIR!!
I TAKE IT BACK, GOD IS SO FAIR!!!
SORRY!
AWAWAWAWAWAWAH!
THUNK
THUNK
WET
SOPPING
SHOULD I SKEWER YOU OR CHOP YOU UP? YOUR CHOICE!!
UWAAAH! A LIFE IS NOT A FAIR PRICE FOR A RUINED HAIRPIECE!!!
STOP THAT, RAIZEN.
DON'T DIRTY YOUR HANDS OVER SUCH A TRIFLING MATTER...
FREEZE
KUZEN.

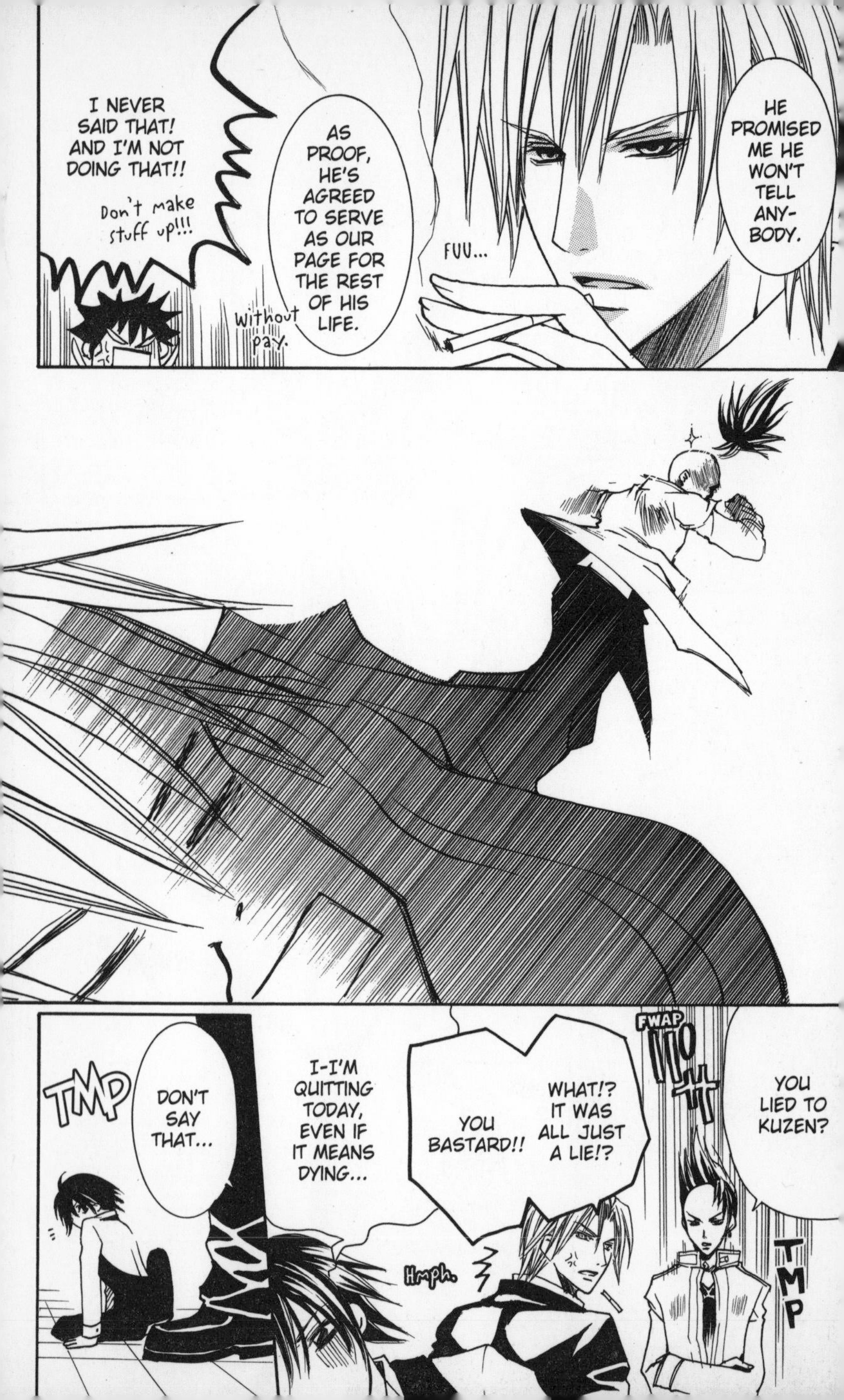
HE PROMISED ME HE WON'T TELL ANY-BODY.
FUU...
AS PROOF, HE'S AGREED TO SERVE AS OUR PAGE FOR THE REST OF HIS LIFE.
Without pay.
I NEVER SAID THAT! AND I'M NOT DOING THAT!!
Don't make stuff up!!!
FWAP
YOU LIED TO KUZEN?
TMP
WHAT!? IT WAS ALL JUST A LIE!?
YOU BASTARD!!
Hmph.
I-I'M QUITTING TODAY, EVEN IF IT MEANS DYING...
DON'T SAY THAT...
TMP

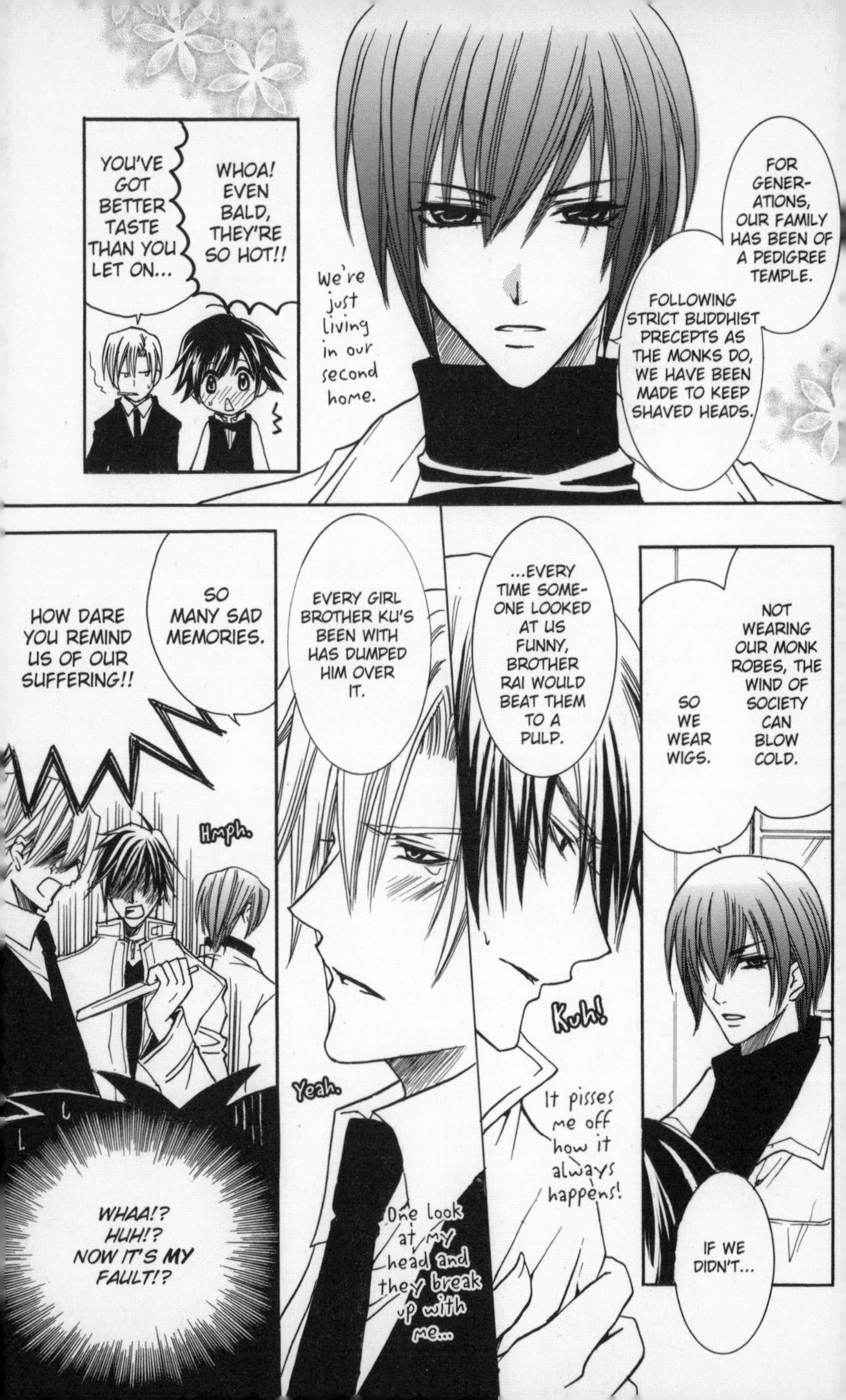

FOR GENERATIONS, OUR FAMILY HAS BEEN OF A PEDIGREE TEMPLE.
FOLLOWING STRICT BUDDHIST PRECEPTS AS THE MONKS DO, WE HAVE BEEN MADE TO KEEP SHAVED HEADS.
We're just living in our second home.
WHOA! EVEN BALD, THEY'RE SO HOT!!
YOU'VE GOT BETTER TASTE THAN YOU LET ON...
NOT WEARING OUR MONK ROBES, THE WIND OF SOCIETY CAN BLOW COLD.
SO WE WEAR WIGS.
IF WE DIDN'T...
...EVERY TIME SOMEONE LOOKED AT US FUNNY, BROTHER RAI WOULD BEAT THEM TO A PULP.
Kuh!
It pisses me off how it always happens!
EVERY GIRL BROTHER KU'S BEEN WITH HAS DUMPED HIM OVER IT.
Yeah.
One look at my head and they break up with me...
SO MANY SAD MEMORIES.
HOW DARE YOU REMIND US OF OUR SUFFERING!!
Hmph.
WHAA!? HUH!? NOW IT'S MY FAULT!?

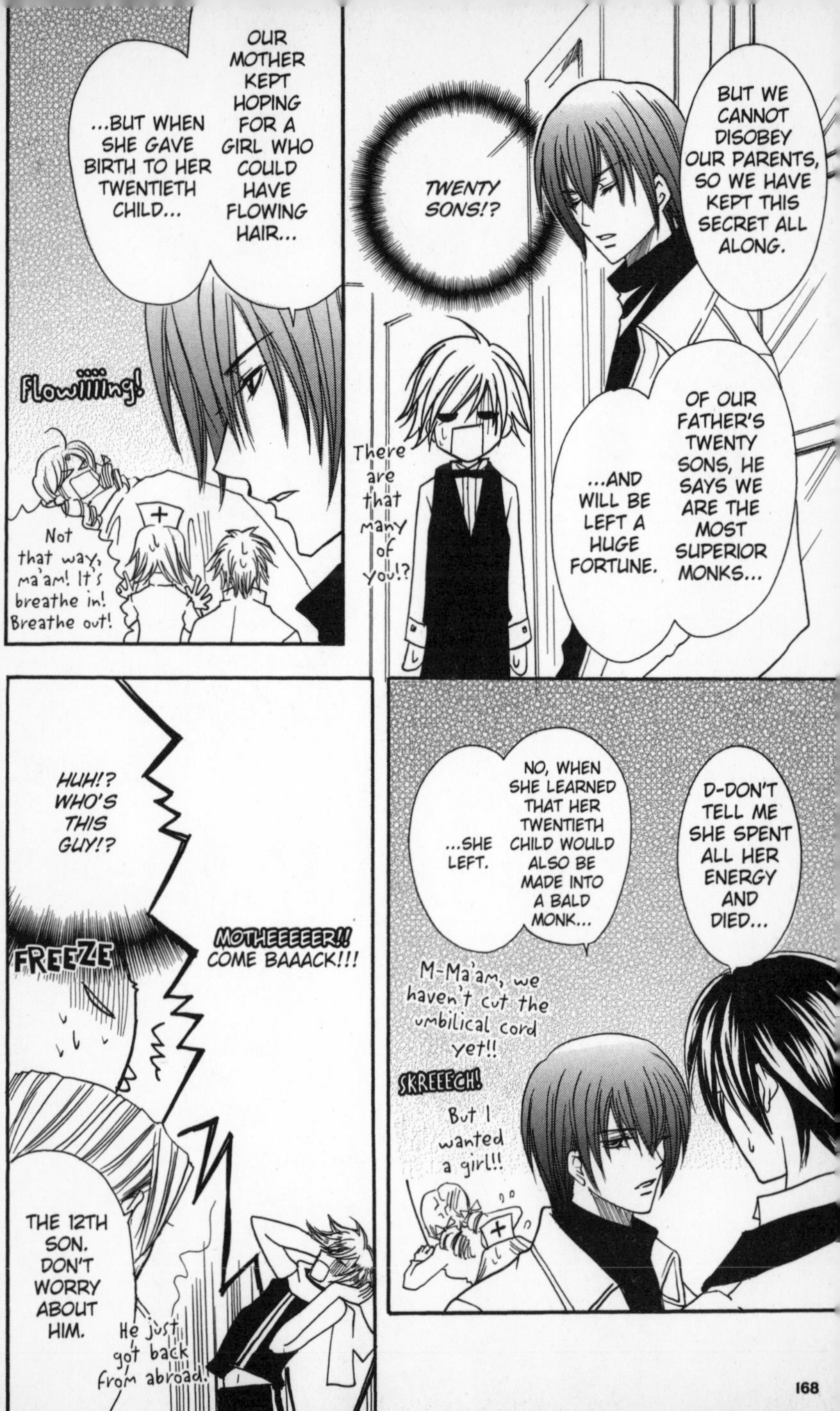
BUT WE CANNOT DISOBEY OUR PARENTS, SO WE HAVE KEPT THIS SECRET ALL ALONG.
TWENTY SONS!?
OF OUR FATHER'S TWENTY SONS, HE SAYS WE ARE THE MOST SUPERIOR MONKS...
...AND WILL BE LEFT A HUGE FORTUNE.
There are that many of you!?
OUR MOTHER KEPT HOPING FOR A GIRL WHO COULD HAVE FLOWING HAIR...
...BUT WHEN SHE GAVE BIRTH TO HER TWENTIETH CHILD...
Flowiiiing!
Not that way, ma'am! It's breathe in! Breathe out!
D-DON'T TELL ME SHE SPENT ALL HER ENERGY AND DIED...
NO, WHEN SHE LEARNED THAT HER TWENTIETH CHILD WOULD ALSO BE MADE INTO A BALD MONK...
...SHE LEFT.
M-Ma'am, we haven't cut the umbilical cord yet!!
SKREEECH!
But I wanted a girl!!
HUH!? WHO'S THIS GUY!?
MOTHEEEEEER!! COME BAAACK!!!
FREEZE
THE 12TH SON. DON'T WORRY ABOUT HIM.
He just got back from abroad.

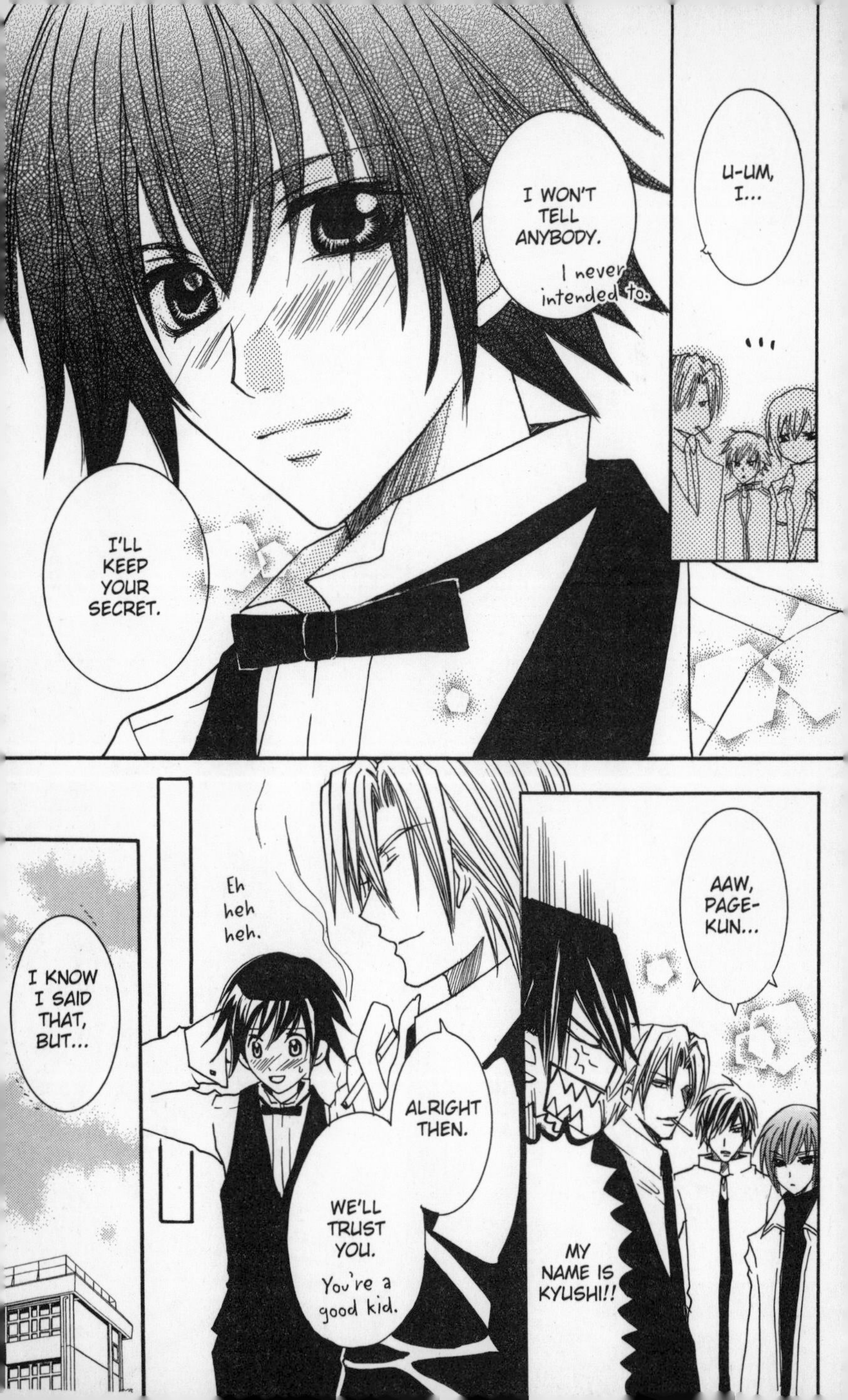
U-UM, I...
I WON'T TELL ANYBODY.
I never intended to.
I'LL KEEP YOUR SECRET.
AAW, PAGE-KUN...
MY NAME IS KYUSHI!!
Eh heh heh.
ALRIGHT THEN.
WE'LL TRUST YOU.
You're a good kid.
I KNOW I SAID THAT, BUT...

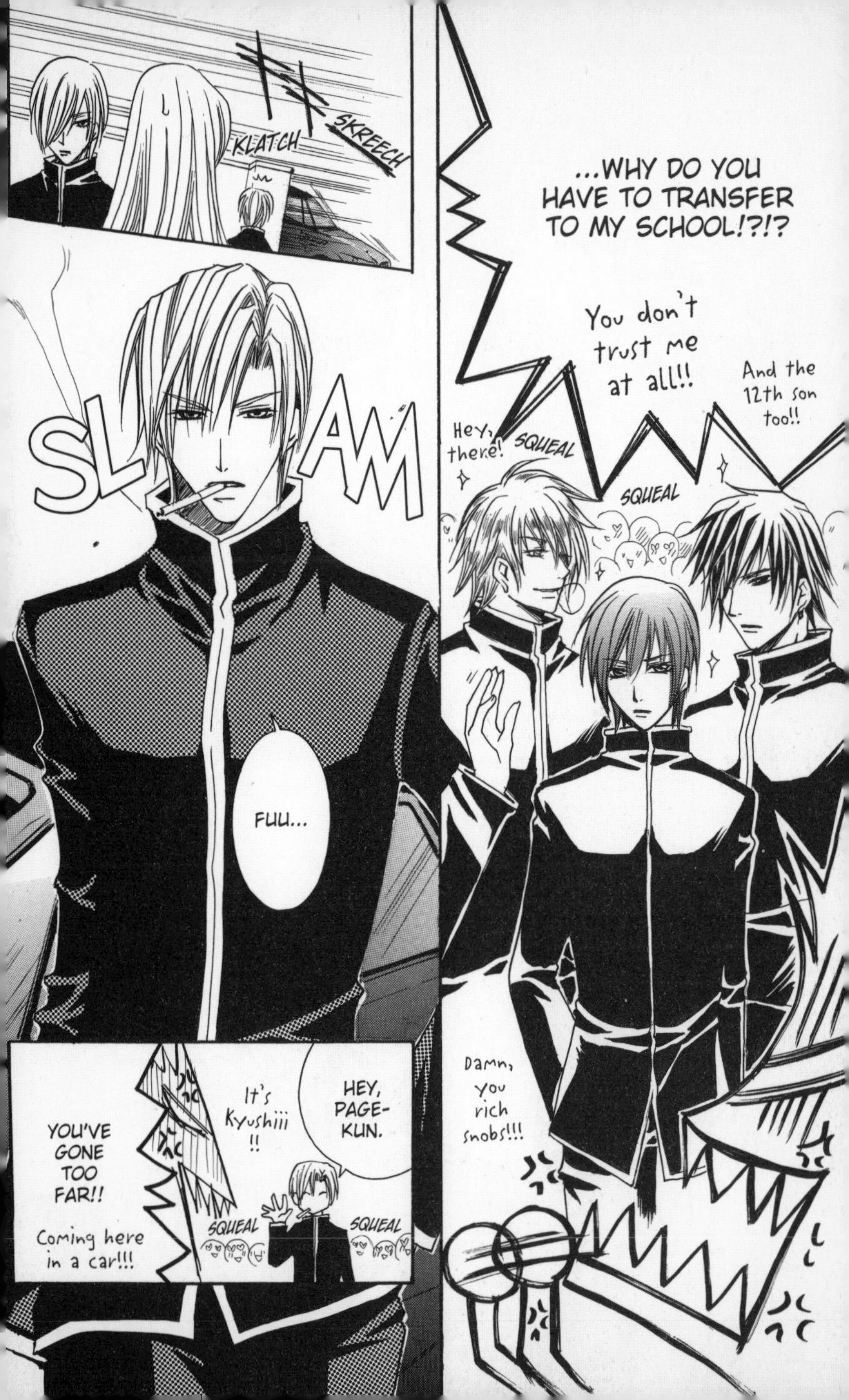
...WHY DO YOU HAVE TO TRANSFER TO MY SCHOOL!?!?
And the 12th son too!!
You don't trust me at all!!
Hey, there!
SQUEAL
SQUEAL
Damn, you rich snobs!!!
SKREECH
KLATCH
SLAM
FUU...
HEY, PAGE-KUN.
It's Kyushiii!!
YOU'VE GONE TOO FAR!!
Coming here in a car!!!
SQUEAL
SQUEAL

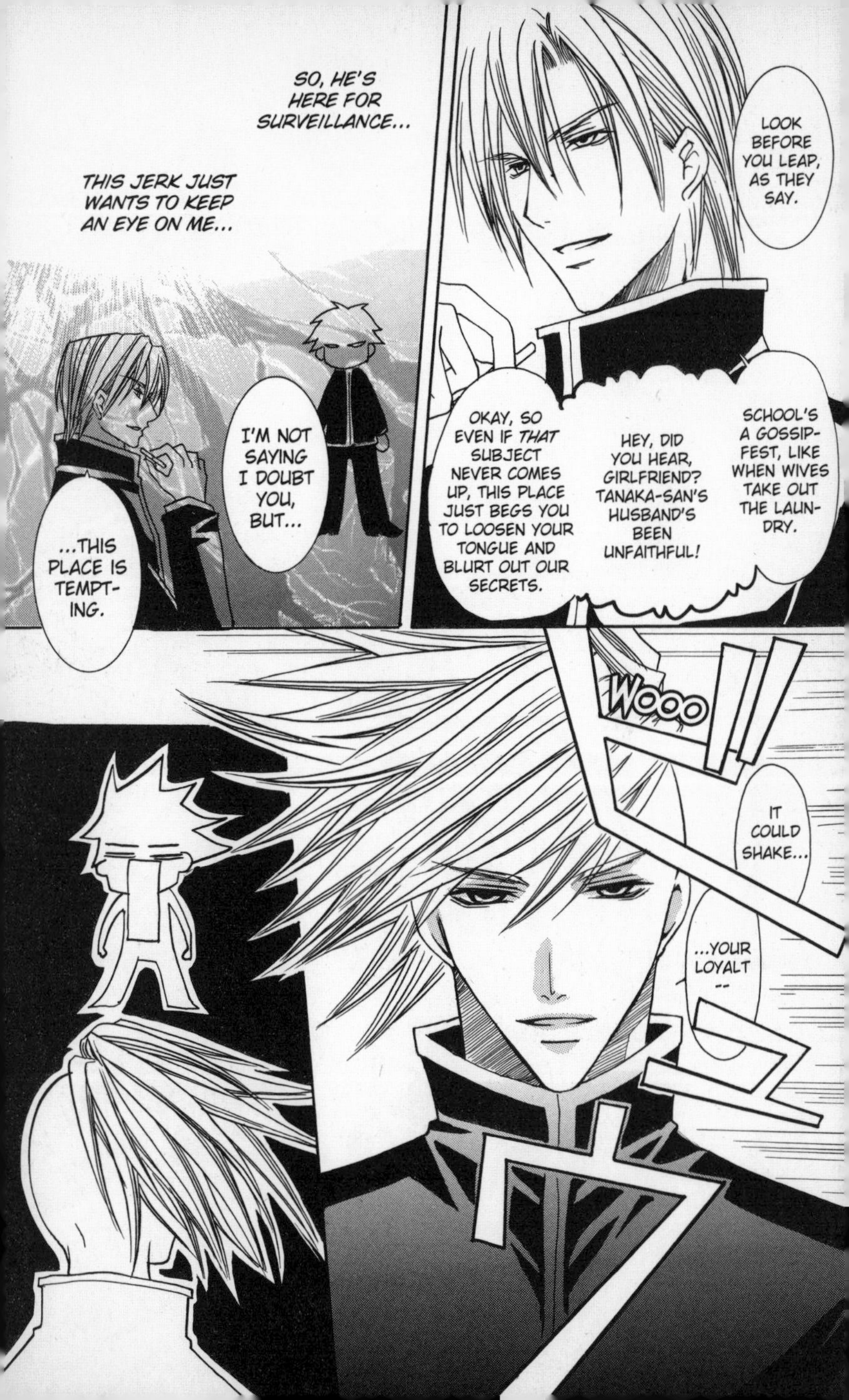

LOOK BEFORE YOU LEAP, AS THEY SAY.
SCHOOL'S A GOSSIP-FEST, LIKE WHEN WIVES TAKE OUT THE LAUNDRY.
HEY, DID YOU HEAR, GIRLFRIEND? TANAKA-SAN'S HUSBAND'S BEEN UNFAITHFUL!
OKAY, SO EVEN IF *THAT* SUBJECT NEVER COMES UP, THIS PLACE JUST BEGS YOU TO LOOSEN YOUR TONGUE AND BLURT OUT OUR SECRETS.
SO, HE'S HERE FOR SURVEILLANCE...
THIS JERK JUST WANTS TO KEEP AN EYE ON ME...
I'M NOT SAYING I DOUBT YOU, BUT...
...THIS PLACE IS TEMPT-ING.
WOOO
IT COULD SHAKE...
...YOUR LOYALT --

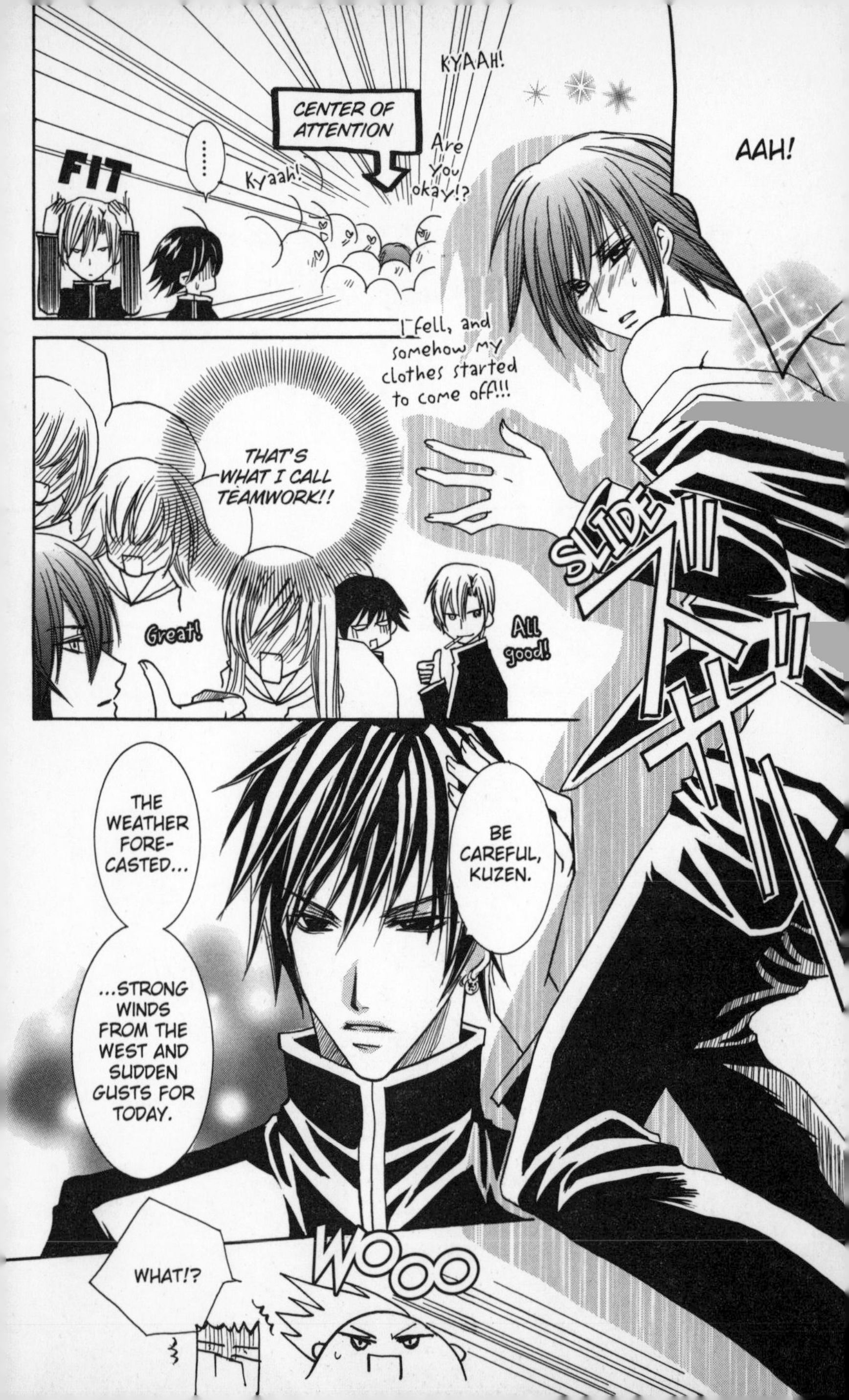
AAH!
I fell, and somehow my clothes started to come off!!!
SLIDE
KYAAH!
CENTER OF ATTENTION
Are You okay!?
Kyaah!
......
FIT
THAT'S WHAT I CALL TEAMWORK!!
All good!
Great!
BE CAREFUL, KUZEN.
THE WEATHER FORE-CASTED...
...STRONG WINDS FROM THE WEST AND SUDDEN GUSTS FOR TODAY.
WOOO
WHAT!?

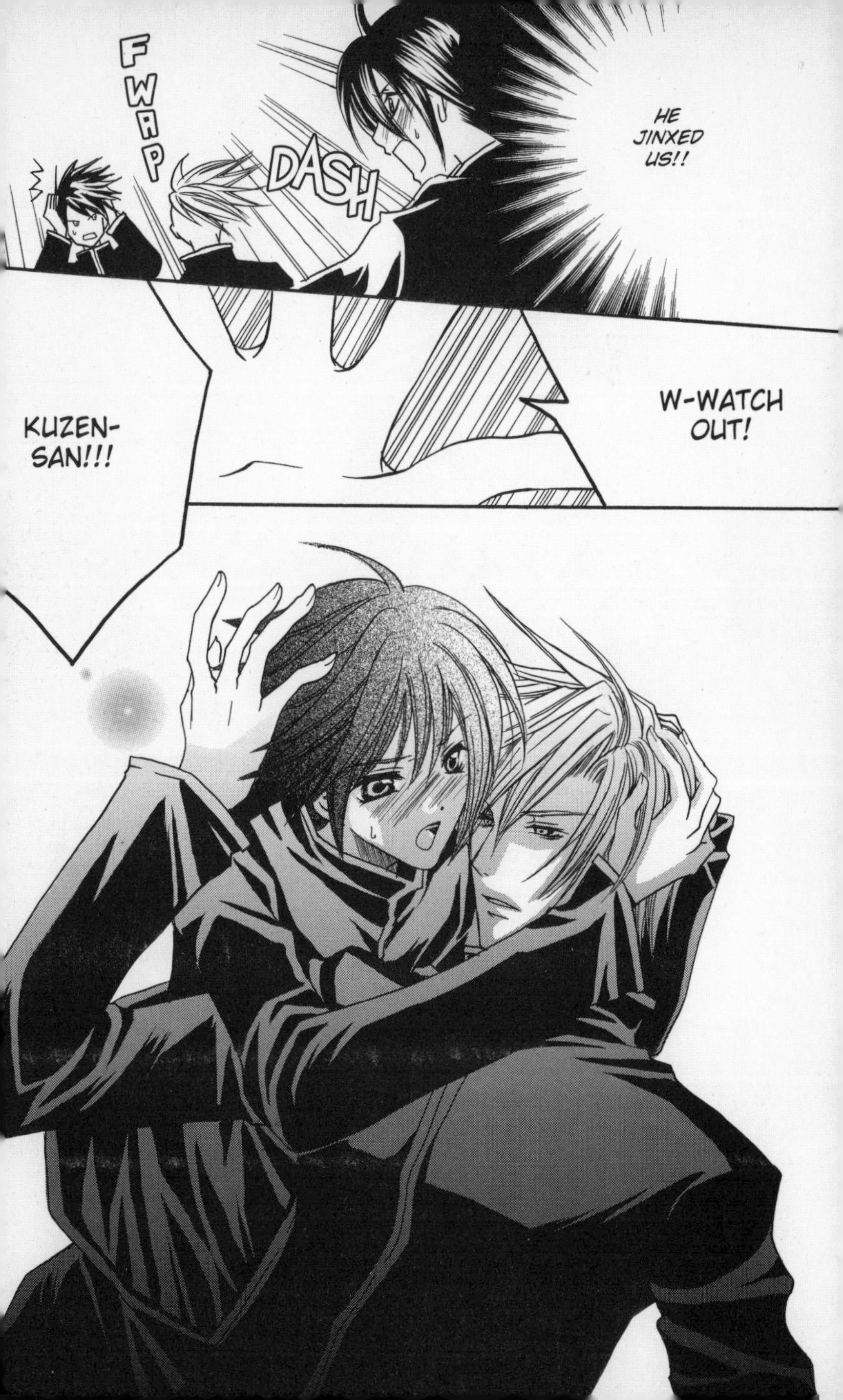
HE JINXED US!!
DASH
FWAP
W-WATCH OUT!
KUZEN-SAN!!!

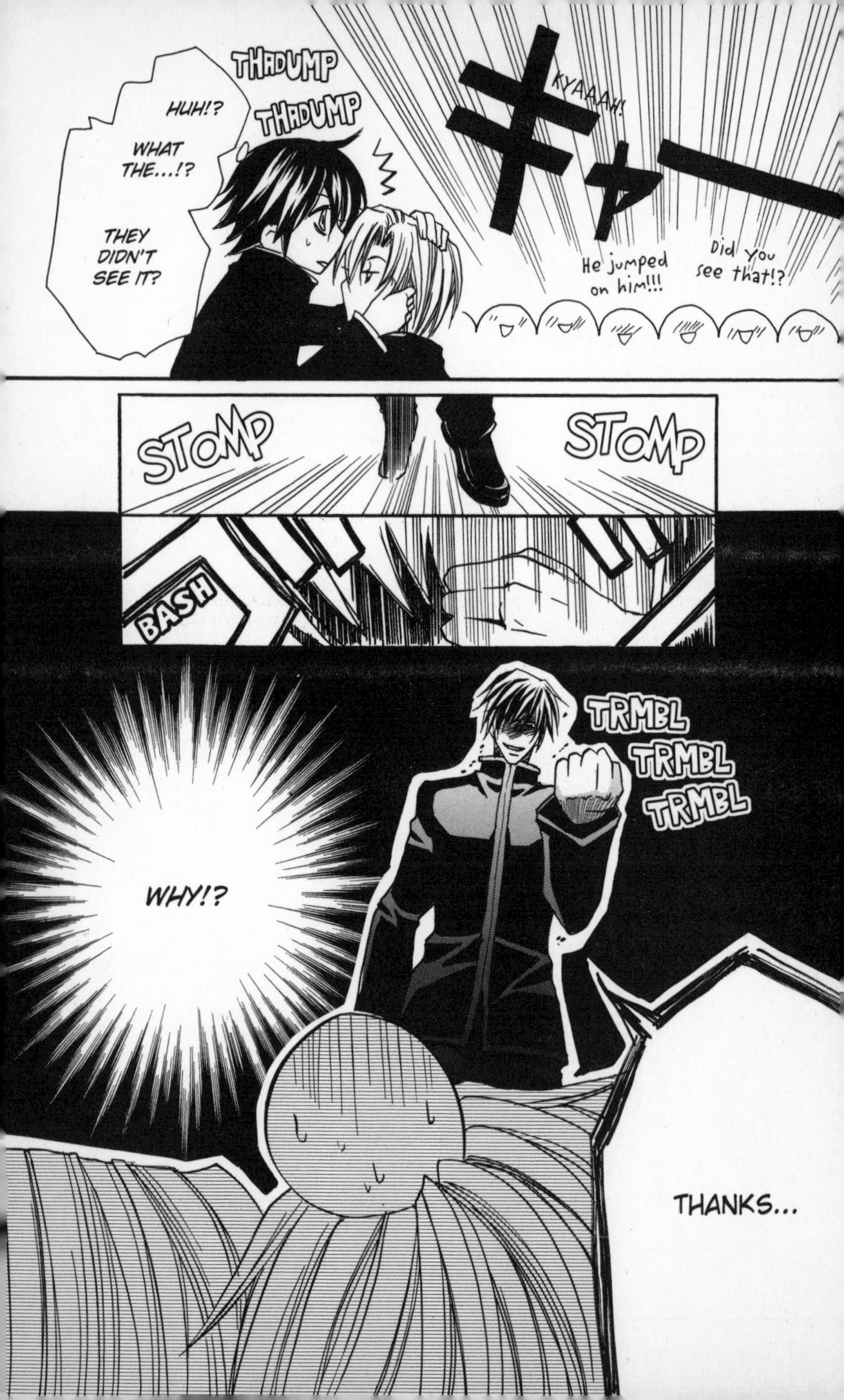

キャー
KYAAAAH!
Did you see that!?
He jumped on him!!!
THADUMP
THADUMP
HUH!? WHAT THE...!? THEY DIDN'T SEE IT?
STOMP
STOMP
BASH
TRMBL TRMBL TRMBL
WHY!?
THANKS...

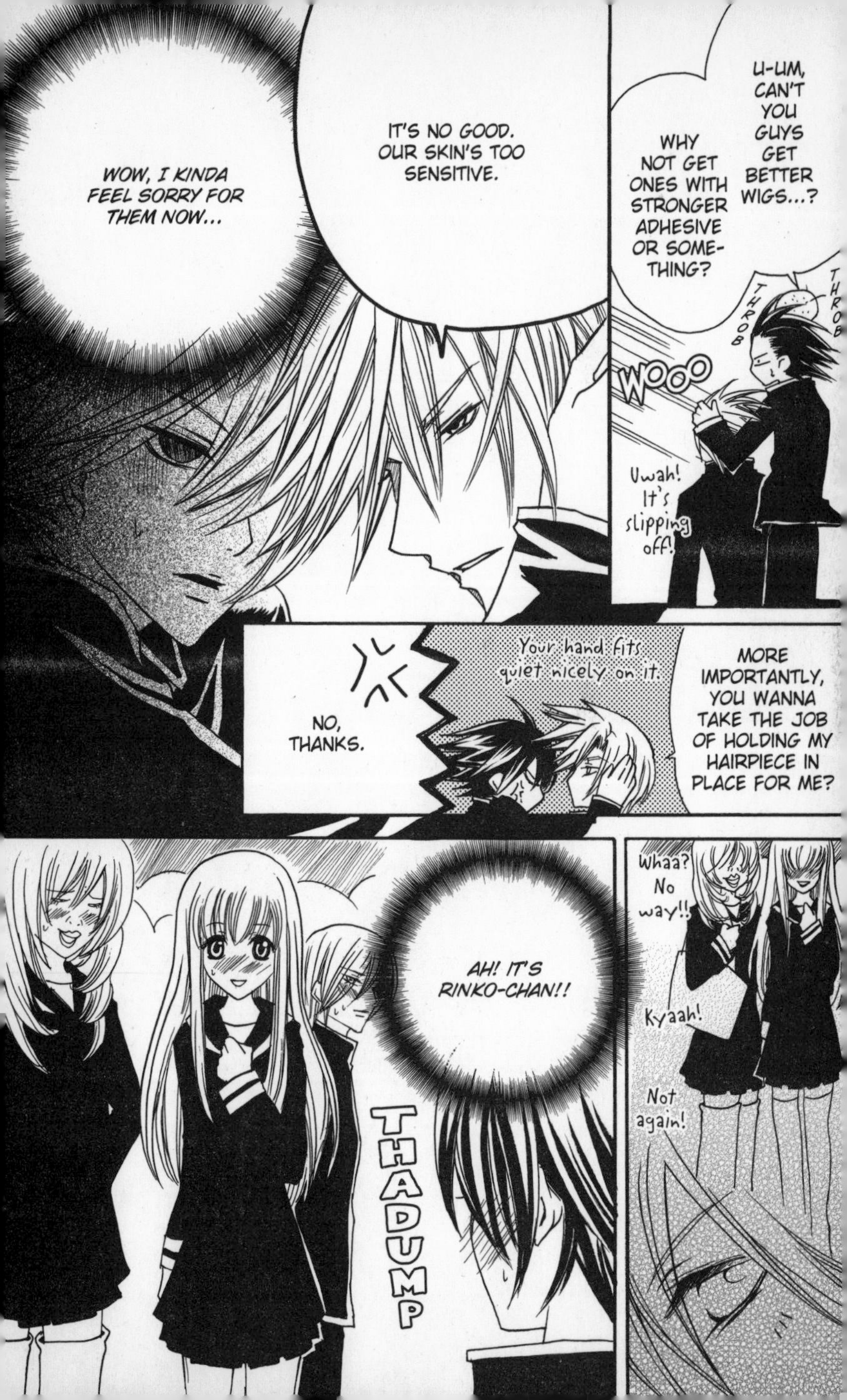
U-UM, CAN'T YOU GUYS GET BETTER WIGS...?
WHY NOT GET ONES WITH STRONGER ADHESIVE OR SOME-THING?
THROB
THROB
WOOO
Uwah! It's slipping off!
IT'S NO GOOD. OUR SKIN'S TOO SENSITIVE.
WOW, I KINDA FEEL SORRY FOR THEM NOW...
MORE IMPORTANTLY, YOU WANNA TAKE THE JOB OF HOLDING MY HAIRPIECE IN PLACE FOR ME?
Your hand fits quiet nicely on it.
NO, THANKS.
Whaa? No way!!
Kyaah!
Not again!
AH! IT'S RINKO-CHAN!!
THADUMP

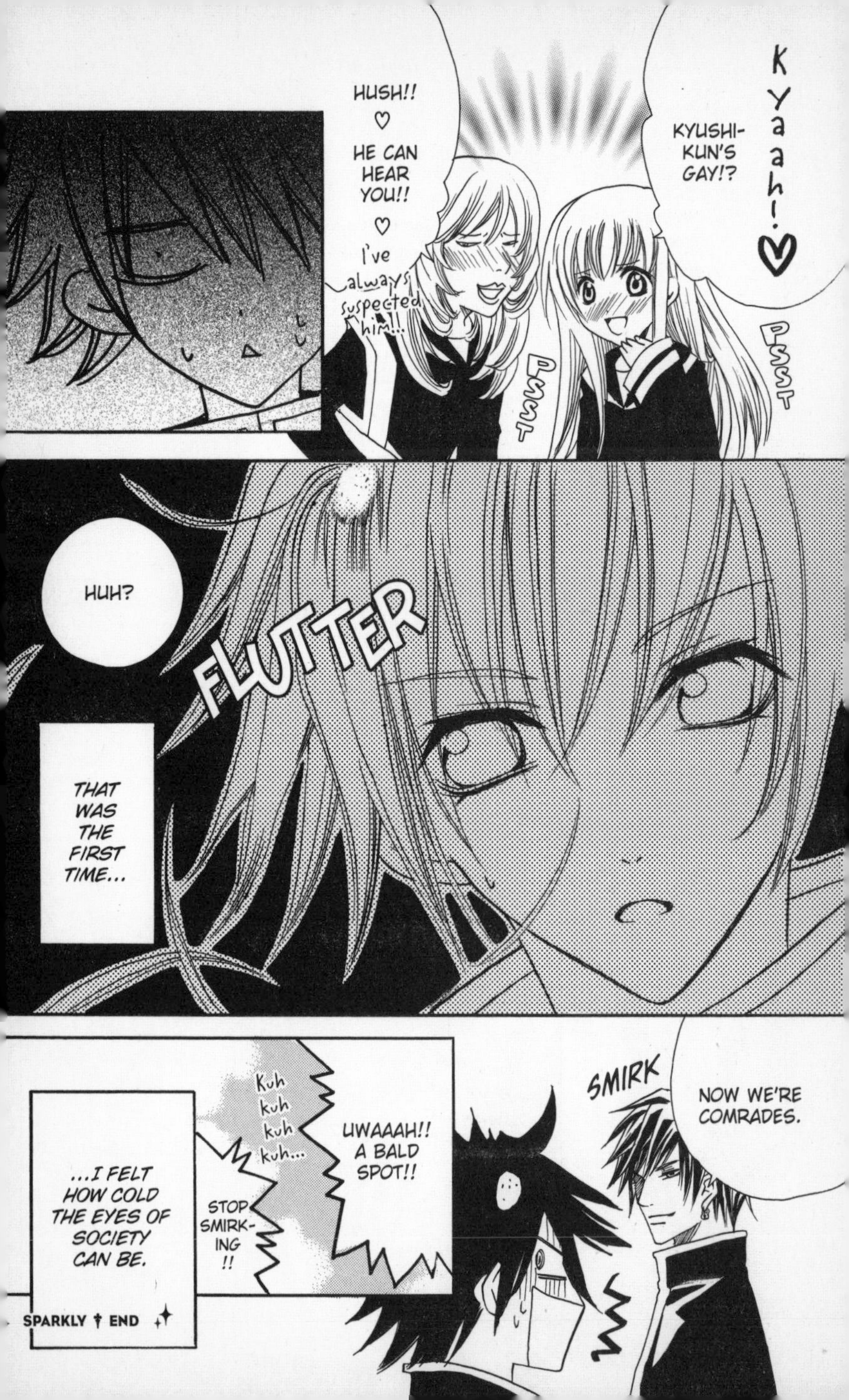
Kyaah! ♥
KYUSHI-KUN'S GAY!?
HUSH!! ♡ HE CAN HEAR YOU!! ♡
I've always suspected him!!
PSST
PSST
HUH?
FLUTTER
THAT WAS THE FIRST TIME...
NOW WE'RE COMRADES.
SMIRK
UWAAAH!! A BALD SPOT!!
Kuh kuh kuh kuh...
STOP SMIRKING!!
...I FELT HOW COLD THE EYES OF SOCIETY CAN BE.
SPARKLY † END

# AFTERWORD

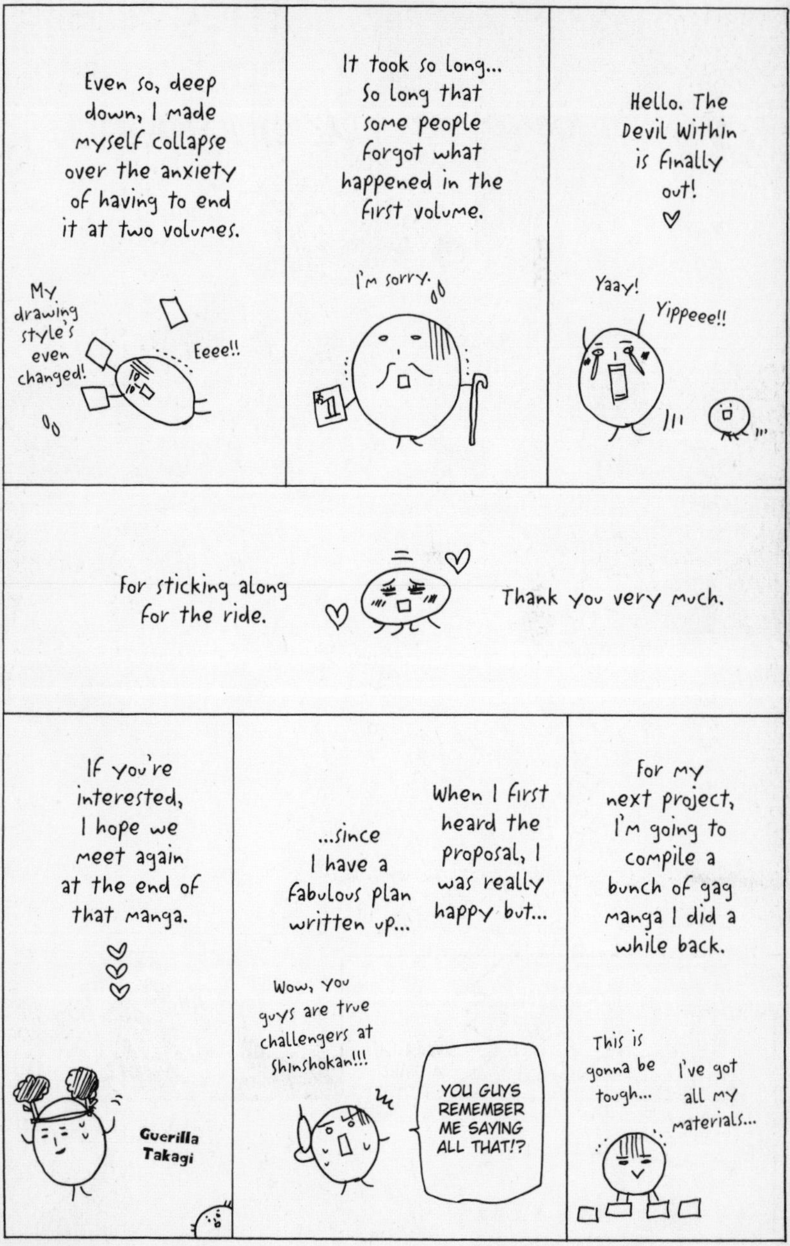
Hello. The Devil Within is finally out!
Yippeee!!
Yaay!
It took so long... So long that some people forgot what happened in the first volume.
I'm sorry.
Even so, deep down, I made myself collapse over the anxiety of having to end it at two volumes.
Eeee!!
My drawing style's even changed!
Thank you very much.
For sticking along for the ride.
For my next project, I'm going to compile a bunch of gag manga I did a while back.
I've got all my materials...
This is gonna be tough...
When I first heard the proposal, I was really happy but...
...since I have a fabulous plan written up...
Wow, you guys are true challengers at Shinshokan!!!
YOU GUYS REMEMBER ME SAYING ALL THAT!?
If you're interested, I hope we meet again at the end of that manga.
Guerilla Takagi

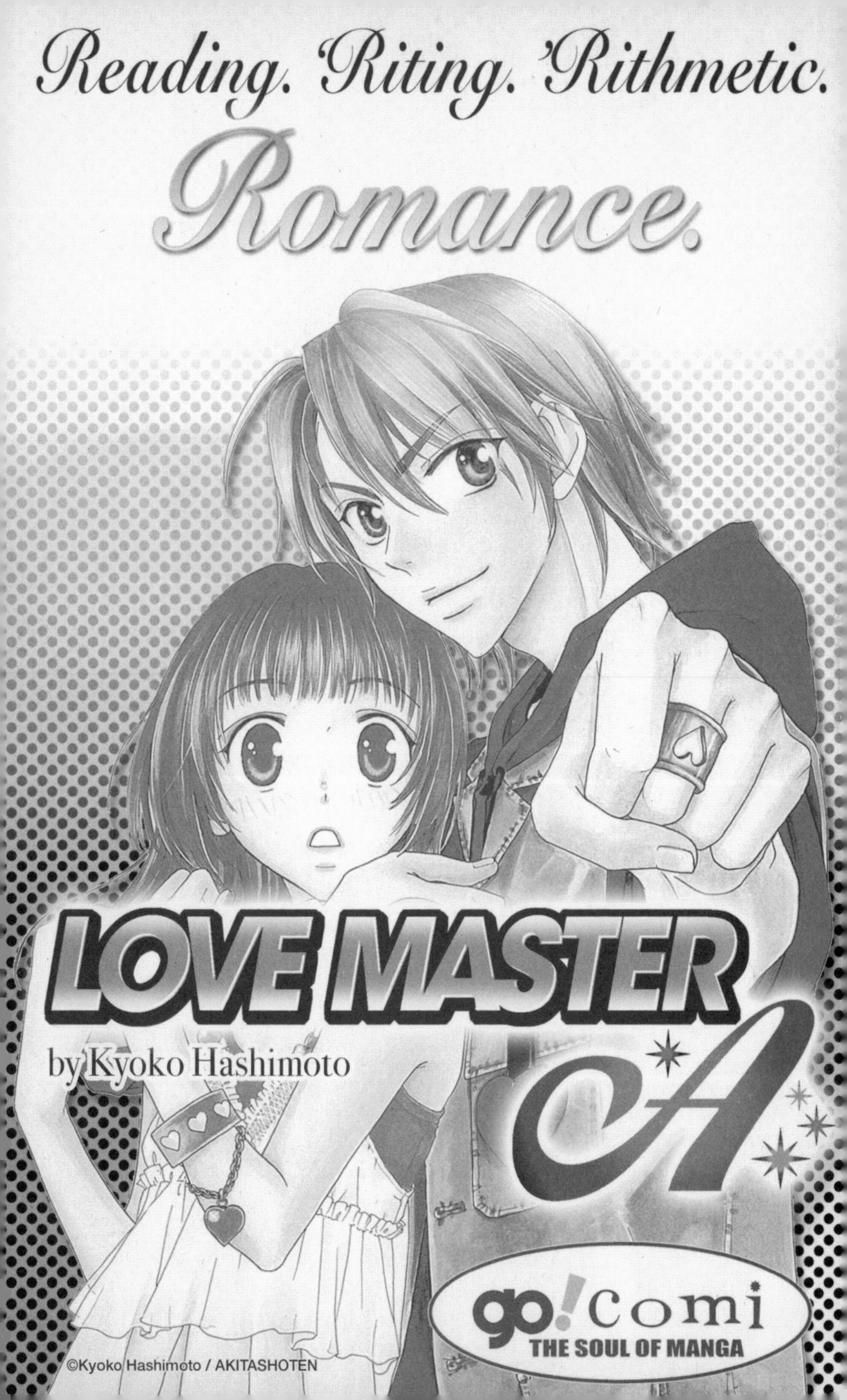
Reading. 'Riting. 'Rithmetic.
Romance.
LOVE MASTER A
by Kyoko Hashimoto
go!comi
THE SOUL OF MANGA
©Kyoko Hashimoto / AKITASHOTEN

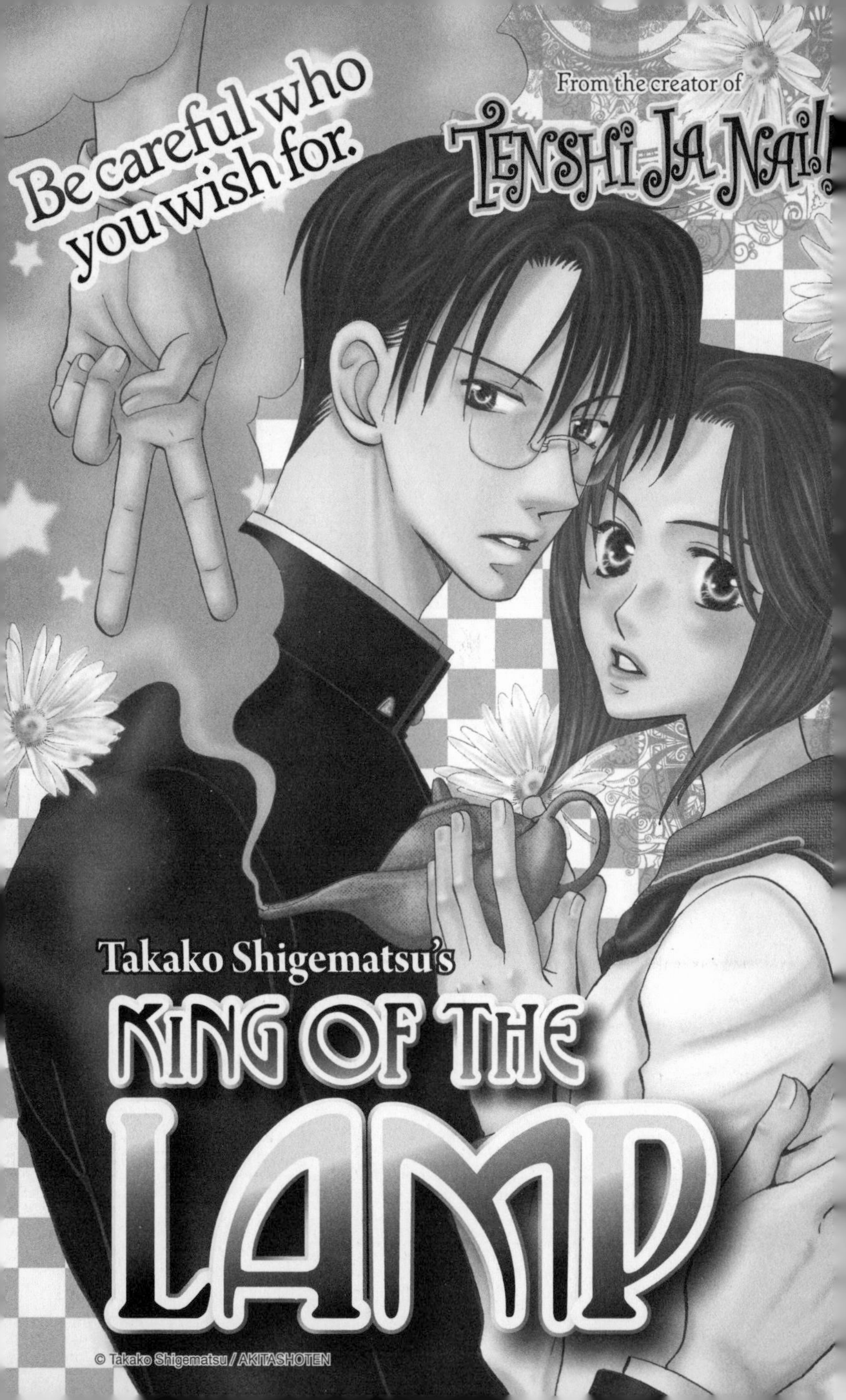
Be careful who you wish for.
From the creator of
TENSHI JA NAI!
Takako Shigematsu's
KING OF THE LAMP
© Takako Shigematsu / AKITASHOTEN

EVIL...

...HAS MET ITS MATCH.

KANNA

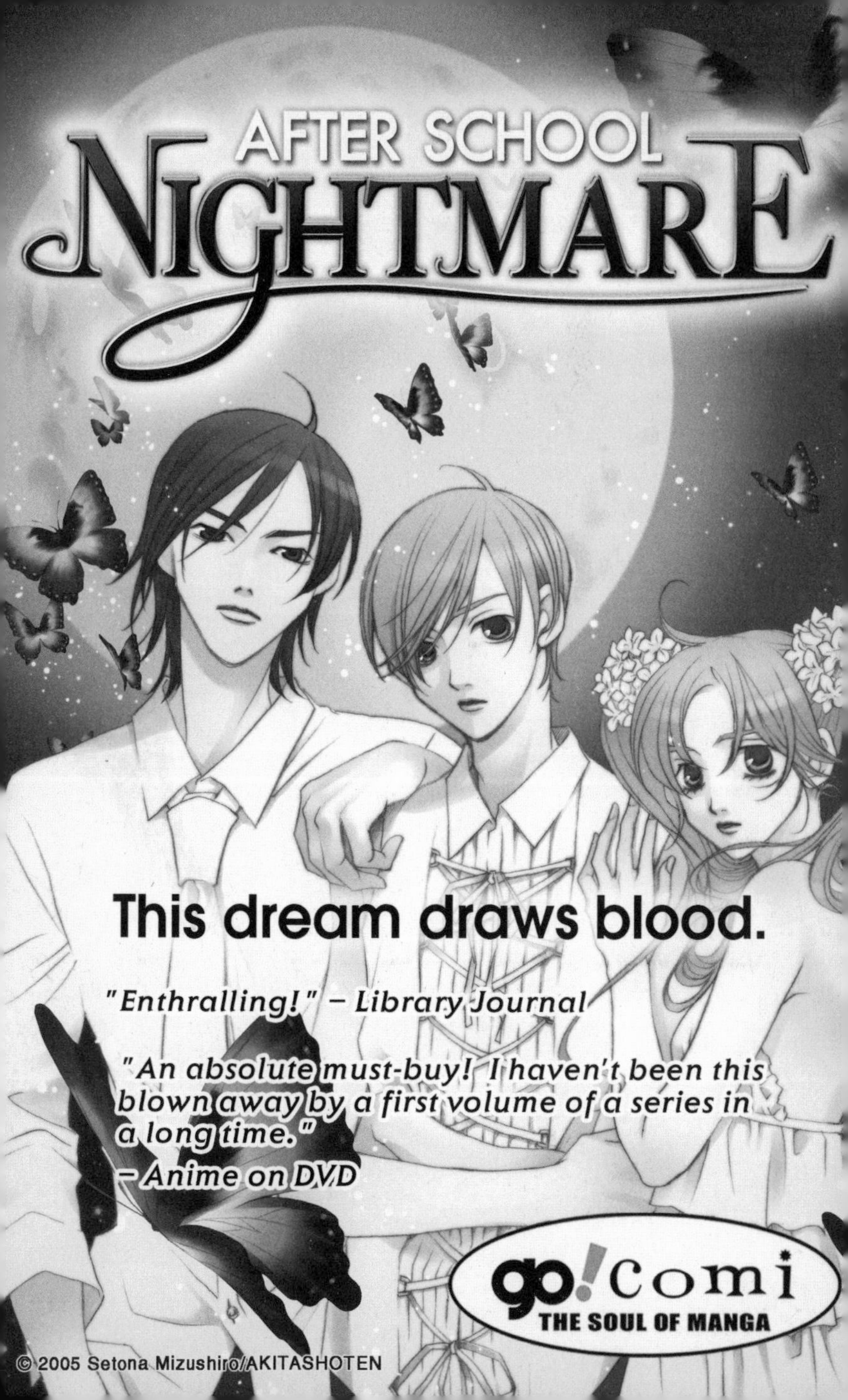
AFTER SCHOOL
NIGHTMARE
This dream draws blood.
"Enthralling!" – Library Journal
"An absolute must-buy! I haven't been this blown away by a first volume of a series in a long time."
– Anime on DVD
go!comi
THE SOUL OF MANGA
© 2005 Setona Mizushiro/AKITASHOTEN

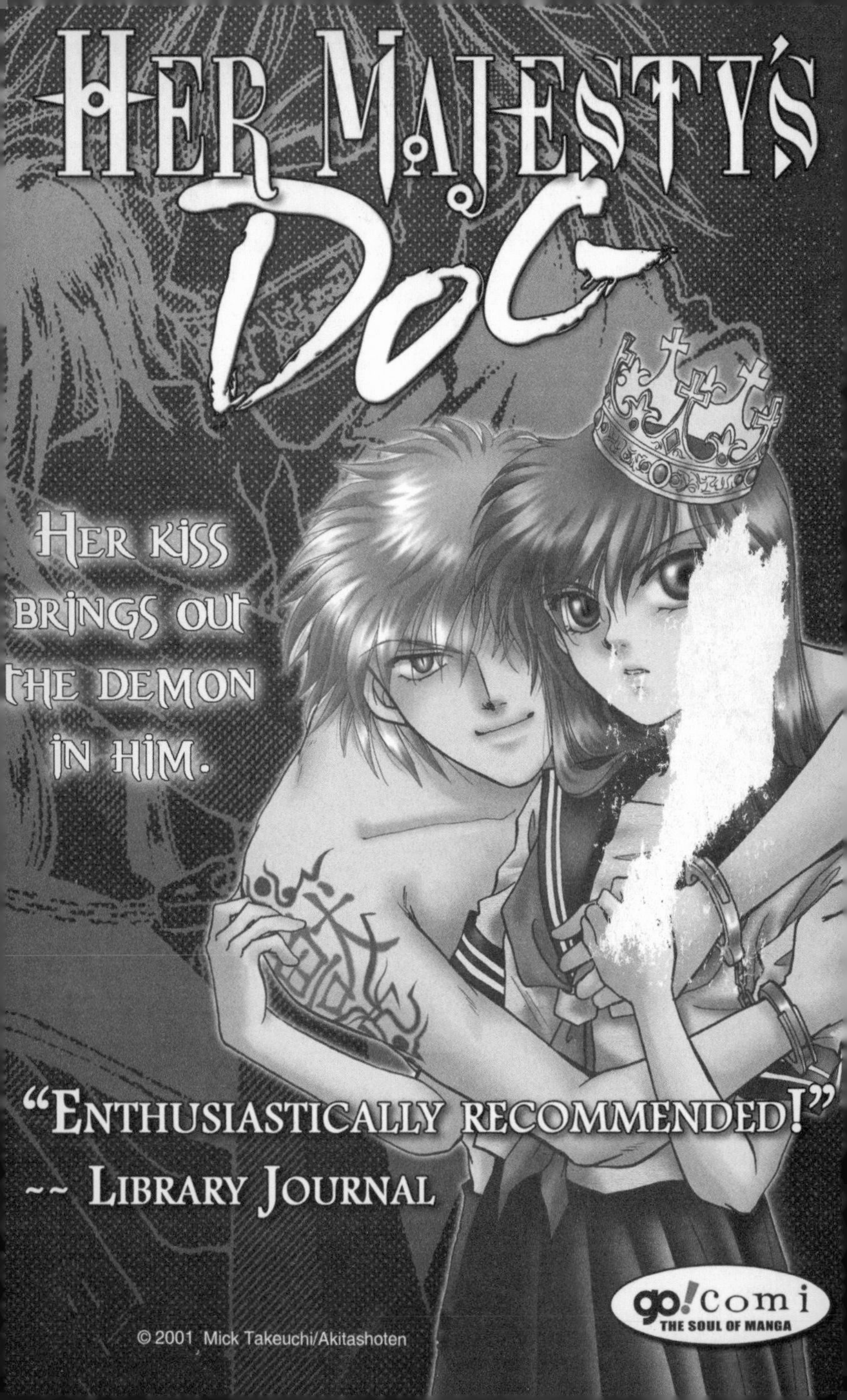
HER MAJESTY'S DOG
HER KISS BRINGS OUT THE DEMON IN HIM.
"ENTHUSIASTICALLY RECOMMENDED!"
~~ LIBRARY JOURNAL
go!comi
THE SOUL OF MANGA
© 2001 Mick Takeuchi/Akitashoten